1ST LT. ROBERT L. STONE

0-696041
Bombardier
United States Army Air Forces
7th Air Force
11th Bomb Group
431st Bomb Squadron (Heavy)

JANUARY 1943 – AUGUST 15, 1945

ISBN-10: 0692495967
ISBN-13: 978-0-692-49596-4

Library of Congress Control Number: 2015951508

Front and back cover photographs by Mark McCarty

This book is not for sale but if you enjoyed reading it please tell your friends, a library, school or World War II enthusiast about it. We hope you will consider a gift to the Wounded Warrior Project for the brave men and women who were not as fortunate as those in our family.

Additional books for this limited first printing can be ordered by writing to our email address: lettersinaboxWW2@gmail.com.

For more information *Letters in a Box* and the Wounded Warrior Project please go to:

https://fundraise.woundedwarriorproject.org/rtt/Fundraising/individual/25512316

Please visit our Facebook page for more information, letters and photographs from our book, *Letters in a Box*:

https://www.facebook.com/lettersinabox

This book has been written with love and nostalgia for a unique time in our country's history that can never be repeated in the same way again. It is to preserve some of the thoughts and feelings that inspired this generation to do their duty by serving their country in so many ways, and how it is reflected in one family's experiences.

ACKNOWLEDGEMENTS

With our special thanks and deep gratitude to Tom Brokaw for his generous permission to quote from his wonderful book, *The Greatest Generation*, and to Herbert Allen, a forever friend for connecting the dots. To members of the Stone family, most particularly Jean and Don, Kate Stone Lombardi, Beth Stone, Suzi Stone, and Jimmy Stone III, for their memories and help.

With extra thanks to Connie Sheehy for her research tips and constant support, and to our many friends most particularly Diane and Michael Taylor and Joe Finnegan who encouraged us along the way. We appreciate the expertise and wonderful work of the extraordinary photographer Mark McCarty for the images on the front and back cover, the large map that was too fragile for us to work with, and the last photo of Bob's '92 hat with the flag. We also want to thank Michael Finnegan and Quad Printers for their excellent work in the printing of our project. Thanks also go to the undiminished enthusiasm and help of Sue Wells and her Pine Cobble School students and faculty for their help in the distribution of the book. We can only hope that the Pine Cobble students learned a little bit about World War II in the process! Our grateful thanks go to Toni Kiser of the National WWII Museum in New Orleans, Louisiana who embraced our idea and was the first World War II expert to think we were doing something worthwhile. Thanks also go to Susan Brown and Katey Winant for their editing skills and knowledge. And to Bill Fenton whose advice is always spot on. Special thanks to John Botts, who took the time to encourage me to write a more personal story that I hope was worth telling.

We want to particularly thank Molly and Sam Baker for encouraging their young son to be inquisitive and ask questions that opened many adult minds to what was important and worth preserving. And to their son, Otis, whose inspiration to do a school project on Bob's World War II experiences added so much insight to an untold story and became such an important part of this book.

But most of all I want to thank my daughter, Ali Adair, because without her this book could never have happened. This is the greatest gift she could ever give to me. When she first saw the letters and read them she was determined that we should do something about them because they were too precious to put back on a shelf (as I might have been tempted to do). Equipped with her strong computer and graphic skills, honed from receiving her Master's degree in Architecture, she assured me that the project was possible and that she and I could collaborate, as we have, to develop the book. For this I shall be eternally grateful. We know that we have both learned a lot along this journey together and we hope you will also learn something about family, patriotism, commitment, intelligence, education, determination, history, or just the power of love.

And, of course, our deepest love and gratitude go to my Bob for the memories he has now finally shared with us all, and to his Dad, who had the wisdom and thoughtfulness to preserve them.

THE FAMILY

JAKE

ISABEL

UNCLE EDDIE

BOB

DON

JIM

BEE

KEN

BARRY

Jake/Dad
Bob/Oldest Son
Bee/Jake's 2nd Wife

Isabel/Mother
Don/Middle Son
Ken/Bee's Oldest

Eddie/Isabel's Brother
Jim/Youngest Son
Barry/Bee's Youngest

TABLE OF CONTENTS

INTRODUCTION

How do we become who we are? In the 1940's many girls and boys in their late teens were asked to make a decision that could either shape their lives or end them. Patriotism, for these youngsters was contagious and they were proud to be able to serve their country. Teenagers enlisted because a family member or friend had signed up or because it was the accepted thing to do, and they gave little thought to what the consequences might be. Bob Stone was one of these young boys and we will journey with him from 1942 to 1945 through his letters home to his Dad and family.

The journey for me started with a vintage 1940's Saks Fifth Avenue brown checked box filled with over 150 letters; my husband's father had kept them since 1943, on a shelf in his Park Avenue apartment. Bob's Dad probably collected and saved these letters because they could have become the last words he would ever hear from his eldest son. The box was given to my husband in the 1970's and for many more years languished untouched on a shelf in our home. We knew they were there, but Bob had no interest in revisiting the memories that they held. After his death, I rediscovered the box. When I read the letters with my daughter and saw the scrapbooks and newspaper clippings, we considered them too important a part of our family and of history to put back on another shelf. And so with astonishing help from my daughter, this book was created from the "Letters in the Box."

During the war years letters were the most efficient way of communicating and keeping up the morale of servicemen overseas. Anyone who wrote was helping in the war effort. Some friendships intensified during these letter-writing years, but dissolved after the war and even within families the bonds that strengthened them during these years sometimes frayed. But what is important is that "letters" are a mirror to those times and one of the only records we have of what it was like to actually be there.

For the sake of those who lived through the World War II years, my daughter, Ali, and I have tried to tell this story accurately. Ultimately, we plan to send Bob's letters and memorabilia to the National WWII Museum in New Orleans where his brother Jim, who was instrumental in the museum's establishment, lived. Perhaps they will help future generations understand the times and the actions of at least one young man and his family during those tumultuous war years.

The Stone family was not a military family, but two generations of eight family members became involved in the war effort. The family included: the Dad, Jake Stone, and his three sons Bob, Don and Jim. In the 1930's Jake was divorced from the boys' mother, Isabel, and in 1937 he married Beatrice Marks, who had two sons, Ken and Barry. In 1943, Ken married Bunny Kahn. Uncle Eddie Greenbaum was Isabel's brother and played a major role in Bob's life. Mildred and Eddie Hilson were close family friends. They are all mentioned in Bob's letters and only after the war did anyone realize that four of the boys were involved in one of the Pacific's bloodiest battles for Iwo Jima. Bob dropped bombs on the island, Ken's destroyer shelled the island, and Jim and Barry led Marine companies onto the beaches. But how did four of the brothers all get to this same place at the same time in the middle of nowhere while the fifth brother fought in the Battle of the Bulge?

The Stone family lived at 375 Park Avenue in New York City in a beautiful old apartment building that was razed in the 1950's for Mies Van Der Rohe's iconic Seagram Building. Jake's three sons all went to the best private schools, and on to Williams College. Their Dad had graduated from Williams in 1914 and had told them they could go to whatever college they wanted, but he would only pay for Williams.

Jake was a partner at Asiel & Co., a banking and investment firm where he was a member of the New York Stock Exchange and specialized in trading bonds. He took a leave of absence from the firm during World War I and graduated from Officer Candidate School as a first lieutenant and served in the infantry in France. He wrote letters home to his mother, but had a friend back in the states mail them so that she would not worry about him being in combat overseas. In 1942 he took another leave of absence and re-enlisted, but because of his age and health limitations he was made a Lieutenant Commander in the Navy's Bureau of Supplies and Accounts stationed in New York City. Although Bee Stone was not in uniform she was an important part of the war effort, writing letters, and fulfilling requests from underwear to watch repairs and food.

Uncle Eddie took a leave of absence from his law firm in 1940 when he was called to active duty more than a year before war was declared. He had been a Major in World War I and was asked to serve as a Lieutenant Colonel and was soon promoted to Brigadier General. For over six years he worked on many strategic and important issues as executive officer to Under Secretary of War Robert P. Patterson, who later became Secretary of War under President Truman.

Tom Brokaw's wonderful book *The Greatest Generation* starts our two year journey with a quote from Air Force Captain Joe Foss, a Medal of Honor winner: "Hey, if we hadn't put up a scrap back there during the forties, you'd be living under the Japs or Germans and I don't think you'd like that very much."[1] Those weren't Bob's words, but they certainly could have been and they encapsulated the thinking of so many during this period. Captain Foss's words were not politically correct. They were not complicated or deeply philosophical. It was a pure and simple reason that made them all want to do something to help in the war effort.

Tom's book follows a young man born in 1920, a year before my Bob was born. He recounts what was happening in the world and has given us permission to use his words to set the scene, which will put the motives and letters in perspective. All the words in italics are Tom's, but we have inserted into this time frame what the extended family, and most particularly what Bob was doing at the time.

> *...1920 was an auspicious year for a young person to enter the world as an American citizen. The U.S. population had topped 106 million people, and the landscape was*

changing rapidly from agrarian to urban, even though one in three Americans still lived on a farm. Women were gaining the right to vote with the ratification of the Nineteenth Amendment, and KDKA in Pittsburgh was broadcasting the first radio signals across the middle of America. Prohibition was beginning, but so was the roaring lifestyle that came with the flouting of Prohibition and the culture that produced it. In far-off Russia the Bolshevik revolution was a bloody affair, but its American admirers were unable to stir comparable passions here.

Five years later, this American child born in 1920 seemed to be poised for a life of ever greater prosperity, opportunity, and excitement. President Calvin "Silent Cal" Coolidge was a benign presence in the White House, content to let the bankers, industrialists, and speculators run the country as they saw fit.

As the 20s roared along, the Four Horsemen of Notre Dame were giving Saturdays new meaning with their college football heroics. Jack Dempsey and Gene Tunney were raising the spectacle of heavyweight boxing matches to new heights of frenzy. Baseball was a daytime game and a true national pastime, from the fabled Yankee Stadium to the sandlots of rural America.

The New Yorker was launched and the place of magazines occupied a higher order. Flappers were dancing the Charleston; Fitzgerald was publishing The Great Gatsby; the Scopes trial was underway in Tennessee, with Clarence Darrow and William Jennings Bryan in a passionate and theatrical debate on evolution versus the Scriptures. A. Philip Randolph organized the Brotherhood of Sleeping Car Porters, the beginning of a long struggle to force America to face its shameful policies and practices on race.[2]

During this time Bob and his two brothers attended The Windward School in White Plains, New York, which was started for them by their mother. Isabel had graduated from Barnard College in 1914 along with 152 classmates who had voted her the "Best All Around," "the Wittiest," and the "Most Versatile." There were 673 students at the college and she was an outstanding athlete who played forward on the varsity basketball team as well as being her class tennis champion and Barnard College tennis champion in 1916-17. She was Editor–in-Chief of the yearbook and was involved in the english, drama, and philanthropic clubs, and there is a scholarship named for her at Barnard. When Bob was old enough to start school, she decided that the existing schools were not acceptable because she wanted a better education for her sons. So she started The Windward School which is now a nationally recognized school whose mission has changed and is now known for developing instructional programs designed specifically to help children achieve language proficiency, academic success, and social and emotional growth. It continues to flourish and now encompasses grades 1-9 and is preparing to expand. Isabel left a wonderful educational legacy for future generations.

By the time this young American who had such a promising start reached the age of ten, his earlier prospects were shattered; the fault lines were active everywhere: the stock market was struggling to recover from the crash of 1929, but the damage was too great. U.S. income was falling fast. Thirteen hundred banks closed. Businesses were failing everywhere, sending four and a half million people onto the streets with no safety net. The average American farm family had an annual cash income of four hundred dollars.

Herbert Hoover, as president, seemed to be paralyzed in the face of spreading economic calamity; he was a distant figure of stern bearing whose reputation as an engineering genius and management wizard was quickly replaced by cruel caricatures of his aloofness from the plight of the ever larger population of poor. [3]

At this time the boys were at the Harvey School now in Katonah, New York. It was a boarding school for boys from 4-9th grades. This was a difficult time in Isabel and Jake's marriage and they divorced in the mid 1930's and Jake knew he could not care for the boys alone. He wanted them to have a good education in a safe environment with good academics, a structured campus life with intelligent role models and athletic opportunities that were not available in the city. Harvey provided the best solution close to home. All the boys played on a team that was suitable for their ability. Bob played football, and baseball and was editor of their yearbook and was in the drama and stamp clubs. Don played baseball, football and soccer. Jimmy played on football and baseball teams and was on the business board of their publications, and was awarded the History Prize. Barry was there for the last two grades and played basketball, football, baseball, was awarded the Latin Prize and was elected Student Council president.

Congress passed the disastrous Smoot-Hawley Tariff Act, establishing barriers to world trade and exacerbating an already raging global recession.

Yet Henry Luce managed to launch Fortune, a magazine specializing in business affairs. United Airlines and American Airlines, still in their infancy, managed to stay airborne. Lowell Thomas began a nightly national radio newscast on NBC and CBS. The Lone Ranger series was heard on radio.

Overseas, three men were plotting to change the world: Adolph Hitler in Germany, Joseph Stalin in Russia and Mao Zedong in China. In American politics, the New York governor, Franklin Delano Roosevelt, was planning his campaign for the 1932 presidential election.

By 1933, when the baby born in 1920 was entering teenage years, the promise of that early childhood was shattered by crashing world economies. American farmers were able to produce only about sixteen bushels of corn per acre, and the prices were so low that it was more efficient to feed the corn to the hogs than take it to market.

...A mass of homeless and unemployed men drifted across the American landscape, looking for work or a handout wherever they could find it. More than thirty million Americans had no income of any kind. The American military had more horses than tanks, and its only action had been breaking up a demonstration of World War I veterans demanding their pension bonuses a year earlier.

Franklin Roosevelt took the oath of office as president of the United States, promising a New Deal for the beleaguered American people, declaring to a nation with more than fifteen million people out of work, "The only thing we have to fear is fear itself."

He pushed through an Emergency Banking Act, a Federal Emergency Relief Act, a National Industrial Recovery Act, and by 1935 set in motion the legislation that would become the Social Security system.

Not everyone was happy. Rich Americans led by the Du Ponts, the founders of General Motors, and big oil millionaires founded the Liberty League to oppose the New Deal. Privately, in the salons of the privileged, Roosevelt was branded a traitor to his class.

In Germany, a former painter with a spellbinding oratorical style took office as chancellor and immediately set out to seize control of the political machinery of Germany with his National Socialist German Workers party, known informally as the Nazis. Adolph Hitler began his long march to infamy. He turned on the Jews, passing laws that denied them German citizenship, codifying the anti-Semitism that eventually led to the concentration camps and the gas chambers, an act of hatred so deeply immoral it will mark the twentieth century forever.

By the late thirties in America, anti-Semitism was the blatant message of Father Charles Coughlin, a messianic Roman Catholic priest with a vast radio audience. Huey Long, the brilliant Louisiana populist, came to power, first as governor and then as a U.S. senator, preaching in his own spellbinding fashion the power of the little guy against the evils of Wall Street and corporate avarice.

When our young American was reaching eighteen, in 1938, the flames of war were everywhere in the world: Hitler had seized Austria; the campaign against Jews had intensified with Kristallnacht, a vicious and calculated campaign to destroy all Jewish businesses within the Nazi realm. Japan continued its brutal and genocidal war against the Chinese; and in Russia, Stalin was presiding over show trials, deporting thousands to Siberia, summarily executing his rivals in the Communist party. The Spanish Civil War was a losing cause for the loyalists, and a diminutive fascist general, Francisco Franco, began a reign that would last forty years.

In this riotous year, the Prime Minister, Neville Chamberlin, believed he had saved his country with a pact negotiated with Hitler at Munich. He returned to England to declare, "I believe it is peace for our time...peace with honor."

It was neither."[4]

During the mid to late 1930's the five boys were all at Deerfield Academy in Deerfield, Massachusetts for their high school years except for Donny's freshman year spent at the Judson School in Arizona. Ken was a cum laude student and was in the chess club and played football, basketball, baseball and tennis. Sports were required and there was a team for every level and ability of play. Bob played varsity tennis his senior year, and also played soccer and basketball and was in the music, chess and stamp clubs—but his interests were in the business and management areas of the school's publications where he held top positions. Don played three years of varsity tennis and was captain his senior year. He also played squash, hockey, and soccer, and was in the chess, dramatic, music and stamp clubs, and held top editorial positions on the school publications. Jimmy played varsity baseball his senior year and was assistant manager of varsity basketball and for the senior play. He also played basketball, lacrosse, and football and was an officer of the stamp club, belonged to the dramatic club each year and was either on the editorial or business board of the school's two publications. Barry blossomed as an athlete in these years and played varsity lacrosse all four years, varsity hockey for three years, and varsity football for two years. He also was head cheerleader, involved in the business boards of school publications, and was in the glee, senate, and press clubs. All of their academic qualifications were excellent as they were at a good school, and they were all good citizens of their school community. I mention their interests and involvements during this time because taken together with their physical fitness these were the only factors on which to judge their ability to serve in the armed forces successfully.

In 1935, when Bob was fourteen and at Deerfield, I was born in New York City. We were not to marry until thirty-three years later in 1968. However, these years are important to us as they shaped the couple we became who shared an amazing love for each other. I often think how impossible it would have been for me to have loved him during this time and wondering every day whether he would come back to me. Then I think of the millions of men and women who had loved ones on the battlefields around the world and managed to get through it all. After all, there is no guarantee that every time you say goodbye to a loved one that you will ever see them again.

> *At home, Roosevelt was in his second term, trying to balance the continuing need for extraordinary efforts to revive the economy with what he knew was the great peril abroad. Congress passed the Fair Labor Standards Act, setting a limit on hours worked and a minimum wage. The federal government began a system of parity payments to farmers and subsidized foreign wheat sales.*
>
> *In the fall of 1938, Dwight David Eisenhower, a career soldier who had grown up on a small farm outside of Abilene, Kansas, was a forty-eight-year-old colonel in the U.S. Army. He had an infectious grin and a fine reputation as a military planner, but he had no major combat command experience. The winds of war were about to carry him to the highest peaks of military glory and political reward. Ike, as he was called, would become a folksy avatar of his time.* [5]

Ken went to Amherst in 1938, and Bob entered Williams College in 1940.

> *America was entertained by Benny Goodman, Glenn Miller, Woody Guthrie, the music of Hoagy Carmichael, the big-screen film magic of Clark Gable, Cary Grant, Katharine Hepburn, Errol Flynn, Ginger Rogers, Fred Astaire, Bette Davis, Henry Fonda.*
>
> *At the beginning of a new decade, 1940, just twenty years after our young American entered a world of such great promise and prosperity, it was clear to all but a few*

delusional isolationists that war would define this generation's coming of age.

France, Belgium, The Netherlands, Luxembourg, Denmark, Norway and Romania had all fallen to Nazi aggression. German troops controlled Paris. In the east, Stalin was rapidly building up one of the greatest ground armies ever to defend Russia and communism.

Japan signed a ten-year military pact with Germany and Italy, forming an Axis they expected would rule the world before the decade was finished.

Roosevelt, elected to his third term, again by landslide, was preparing the United States, pushing through the Export Control Act to stop the shipment of war materials overseas. Contracts were arranged for a new military vehicle called the jeep. A fighter plane was developed. It would be designated the P-51 Mustang. Almost 20 percent of the budget FDR submitted to Congress was for defense needs. The first peacetime military draft in U.S. history was activated.

Roosevelt stayed in close touch with his friend, the new prime minister of England, Winston Churchill, who told the English: "I have nothing to offer but blood, toil, tears and sweat." And "we shall not flag or fail...we shall fight on the seas and oceans... we shall fight on the landing grounds, we shall fight in the fields and on the streets, we shall fight in the hills, we shall never surrender."

Our twenty-year old American learned something of war by reading <u>For Whom the Bell Tolls</u>, by Ernest Hemingway, and something else about the human spirit by watching <u>The Grapes of Wrath</u>, the film based on John Steinbeck's novel, directed by John Ford and starring Henry Fonda.

The majority of black Americans were still living in the states of the former confederacy, and they remained second-class citizens, or worse, in practice and law. Negro men were drafted and placed in segregated military units even as America prepared to fight a fascist regime that had as a core belief the inherent superiority of the Aryan people.

It had been a turbulent twenty years for our young American, and the worst and the best were yet to come. On December 7, 1941, the Japanese attacked Pearl Harbor. Across America, on that Sunday afternoon, the stunning news from the radio electrified the nation and changed the lives of all who heard it. Marriages were postponed or accelerated. College was deferred. Plans of any kind for the future were calibrated against the quickening pace of the march to war.

Shortly after the attack, Winston Churchill called FDR from the prime minister's country estate, Chequers. In his book The Grand Alliance, Churchill recounted the conversation. "Mr. President, what's this about Japan?" Roosevelt replied, "It's quite true. They have attacked us at Pearl Harbor. We're all in the same boat now."

Churchill couldn't have been happier. He would now have the manpower, the resources, and the political will of the United States actively engaged in this fight for survival. He wrote, "So we had won after all." A few days later, after Germany and Italy had declared war against the United States, Churchill wrote to Anthony Eden, his foreign secretary, who was travelling to Russia, "The accession of the United States makes amends for all, and with time and patience will give us certain victory."

In America, young men were enlisting in the military by the hundreds of thousands. Farm kids from the Great Plains who never expected to see the oceans in their lifetimes signed up for the Navy; brothers followed brothers into the Marines; young daredevils who were fascinated by the new frontiers of flight volunteered for pilot training. Single young women poured into Washington to fill the exploding needs for clerical help as the political capital mobilized for war. Other women, their husbands or boyfriends off to basic training, learned to drive trucks or handle welding torches. The old rules of gender or expectation changed radically with what was now expected of this generation.

...1940...was the fulcrum of America in the twentieth century, when the nation was balanced precariously between the darkness of the Great Depression on one side and the storms of war in Europe and the Pacific on the other. It was a critical time in the shaping of this nation and the world, equal to the revolution of 1776 and the perils of the Civil War. Once again the American people understood the magnitude of the challenge, the importance of an unparalleled national commitment, and, most of all, the certainty that only one resolution was acceptable.[6]

At this time Uncle Eddie was called into active duty and served in many capacities helping to prepare our nation for war. He was responsible for rewriting the tax laws to encourage manufacturers to change their products from peacetime to wartime materials and he encouraged good lawyers to enlist and help in the procurement of contracts with manufacturers and businesses in all fields. He was instrumental in the wording of many important documents such as the Lend-Lease Act and the G.I. Bill of Rights. All of this was before Pearl Harbor. He helped to set up the Army Correction Division, the point system for discharge, and was involved in the delegating of funds for the "Manhattan District" with General Leslie R. Groves. Later this top-secret plan became publicly known as the "Manhattan Project" which developed the atomic bomb.

The nation turned to its young to carry the heaviest burden, to fight in enemy territory and to keep the home front secure and productive. These young men and women were eager for the assignment. They understood what was required of them, and they willingly volunteered for their duty.[7]

Ken enlisted in the Navy after his Junior year at Amherst and before Pearl Harbor to join the U.S. Naval Reserves as a midshipman in training known as a "90-Day Wonder"—this was an officer commissioned after a three month training period at specific colleges that culminated in a commission as an ensign. This was a necessary program to quickly fill jobs necessary to the war effort, but there was a distinction in the minds of veterans between the "90-Day Wonders" and those who had gone through the more rigorous training channels. After completing this program he was assigned to anti-submarine duty in the Atlantic aboard the Destroyer USS McCormack that also helped in the landing of troops in Morocco.

It was not until Bob's eleven-year-old friend, Otis Baker, visited in 2008, and asked Bob about his wartime experiences that he began to open up and talk about them. He was then 85 years old. Otis had decided to write a paper for a school assignment about Bob's experiences in the war. Bob's memories and words were so honest and insightful after 57 years that we added them here and to the notes at the back of the book. This way you will know where and what he was doing—words that would have been censored out of his letters during the war.

As Bob spoke to me answering questions that Otis had asked for his project I was rapidly typing so that we would have some record of what he was finally telling us about his experiences. I then emailed them to Otis's Mom who gave them to Otis for his project, and that is why I, fortunately, have many of Bob's own words to quote.

Bob said that "On December 8, 1941 I was a sophomore at Williams College studying in my room with the radio on (there was no TV in those days) and I heard President Roosevelt announce that the Japs had made a sneak attack dropping tons of bombs on Pearl Harbor where virtually our entire Navy was berthed. The devastation of our navy's ships plus the enormous loss of American lives upset and angered me so much that I immediately enlisted in the aviation cadets as an entry into the Air Forces. The unprovoked and dastardly act by the Japanese is something that I will never forget!"

On this same day in 1941, I was six years old and vividly remember sitting with my family on a glass sun porch with snow outside, listening to the very same broadcast. I recall that I knew that something momentous was happening but didn't know what or why. My father at that time was president of the National Union Radio Company, formed by RCA (the Radio Corporation of America), specifically to make radio and cathode ray tubes for the war effort. We had moved from New York City to Montclair, New Jersey because he needed to be near the factories in New Jersey and Pennsylvania; at that time cars and gas were rationed making a commute from New York City difficult. In 1944, the plants received an "Army and Navy E"[8] for effort, and I remember how proud we felt when the award was given to my father and his company employees in an impressive ceremony, complete with brass bands and flags waving.

As I was entering the second grade at The Brearley School in New York City, Bob was waiting to be called into the pilot training program. There was a waiting period to get into this program, so he finished his sophomore year at Williams and then lived at home in New York City working as a clerk for Lehman Brothers until his enlistment orders came through.

Bob kept track of his many bases and missions overseas through a large 3'x4' map, a log of his bombing runs and two scrapbooks of photographs and memorabilia—all containing information he could not include in his letters. In the 1940's there were only newspapers, books, telephones, telegrams, letters and radios that kept us informed. Letters that you mailed were the most efficient way of communicating when someone was overseas. Letters home also filled lonely hours and eased boredom for the men in service. Receiving them was usually the high point in a day and an existence far from home. So when Bob left New York for Nashville, Tennessee, his postcards and letters and this journey started with the words "Dear Dad...

FIRST STOP: NASHVILLE, TENN

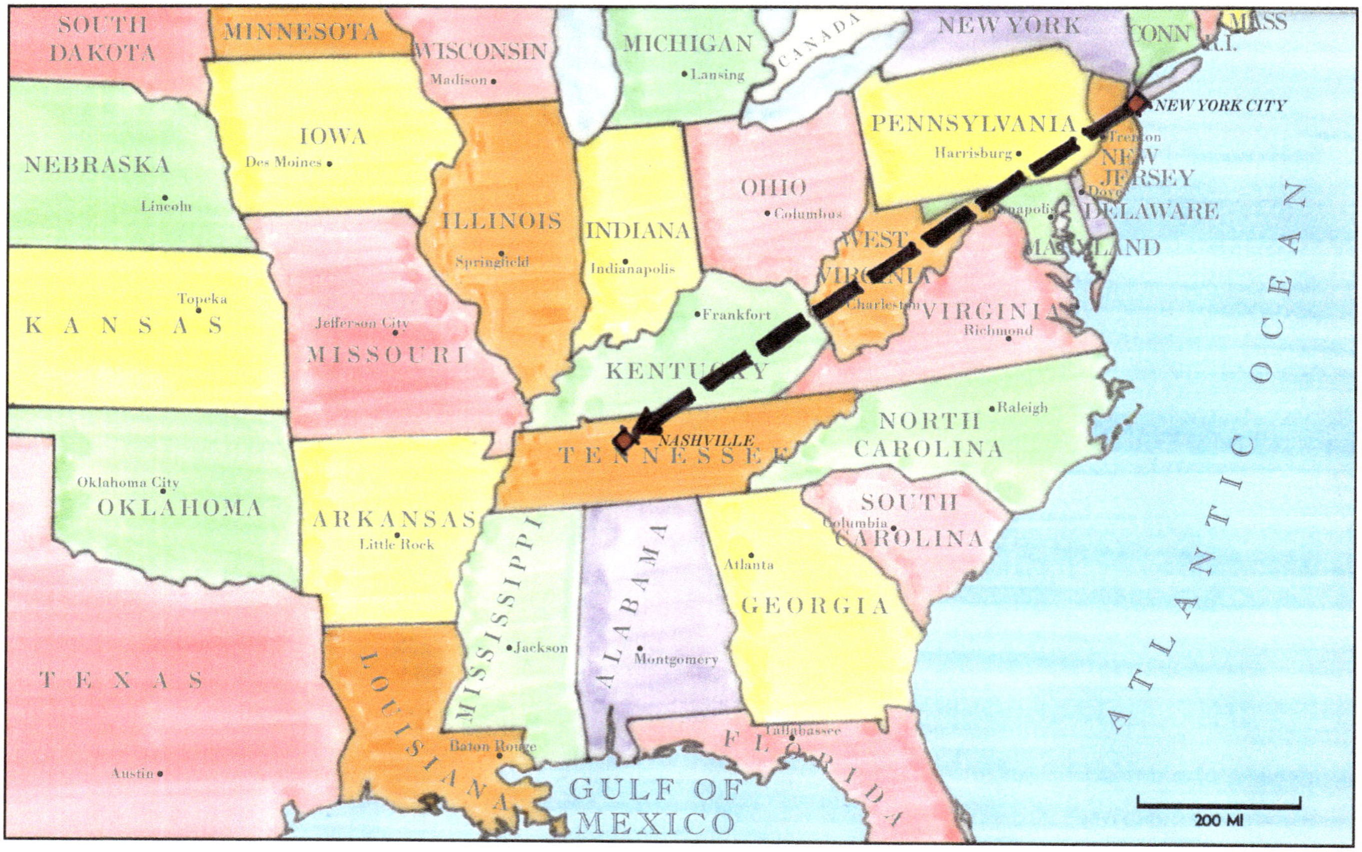

FEBRUARY 1943–MARCH 1943

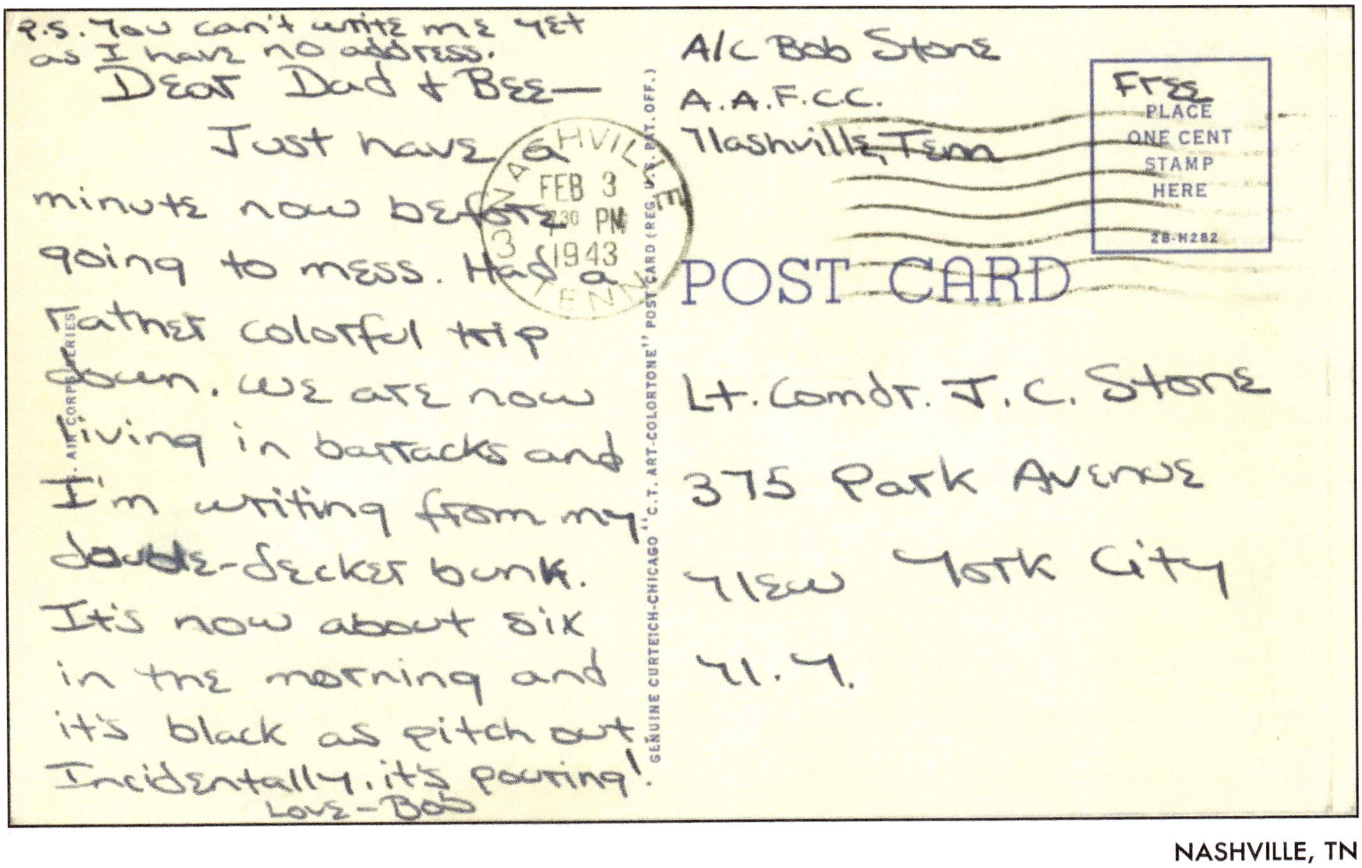
P.S. You can't write me yet
as I have no address.
Dear Dad & Bee—
Just have a
minute now before
going to mess. Had a
rather colorful trip
down. We are now
living in barracks and
I'm writing from my
double-decker bunk.
It's now about six
in the morning and
it's black as pitch out
Incidentally, it's pouring!
Love—Bob

A/C Bob Stone
A.A.F.C.C.
Nashville, Tenn

Free
PLACE
ONE CENT
STAMP
HERE
2B-H282

NASHVILLE
FEB 3
7:30 PM
1943
TENN

POST CARD

Lt. Comdr. J. C. Stone
375 Park Avenue
New York City
N.Y.

GENUINE CURTEICH-CHICAGO "C.T. ART-COLORTONE" POST CARD (REG. U.S. PAT. OFF.)
AIR CORPS SERIES

NASHVILLE, TN

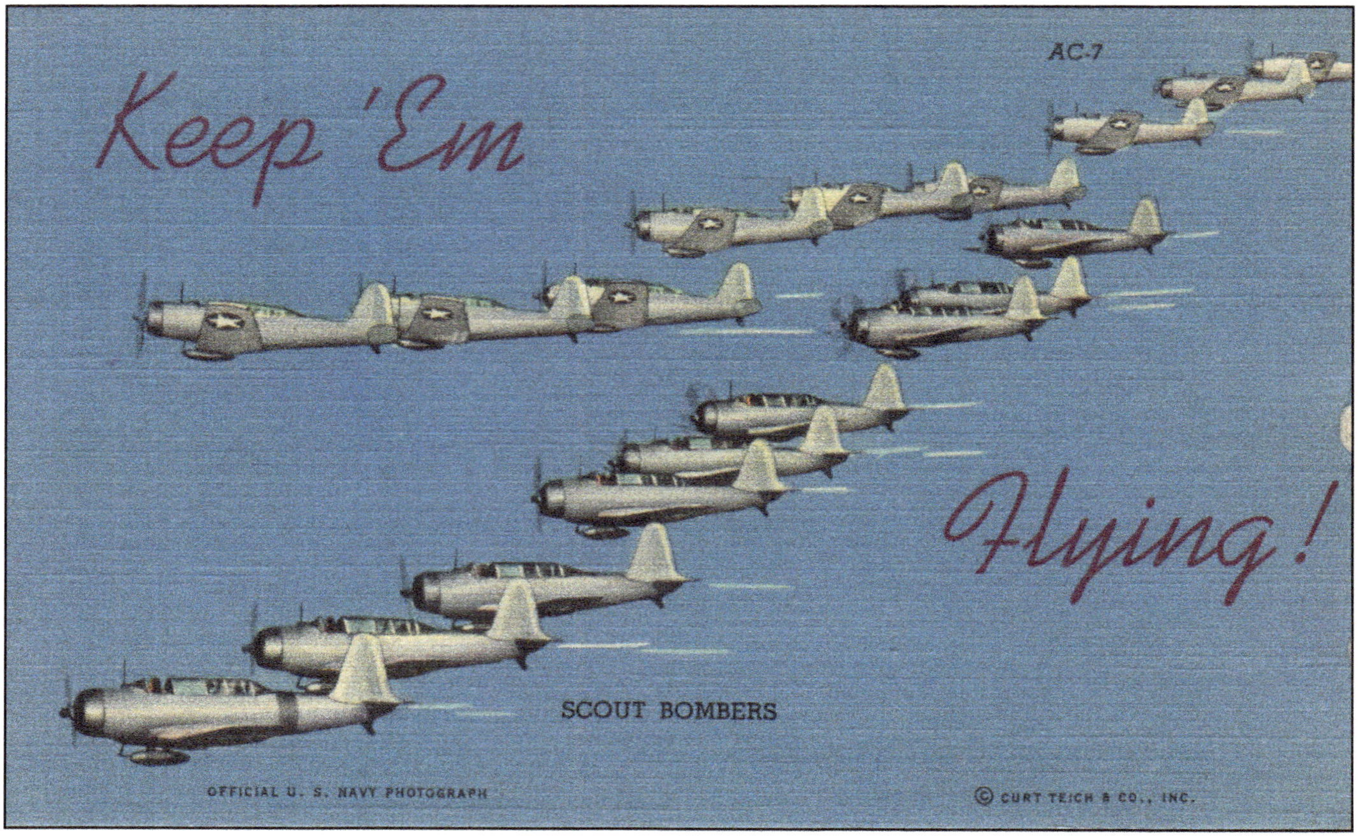

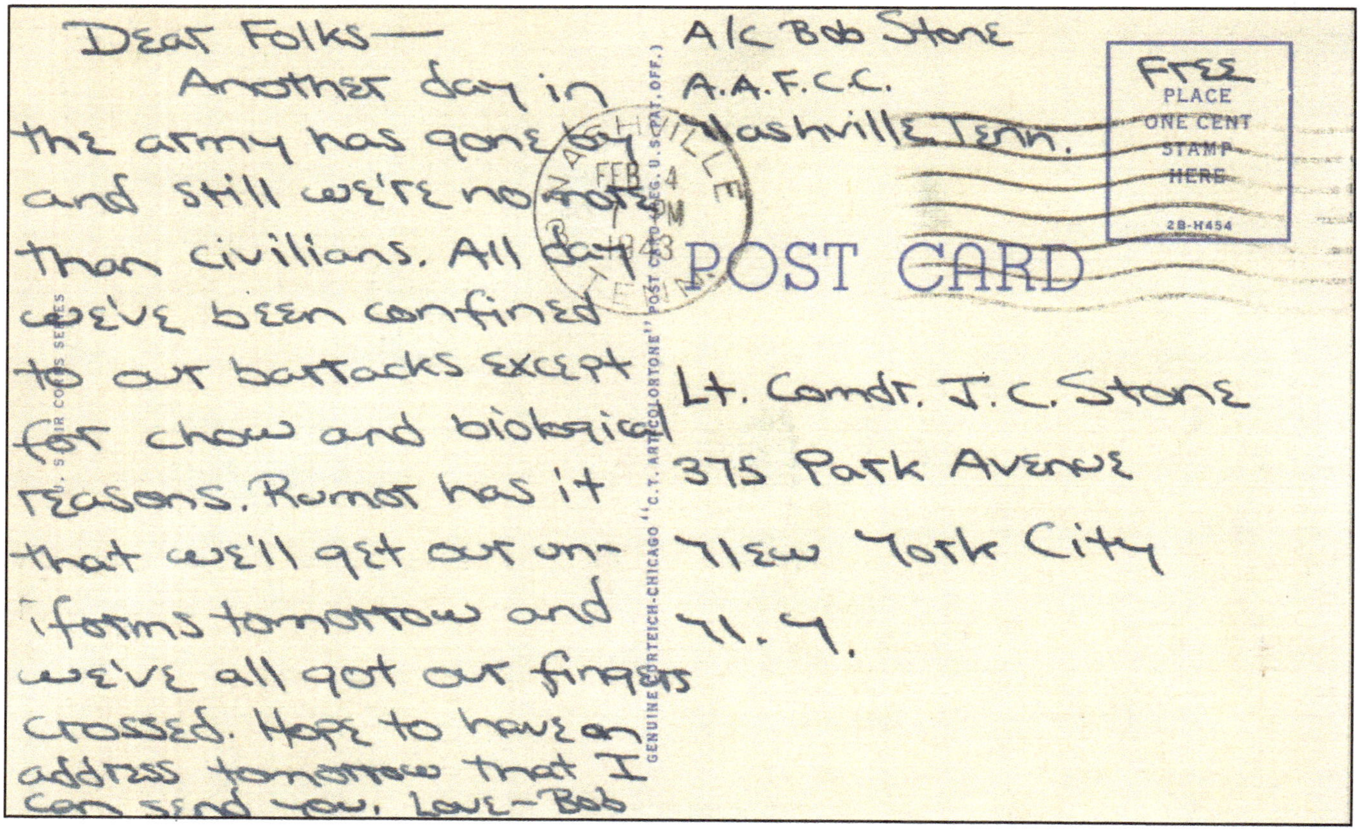

Dear Folks—
Another day in the army has gone by and still we're no more than civilians. All day we've been confined to our barracks except for chow and biological reasons. Rumor has it that we'll get our uniforms tomorrow and we've all got our fingers crossed. Hope to have an address tomorrow that I can send you. Love—Bob

A/C Bob Stone
A.A.F.C.C.
Nashville Tenn.

FREE
PLACE ONE CENT STAMP HERE
2B-H454

NASHVILLE FEB 4 7 PM 1943 TENN.

POST CARD

GENUINE CURTEICH-CHICAGO "C.T. ART-COLORTONE" POST CARD (REG. U.S. PAT. OFF.)

U. S. AIR CORPS SERIES

Lt. Comdr. J. C. Stone
375 Park Avenue
New York City
N. Y.

FEBRUARY 4-6, 1943

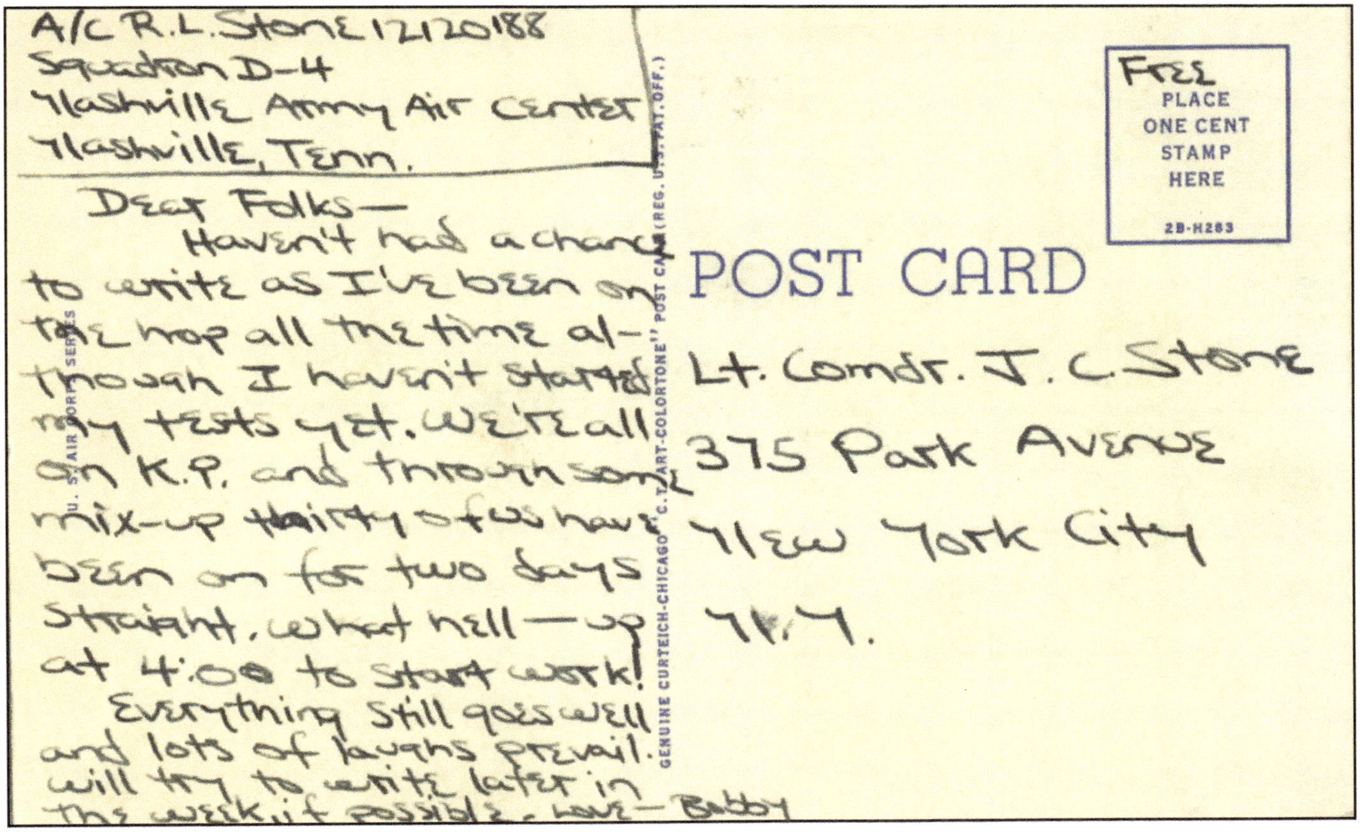

A/C R.L. Stone 12120188
Squadron D-4
Nashville Army Air Center
Nashville, Tenn.

Dear Folks—
Haven't had a chance to write as I've been on the hop all the time although I haven't started my tests yet. We're all on K.P. and through some mix-up ~~thirty~~ of us have been on for two days straight. What hell—up at 4:00 to start work!
Everything still goes well and lots of laughs prevail. Will try to write later in the week, if possible. Love—Bobby

U. S. AIR CORPS SERIES

GENUINE CURTEICH-CHICAGO "C. T. ART-COLORTONE" POST CARD (REG. U. S. PAT. OFF.)

Free
PLACE ONE CENT STAMP HERE
2B-H283

POST CARD

Lt. Comdr. J. C Stone
375 Park Avenue
New York City
N.Y.

NASHVILLE, TN

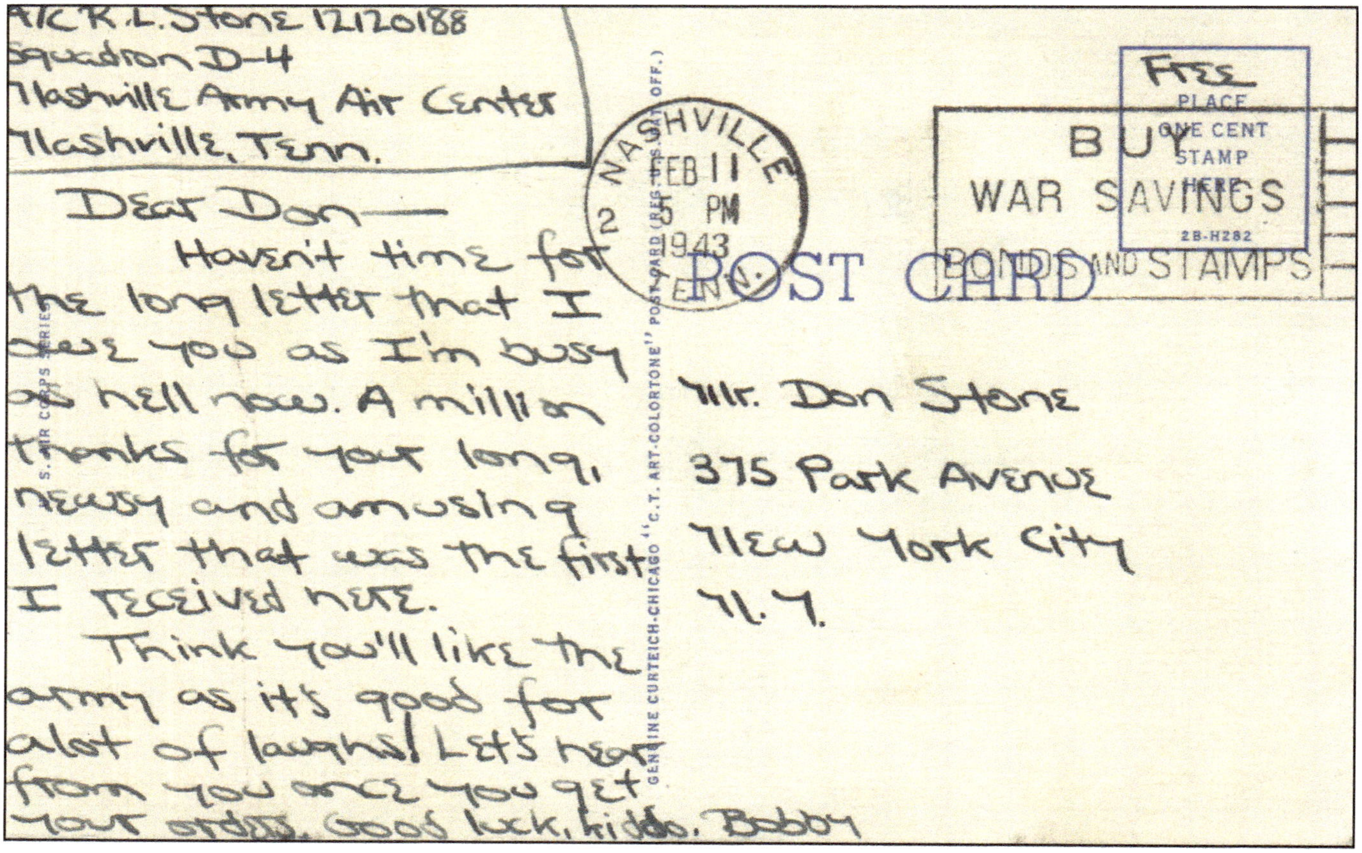
A/C R.L. Stone 12120188
Squadron D-4
Nashville Army Air Center
Nashville, Tenn.

Dear Don—
Haven't time for the long letter that I owe you as I'm busy as hell now. A million thanks for your long, newsy and amusing letter that was the first I received here.
Think you'll like the army as it's good for alot of laughs! Let's hear from you once you get your orders. Good luck, kiddo. Bobby

NASHVILLE FEB 11 5 PM 1943 TENN. 2
BUY WAR SAVINGS BONDS AND STAMPS
Free
PLACE ONE CENT STAMP HERE
2B-H282
POST CARD
U.S. AIR CORPS SERIES
GENUINE CURTEICH-CHICAGO "C.T. ART-COLORTONE" POST CARD (REG. U.S. PAT. OFF.)

Mr. Don Stone
375 Park Avenue
New York City
N.Y.

FEBRUARY 11, 1943

U. S. ARMY AIR FORCES

Friday the 11th [9]

Dear Dad, Bee, and Don (if he's still home)—

Sorry I haven't gotten a letter off to you before this but as you can imagine I've been on the go ever since I left. The train ride down was uneventful and very tiring and it was a relief to get off at Berry Hills. We all marched up to a place where we were assigned to barracks, that had double-decker beds. We stayed here for a couple of days until we marched over for processing. Here we were issued two duffle bags and stripped to the skin when we entered. After a couple of hours when we came out we were completely dressed and outfitted as a soldier. We got everything from shoes and toilet articles all the way to a gas mask. After being outfitted we moved to other barracks in a quarantine area where we are now confined for two weeks.

At the start of this week ~~week~~ most of the fellows started on their psychs, physicals, and interviews and are finishing them up today as they take four days. There are so many of us that they couldn't take us all and so about 60 of us still have everything to take. It's rotten this way as we feel left out of things not having started anything yet.

On monday and tuesday I was on K.P. We all have to take a crack at it and it's no punishment. Those of us not taking tests yet got stuck and had it two days in a row. It was really something as a guard routs you out of bed at four o'clock and you work all through the day without a let-up. It's certainly a heck of a grind!!!

This place continues to be lots of laughs. The fellows are really a riot and always good for chuckles. Life in the barracks is really something. It's just like Monte Carlo. Since we can't go anywhere, there are all kinds of gambling games perpetually in session.

The fellows in my barracks are a good lot and although there are about 35 of us we nearly all know each others first name. Pete's in another barracks but I see alot of him anyway. There's a kid about five bunks away from me who went to Weslyan and is a damn nice guy.

Never have I been with such a funny bunch of fellows. Each one is cleverer than the next and the repartee that floats around is truly something. Of course, the language is not that of the king's court, but none the less it's a riot!

Must run to formation in a minute so I'll halt here. Am sending my watch home as it's on the blink again. Please get it back to me as soon as possible cause I miss not having it. Write soon——

All love— Bobby

FEBRUARY 11-12, 1943

NASHVILLE ARMY AIR CENTER (A.A.F.C.C.)
NASHVILLE, TENNESSEE

Friday the 12th

Dear Don——

Really haven't time to write you a decent letter today cause I'm busy as hell, but still I want to drop you a line before you leave to help win the war.

The St. Chris arrived yesterday and it's really beautiful. Really kiddo, it's just the kind I wanted and that's not alot of bull. The nylon chain is very comfortable and I'd hardly know I was wearing anything at all—much more practical than a metal chain.

This place is really alot of laughs. The life in the barracks is funnier than a musical comedy on broadway as the fellows are a howl. There are all kinds of guys and they really make quite a conglomeration.

As yet I haven't had any classification tests although most of the fellows have. Probably the rest of us will start ours on monday. In the barracks you'd think it was Monte Carlo.

There are always two seven-hand poker games in session, gynn games galore, and a bunch of the kids play pinochle. We're in quarantine in a restricted area for two weeks and so everybody has alot of money with nothing to spend it on and so gambling runs rampant. The other night one kid was playing crap with two other guys and he cleaned them to the tune of $45—nice haul, eh? You'd have a field-day as there's a perpetual poker game to interest you—gosh how Jimmy would love it!

So far I've been on K.P. (we all have to take turns at it and its no punishment) twice. We had to get up at 4:00 and work all day till the evening and boy is it a tough grind!!!

No more now as I must run to a formation. Again thanks millions for the St. Cris and the inscription on it. Also thanks muchly for the long letter. It came in the first mail any of us received and it was my first letter! Best o' luck to you in the army and let me hear from you once you get settled somewhere and I'll do likewise.

Again all luck — Bobby

FEBRUARY 12-16, 1943

A. C.-4
Keep 'Em
Flying!
LIGHTNING INTERCEPTOR
© CURT TEICH & CO., INC.

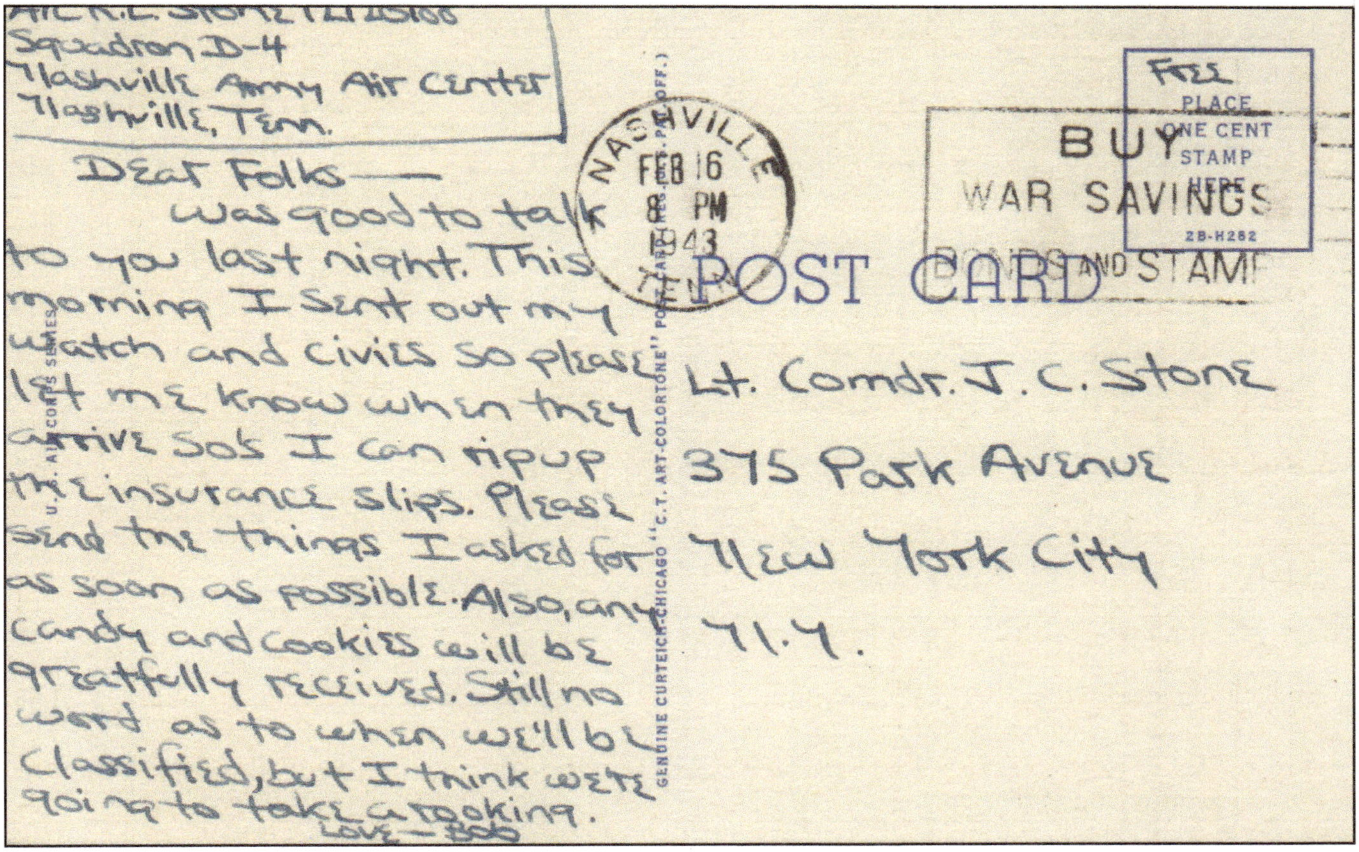
A/C R.L. Stone
Squadron D-4
Nashville Army Air Center
Nashville, Tenn.

Dear Folks—
Was good to talk
to you last night. This
morning I sent out my
watch and civies so please
let me know when they
arrive so's I can rip up
the insurance slips. Please
send the things I asked for
as soon as possible. Also, any
candy and cookies will be
greatfully received. Still no
word as to when we'll be
classified, but I think we're
going to take a rooking.
Love — Bob

NASHVILLE
FEB 16
8 PM
1943
TENN.

FREE
PLACE
ONE CENT
STAMP
HERE
2B-H262

BUY
WAR SAVINGS
BONDS AND STAMPS

POST CARD

Lt. Comdr. J. C. Stone
375 Park Avenue
New York City
N.Y.

U. S. AIR CORPS SERIES
GENUINE CURTEICH-CHICAGO "C.T. ART-COLORTONE" POST CARD (REG. U.S. PAT. OFF.)

A/C R.L. Stone 12120188
Squadron D-4
Nashville Army Air Center
Nashville, Tenn.

Dear Dad—
Just a hasty card to say that about 50 of us are taking an awful rooking as they said we won't take our psychs until the 23rd at earliest while the rest of the squadron will be classified and shipped out any day now. C'est la guerre.
Love—Bobby

Lt. Comdr. J.C. Stone
375 Park Avenue
New York City
N.Y.

FEBRUARY 17-18, 1943

NASHVILLE, TN

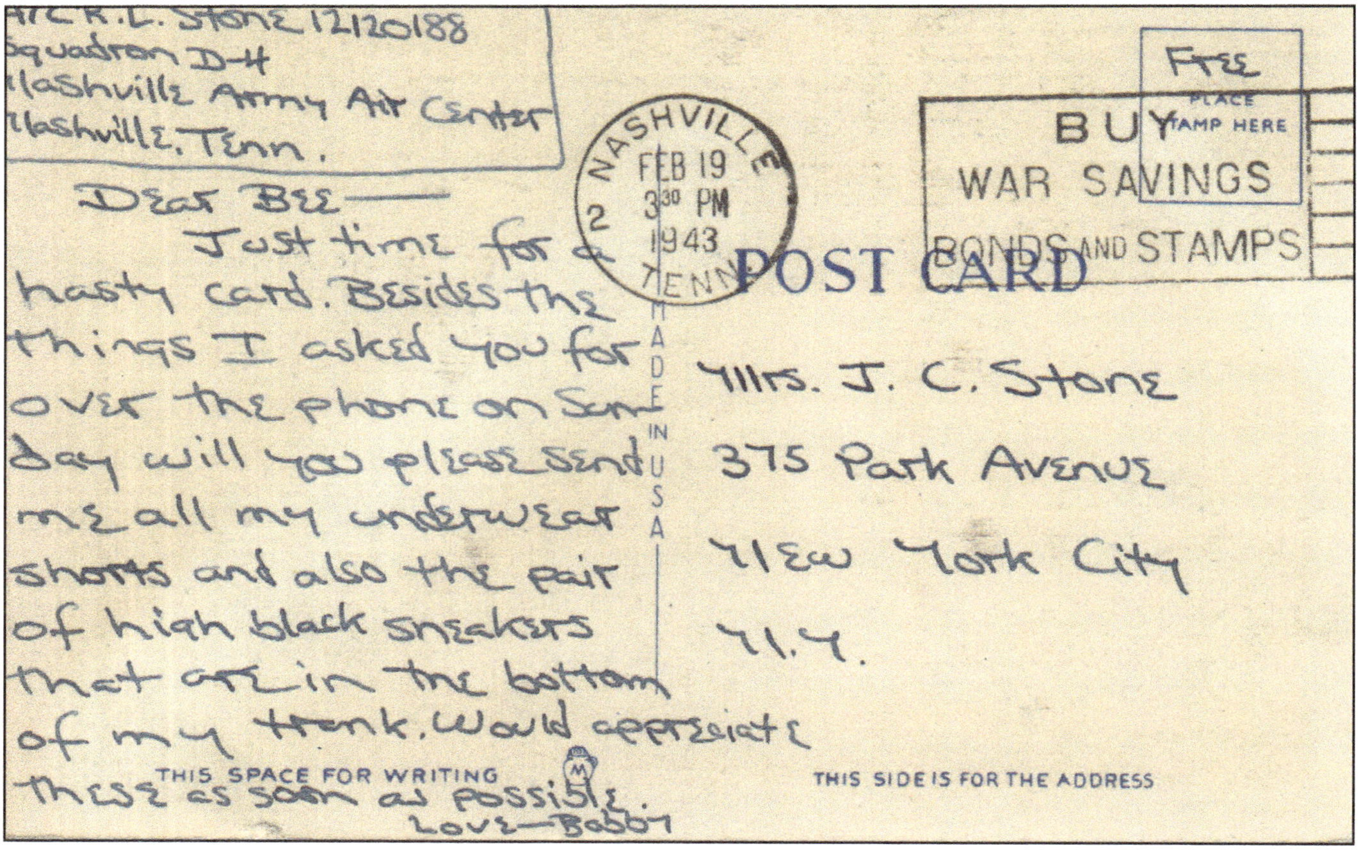
A/C R.L. Stone 12120188
Squadron D-4
Nashville Army Air Center
Nashville, Tenn.

NASHVILLE FEB 19 3³⁰ PM 1943 2 TENN.

BUY WAR SAVINGS BONDS AND STAMPS

Free

PLACE STAMP HERE

POST CARD

MADE IN USA

Dear Bee——
Just time for a hasty card. Besides the things I asked you for over the phone on Sunday will you please send me all my underwear shorts and also the pair of high black sneakers that are in the bottom of my trunk. Would appreciate these as soon as possible.
Love—Bobby

Mrs. J. C. Stone
375 Park Avenue
New York City
N.Y.

THIS SPACE FOR WRITING

THIS SIDE IS FOR THE ADDRESS

FEBRUARY 19-20, 1943

U. S. ARMY AIR FORCES

Saturday

Dear Dad + Bee—

Today I have some time to write although it may be a bit interrupted. You see I'm on a detail as a runner in Section headquarters today, and when we're not out we just sit put.

Still no word as to when we'll start our psychs but it's possible we may at the start of next week. All week the other fellows in the squadron have been getting back their classifications—also their disqualifications. Already about 35 have been washed out and not nearly all of the classifications are back yet. Some of the boys in the barracks were really broken up last night when they heard they'd been disqualified. By the way, Pete was classified as a pilot.

We got off quarantine last Wednesday and that was our first open-post night. I went to Nashville and met Phil and Lois for cocktails (can't buy anything but beer unless you bring your own bottle.) Had supper with a bunch of the boys in the Hotel Hermitage and stuck around until about 10:00 when we had to come back on the bus. Was really great to go into Nashville and be free for a few hours after our long confinement.

Last night I went to Nashville again and met Phil and Lois for dinner at the Andrew Jackson. We really had a swell time and they drove me home afterwards. It's such fun having them down here when we get off on Wednesday and Fridays.

Bee, thanks so much for sending me the towels and handkerchiefs so promptly—they're both perfect, and fit the bill to a T. I hope by now you've ~~gotten~~ received my watch which I'd like back as soon as possible, as I miss it very much. Also, I hope my clothes have arrived and that you'll have them laundered and put away for me. I sent you a card asking for my black sneakers in the bottom of my trunk and also please send with them all my underwear shorts that are in my big suitcase with my ~~ut~~ shirts ~~etc~~ and summer clothes etc.. Thanks muchly, Bee.

All week we've kept extremely busy with a rigorous program of two lectures (illustrated with movies), long periods of drilling, and mass calesthenics every day. We hardly have a minute to ourselves cause they've got us on the jump at all times. Besides all this we still pull K.P., guard duty (which I haven't had yet), latrine and various other duties.

No more now as I must be off. Thanks for your letters and also for forwarding my mail from 375. Incidentally, I should have a bill from the florist or hasn't it come yet. If so, please send it on.

All love—

Bobby

FEBRUARY 20-22, 1943

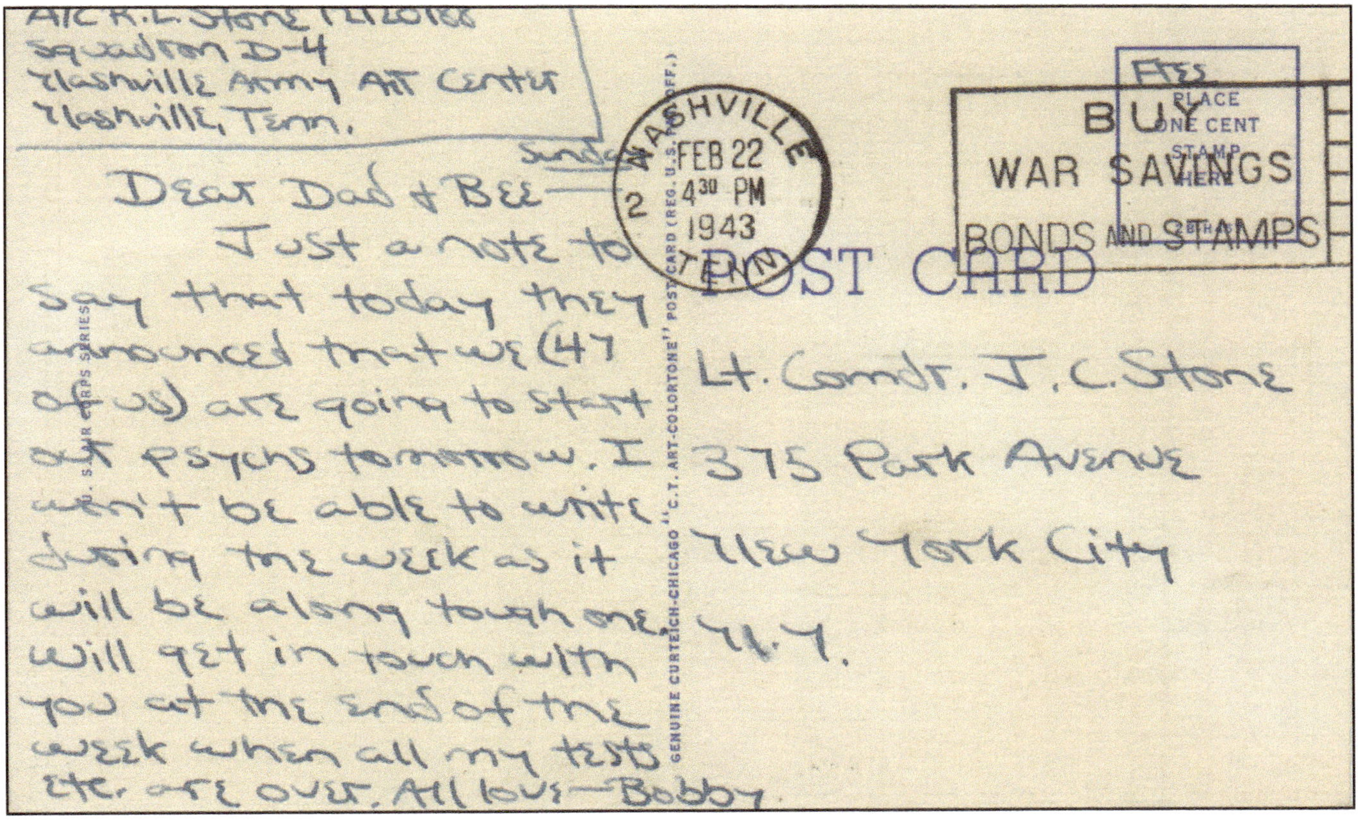

NASHVILLE, TN

U. S. ARMY AIR FORCES

Friday Nite

Dear Dad + Bee——

I imagine you've given me up as a lost soul since I haven't written for so long. Last week, however, I was tied up with all my tests etc and so far this week they've kept us on the hop with constant details and duties.

Last monday I started off with a day of written psychs that lasted for eight hours. It was the multiple choice type based on everything imaginable. Nobody is ever washed out as a result of this part of the test and it's merely used to help in your classification. The next day we took our individual psychs that can best be described as "penny arcade day." They have the damnest contraptions with lights and levers and buttons to push on and off. These tests were very interesting and are used to test your coordination. The next day and the most important I took my "ARMA" (adaptability relative to military aeronautics). This was an interview with a psychiatrist in which he asks a million and one different questions. This is the part of the tests that the majority of the fellows are washed out on. I really had fun talking with my fellow and I think I did quite well. The following day the actual

MARCH 5, 1943

physical came. Never have I had such a complete going-over. The most extensive thing is the eye test in which they give you depth perception, prism divergence and convergence, as well as a number of other things. I went through the whole exam without a recheck until I came to the last room where I got a recheck on my leg cause they wanted to have it X-rayed. Had this done right away and took the pictures and the report to the captain who is the orthopaedic surgeon. He said he thought that the plate would have to come out not because anything was wrong with it but because if anything ever happened to my leg it might cause complications or some such rot. Then I reported to the flight surgeon who told me to come back the next day which I did. Went to the original captain who had eight medical officer sitting in his office like a jury. He told them about my leg etc. and the verdict was rendered not guilty — i.e. that I didn't have to have it out. Then reported back to the flight surgeon who said my papers were o.k. to go on to classification and that was that. As yet no word has come through but it's not too bad a sign as some fellows have had to wait as long as two weeks to get any word as it's a long procedure. Waiting anxiously for some word one way or the other is absolute hell but there's not a darn thing you can do about it.

Page 3

U. S. ARMY AIR FORCES

On Friday a big shippment of several thousand men went out as pilots and Pete was among them. We've heard from them already from Maxwell Field, Alabama. Right now another bunch of pilots and navigators are on orders to leave any time, destination unknown. Slowly but surely most of my friends are taking off and I'd certainly love to join them.

The number of wash outs is increasing daily and some of the kids are really broken up. After being reverted to a private they get an automatic three day pass as well as open-post every night until twelve—hardly worth it, though!!

On Wednesday I went to Lois and Phil's apt. for dinner. Lois really outdid herself and cooked up one super meal. I was so surprised to find she was such a wonderful cook. I hadn't eaten so well in a month. It's certainly swell to have them around to visit with on open-posts.

Don't know if I've thanked you or not but many thanks now for the hanks, underwear, towels, sneakers, and cookies Bee. The last of which will be muchly appreciate any time again. Also, thanks Dad + Bee for your letters that are more than welcomed.

MARCH 5, 1943

The last week or so the weather has been absolutely miserable in this hell-hole. The temperature has been down around zero and it's most uncomfortable since we have such crummy barracks. Last night it snowed like anything and today we have a good four inches on the ground—no kidding this place really stinks and I'll certainly be glad to leave it.

Had a taste of real drudgery a week ago when I was on guard duty. It's a 24 hour proposition with two hours on and four off. Believe me it's no fun to be up most of the night pounding a beat all alone out in the cold—not my idea of a good time.

Last Sunday I had my first ~~ty~~typhoid and tetanus shots. They really dish them out wholesale. You roll up both sleeves and you're hit from both sides at once by a needle—most unpleasant!

I hope by now my watch is about ready as I'm lost without it. Please send all my letters to the boys at Deerfield as well as to Don and Ken so I won't have to write everybody separately cause I just haven't the time.

Keep your fingers crossed that my classification comes through alright and that I get by. I'll let you know as soon as anything comes through. My love to you all—

Bobby

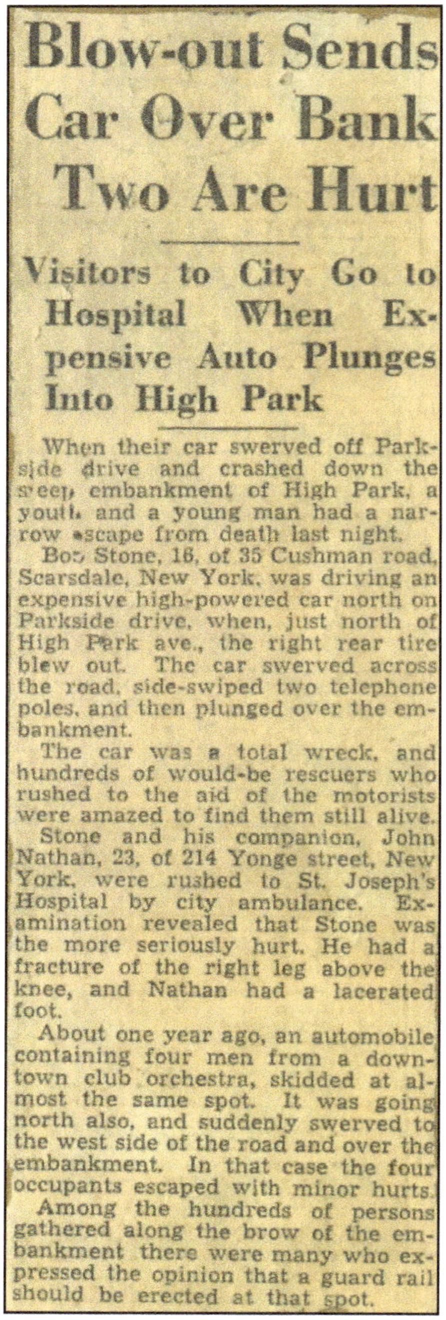

Blow-out Sends Car Over Bank Two Are Hurt

Visitors to City Go to Hospital When Expensive Auto Plunges Into High Park

When their car swerved off Parkside drive and crashed down the steep embankment of High Park, a youth and a young man had a narrow escape from death last night.

Bob Stone, 16, of 35 Cushman road, Scarsdale, New York, was driving an expensive high-powered car north on Parkside drive, when, just north of High Park ave., the right rear tire blew out. The car swerved across the road, side-swiped two telephone poles, and then plunged over the embankment.

The car was a total wreck, and hundreds of would-be rescuers who rushed to the aid of the motorists were amazed to find them still alive.

Stone and his companion, John Nathan, 23, of 214 Yonge street, New York, were rushed to St. Joseph's Hospital by city ambulance. Examination revealed that Stone was the more seriously hurt. He had a fracture of the right leg above the knee, and Nathan had a lacerated foot.

About one year ago, an automobile containing four men from a downtown club orchestra, skidded at almost the same spot. It was going north also, and suddenly swerved to the west side of the road and over the embankment. In that case the four occupants escaped with minor hurts.

Among the hundreds of persons gathered along the brow of the embankment there were many who expressed the opinion that a guard rail should be erected at that spot.

In July of 1938, Bob and Jack Nathan (an older friend and substitute parent) were driving north on a fishing trip to Canada when a rear tire on their LaSalle car blew out and, because there was no guardrail, the car somersaulted down a ravine. Miraculously, their injuries were a broken femur for Bob and a lacerated foot for Jack. Fortunately, there was a doctor in Toronto who had knowledge of the operation with a Lane Plate that could be screwed onto bone and would facilitate healing on Bob's femur. He was in a body cast that was modified after several months so that he could return to Deerfield, where he had to be lowered out of the train window onto the platform. For many months or even years, a Toronto tire store featured a photo of their wrecked car with this heading: "THIS...might have happened to you...but... it can't happen if you ride on Goodyear Lifeguard Tires" and with that warning I'm sure their tire sales increased.

CAR ACCIDENT EXPLANATION, JULY 1938

Youths Injured When Car Makes Plunge

—(Telegram photo. Copyright, 1938.)

Here is the wreckage of a motor car in which two U.S. youths, bound for northern Ontario on a fishing trip, narrowly escaped death when it plunged into the ravine along High Park avenue just south of Bloor street after a blowout, according to police. Both were rushed to hospital, John Nathan, of Pelham, N.Y., with a cut foot, and Robert Stone, of Scarsdale, N.Y., with a leg fracture that will keep him confined two months.

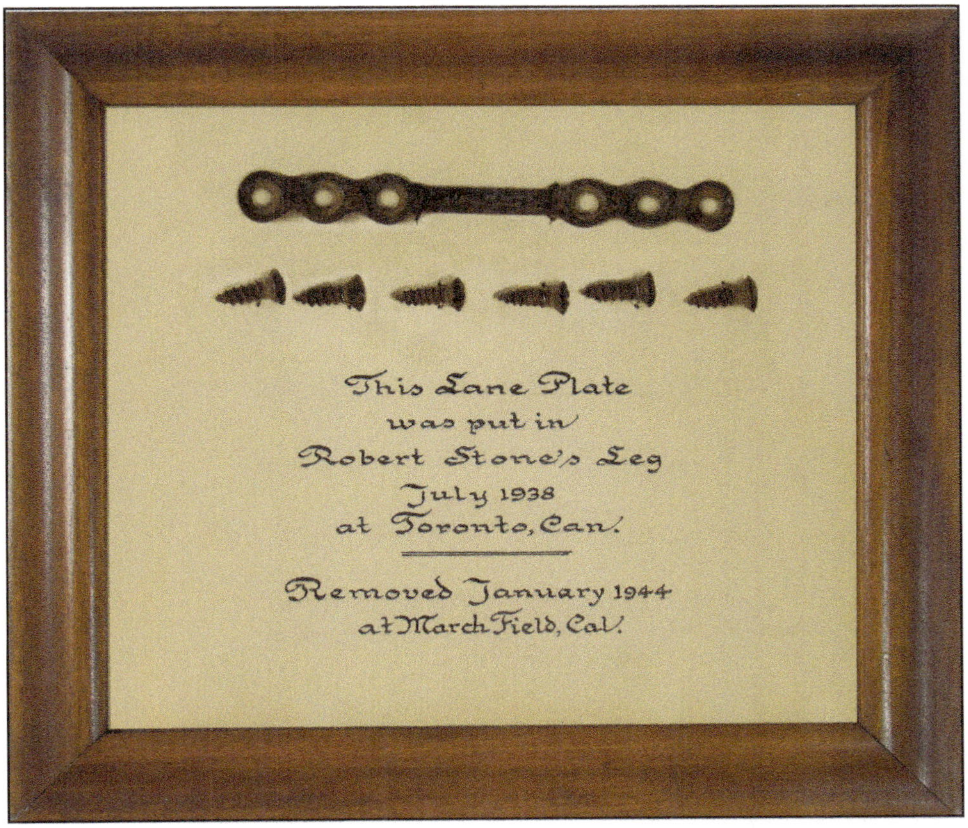

U. S. ARMY AIR FORCES

Sunday

Dear Dad & Bee (also the frères if home)——

I hope you'll excuse the long wait without mail but unfortunately nothing has broken my way of late and consequently I haven't felt up to writing. As a matter of fact, I just got out of the hospital last night after being in for five days with a temp. of 102 and a very bad sore throat. Never have I spent a more miserable few days or under worse conditions.

A week ago today I got another one of those disappointments that the army is so free with. We were put on shipping orders and were to leave last sunday, that is until they took us off orders and so here we sit. Right now our original squadron of 210 men has been narrowed down to about 30 poor souls who are left here in Nashville—all the rest have been shipped out. There are so few of us left that we're all in one barracks when formerly we occupied seven. It's really rotten to have all your friends sent away cause you get used to live with one another and then your friendship is broken up.

I'm told that today is the first day of Spring and believe it or not it's snowing outside. This place

MARCH 21, 1943

has the damnest weather of any spot I've ever been. That's why so many of the kids spend half of their time in the hospital—it's really miserable!

There's very little to write in the way of news since our days are so very routine. The main accent is on continual guard duty, K.P., and many other odd details. Of course we drill, have gas mask practise and do calisthenics.

Since I was sick last week, I wasn't in town at all, but before that I saw quite a bit of Lois and Phil. It's swell having them here since the town of Nashville has so little to offer. When the war is over, Tenn. is one state I will never visit again.

Can't think of any more news to write ~~and~~ but I'll let you know as soon as I have any idea of moving out although I can't tell you exactly the day cause it's all very secret. As a matter of fact, they threaten to take away our cadet appointment if we tell anyone our date or destination of shippment.

Write often!

Lots of love to all →

Bobby

P.S. Think it's swell about your making the marines, Jim!

U. S. ARMY AIR FORCES

Wednesday Nite

Dear Dad + Bee—

'Twas good to talk with you tonight, Dad, after missing you the other times. I'm sorry you didn't get the letter I mailed Saturday because I explained that I'd been in the hospital and why I hadn't written etc. I hope by now that it has arrived.

As I said tonight I've only got a few more days to spend in this god-forsaken place. Out of our original squadron of 210 there are only about twenty-five of us left. Why I had to be one of the forgotten few, I will never know!

I honestly don't know where we'll be sent although I imagine it will either be Santa Ana, California or Elington Field, Texas as there are two large bombardier schools there. Heard a rumor that there's a new school in Georgia that we might be sent to—god, I hope so cause then I'd have a chance to get home if I got a few days pass while if I went west my chances would be nil. Cross your fingers I stay in the East although my chances are slim.

MARCH 24, 1943

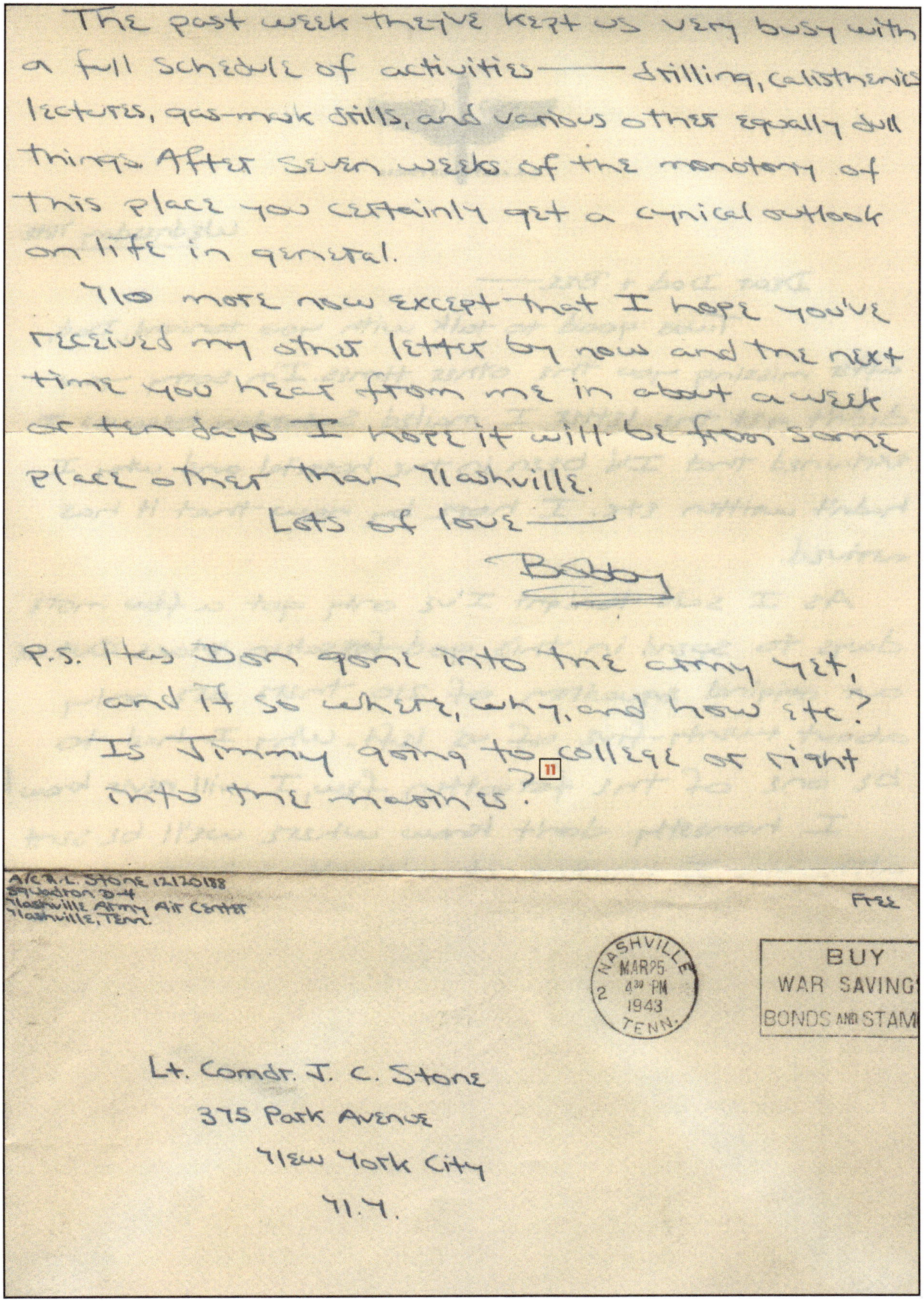

The past week they've kept us very busy with a full schedule of activities —— drilling, calisthenics lectures, gas-mask drills, and various other equally dull things. After seven weeks of the monotony of this place you certainly get a cynical outlook on life in general.

No more now except that I hope you've received my other letter by now and the next time you hear from me in about a week or ten days I hope it will be from some place other than Nashville.

Lots of love ——

Bobby

P.S. Has Don gone into the army yet, and if so where, why, and how etc?

Is Jimmy going to college or right into the marines?[11]

A/C R. L. Stone 12120188
Squadron D-4
Nashville Army Air Center
Nashville, Tenn.

Free

NASHVILLE MAR 25 4³⁰ PM 1943 TENN.

BUY WAR SAVINGS BONDS AND STAMPS

Lt. Comdr. J. C. Stone
375 Park Avenue
New York City
N.Y.

BOMBARDIERS in the 1940's

Somewhere during this period Bob was selected to be a bombardier rather than a navigator or pilot and so his courses were made more specific to his future responsibilities. In training bombardiers before 1942 there were no screening tests. That is why so many unqualified men were sent to pilot, navigator, or bombardier classes and why so many were disqualified or flunked out.

Devising a valid test to select prospective bombardiers turned out to be a much more difficult problem than those developed to single out prospective pilots or navigators. Pilots required high psychomotor skills, but not necessarily excellence in mathematics; navigators required a facility with mathematics but not nearly the motor skills required of the pilots. The bombardier turned out to be a quite different breed. In addition to understanding the laws of physics he needed math skills that approached those of the navigator and motor skills more delicate than those required of the pilot.

Before 1940 the pilot was in command of flying low over enemy targets and deciding when and where to drop the bombs and either doing it himself or directing one of his crew to do so. In the 1940's, "bombardier" was a new title for a different brand of soldier. Brig. Gen. Eugene L Eubank, USAAF, described him this way: "…the most important of all our fighting men today—he is most important because upon him rests the success of any mission in which he participates. The greatest bombing plane in the world with its combat crew take him into battle through weather and through enemy opposition just so he may have 30 seconds over the target, in those 30 seconds he must vindicate the greatest responsibility ever placed upon an individual soldier in the line of duty."[12]

In the B-24 Liberator the bombardier sat below the pilots with a view ahead and to the ground below, and with a Norden Bombsight through which to aim his payload of bombs. The bombardier put the air speed, wind speed, direction and angle of drift information into the Norden Bombsight. Then, based on this information, the pilot turned the plane onto autopilot which flew the plane to the precise target and the bombsight calculated the trajectory of the bomb. [13]

Since the Norden was considered a critical wartime instrument, bombardiers were required to take an oath during their training stating that they would defend its secret with their life if necessary. In case the bomber plane should make an emergency landing in enemy territory, the bombardier would have to shoot the important parts of the Norden with a gun to disable it. This action would still leave a nearly intact apparatus to the enemy, so a thermite grenade was installed; the heat of the chemical reaction would melt the Norden into a lump of metal.

After each completed mission, bomber crews left the aircraft with a bag that was deposited in a safe called the Bomb Vault. This secure facility was typically in one of the base's Quonset hut support buildings. The bombsight shop was manned by enlisted men who were members of a Support Depot Service Group attached to each USAF bombardment group. These shops not only guarded the bombsights but performed critical maintenance on the Norden and related control equipment. [14]

That is why on Bob's "scariest mission", when they had to throw all their heavy equipment overboard, they threw everything but the Norden Bombsight into the sea. I don't even know if they kept their parachutes.

USAAF BOMBARDIER SCHOOL
ELLINGTON FIELD, TX

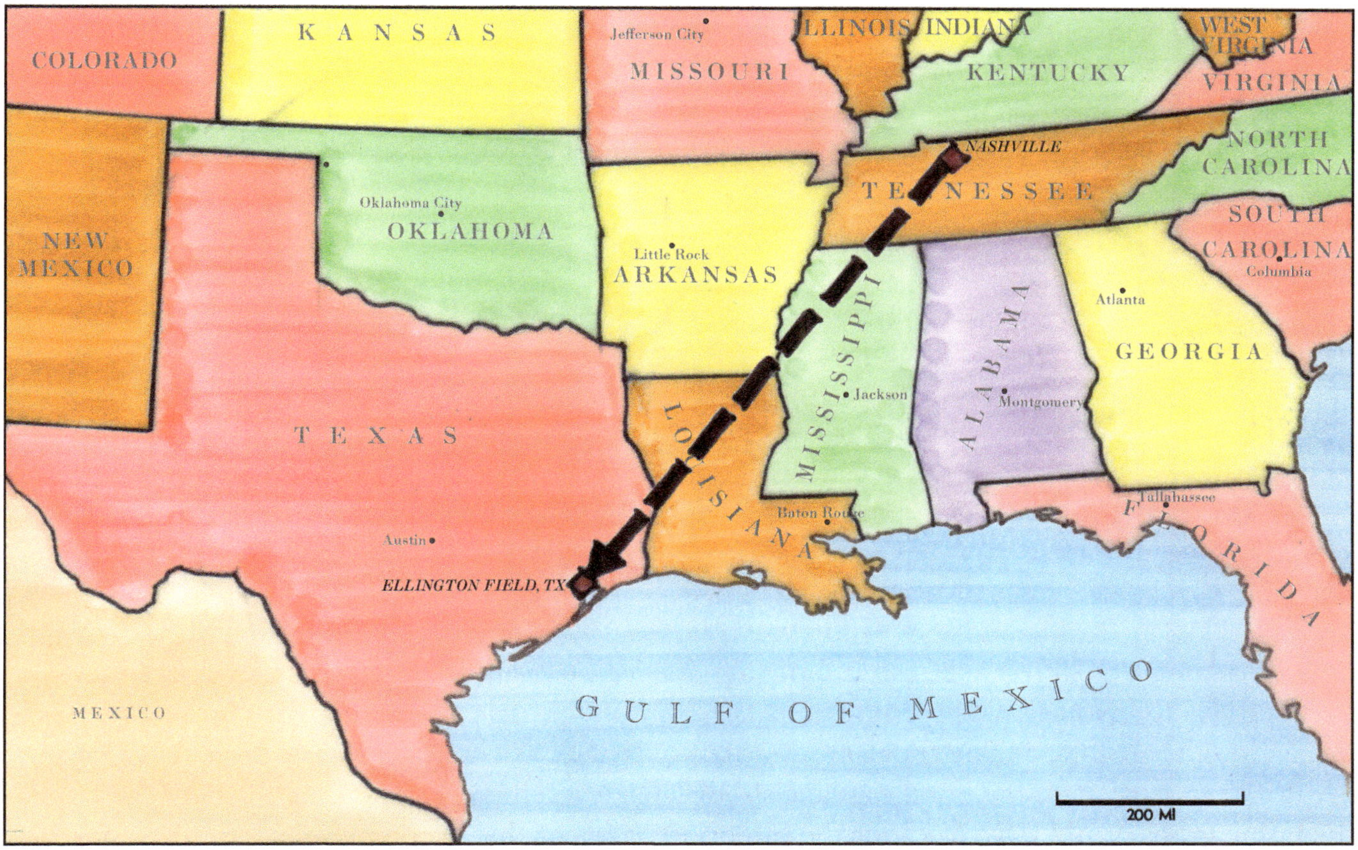

MARCH 1943–JUNE 1943

PREFLIGHT SCHOOL
BOMBARDIER
U. S. ARMY AIR CORPS
ELLINGTON FIELD, TEXAS

Saturday Nite

Dear Dad + Bee —

After my first few days, Ellington seems to be a swell place. Our routine here is really something. Every day we get up at 5:30 and make up our bunks etc. and go to breakfast at 6:15. Then we go to calisthenics for an hour after which we go to a class on military science. Next comes lunch followed by four hours of classes. Then we have an hour of drill and then supper. You don't have a free minute all day and in fact you can't sit on your bunk from 5:30 till 5:00 in the afternoon. Lights go out at 10:00 but believe me you're glad to get to bed because you can't help being completely exhausted.

If I ever get through the courses here it will be a miracle because all of them are subjects I avoided taking at college and was weak on in prep-school. I have maps and aerial photography, arithmetic, code, and physics which is a stinker. The math and physics look as though they'll be tough as heck because they have to cram alot of college work into a very short period of time since they try to rush us through.

APRIL 3, 1943

So far the weather has been brutally hot with a bright sun shining down all day. Several times I almost blacked out while marching. Would you be good enough to send me some salt tablets, Bee? I tried to buy some on the post and can't, and we won't get to town for the next three weeks.

Today all of the cadets in both the bombardier and and navigator wings had a big parade and we passed in review before all the top-officers of the post. It was really tough in the boiling sun. I hope that I get used to it soon because it really takes it out of me right now coming from a cold climate.

The food continues to be terrific! Today we had a large steak for lunch plus our choice of four vegetables etc. I have never had such meals before even at Deerfield. It's just like going to one of the best restaurants in New York. When we have eggs and hotcakes, they're hot because they take them off the stove as you come by in line.

From now on I doubt if you'll hear from me at all during the week because we have no time to ourselves except for a few hours at night when I'll have to be studying if I ever expect to get by. So, don't worry if you don't hear from me, and please you write cause mail is always swell.

My love to all — Bobby

P.S. Please send all my letters on to Don and Jim as I haven't time to write them too. Please don't forget.

U. S. ARMY AIR FORCES

Sunday

Dear Dad & Bee —

It was only last night that I wrote you but since then I recall several things that I'd meant to ask you to send me as soon as possible. All of the following I can't get at the PX and I'd really appreciate your sending me —— 1.) A Yardley Shaving Bowl.

2.) Some Yardley Shaving Talcom.

3.) Five wooden hangers (which can't be bought here for love nor money.)

4.) Some salt tablets.

I hate to bother you with these things but I just can't get them and if possible would like to have them. Thanks loads, in advance.

While on the subject of sending things, I wonder what's happened to my subscriptions of Life, the Williams Record, and Deerfield Scroll. If they're coming to 375, I'd appreciate your forwarding them.

Haven't any more news since last night so I'll hang up now. Thanks for all my various requests, and I hope they're not too much trouble.

Lots of love ——.

Bobby

Monday Nite

Dear Dad + Bee—

This is gonna be short and snappy because I have lots of work to do. Things are going only fairly well since the class work is very hard for me. Physics and math are really college calibre courses that they try to cover in a short time.

This week-end our squadron was surprised when they gave us open-post when we weren't supposed to get it for three weeks. I didn't go to town but stayed here and studied over the week-end. It was really dead in the barracks because nearly all of the gang beat it for Houston. I'd loved to have gone but didn't feel I could afford to with the work moving so fast.

Thanks loads for all the various things that I received this afternoon. Everything was perfect and muchly appreciated. Also, thanks for your various letters. I'm glad that you're over the measels now, Bee. What a silly disease to catch at your age!

The weather continues to be very warm and at times quite uncomfortable—it's more bearable now that we're wearing sun-tans. It's just as warm here as it is at home in the middle of the summer.

The fellows here are really the best. We have a swell bunch in our barracks and we all get along fine. The food continues to be great and it's a treat to go to each meal.

Gotta run now but I did want you to at least hear from me. Please continue to write often cause your letters are really appreciated.

Lots of love

Bobby

PREFLIGHT SCHOOL
BOMBARDIER
U. S. ARMY AIR CORPS
ELLINGTON FIELD, TEXAS

Sunday

Dear O'ma[15] —

It was good to hear from you again and to know that you're back in New York. I'm sure I don't know the occasion for my deserving such a generous check but none the less I do appreciate it very much and can't thank you enough. You can be certain that I'll find some good use for it in one way or another. It was really so swell of you O'ma, and I can't express how grateful I am — a millions thanks!

Life here at preflight is swell although it's quite tough. The classes are very difficult for me and they move darn fast trying to cram alot of work into a small period of time. Right now I'm taking math, physics, code, maps and charts, and military science.

Besides our classes we have an hour of calisthenics and drill every day. From 5:00 in the morning until 5:30 at night we haven't a minute to ourselves — we're really busy!

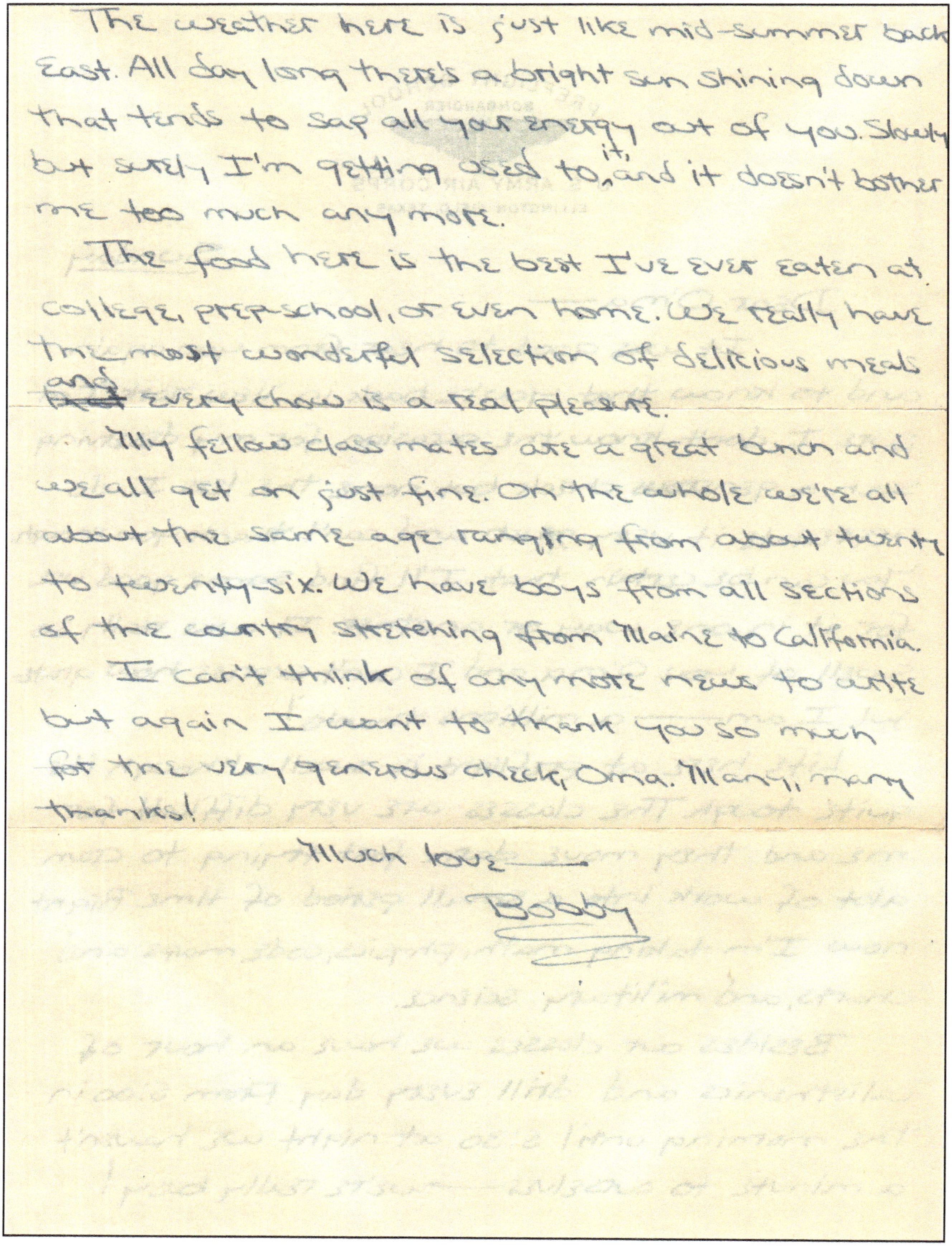

The weather here is just like mid-summer back East. All day long there's a bright sun shining down that tends to sap all your energy out of you. Slowly but surely I'm getting used to it, and it doesn't bother me too much any more.

The food here is the best I've ever eaten at college, prep-school, or even home. We really have the most wonderful selection of delicious meals ~~that~~ and every chow is a real pleasure.

My fellow class mates are a great bunch and we all get on just fine. On the whole we're all about the same age ranging from about twenty to twenty-six. We have boys from all sections of the country stretching from Maine to California.

I can't think of any more news to write but again I want to thank you so much for the very generous check, Oma. Many, many thanks!

Much love—

Bobby

APRIL 18-25, 1943

U. S. ARMY AIR FORCES

Sunday

Dear Dad and Bee—

There's not much news to report from Ellington, but I thought I'd at least drop you a line saying that all goes well. The work continues to be interesting but none the less tough as hell. The physics here is darn rough and the instruction is far from good. In most courses we have enlisted men who are not great.

As yet I haven't been off the post because I've been stuck with guard duty, studying, and this week-end a big parade for some women flyers who received their wings. Frankly, I'm going just a bit stir crazy being confined here on the post not seeing civilians and the other symbols of free living that still exist. Just to see a car that isn't painted olive drab would be a treat in itself.

Thanks for sending me that picture of Don, Bee. Frankly I don't like it ~~too~~ much cause I don't think it does him justice. Incidentally what's happened to the picture of Mom, Don, and you in uniform that you were going to send me, Dad? Remember I was having one made of Mom 4½ x 6½ I think it was?

I'm getting more accustomed to the weather even though it continues to be extremely warm. So far we've only had one rain in three weeks and it really poured then.

Can't think of any more to write now so I'll stop here. Thanks loads for your letters — please keep them up cause they're muchly appreciated. Incidentally, they've changed our address a little and it now reads as follows —

A/C R.L.S 12120188
Bombardier Wing
Group 21 Squadron D.
Ellington Field, Texas

If you use this address it will be easier for the clerks and we'll get the letters that much sooner. Please notice it's group 21 and not 20 and I didn't make a mistake in writing it. It's changed now because one class just graduated last wednesday.

Must run now —

Lots of love —

Bobby

APRIL 25-27, 1943

U. S. ARMY AIR FORCES

Thursday Nite

Dear Dad + Bee—

Just a hasty note cause I'm very busy with alot of work for classes tomorrow. I guess my last letter crossed yours Dad because the pictures arrived. Many thanks! I really think that one of Mom is swell and Doris is good also.

I'm sending you a picture-book of Ellington which gives only a fair idea of what goes on here. I think, however, you'll enjoy seeing it anyway.

As yet I haven't gotten to town but plan to go to Houston on Saturday night and a bunch of us hope to go to Galveston swimming on Sunday, if all goes well. I'm really looking forward to getting off the post for some diversion from the routine of army-life.

Must run now—

Lots of love,

Bobby

P.S. Again thanks for the pictures, Dad. Please don't forget to send me the one of the Comdr. when it comes.

ELLINGTON FIELD, TX

U. S. ARMY AIR FORCES

Sunday Night

Dear Dad and Bee:

Have a few minutes before retreat and so I'll bat out a or two before retiring. The past week was a tough one scholastically as well as physically since we had several tests and two parades. It has gotten lots warmer (if possible) and so I didn't relish doing anything strenuous.

Last week I got a rather nice break when I was made Squadron Supply Sgt. What it means is that I'm in charge of the supply room and to see that we have all the mops, brooms, soap, buckets, etc. that we need. I also have to take charge of having all the squadron's shoes sent up to the repair dept. It's really quite a repponsible position and the work is good experience. Also, it makes me one of the squadron officers and so I'm excused from the hour of drill every afternoon. Also, we get out first on open post and also get an extra open post every wednesday night. The last, and most welcomed, of the priveledges is that all of the officers were put into little rooms instead of living right in the row of bunks in the barracks. In each barracks there is small room at one end that is shut off from the rest by a door. It's swell to have our own room because you can get lots more work done in the quiet of a room instead of amidst the hubbub of the barracks. I'm in a four man room with the squadron commander, a flight lieutenant, and our squadron first sgt. As you can imagine, I welcome the new authority and the breaks that go with it. Also, if you're a cadet officer it goes on your record that follows you from field to field, and if you do a good job it speaks well for you.

Last night I left the post for the first time since I've been here. I went to Houston which isn't a bad town although I'd take any eastern town at the drop of a hat. Today I had a really swell time when three of us went

MAY 2, 1943

up to Galveston for the day swimming. It was really loads of fun to don a bathing suit and loll on the beach. Of course I was a dope and stayed too long in the sun and am really miserable right now. From head to toes I'm as red as a lobster. I've never had such a bad burn, and I only hope that it feels better in the morning. Frankly, I doubt if I get any sleep tonight. Incidentally, we hitch hiked all the way which is about forty miles. We got rides up and back without even holding up our thumb. The people were surely swell. On the way down a young major from Camp Wallace took us most of the way.

Thanks loads, Bee, for attending to my pen. It works fine now. I'm using the typewriter only because I feel too punk to push a pen tonight. If you can find my swimming trunks, I'd appreciate it if you'd send them to me in case we go swimming again. They are a light tan canvas-like pair of trunks with a removable belt. I think they're in my trunk with my white tennis shorts. Thanks muchly.

Must run now as bed-time is nearing. I won't get much sleep but at least I'm going to give it a try. Thanks loads for your letters.

Lots of love,

Bobby

U. S. ARMY AIR FORCES

Monday Night

Dear Dad:

Even though I wrote you last night, I want to thank you now for the pictures that arrived today. I really think the picture of the commander is the "nuts". As a matter of fact, I think it's the best picture you've ever had taken. That uniform certainly is impressive! It's funny being in the cadets and having a Dad in the navy. Needless to say it provokes untold comment among my friends when they know that I have a Dad wearing the blue and gold.

I just got out of the hospital a few minutes ago after being in since last night at about one o'clock. I had such a miserable sunburn that at about twelve-thirty last night the ambulance took me in. All night I was awake and they treated my burns, so that tonight I feel lots better although I'm still not wholly cured. This damn Texas sun is very disceptive and you don't know that you're being burned until it's too late.

Again thanks for the picture of both you and Don. Incidentally, this picture of him is lots better than the first one Bee sent me. I've got to get to bed now and try to make up for all the sleep I lost last night.

Lots of love,

Bob

MAY 3-4, 1943

THIS SPACE FOR WRITING MESSAGES

A/C R.L. Stone
Bombardier Wing
Group 21 Squadron D
Ellington Field, Texas

GALVESTON MAY 4 6:30 PM 1943 TEXAS

Dear Folks—
A few of us were down here today and I'm now as broiled as a lobster. It was to go bathing and sunning for a change from our routine—Bobby

PUB. BY GALVESTON WHOLESALE NEWS CO., GALVESTON, TEXAS

"TICHNOR QUALITY VIEWS" REG. U.S.PAT.OFF. MADE ONLY BY TICHNOR BROS., INC., BOSTON, MASS.

FREE
PLACE ONE CENT STAMP HERE
MADE IN U.S.A.

POST CARD

Lt. Comdr. J.C. Stone
375 Park Avenue
New York City
N.Y.

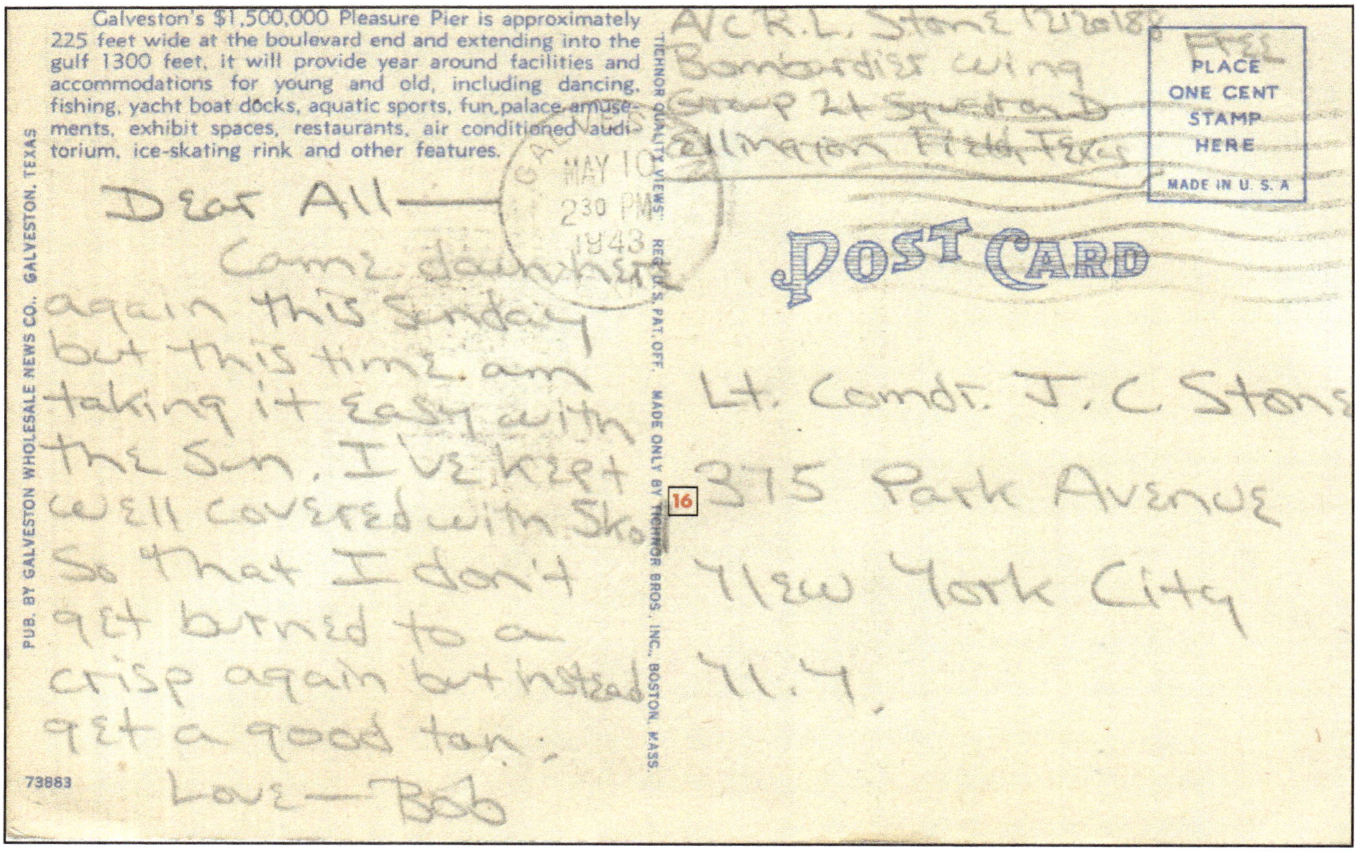
Galveston's $1,500,000 Pleasure Pier is approximately 225 feet wide at the boulevard end and extending into the gulf 1300 feet, it will provide year around facilities and accommodations for young and old, including dancing, fishing, yacht boat docks, aquatic sports, fun palace amusements, exhibit spaces, restaurants, air conditioned auditorium, ice-skating rink and other features.

PUB. BY GALVESTON WHOLESALE NEWS CO., GALVESTON, TEXAS

"TICHNOR QUALITY VIEWS" REG. U.S. PAT. OFF. MADE ONLY BY TICHNOR BROS. INC., BOSTON, MASS.

GALVESTON MAY 10 2:30 PM 1943

A/C R.L. Stone 12120188
Bombardier Wing
Group 24 Squadron D
Ellington Field, Texas

FREE

PLACE ONE CENT STAMP HERE
MADE IN U. S. A

POST CARD

Dear All—
Came down here
again this Sunday
but this time am
taking it easy with
the Sun. I've kept
well covered with Skol
So that I don't
get burned to a
crisp again but instead
get a good tan.
Love—Bob

Lt. Comdr. J. C Stone
375 Park Avenue
New York City
N.Y.

16

73883

MAY 10, 1943

PREFLIGHT SCHOOL
BOMBARDIER

U. S. ARMY AIR CORPS
ELLINGTON FIELD, TEXAS

Monday Night

Dear Dad—

Have no time to write because we have a math test tomorrow. I do, however, want to answer a few questions from your letter I received today. First off, I plan to have a picture taken but as I've told you I've only been in Houston once. I'll get you one as soon as I get one taken which will probably in a week or so. O.K.?

You asked if I'd gotten the picture of you and Don and I wrote you a thank-you letter upon receiving them. Didn't you get it? If not, again a million thanks for both. I thought the one of you was darn swell and the uniform is very handsome and most impressive! A million thanks, Dad.

I didn't go to town Saturday but did go up to Galveston swimming again Sunday. Not very exciting but lots of fun ~~bath~~ sunbathing and swimming. Haven't any more time now cause I've got to get studing. Many thanks for writing—I really appreciate you're being such a swell correspondent and writing so often. S'long. Lots of love—

Bob

ELLINGTON FIELD, TX

Saturday Night the 22nd.

Dear Dad and Bee:

Excuse the long absence without mail, but for the last week or so I've been busy as heck with tests and one thing or another. Life goes on as usual with classes following on day after day.

This week I completed two of my courses with flying colors. I got a 93 on the Aerial Photography and Maps and Charts final for a final average of 95. I also surprised myself on the math final by getting a perfect paper on vectors for a final average of 95 in math also. Vectors has to do with plotting flight courses allowing for the wind drift and the other atmospheric phenomenon that enter into flying.

From now till the rest of the time I'm here I'll be concentrating on the Physics which is coming along lots better now. That course is longer than all the rest and lasts for the entire time we're at pre-flight. This week we started a course on Aircraft Identification and one on Naval Identification. In Aircraft we have to learn to recognize all the U.S. Army planes as well as most of the enemy ships. On the whole a most important course for when we actually get into the fray. In Naval Forces they teach us a little baskground of the navy as well as the recognition features on our major ships, so that we won't be out some time and bomb our own navy as the Italians did.

I was certainly envious when I heard that Don was home for a few days. I'd surely give alot just to get home for even a day. I haven't heard from him this week and so I imagine he's probably moved on by now. I do hope he gets to a decent field so it isn't too tough for him. It was certainly a shame he couldn't have gotten into something he really would have liked a little more!

Thanks both of you for being such good correspondents. All your letters are really appreciated even though I don't get a chance to answer them as often as I'd like to. Your trip to Deerfield sounded fun Bee, as did yours to Atlantic City Dad.

MAY 22, 1943

This week the field was visited by Pat O'Brien and several other movie stars. You see he is in a new movie that just opened called "Bombardier". He and the leading lady [17] were out here on Thursday and they rode by in an open jeep waving to all the cadets who were lining the streets in their honor. All in all it was a pretty sour affair to stand around and gape at a broken-down actor, but orders are orders. None the less we're all looking forward to seeing the picture because it's supposed to be quite good.

Didn't leave the post last week-end as I had to stay put to study for my two exams this wek but needless to say it was more than worth it. I almost died when I got back a 100 on the vector exam. If the weather is good tomorrow I plan to go to Galveston tomorrow to get some more sun. It's far from an exciting place but it's such fun and relaxation to get away from army life for a few hours.

Can't think of anything more now so I'll stop here.

Lots of love,

Bobby

A/C R. L. Stone 12120188
Bombardier Wing
Group 21, Squadron D
Ellington Field, Texas

FREE

HOUSTON, TEXAS
MAY 23
9 AM
1943

BUY
WAR SAVINGS
BONDS AND STAMPS

Lt. Comdr. J. C. Stone
375 Park Avenue
New York City

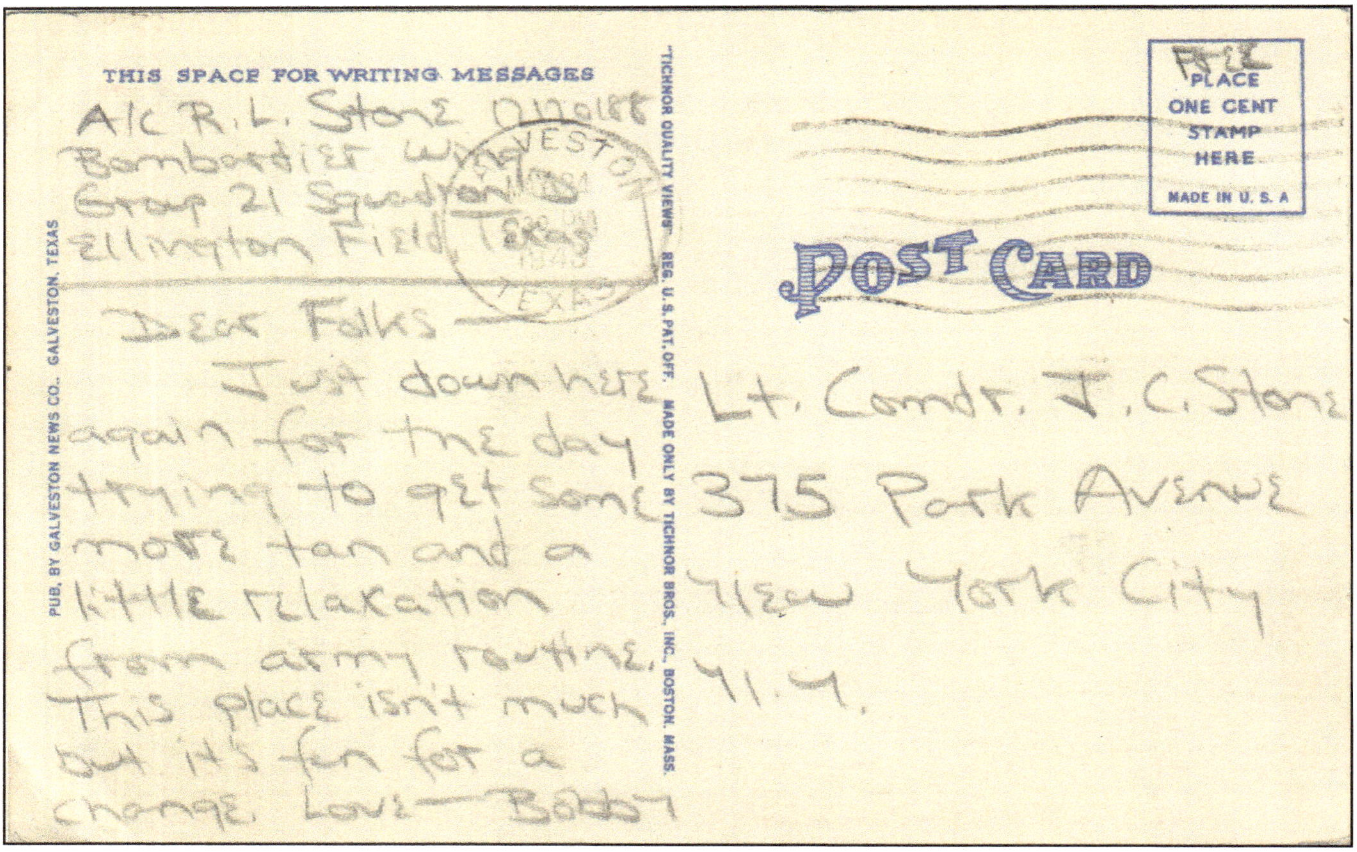

MAY 24-25, 1943

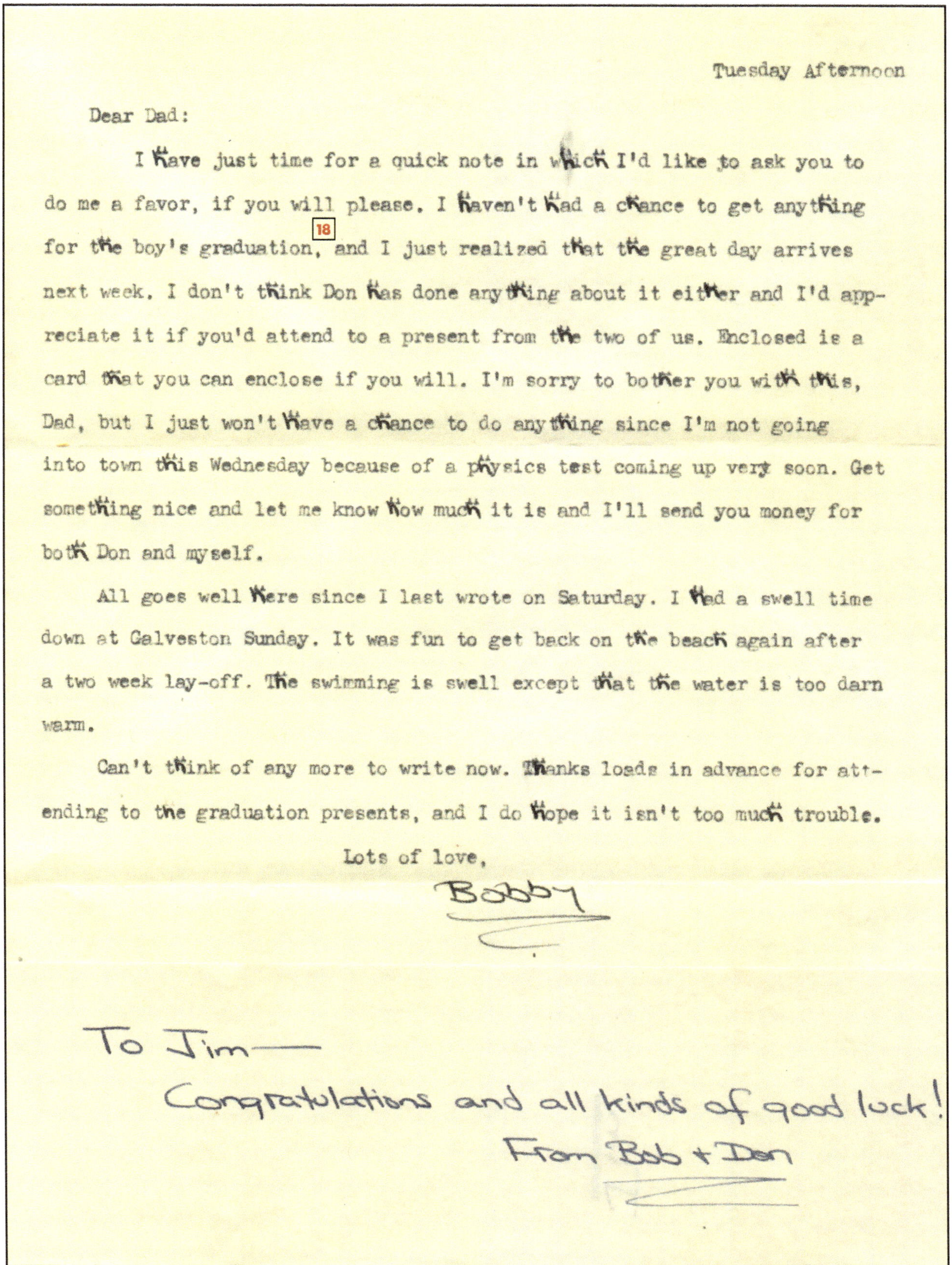

Tuesday Afternoon

Dear Dad:

I have just time for a quick note in which I'd like to ask you to do me a favor, if you will please. I haven't had a chance to get anything for the boy's graduation,[18] and I just realized that the great day arrives next week. I don't think Don has done anything about it either and I'd appreciate it if you'd attend to a present from the two of us. Enclosed is a card that you can enclose if you will. I'm sorry to bother you with this, Dad, but I just won't have a chance to do anything since I'm not going into town this Wednesday because of a physics test coming up very soon. Get something nice and let me know how much it is and I'll send you money for both Don and myself.

All goes well here since I last wrote on Saturday. I had a swell time down at Galveston Sunday. It was fun to get back on the beach again after a two week lay-off. The swimming is swell except that the water is too darn warm.

Can't think of any more to write now. Thanks loads in advance for attending to the graduation presents, and I do hope it isn't too much trouble.

Lots of love,

Bobby

To Jim—

Congratulations and all kinds of good luck!

From Bob + Don

An example of one of the notes Bob wrote to Jimmy & Barry.

PREFLIGHT SCHOOL
BOMBARDIER
U. S. ARMY AIR CORPS
ELLINGTON FIELD, TEXAS

Sunday

Dear Dad—

I was quite surprised when Jim wrote me about the change in the date of your birthday. No matter what the date, I want to wish a great Dad all of the best on his forty-? birthday. I really wish we could all be together for the day but of course war makes that, along with many other things, impossible. Even so Dad, you can be sure that I'll be with you at 375 in spirit though not in body to wish you all of the luck and congratulations in the world for the years to come—and lord hope that they're more pleasent and less depressing than the last one!

I won't go into a long ado of how very proud I am of my old (apolgies) "Pop" and what he's doing to help end this damn war. You already know that I, along with everyone else you know, think you're a great guy and you're doing more than your share to end the mess we're in—you're a great guy, Dad,

JUNE 13, 1943

and you've certainly made a tough goal for your three sons to live up to and attain. If they only half way reached it, they could hardly be called unsuccessful.

Again Dad, I wish we could all be together for the day but none the less I'll be thinking of you and hoping you're having a very, very happy birthday.

With lots of love from,

Your loving Son—Bobby

Monday

Dear Dad, Bee, Jim, and Barry—

This will have to be one of those long joint affairs because I owe everyone letters, and I just haven't time to write.

Classes have just about come to an end and I really outdid myself by finishing up with a real set of grades. In Chemical Warfare, Ground Forces, First Aid, and Code we didn't get a grade but merely the notation of "Satisfactory" or "Unsatisfactory". The following, however, make up our actual courses and we get a numerical grade in each. Math 95, Naval Forces 95, Aircraft Identification 98, Maps and Charts 95, and 85 in physics. In the physics final I really delivered the goods and got a 98 to pull up my first test which was below seventy. Although these grades are well above average, they don't mean too much because the real thing comes at Advanced. What you do at preflight doesn't count too much unless you're on the ball at Advanced. There we have twelve weeks of training most of which is spent in actual bombing. The first three weeks we're on the ground going to class and then we sprout wings. Advanced is one heck of a tough proposition and the wash-outs are numerous—all I can do is hope for the best.

A week from this wednesday the first fellows

JUNE 14, 1943

in our group will go to Advanced. There's only room for about $\frac{1}{3}$ to go and so they have to pick the lucky ones. I ought to be picked as they always give preference to Cadet officers. The remaining $\frac{2}{3}$rds go to gunnery school for seven weeks. The ones who go to Advanced first go to gunnery later as officers.

Before I forget it, please thank O'ma for her sweet letter and explain to her that I just haven't had time to write and will have even less in the near future. I feel like such a heel not answering letters but I have all I can do to write you folks and Pam [19] occasionally as it is. Please don't forget to tell O'ma.

Many congrats on making "Cum Lousy", Barry. I really think it's swell. Also, nice going Jim on the varsity "D". It must feel funny to have the last of our long line of Deerfielders graduated.

There's not too much in the way of news from here because I've spent most of my time with the books, even on the week-ends. I have been up to Galveston a couple of more times but nothing much besides that. I did use my officers open post to go to town last wednesday night for dinner and a show. Think I'll go in again this week cause I have nothing else to do.

Last week we went out on the range and fired a few rounds with a .45. We also had a day of gas drill where they threw a sample of every known gas at us so's we'd know what it's like. This week we'll go up in the pressure chamber to determine whether we'll be high or low altitude bombardiers. It's supposed to be quite something and I'll write you all about it after I've been up.

The weather continues to be unbearably hot and I hate to think what it will be like when summer comes, because it's really miserable now.

Can't think of any more to write cause all we're doing now is loaf. We go to a few movies and demonstrations each day, but otherwise nothing cause classes are all over.

Let's hear from you.

Lots of love—

Bobby

EN ROUTE FROM ELLINGTON FIELD, TX

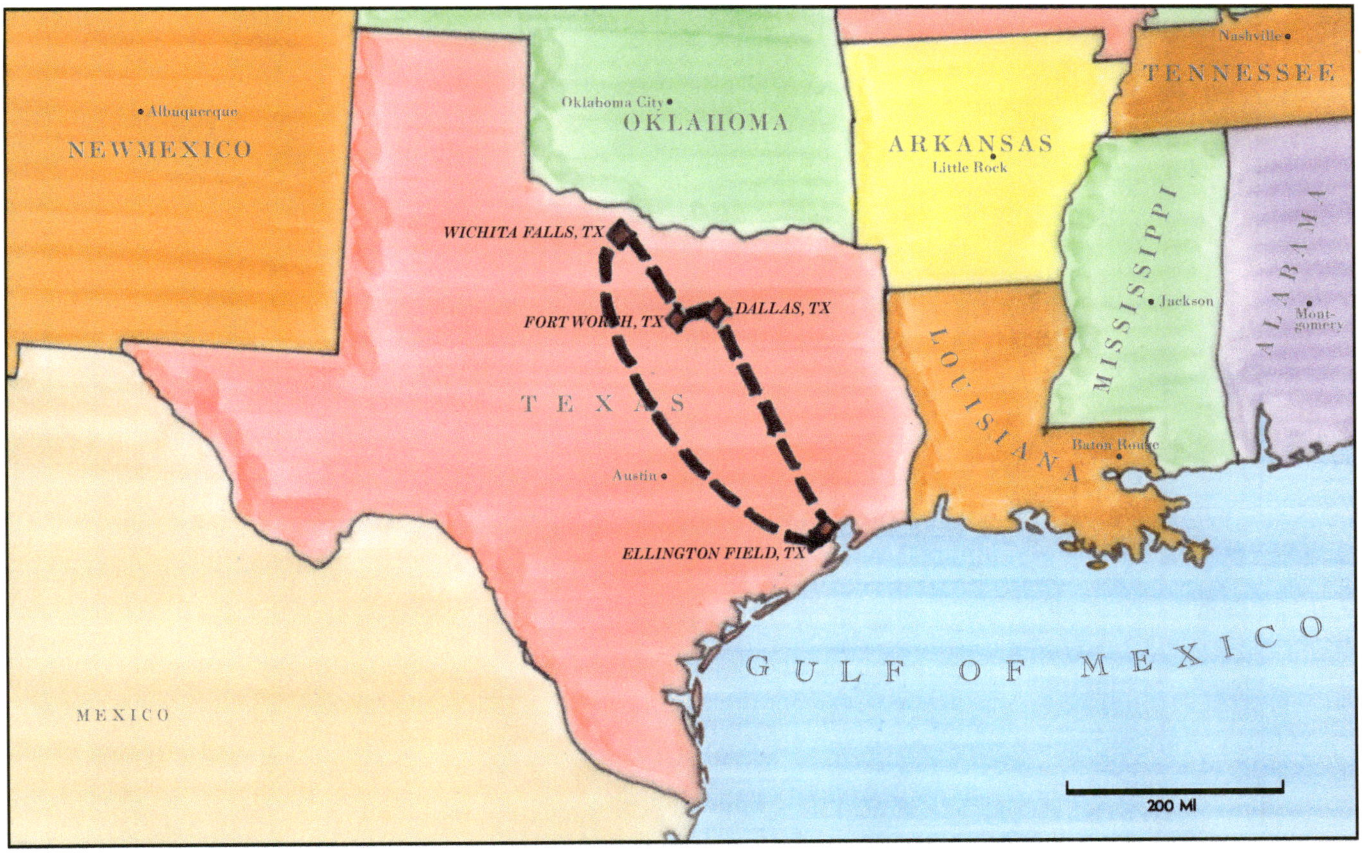

JUNE 1943

Sunday Aft.

Dear Folks—

Right now I'm so annoyed that I shouldn't be writing you but I have several hours to kill with nothing to do.

As you can see I'm in Dallas writing from the USO in the railroad station. Spoke to Don earlier in the week and we agreed to meet here in Dallas for a few hours today.

I arrived here about 9:00 last night after taking a heck of a chance of being picked up by an M.P. because I couldn't get a pass to travel out of our 50 mile radius.[20] I didn't want to let Don down and so I risked it and so far so good although I'm

THE YOUNG MEN'S CHRISTIAN ASSOCIATIONS • THE NATIONAL CATHOLIC COMMUNITY SERVICE
THE SALVATION ARMY • THE YOUNG WOMEN'S CHRISTIAN ASSOCIATIONS
THE JEWISH WELFARE BOARD • THE NATIONAL TRAVELERS AID ASSOCIATION

JUNE 20, 1943

not back home yet.

On arriving here last night I was amazed when there wasn't a room to be had from the largest to the smallest hotel — the town was packed. 'Twas a a long funny story and I'll tell you sometime how I got a bed with the nicest people — really worked out swell. Came to the station at about 9:30 this morning where I waited for Don's train that didn't come in until 11:00 and oddly enough Don wasn't on it. I can't imagine why he didn't come and I hope he has a good reason because I gave up going to our graduation party to come all this way only to be stood up. After I had lunch today, I came back here to meet another train from Missouri but still no Don. Now I've got to wait till 5:00 to get my train back to Houston. Not what I'll call a successful weekend!!!

THE YOUNG MEN'S CHRISTIAN ASSOCIATIONS • THE NATIONAL CATHOLIC COMMUNITY SERVICE
THE JEWISH WELFARE BOARD • THE NATIONAL TRAVELERS AID ASSOCIATION

ELLINGTON FIELD, TX

page 3

Placed a call to you this morning for fathers day, Dad, but I was disappointed on that too when I found you out. The maid (of rather dubious intelligence) got your number all bawled up and so I had no idea of where you were. I'm going to try the call again at 4:00 before I leave hoping you'll be home by then. If not here's wishing a very happy father's day to the greatest Dad in the world!!

Don't know any more about when I'll be pulling out but I have hopes that the next time you hear from me I'll be at Advanced. Cross your fingers for me. Lots of love—

Bobby

THE YOUNG MEN'S CHRISTIAN ASSOCIATIONS • THE NATIONAL CATHOLIC COMMUNITY SERVICE
THE SALVATION ARMY • THE YOUNG WOMEN'S CHRISTIAN ASSOCIATIONS
THE JEWISH WELFARE BOARD • THE NATIONAL TRAVELERS AID ASSOCIATION

JUNE 20-23, 1943

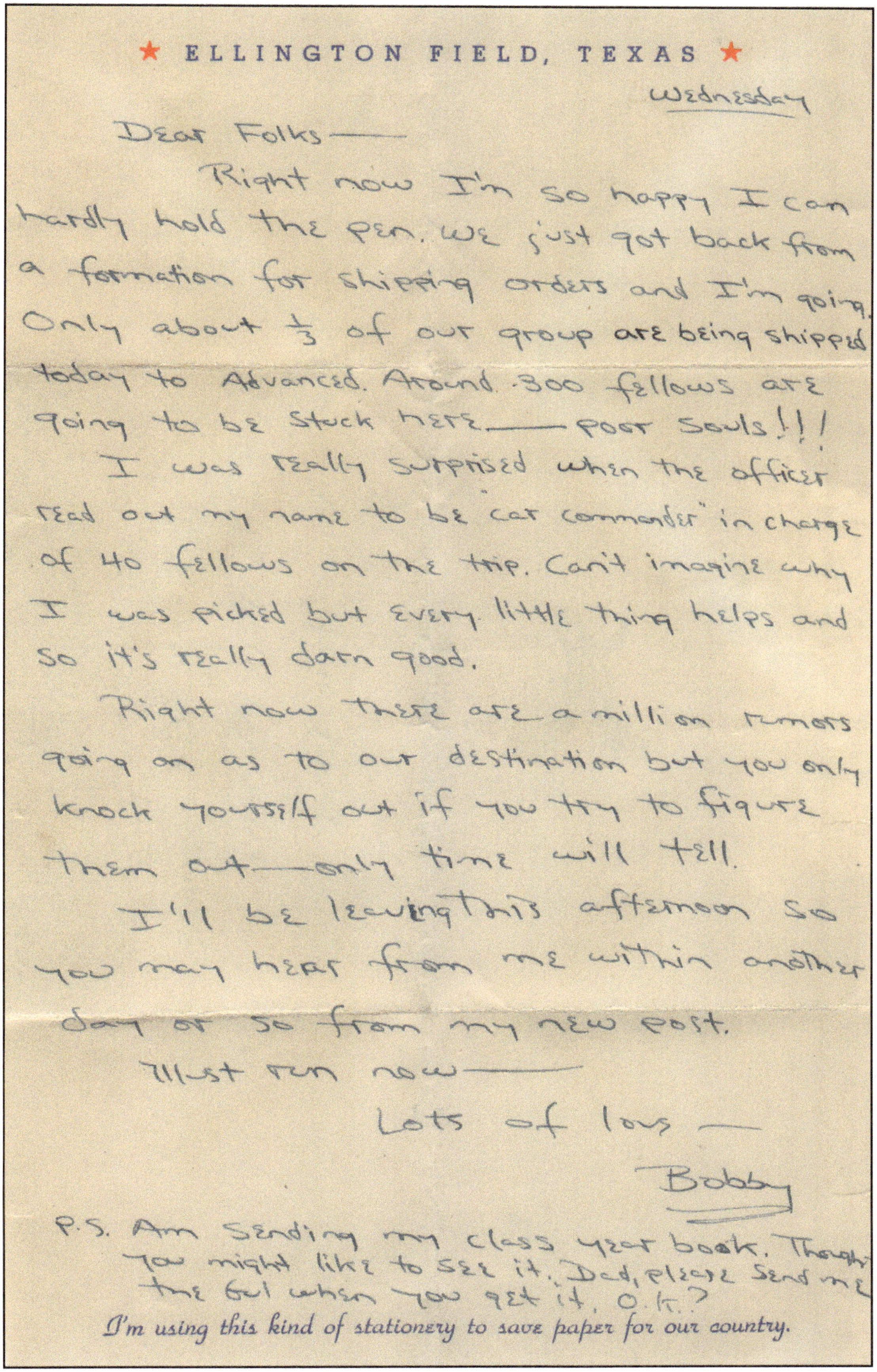

★ ELLINGTON FIELD, TEXAS ★

Wednesday

Dear Folks—

Right now I'm so happy I can hardly hold the pen. We just got back from a formation for shipping orders and I'm going. Only about 1/3 of our group are being shipped today to Advanced. Around 300 fellows are going to be stuck here—poor souls!!!

I was really surprised when the officer read out my name to be "car commander" in charge of 40 fellows on the trip. Can't imagine why I was picked but every little thing helps and so it's really darn good.

Right now there are a million rumors going on as to our destination but you only knock yourself out if you try to figure them out—only time will tell.

I'll be leaving this afternoon so you may hear from me within another day or so from my new post.

Must run now—

Lots of love—

Bobby

P.S. Am sending my class year book. Thought you might like to see it. Dad, please send me the bill when you get it, O.K.?

I'm using this kind of stationery to save paper for our country.

ELLINGTON FIELD, TX

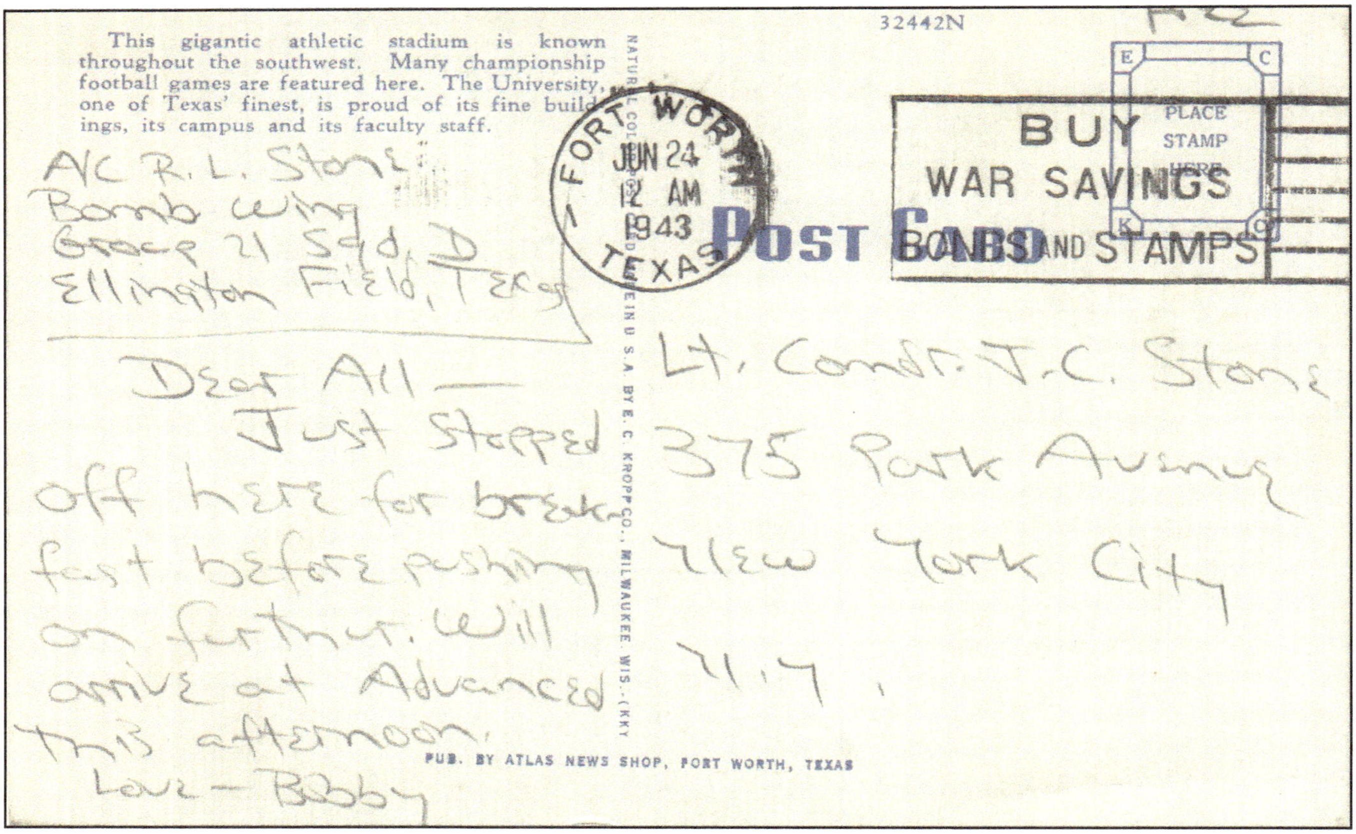

This gigantic athletic stadium is known throughout the southwest. Many championship football games are featured here. The University, one of Texas' finest, is proud of its fine buildings, its campus and its faculty staff.

32442N

FORT WORTH JUN 24 12 AM 1943 TEXAS

BUY WAR SAVINGS BONDS AND STAMPS

PLACE STAMP HERE

POST CARD

A/C R. L. Stone
Bomb Wing
Group 21 Sqd. D
Ellington Field, Texas

Dear All —
Just stopped off here for breakfast before pushing on further. Will arrive at Advanced this afternoon.
Love — Bobby

Lt. Comdr. J. C. Stone
375 Park Avenue
New York City
N.Y.

PUB. BY ATLAS NEWS SHOP, FORT WORTH, TEXAS

JUNE 24, 1943

ELLINGTON FIELD, TX

FORD-MONTGOMERY COMPANY

WICHITA FALLS, TEXAS — CHILDRESS, TEXAS — DALLAS, TEXAS

WRITTEN FROM

Thursday Aft

Dear Folks—

We were unexpectedly held over here in Wichita Falls and so we have a few hours to bum around town.

So far the trip has been a pleasant one and my job as car commander a veritable cinch since the fellows have been most cooperative. This morning when we awoke (that is those who were able to sleep) we were in Ft. Worth where we got off for breakfast. We marched the gang, 80 strong down the main street to a restaurant where a welcomed meal was awaiting us. Got right back on the train after eating and came directly here where we got off for lunch here at the hotel.

This is a small town as I said in my postal to you but it's surely swell to get

"Come as you are"

JUNE 24, 1943

off the train awhile.

Yesterday the Lt. in charge of our shipment open his sealed orders in front of R.L.S. and the other car commander. We couldn't tell the fellows yesterday but now they all know we're going to Childress, Texas. It's meant to be a lousy little town and a very tough Advanced School. From all we hear it isn't ~~#~~ at all good. I'll have to find out for myself. Incidentally, I don't know my address but if you write me to Advanced Bombardier School
Childress, Texas
I'm sure I'll get it. As soon as I know my address I'll, of course, send it to you.

Speaking of writing please be sure to tell O'ma and various other people who've written me that I just don't (and won't have) any time to write. I hope they'll understand cause that's how it is. For that matter I imagine I'll be writing you lots less now because Advanced is lots lots tougher than preflight. S'long now while I go out and give the town the once over.

Lots of love — Bobby

USAAF ADVANCED BOMBARDIER SCHOOL CHILDRESS, TX

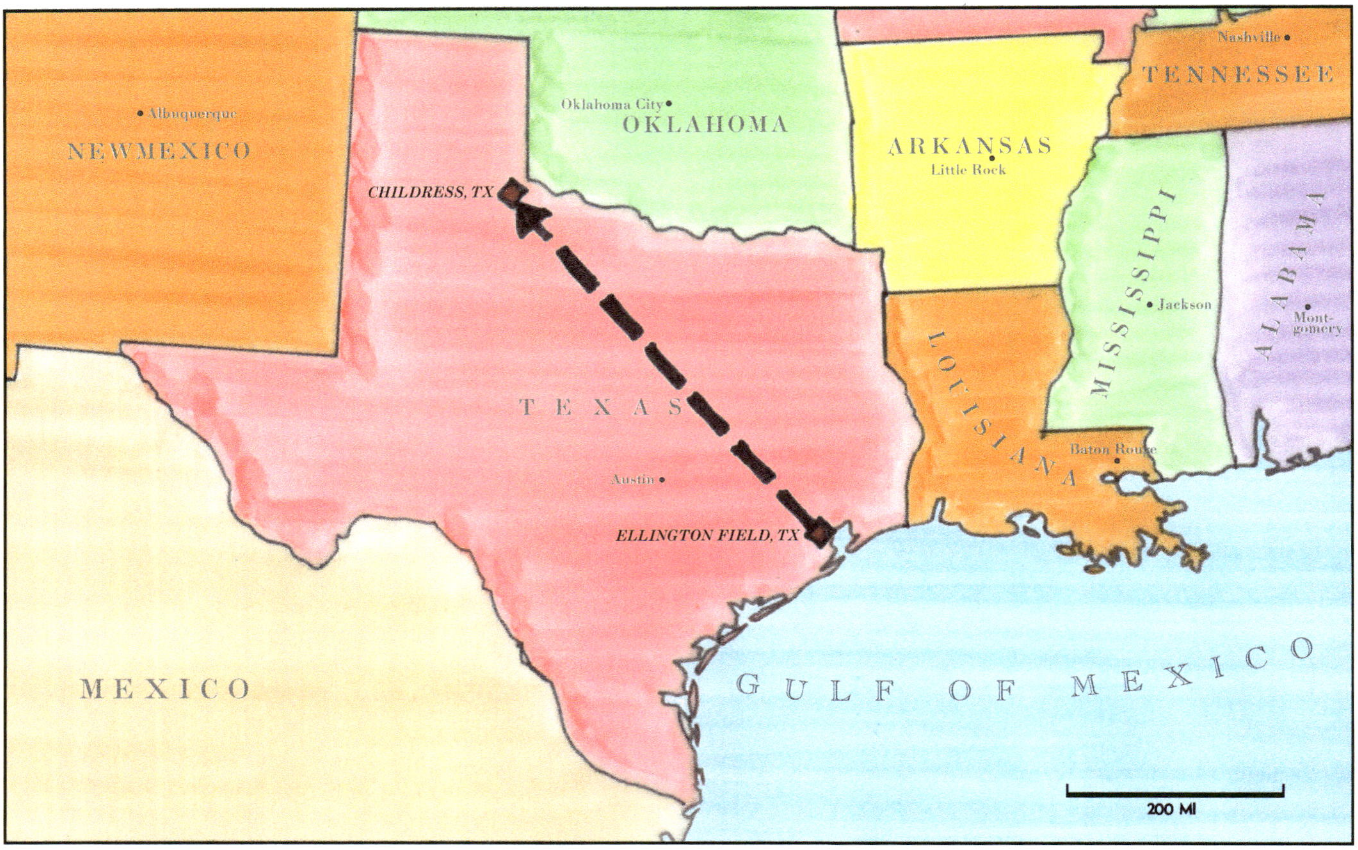

JUNE 1943–NOVEMBER 1943

ARMY AIR FORCES BOMBARDIER SCHOOL
CHILDRESS, TEXAS

Sunday

Dear Dad, Bee, Don, and Jim—

Was good to talk you this morning and tell you about my whereabouts. Had quite a bit of excitement after I wrote you from Wichita Falls where we were held over for 9 hours due to a wreck down the road. We sat up all night and finally pulled into a cross roads on the tracks at about five the next morning. Upon inquiry we were told it was the town of Childress. It's a small place with a main street quite comparable to Bloomingdale.[21] It's a dry town run by church people so that you can't even buy beer. No kidding it is really an incredible set-up and I can't describe how miserable it is. Open-post means nothing here because we're restricted to 25 miles and so nobody goes to town, because there is really nothing.

Pretty soon some G.I. trucks brought us out here to the field which is really something. It's very flat desert country which is dusty as anything and extremely hot. We live in single story barracks that aren't too hot. The food isn't comparable to Ellington but it's not bad. About the only good thing so far is the fellows. We have a class of about 120 and there really great guys.

Starting with our class the course has been changed from 12 to 18 long weeks. We will graduate as "Bombagators" (Bombardier-Navigator). In fact, the first thing we take up is navigation which is meant to be mighty tough. The upper class say that the work here is really tough and washouts are frequent. All our officers have told us the courses and flying are incomparable to anything we've ever done before. Incidentally are C.O. is a Captain who's hard as nails and known to be a stinker. The discipline here is very strict since they turn out good officers as well as bombardiers.

Our course is so tough and keeps us so busy that we never have a minute to our self. This time I really mean it when I say you won't hear from me because I know we'll have no free time. I'd really appreciate it if you'd tell all my friends that I'll really appreciate mail but won't be able to write back, as much as I'd like to. Please ask everyone to write because it's really lonely

JUNE 27, 1943

Pg. 3

and mail will be especially welcomed. I hate to lose contact with everyone but writing will be an impossibility from all indications.

The day we arrived we were issued alot of new equipment. Each man got a waltham wrist watch, a stop watch, a series of complicated computers and dials, bombing tables, a lawyers brief case, rulers and compasses, a drawing board, lots of tech manuals, and a box of books and small gadgets none of which mean anything to us. It was just like Xmas opening box after box of instruments etc..

Just had a thought. One of the boys has a camera here, most illegal of course. We thought we'd take some snaps and send them home but unfortunately we can't get film. If you could get us some "XX 828" Kodak film I'd really appreciate it. If you can send some, wrap it in a box that has nothing to do with photography because we'd be in a real mess if detected.

Guess I've told you just about everything that's happened so far. I hope you'll understand the setup here because it's going to be rough and getting through will be a really accomplishment. Please write often because it's really lonely out here and I do mean lonely. Be sure to send any letters I write you on to Don and Jim.

Lots of love———

Bobby

P.S. In case my address is blurred on the envelope and you didn't get it on the phone.

A/C R.L.S. 12120188
Class 43-13 Sqdn 7 Flight D
AAFBS
Childress, Texas.

ARMY AIR FORCES BOMBARDIER SCHOOL
CHILDRESS, TEXAS

Saturday Nite

Dear Dad, Bee, Don, Jim, and Betty—

With the week-end at hand I find myself with a few spare hours, which is unusual for this place This past week was the fullest that I have ever spent. I'll go through a typical day, and every day is just alike.

Up at 6:20 with breakfast at 7:00. We go to class, where we each have our own permanent desk, at 8:00 and remain there working steadily until 12:00 when we go to lunch. Every hour we go outside for a ten minute smoke and stretch. At 1:00 we come back to class where we remain until 5:00 when we go to retreat. Following retreat we get into athletic clothes and go to P.T. for an hour. Supper is at 6:45 and then back to class at 7:30 until 9:30 when our day is over. We have one hour a day to do as we like from 9:30 to 10:30 when lights go out.

It's really some grind sitting at the same desk in the same room for 10 hours of classes every day. This new plan of giving us six weeks of navigation first is mighty rugged. Every day we have an exam that lasts for about an hour and every Saturday we have a four hour exam on the week's work

The work is interesting, different, and absorbing. They throw it at us so darn fast that you've got to be on the ball every minute. I worked hard all week and did very well on the daily tests which count $\frac{1}{4}$ of our weeks grade. The long 4 hour exam we took this afternoon counts $\frac{3}{4}$. It included everything we did all week and you really had to know your stuff to do well. I have no idea how I did but I'll find out tuesday. Cross your fingers!

We have three instructors who teach us everything. They are all three princes to say nothing of being A-1 teachers. They were once cadets and they're young and can get the work across to us in a way that we can understand and appreciate.

The type of work we did had to do with plotting courses on various projections, mainly the mercator. The other main bulk of the work had to do with learning how to work a computer that figures airspeed, temperature altitude, calibrated altitude, and lord knows what all else. I can honestly say that I learned more this week than I did in a half a year at college or prep-school. I can't impress you enough the amount of work that they give us in ten hours each day. You have to understand and learn the work as you go along since we don't get any free time to study things, if we miss them.

I must say that the work is interesting even though tough as heck. They keep telling us how the washout rate is going up and the course becoming tougher. If I get through it will be due to damn hard work and alot of luck when it comes to dropping the bombs. If I get my wings and a commission I can certainly tell the world I worked for it. That's the way we all feel and doff our hats to any man with navigator, bombardier, or pilots wings. It's a real pull.

With only an hour off a day you can see that we don't have any time to do any personal things at all. Our day is the fullest and busiest you can imagine.

The camp here has nothing to offer except alot of dust and warm weather. Actually it doesn't matter too much because we don't have any time to do anything except go to class. Our open-post (which hardly anyone uses since Childress is nothing) doesn't start until after

Supper Saturday night until 12:00. You'd think we were back at grade school. Tomorrow on our great day of independence we've got to put on a parade for the towns people in the afternoon. Then from 7:30 till 9:30 we have to go to class. That's no exaggeration and wouldn't you think that's taking things a bit too far? It ought to be a pleasant 4th, says who!

One swell thing is that we have a great bunch of fellows in the barracks. We really have the best flight in our class and the kids are tops. We all get on just fine and that's damn important when you're working under such a strain and tension as we are.

Guess that about takes care of all that happened this week. This was the first time I had a chance to write you and I'm sure you'll appreciate not hearing from me more often. Please be sure to send all my letters around to the various brothers. Hope you have a swell time at Alderbrook.[22] Catch some big ones for me, Dad.

Loads of love ——

Bobby

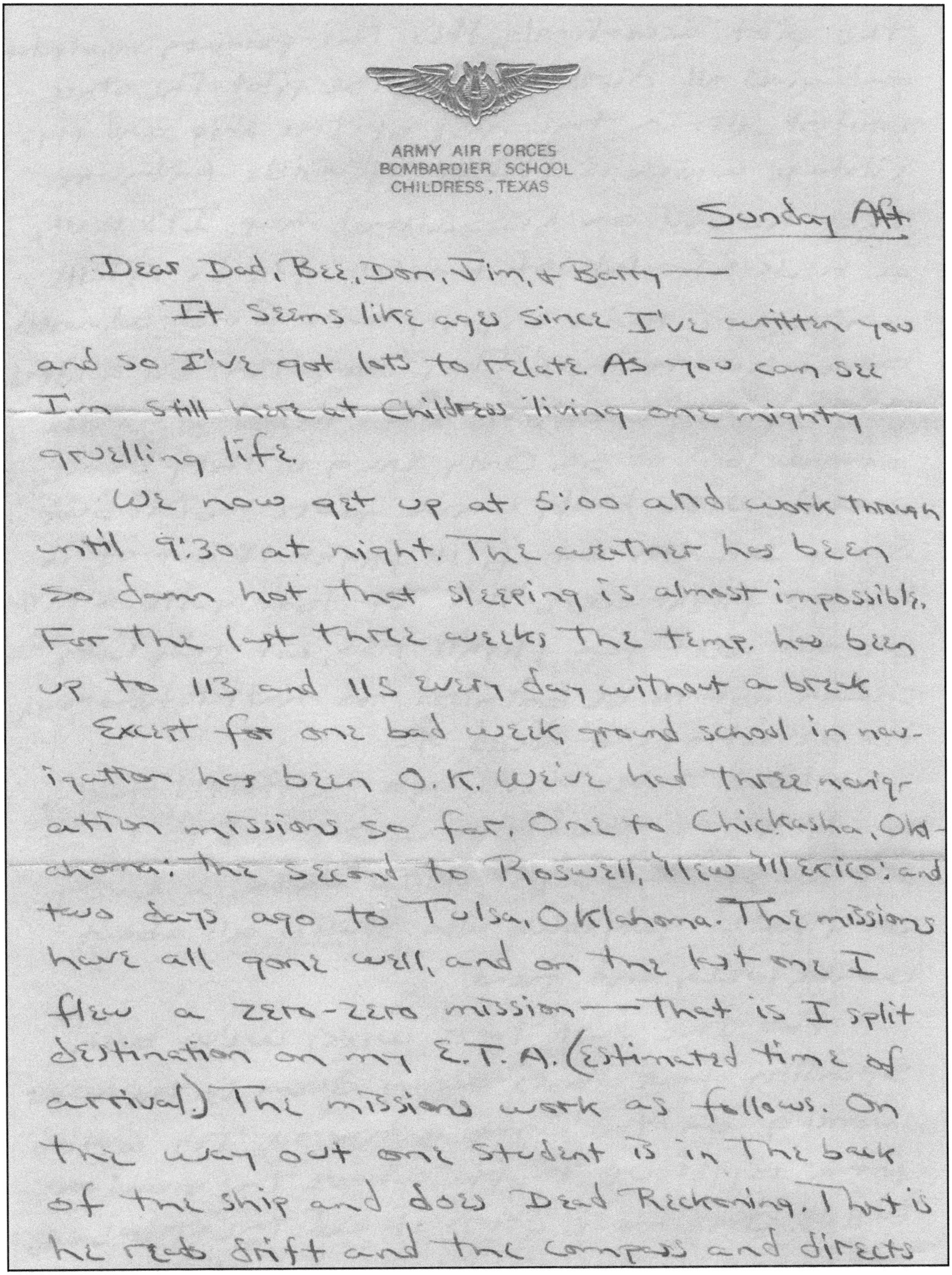

ARMY AIR FORCES
BOMBARDIER SCHOOL
CHILDRESS, TEXAS

Sunday Aft.

Dear Dad, Bee, Don, Jim, & Barry—

It seems like ages since I've written you and so I've got lots to relate. As you can see I'm still here at Childress living one mighty gruelling life.

We now get up at 5:00 and work through until 9:30 at night. The weather has been so damn hot that sleeping is almost impossible. For the last three weeks the temp. has been up to 113 and 115 every day without a break

Excest for one bad week, ground school in navigation has been O.K. We've had three navigation missions so far. One to Chickasha, Oklahoma; the second to Roswell, New Mexico; and two days ago to Tulsa, Oklahoma. The missions have all gone well, and on the last one I flew a zero-zero mission—that is I split destination on my E.T.A. (estimated time of arrival) The missions work as follows. On the way out one student is in the back of the ship and does Dead Reckoning. That is he reads drift and the compass and directs the pilot accordingly. He's the primary navigator and gives all directions to the pilot. The other student sits in the nose of the ship and flys pilotage which is flying by visible landmarks that he sees on his sectional map. It's really a heck of alot of fun. We fly in AT-11's which are twin engine, twin finned advanced bombardier trainers. They carry ten one hundred pound practice bombs. These ships that cruise around 160 or so. Only thing's they bounce around quite badly when you're in the back doing DR. On our first flight 18 out of 26 in our flight were sick. It took quite a toll on our next two flights too, but I'm lucky enough not to be bothered no matter how rough its been. Hope it keeps up.

About three weeks ago we started taking bombing in ground school. We had to learn all about the sight itself which is a very [23] complicated gadget. We also studied all about bombs, fuzes, and racks.

For the past three weeks we've been spending four hours a day down in the hangar working on the bombing trainer. It's a platform rigged up 10 ft. above the ground on rollers. One man drives it and the other bombs with the sight which is rigged up to simulate

AUGUST 8, 1943

actual bombing conditions. We work down there so's to learn the bombing procedure before going into the air.

Tomorrow we go down on the line to fly our first bombing mission. For the first week we'll fly "dry runs" every day before we drop our first bomb. From now on we'll be flying every day including sundays. Fun but rough!

This grind is really something. Our flight has been lucky enough to lose only two men so far. One other is asking to be washed out because the strain is too much for him. Alot of us feel that way but we'd never quit until they forced us to, and I hope that will never be.

Aside from the work here there is nothing to report because that's all we do. Week-ends are a non-existent creation not made for cadets. It's really rough and most of the time seems like a futile existence. I won't start philosophizing or I'll be rambling for pages.

Please keep writing cause I love to hear from you all, even though I can write back. I miss you all and only wish there was some way I could get home, but in the cadets that's unheard of.

I've tried to reach you by phone the last few nights but haven't succeeded yet. I have another call in for tonight. Perhaps I'll reach you then.

Love to you all——

Bobby

P.S. Please be sure this letter goes the rounds!

AUGUST 8, 1943/PHOTOGRAPH

Advanced AT-II Bombardier Training Plane, used by Bob for flights at Childress, TX.

THE NORDEN BOMBSIGHT

The Norden Bombsight was a tachymetric bombsight used by the United States Army Air Forces during World War II. There was a lot of political controversy surrounding the production and use of the bombsight between politicians and the different branches of the service so that early production of the bombsight was delayed and used for the first time in March 1943, at a cost of $8,800.

Key to the operation of the Norden were two features: an analog computer that constantly calculated the bomb's trajectory based on current flight conditions, and a linkage to the bomber's autopilot that let it react quickly and accurately to changes in the wind or other effects. Together

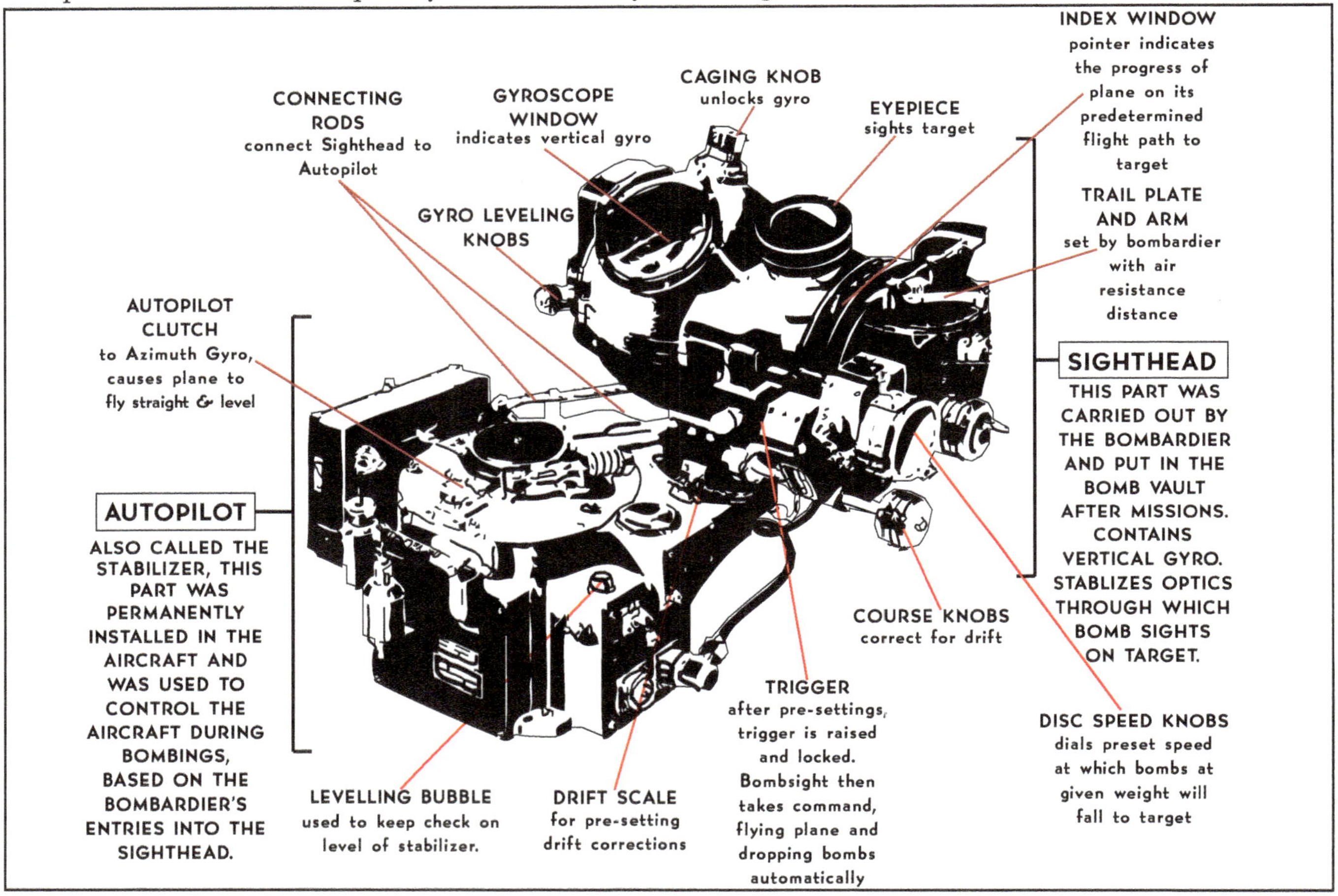

these features allowed for unprecedented accuracy in day bombing from high altitudes.

The bombardier first looked up the expected time it would take for the bombs to fall from the current altitude. This time was set into a countdown stopwatch, and the bombardier waited for the target to line up with a set of iron sights at the front of the bombsight. When the target passed through the sights the timer was started and the bombardier then rotated the telescope around its vertical axis to track the target as they approached it. The movement was linked to a second sight through a gearing system that caused the second sight to move twice as fast as the first. The bombardier continued moving the telescope until the timer ran out. The second sight was left in the correct position for aiming; the bombardier moved his eyes to look through this second set of sights to time the drop, and had 30 seconds over the target area.[24]

NORDEN BOMBSIGHT/AUGUST 14, 1943

ARMY AIR FORCES
BOMBARDIER SCHOOL
CHILDRESS, TEXAS

Saturday Nite

Dear Dad—

I can't tell you how swell it was to talk to you last night. I've wanted to call for quite some time but getting a call through is a real orgy—well worth it though, when the call finally got through.

This past week was a very tiring but interesting one. Every day we reported to the flight line at 12:00 and didn't get through until 5:30. There's an operations board where our missions are posted. Every day I flew at least one bombing mission. All week we flew dry runs until yesterday when I dropped my first bomb—quite exciting! From now on we'll being dropping several every day until we're through. The pilot and bombardier instructor assigned to me are just swell. Two great guys! After awhile we'll fly solo mission with only the pilot and no instructor along.

On each missions two student bombardiers go along. While one bombs the other takes pictures of the impact. There's a camera hatch in the rear of the ship and you stick the movie camera out of it when you hear "bombs away" over the interphones, and start grinding. We take pictures to give statistics an accurate record of the impact.

Since we've started bombing I've become comfortable for the first time since I've been in this god-forsaken state. On the ground the temperature is anywhere from 105°-115° while up at 12,000 feet we're actually cold when the mercury drops down to 60°. Believe it or not we take a sweater along cause its so cold up there. The heat has been unbearable out here, and they say it's the hottest spell they've had here in years—just our luck!!

Before I forget, I wonder if you'd do me a big favor, Dad? I'd really appreciate it if you could get me a thermos bottle to take along when we fly. 'Twould be swell if you could arrange it. Also, I'm in dire need of a good shaving brush and the P.X. hasn't much to offer. If you could get me one I'd really appreciate it, Dad.

The grind out here continues unrelentingly day after day. We lost two more kids out of our class cause they just couldn't take it, so they quit. We've lost an amazing number because of airsickness. Riding in the rear of an AT-11 is no joyrides on a rough afternoon. It's not like any other plane and even fellows who've had alot of time at pilot training just can't take it. Our instructors and pilots say they'd be sick too if they had to ride in the back. On this score I've been darn luck in not being effected even on the roughest days we've had.

That certainly is swell news about Ken. I certainly think he's a lucky guy and can't envy him enough. Being stuck out here in Texas without a chance of getting home, doesn't make for too bright a future. I really think he has a swell set-up and his getting engaged just makes it perfect.

Tomorrow our class has to take the "64" which is the long complete physical you get if you are a member of an aircrew. It's the one we took about six months ago down at Nashville when we were classified.

Can't think of any other news to report from Shangri-La. We don't do a darn thing here but go to ground school and fly. I've been to town (which is nothing) only once in seven weeks. It just isn't worth it. This is really an indescribably miserable place. In fact we don't understand why we're not getting overseas pay. After this, combat ought to be easy.

Every morning for P.T. they run us around the track 8 times making a little over a mile. Then some days we get the obstacle course which is a loopo. They have us doing things I never thought possible before. We do 'em though!

Again Dad, it was swell to talk to you and we'll have to do it again some time before too long. It's so darn lonely here that it's good to hear from home.

My love to all ——

Bobby

P.S. I'm writing Ken and Bunny a joint letter that I'd appreciate you're getting to Bunny cause I don't know her address. Have her be sure to save it for Ken until he's in again.

ARMY AIR FORCES
BOMBARDIER SCHOOL
CHILDRESS, TEXAS

Monday Nite

Dear Dad—

Just a quickee to say thanks a million for the generous check that came today. I don't know what the occasion was but I certainly appreciate your thoughtfulness. Thanks a heck of alot, Dad

Flew again this afternoon and dropped two more instructional bombs. This flying every day is really darn tiring although lots of fun. It was tough bombing today because of the low clouds that constantly obscured the vision to the target.

On Sunday our class took our "64" and I got by it O.K. My eyes were considerably weaker than they were six months ago although this was to be expected after all our hours of concentrated study. Most all of us have lost quite alot of weight since we've been out here. The food isn't too good and we don't get nearly enough sleep.

Must get to bed in a few minutes, but I did want to get this off to thank you ever so much for your swell present. Can't express how much I appreciate it—I'm sure you understand. You're a great guy, Dad.

Please thank Bee for her letter that I

also received this morning. Also congratulate her for me about Ken and Bonny.

Lots of love —

Bobby

A/C R.L. Stone 12120188
Class 43-15
Squadron 1 Flight D
Childress Texas

Free

CHILDRESS TEX
AUG 17
2-PM
1943

Lt. Comdr. J. C Stone
375 Park Avenue
New York City
N.Y.

Sunday

Dear Dad and Bee—

Here it is Sunday again and I have a chance to bring you up to date on all the latest from Shangri-La.

The thermos bottle arrived this week and I can't thank you enough for it. I'm the envy of my flight because it's such a treat to have a swallow of something cold while on a long bombing or navigation mission. Many, many thanks! Also, thanks for sending me my class year book. It was fun reading it, but that all seems so long ago that it almost seems unreal. Things have changed so, since then.

Had a tough week on the line since I flew double missions three days. You see one mission goes out at 12:15 and returns at about 3:00 and then if you're on the operations board you go out again at 3:15 until 5:45. When you fly navigation, once a week, thats about a four hour mission in itself.

This week they took quite a toll on our class down on the line. Five kids were washed out on their check-rides. Their ground school grades were good and their bombing wasn't too bad and yet out they go. Nobody seems to know why but they're sure cracking down. We seem to live from day to day down on the line and you're never sure of your status.

My bombing was O.K. this week but it only takes one bad mission to put you up for an elimination ride. There's no human element to ~~this~~ game — it's all cut and dried!

To make things more bearable for us they've scheduled a parade for this afternoon. It seems that we have too much free time on Sunday so that they're remedying that by having a parade.

Can't think of any more now. Thanks for your letters. Keep 'em up.

Lots of love —

Bobby

P.S. ~~E~~ Give my best to O'ma and explain that I haven't time to write. She's written me several times.

Sunday

Dear Dad, Bee, Don, Jim, Ken, and Barry—

Here another two weeks have elapsed and believe it or not I'm still plugging along. It's been a particularly tough period since we've been getting up at 4:20 in the wee hours of the morning and we're in the air by 6:00 when it's still pitch black. We fly until noon when we go to lunch. In the afternoon we go to ground school and have P.T. Then by 6:00 we're all through for the day since we don't have any more night classes.

Our class hasn't done too well in the last two weeks and we've lost quite a few more. Right now our class is about 70 when we started with 105 just twelve weeks ago. I've had several close calls but have been lucky enough to have just squeaked by. It's just a little over six weeks to go and we'll graduate. You'll really have to keep 'em crossed that I can stick it out and be here when the wings are passed out. I've never worked or wished so hard for anything like this before and I only hope and pray that enough breaks are with me to get by. I'm not kidding when I say that we live day to day in fear that we may throw a wild bomb or mess up a navigation mission and be out on our ear. You've just got to be

CHILDRESS, TX

on the ball all the time. With the constant mental strain on us it's tough not to bungle occasionally. Here, however, you just can't afford to.

Before I forget, Dad, thanks loads for the shaving brush, which was just what I wanted. I hate to bother you with something like that but you can't get anything at all out here. At least not such a nice soft brush as that one.

Thanks all of you for your various letters. I'm afraid I owe everyone mail but this joint letter will have to go the rounds, as much as I'd like to write you all separately.

I was certainly jealous when I heard that you'd been home, Don. I'd give anything you can name, [redacted] to get home, even for just a day. I guess I'm silly even to think about it, so I'll just say you're a lucky guy Don, and it's swell you got such a break.

Last week we started in on our combat bombing in which we bomb battleships, docks, truck convoys, and oil refineries that are painted on the ground. This isn't score bombing and it's either a hit or a miss. We throw 60 combat bombs and must have a certain percentage of hits if we are to graduate. In combat bombing we do evasive action and the bombardier flies the ship by means of automatic flight control which is operated through the bomb sight.

SEPTEMBER 12, 1943

Bee, you asked about our navigation. Well, when we're bombing the pilot just flies straight out to the targets since they're only 50 or 60 miles out. We do, however, fly one long straight-navigation mission a week. In a few weeks we may fly combination missions and navigate out to Midlands targets and bomb them and then navigate back.

A week from tomorrow our squadron is going out on maneuvers which last for about five days. It's meant to be quite an experience since you live and fly under combat conditions. Live in tents, do K.P., load, fuse, and prepare our own bombs. It's really meant to be tough but it's an unbeatable experience since it is just what we'll be up against in combat. I'll write you all about it when I know more myself.

Have very little to write in the way of interesting news since our life is so routine with flying and ground school day after day. For one more week we'll get up at 4:20 and then we start night bombing and sleep most of the morning since we're bombing most of the night. Still don't do anything over the weekends since the facilities around here are non-existant. We see an occasional movie on the post and spend alot of time playing cards. It's not a very varied or enviable life, but there just isn't anything else to do.

I won't drag, this already too long letter, out any more. Please be sure that this goes the rounds 'cause I just can't write you all. I think of you and miss you all—

Lots of love—

Bobby

ARMY AIR FORCES
BOMBARDIER SCHOOL
CHILDRESS, TEXAS

Sunday Aft

Dear Dad & Bee—

Twas so swell to speak to you this morning that I thought I'd just scribble off a short letter.

Am looking forward to going on maneuvers tomorrow. They say its a real test of whether you can fly under combat conditions. It's really rough living in pup tents way out in nowhere. We do K.P., guard duty, fill and fuse actual demolition bombs—all this besides flying bombing and navigation missions. We'll have to wear gas masks at all times because ships fly over and drop gas bombs on us just to make things a little more realistic.

Yesterday we were issued a wonderful piece of equipment. We got those heavy leather flying pants and jackets. They have a big sheep skin collar and are completely lined with sheep skin. They're great big heavy things but oh so warm. They're just like the outfits you see pictured in the movies of high altitude flying. We all look like Polar explorers!

As I said on the phone we lost two more boys from our flight this week. Poor kids working for 13 weeks only to go back to the G.I.'s as a buck private. I'm not ~~trying~~ to make it sound tough when I say that it was nip and tuck for me the past ten days. You're never sure of your status and they give you axe for practically the smallest failing. All I can do is give my all and hope for the breaks for the next 39 days. It would really kill me to miss out on a commission and my wings after getting so close and yet so far from my goal.

No more now 'cause I've got to whip together some warm clothes and equipment before 0600 tomorrow.

Again 'twas swell to talk with you—

All love—

Bobby

A/C R.L. Stone
Class 43-15
Squadron 7 Flight D
Childress, Texas

Fr

CHILDRESS, TEX.
SEP 20
7-PM
1943

Lt. Comdr. J. C. Stone
375 Park Avenue
New York City
N.Y.

SEPTEMBER 19–21, 1943

UNITED STATES ARMY AIR CORPS

9/21/43

Dear Dad, Bee, Bob, Jim, Barry, Ken, and anyone
else who is around -

Nothing very much to report from the northwestern sector. Our classes have begun in full force with 2 hours of Spanish one day and 4 hours the next. Don't know whether I previously told you about our profs, but we have five in Spanish who alternate in each class all using the same system of conversational instruction. The head of the Spanish department, a Captain Eduardo Nile-Silva from the U. of Madrid and Pulitzer and Guggenheim followships winner, is the best language teacher I've ever had. The head geographist, Prof. Waibel, former member of the German Supreme Court, is one of the foremost geographists in the world. He has many excellent assistants, Durand, etc. Another famous name is Becker who teaches anthropology and sociology. He is very interesting and gives faint recollections of Billy Evirett without many of Billy's - er um - superfluous material. The historian is quite good although I have had most of the material. They treat it here in a more mature manner and are not as concerned so much with facts as with trends. We had P.T. today and had to take some G.I. tests with old fat Uncle Don grunting under 25 pushups and turning in a miraculous 53 "burpees", an Army specialty. Was doing them with a Wesleyan boy who roomed with Bill Dadowski.

Last weekend I took one of those trips for which I am famous and buzzed down to Minneapolis to meet Andy Hunter. After spending most of the evening talking over old times at a beer bistro we took a bus back to Northfield late at night. In the morning I saw a group of ex-Williams boys. Maybe you remember Ed Mulcahy and Paul Deteis in your class, Bob. They took me all over the canyons which is very beautiful. Naturally much smaller than Wisconsin but comparable in beauty. Unfortunately all the summer school girls had gone home as school had not yet begun. They were boasting of the numerous "queens" they had accumulated, and I for one would never doubt a Williams wolf. Then I caught a train directly from Northfield to Madison on which I met some foolish devoted wife who was travelling from Oakland, Cal. to Miami, Fla. which just proves the already officious statement that "woman is the weaker sex" - mentally - all due deference to you, Bee.

As you may have read in the papers, Wisconsin opened their football season miserably getting thoroughly trounced by Marquette. For all you football strategists, Jimmy in particular, don't bet on Wisconsin this year. Michigan is the team in the west.

The college was much better populated last weekend due to the game, and every day more girls are seen lugging bags around. Naturally all the soldiers would like to break ranks and be of assistance but then that is breaking article 173, par. 4.

- 1 -

Dad, I spoke to the company representative on the college paper again about your subscription but he is uncertain now whether there will be any more papers or whether they will end, but I will see to it that you do get one if it's printed.

Of late the weather has been perfect but cool and very similar to New England falls. If you get the record still, Dad, would you forward it, please. Oh, Bee, I got the Lawn Tennis Magazine. Thanks lots. Saw where my little amigo francais, Henri Salaun, was beaten in 3 rounds of the nationals.

Nothing to say now except many congratulations, Bob, on your good work. Keep it up.

My love to all,

Don.

Cpl. Don Stone
Co. F, Bks. 13
717 Langdon St.
Madison, Wisconsin

SEPTEMBER 21-25, 1943

P.S. Thanks loads for the picture of Jim in uniform. He really looks swell in his marine outfit.

ARMY AIR FORCES
BOMBARDIER SCHOOL
CHILDRESS, TEXAS

Saturday Nite

Dear Dad, Bee, Don, Jim, + Barry—

Well here I am back at camp again and believe it or not I'm mighty glad of it. This might be a second-rate dump but it looks like paradise after spending six days in the wilds of West Texas.

Had quite a thrill when 14 of us flew out with our squadron commander in the B-18 which is a large twin-engined bomber that preceded the present B-17. It's the only one on the field and they use it for transportation purposes since it's so spacious. Twas fun to have our first ride in a real bomber.

Arrived out at the maneuver area where the other ships gathered all morning. It was a little spot out in the middle of nowhere with two dirt runways that were in fair condition—our landings and take-offs were bumpier than off the concrete here at Childress but not too tough since our pilots are all tops. There was a small control tower and two dugouts that made up our operations headquarters.

First off we set up our shelter-halves with two men to a tent. Our duties were numerous and hard and my first day was spent at the end of a shovel digging slit trenches and garbage disposal pits. Incidentally, Texas has the hardest rockiest soil I've ever tried to penetrate. By evening we were all weary when we gathered for supper.

Great sorry came over the whole camp when our squadron commander announced that one of our planes had been lost in an accident on the way to maneuvers. One ship came up under another and it's props cut the tail fins off the other ship. The AT-11 is a twin finned ship and so the pilot didn't have any control over his plane and it went right to the ground without a chance for safety. Our hearts were saddened when he announced the death of all the men — two cadets, the pilot, and the crew chief. After a few simple words it was dismissed as one of those tragedies that accompany war. It was hard for all of us to take but we had to be philosophical.

Comes tuesday morning and I went on a four hour navigation flight up to Oklahoma. Got back in time for lunch after which two of us loaded 10 bombs into the ship and went out bombing. Came back and loaded 10 more bombs which we dropped and repeated this once more until we had completed three bombing missions and had dropped 30 bombs. Believe me it was the roughest day of flying I've ever spent.

SEPTEMBER 25, 1943

page 3

Even though I was dead tired by this time I was rudely awakened at 12:00 to go on guard duty until 3:00. It was a cold, lonely tour of guard and 'twas swell to get back to bed.

The next day was my toughest of all. I was on an ordinance detail. We worked in the sand pits loading bombs with 100 lbs. of sand and putting them on a truck to be carried away to the ammunition dump. We worked all day without let-up and I can honestly say it was the hardest days work I've ever put in. Lifting bomb after bomb into a truck is no cinch, when it weighs 100 lbs.

On Thursday morning I had a moderately easy time when I flew two bombing missions as I did also in the afternoon. Wasn't too rushed and got in some pretty good missions. Up that night at 3:00 for guard duty until 6:00 and as usual that was no fun.

On Friday I was on K.P. for the entire day. It wasn't bad compared to ordinance or some of the other details. After supper the camp was hit by the greatest blow any of us had ever received. We were playing ball against the officers out on the landing field. Our Squadron commander, who's one of the greatest guys you'd ever want to know, and a major who was the head of our maneuvers, were buzzing around the vicinity in a little basic trainer that we had along to go for the mail every day. All of a sudden the ship made a sharp turn about 200 ft. above the ground and went into a spin when the engine stalled. The wing flew apart like paper in mid air and the ship crashed into the ground. It was horrible when it immediately broke into flames right on the end of the runway not 300 yards away from us. Of course, both of the poor devils were killed instantly as the plane burned to a cinder before our very eyes. It was horrible and at first we couldn't believe what had happened although we saw the whole thing unfold before us.

This was a tragedy that left the camp deep in sorrow and mental dejection. There was just nothing to say since we'd all seen it happen and it was nothing but an indescribable catastrophe. One of the pilots tried to say a few words to us but he choked up and had to stop so we all dispersed and returned to our tents in silence. Everyone was deeply affected by the blow of such a loss as was that of Lt. Sayer. All of us, both cadets and pilots were crazy about him since he was a real square guy. Because of his eagerness our squadron is admitted to be the best on the line. Actually, Lt. Sayer died a Captain since his promotion came through the day following his death.

SEPTEMBER 25, 1943

page 5

He was a fellow who would go far in the
army because of his likeable personality and ability
to get things done the way the higher ups wanted.
He was so close to several of the pilots that
a few of them were broken up as much as if
one of their own family had passed away. This
was a tragedy that only a long time will erase
from our memories. Our squadron will never be the same!
The next morning a heavy fog rolled in over
camp and so we couldn't fly. It was a blessing,
since we'd all decided to finish out maneuvers
the way Lt. Sayer would want us to, although none of
us were in any mood or shape to fly that day.
Nobody said a word of it and we played ball
against the officers in an attempt to forget the
the disaster of the previous evening. It was slow,
but we finally put it in the back of our minds
and things were somewhat back to normal again.
This morning the ceiling was too low for us
to bomb and so we came back to camp rather
~~that~~ than waiting until Monday as originally planned.
We were all tired, dirty, and mighty anxious
to get away from that place. We got back here
and right now I feel like a new man. Had a
shave, shampoo, and haircut and good hot shower
which did wonders to remove the grime of sleeping
and eating out in the field. When we got back we

looked like men from the north pole with long beards and dirty bodies.

Thanks for your letters which were most welcomed out at maneuvers. Incidentally, I didn't get the package you sent Dad, either out there or here when we got back. Perhaps it will come in a day or so. About the sweater, Bee, I don't think it would be too good an idea since we are issued one that we're supposed to wear. Thanks anyway.

Starting monday night we go on a new schedule of flying from 12:00 at night until 6:00 in the morning. It will be a screwy set-up and I'll write more about it when I see what's what's.

Think I'll be off to bed for some much needed sleep. Maneuvers really took alot out of us in many ways. The two disasters were horrible, beyond compare, but they do serve to show us that this is war and not a game for weaklings. It's something we're playing for keeps and the sooner it's over the better it will be for all. It's an absolute crime that men like Jack Sayer and those cadets and pilot have to die that way but I suppose all we can say is c'est la guerre and let it go at that. I hope you'll excuse my rambling on this but it made such a deep impression on us all that it will take lots of time to erase.

S'long now.

P.S. With lots of love to you all — Bobby

SEPTEMBER 25-30, 1943

ARMY AIR FORCES
BOMBARDIER SCHOOL
CHILDRESS, TEXAS

Thursday

Dear Dad + Bee —

This will have to be a quickee asking you to do me a favor, Bee. A directive came out that we're going to have to turn in our O.D.'s [25] when we graduate and so I'd appreciate it if you'd send me all the winter clothing I sent home from Ellington. Please attend to this as soon as possible because I'll have to have them very soon.

Our new schedule turned out to be a darn good one although quite screwy — very unlike being in the army. We get up at 10:30 in the morning with breakfast at 11:15. We go to P.T. at 12:20 and then have three hours of classes from 3:00 until 6:00. We then have lunch at 6:00 and are free until 9:00 when we go to the flight line where we fly until 3:00 in the morning. Then we have our supper and go to bed. It's an odd schedule for the army, but it's really swell because it affords us lots of extra free time. We feel like a bunch of bankers getting out of bed at 10:30.

This past week we've had a tough break

on the weather. As a matter of fact I haven't flown for exactly a week now. All summer we had clear blue skies and never lost a day of flying. However, for the past week the field has been closed in due to a 500 ft. ceiling. I've never seen anything like it — there's been a solid blanket of dark clouds over the whole sky so that you can't see through to the sky at all.

It certainly feels great to be coming down the home stretch. The class ahead of us got all their equipment (parachutes, flying suits, etc) yesterday and they graduate in six days. Then we're next. These last days are just as tough as ever and we're all on our toes doing our best to finish out this orgy without a mishap. As each day goes by we all heave a sigh of relief since it's one less day to sweat out.

In ground school we're studying celestial navigation and meteorology which are our last two courses.

Can't think of any more now except congratulations to all of you about Ken and Benny. I tried to wire him last night but western union wouldn't take the wire. Please tell him for me. Wish I were home to congratulate them in person.

S'long all — Bobby

ARMY AIR FORCES
BOMBARDIER SCHOOL
CHILDRESS, TEXAS

Sunday

Dear Dad + Bee—

Here tis another week gone by which brings us just 12 days away from those coveted wings. It's so exciting that it's hard to believe that we've come all this way.

I put a call in to you this morning and as yet at 2:10 I haven't been called back. I still hope that it gets through cause I'd sure like to speak to you again. I haven't heard from you Dad, since maneuvers but I guess it's cause you're so busy. As yet I haven't received my O.D.'s but I imagine they'll come in a day or so, Bee. The Grapevine came and it really was swell. I think Ann did a good job on it. Many thanks. Before I forget Dad, would you please send me Eddie Greenbaum and Aunt Grace's addresses? Please don't forget this.

We've just finished up all our ground school classes except for meteorology which we'll wind up this coming week. We've been flying from 6:00 until 1:00 ~~at~~ night all this past week. It's been a long hard routine and it's been most tiring. We're behind due to bad weather and so last night we flew three missions and didn't get off the line until after 3:00. We don't have any open post and we've got to report to the line again at 7:00 tonight. For the next 12 days we'll be in the blue most of the time trying to get all our bombs dropped.

Starting monday we'll begin our worst schedule so far. We get up at 3:00 in the morning of all hours and fly from 4:00 until 12:00. Talk about your round-the-clock bombing, that's certainly it. What they won't do to tire us out.

That certainly is wonderful news about Ken's promotion. Everything good seems to happen at once. Please congratulate him for me, but really I have no time to write. I'm sure he'll understand. Be sure to let me know if he's going to get married any sooner than he'd originally planned. I'd give anything to be home for that day. If all goes O.K. we ought to get a 10 day leave before going with a tactical unit. It would be too wonderful to think about. Cross your fingers. Hope I can get my call through. By the way, do you think you can dig up an extra shoe stamp?[26] If so I could put it to good use.

Write often— Lots of love—

Bobby

OCTOBER 10-11, 1943

ARMY AIR FORCES
BOMBARDIER SCHOOL
CHILDRESS, TEXAS

Monday Nite

Dear Dad—

Just a note to say it was swell to talk to you and Ken awhile ago. Was sorry you weren't home, Bee.

As I told you, Dad, they changed our schedule today, and this week its as follows.

Reveille 1:30 (at night)
Breakfast 2:00
Flying 3:00-7:00
Dinner 7:30
Flying 8:30-10:30
Ground School 11:00-2:00
P.T. 2:00-3:00
Supper 4:00
Taps + To bed 6:00

If that isn't the worst schedule you've ever heard of getting up at 1:30 and going to bed at 6:00 in the evening. We have to have these terrible hours so that we can get all our bombs dropped before the 23rd. The bad weather got us way behind on our night bombs.

Just wanted you to know what's what

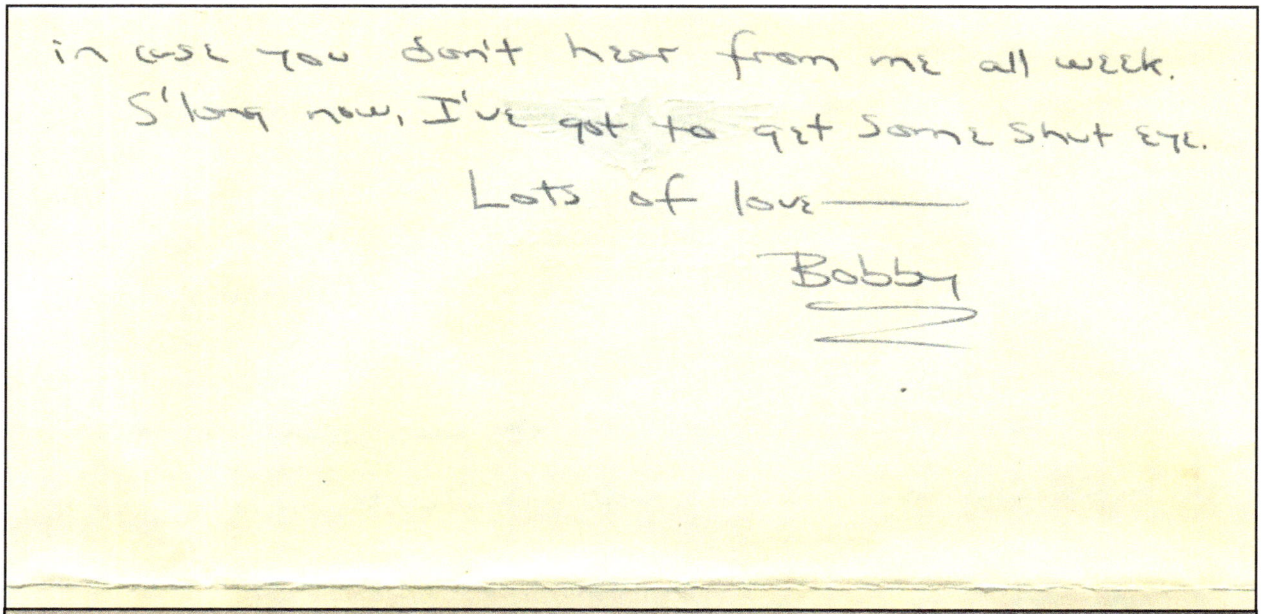
in case you don't hear from me all week.
S'long now, I've got to get some shut eye.
Lots of love ——
Bobby

A/C R. L. Stone 12120188
Class 43-13
Squadron 7 Flight D
Childress, Texas

CHILDRESS, TEX.
OCT 12
7-PM
1943

AIR 6 MAIL
CENTS
UNITED STATES OF AMERICA

AIR MAIL

Lt. Comdr. J. C. Stone
375 Park Avenue
New York City
N.Y.

OCTOBER 11-16, 1943

ARMY AIR FORCES
BOMBARDIER SCHOOL
CHILDRESS, TEXAS

Saturday Nite

Dear Dad, Bee, and Ken (if he's still home) —

Congratulations to all of you on the big news of the week. As I've written before I think it's swell and I think Ken and Bunny are darn lucky kids. Am sure sorry I wasn't on hand to say so in person.

Very little news since I wrote you two days ago. We've really had a tough break on the weather and consequently haven't been in the air for over a week now. The thick blanket of dark clouds hasn't yet lifted, and so we've been grounded for awhile. From now on we'll really be rushed trying to catch up again. You see we have a certain number of bombs to drop from each altitude and on each type of target. Laying off for a week does wonders to pile things up. From now on we'll have to fly as many as three missions a night in order to catch up. Every night this week we've been on the trainers from 9:00 until about 1:30 trying to get in our required forty hours.

We got a great surprise and welcomed break when our graduation was moved five days nearer. If all goes well we'll get our wings on Saturday the 23rd instead of the 28th as previously planned. It's swell because it cuts five extra days of worry from our list. Each day is an orgy in itself and so it's good to have only 21 left to go. It isn't in the bag yet and I doubt if it will be until our last bomb is dropped. We've come a long way and to miss now would be awfully tough to take — I doubt if I could.

Before I forget, thanks loads for the box of eats, Dad. They came in fine shape and were particularly welcomed. You see the Cadet Detachment went on field rations and our food isn't too hot.

Can't think of any more now. Let's hear from you all. It's always swell to get letters. Will really be busy flying all the time this coming week and doubt if I'll have time to write. Know you understand.

My love to all —

Bobby

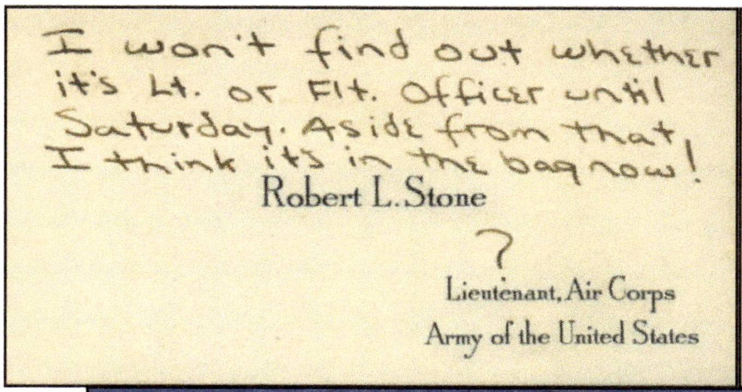
I won't find out whether it's Lt. or Flt. Officer until Saturday. Aside from that, I think its in the bag now!
Robert L. Stone
?
Lieutenant, Air Corps
Army of the United States

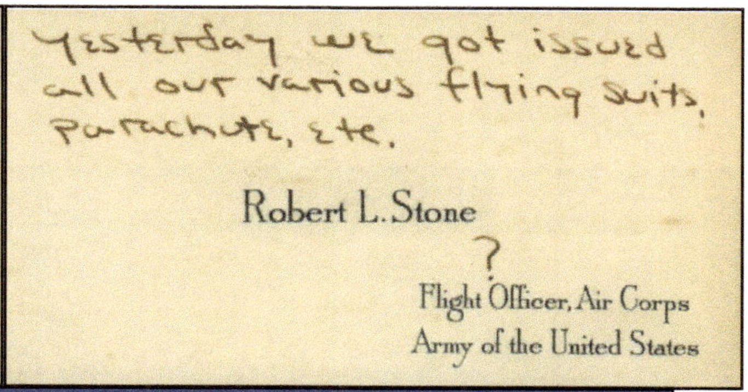
Yesterday we got issued all our various flying suits, parachute, etc.
Robert L. Stone
?
Flight Officer, Air Corps
Army of the United States

CHILDRESS, TX

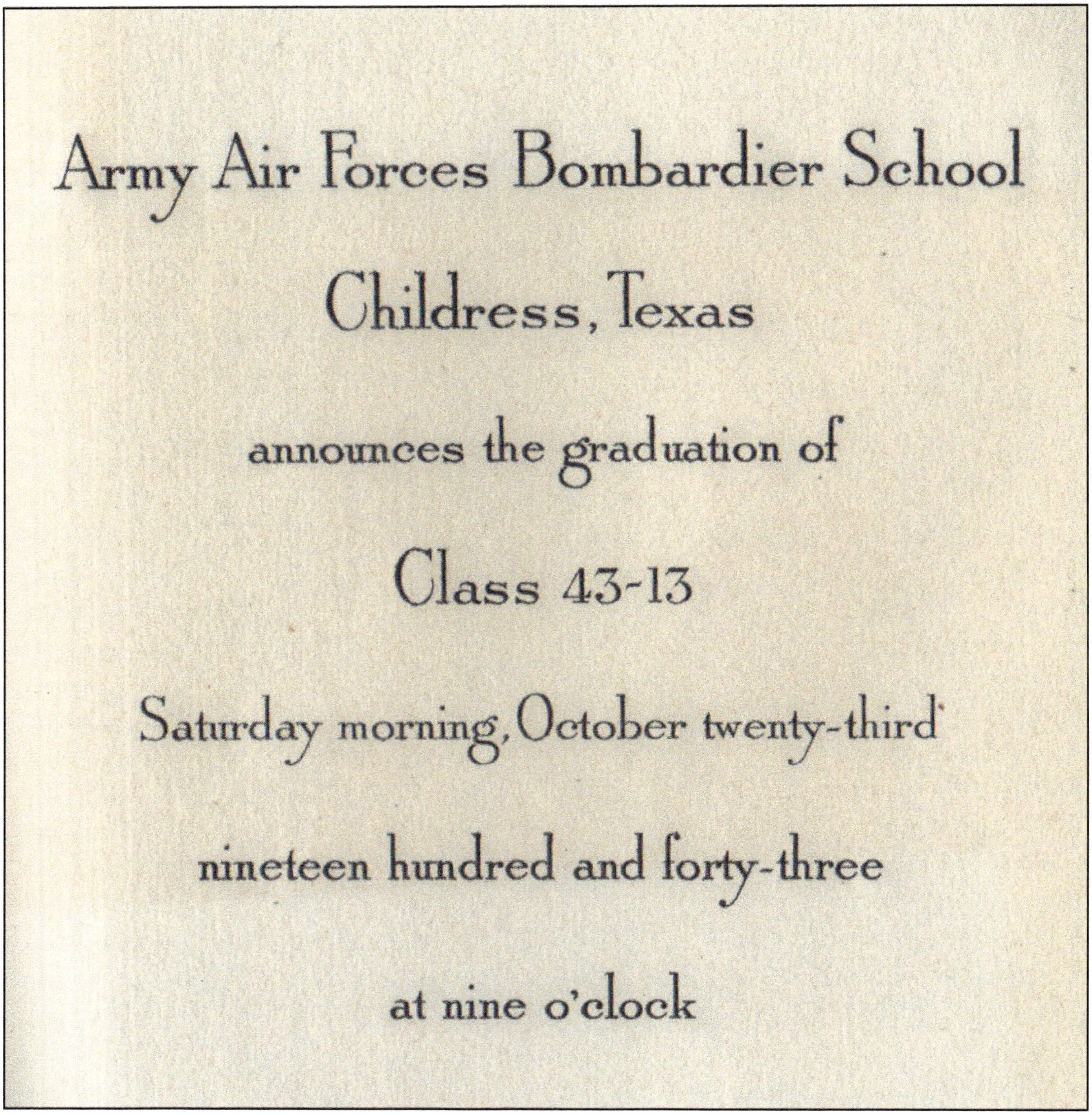

Army Air Forces Bombardier School

Childress, Texas

announces the graduation of

Class 43-13

Saturday morning, October twenty-third

nineteen hundred and forty-three

at nine o'clock

OCTOBER 23, 1943

HEADQUARTERS
ARMY AIR FORCES CENTRAL FLYING TRAINING COMMAND 1FY-ss
Office of the Commanding General

Randolph Field, Texas
23 October 1943

In reply
refer to: AG 201 Stone, Robert Lewis

Subject: Temporary Appointment.

To: A 0-696,041

Aviation Cadet Robert Lewis Stone,
U.S.A.,
Childress, Texas.

1. The Secretary of War has directed me to inform you that the President has appointed and commissioned you a temporary Second Lieutenant, Army of the United States, effective this date. Your serial number is shown after A above.

2. This commission will continue in force during the pleasure of the President of the United States for the time being, and for the duration of the war and six months thereafter unless sooner terminated.

3. There is inclosed herewith a form for oath of office which you are requested to execute and return. The execution and return of the required oath of office constitute an acceptance of your appointment. No other evidence of acceptance is required.

4. This letter should be retained by you as evidence of your appointment as no commissions will be issued during the war.

By Command of Major General BRANT:

J. E. McCord
J. E. McCORD
Lieut. Colonel, A. G. D.
Assistant Adjutant General

Inclosure:
Form for oath of office.

ITINERARY CHILDRESS, TX – WENDOVER FIELD, UT

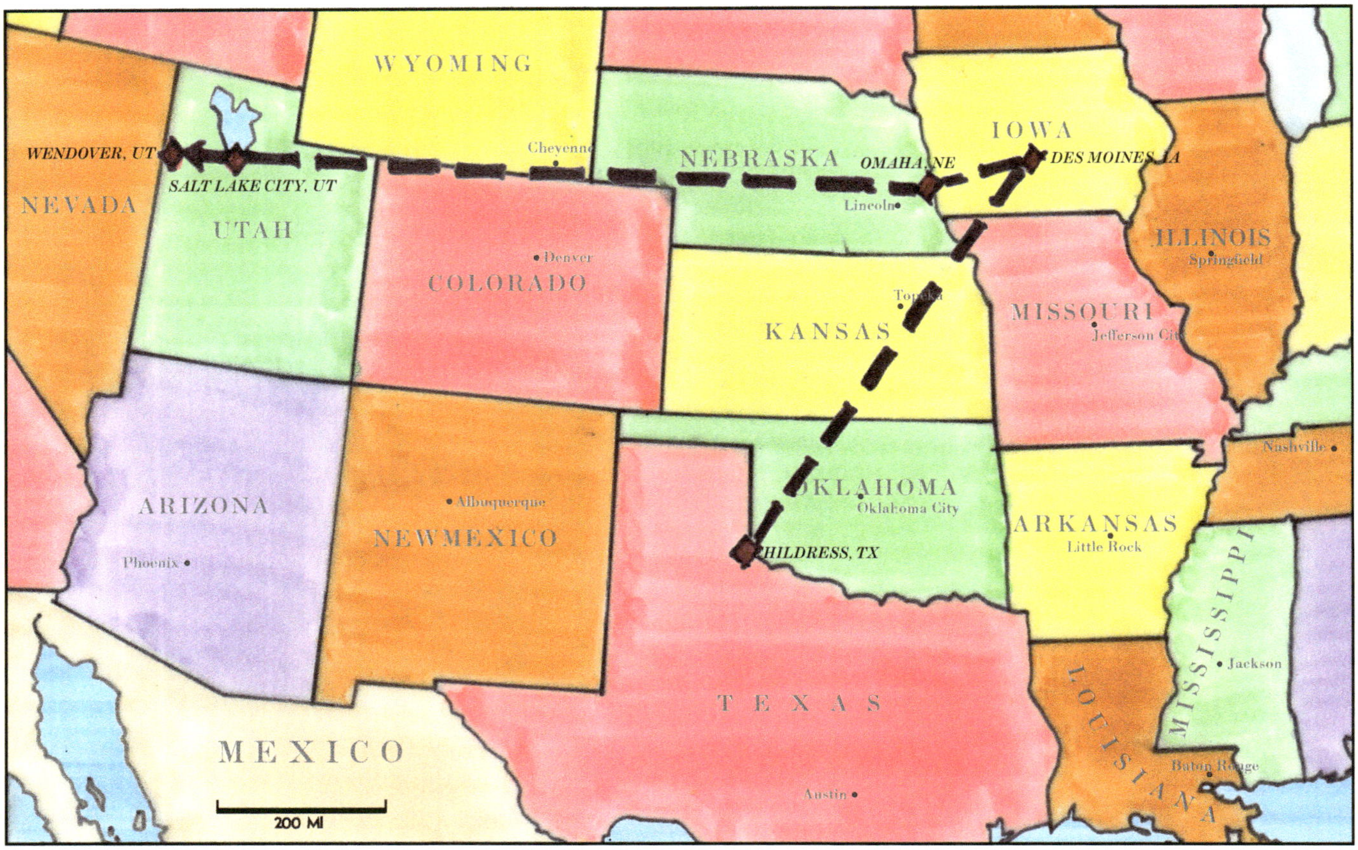

NOVEMBER 1943

Thursday

Dear Dad + Bee—

We just left Des Moines on our way west on what has been a very smooth and uneventful trip. Only slept a few winks during the night but I don't feel too worse for wares as yet. I'll probably be dead tired by this afternoon.

I can't begin to adequately tell you how much I enjoyed my 10 short days at home. Although I didn't do much in the way of excitement, it was wonderful to see you, Jimmy, and Pam again. Eating good meals and just taking it easy made for my best vacation ever. Both of you were just swell about everything and made my stay a real pleasure and much needed change. My only regret is that it couldn't have lasted much longer. I guess you never really appreciate home and a million and one little things you've always taken for granted until you've been away for awhile—it sure does the trick.

In a few minutes we'll be coming into Omaha and so I'll end this so

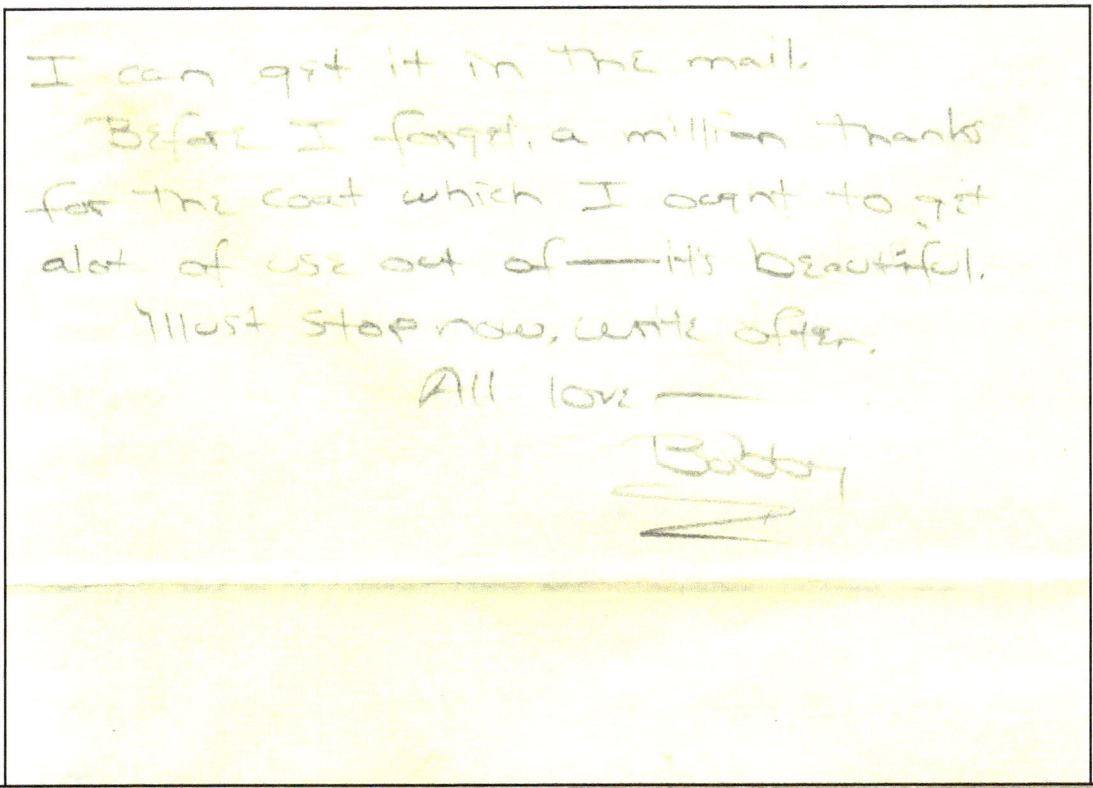

I can get it in the mail.
Before I forget, a million thanks
for the coat which I ought to get
alot of use out of — it's beautiful.
Must stop now, write often.
All love —
Bobby

Sunday Nite

Dear Dad + Bee —

Since you last heard from me, quite alot has happened. Arrived here alright after a rather eventful plane trip. Just after I wired you from Denver, I was given a scare when four fellows were bumped off the ship. Both of those kids from Childress were removed. You see they had to put on more gas since there was a possibility we couldn't land at Salt Lake City due to bad weather but would have to fly 300 miles further on to Boise. From Denver to Salt Lake we had a very rough trip and as a matter of fact they had us leave our seat belts fastened and couldn't serve lunch. It was an extremely bumpy trip over the mountains but on arrival at Salt Lake the visibility was O.K. and we were allowed to land.

Salt Lake City is a very beautiful place located in a valley with a wall of high snow-capped mountains surrounding it. It's really lovely! The city is swell with many theaters, lots of nice stores, and several really good hotels. To say the least I was most pleasantly surprised.

Upon reporting Thursday I was told to return the following day. I went to town, which is only ten minutes from the field, and met up with a gang of kids from Childress. Had a good dinner and a movie and stayed in their apartment that they had already rented—darn nice place with lots of beds and an icebox and kitchenette.

Returned to the field the next morning where I had to fill in alot of papers etc. Was assigned to a barrack with all the gang. Incidentally my present address is —

Lt. R.L.S. 0-696041
Provisional Squadron F
18th Replacement Wing
Salt Lake City, Utah

Again I left the post and haven't been back since. We've lived the life of kings in town without even bothering to report to the post at all. It's absolute bedlam out there with loads of pilots, bombardiers, and gunners all reporting in. It's been like old-home-week running into kids I haven't seen for 10 months since Nashville days. I got my biggest surprise when I bumped into Bink Hemphries, a friend of mine from Williams.

Have no idea when or where I'll be shipped. Some fellows have been here for over five weeks and no one knows anything about anything as to shipping etc.. The only thing I do know is that I was classified for heavy bombardment in either a B-24 or B-17. I hope its the latter.

So far we've gotten lots of sleep, eaten like pigs, and seen lots of movies and in general had a swell time. Went up to the University Saturday to see Utah play Colorado. It wasn't too good a game although it was lots of fun being out in the fresh air and wandering on a college campus. Incidentally it's been quite cold here and already there is wonderful skiing up on the mountains. If I'm here any length of time, I'm going to look into it and possibly go skiing some week-end.

Really can't think of any more for now except, again many thanks for such a swell leave. I only regret it was so short. Please be sure to send my letters around to all the boys so that I won't have

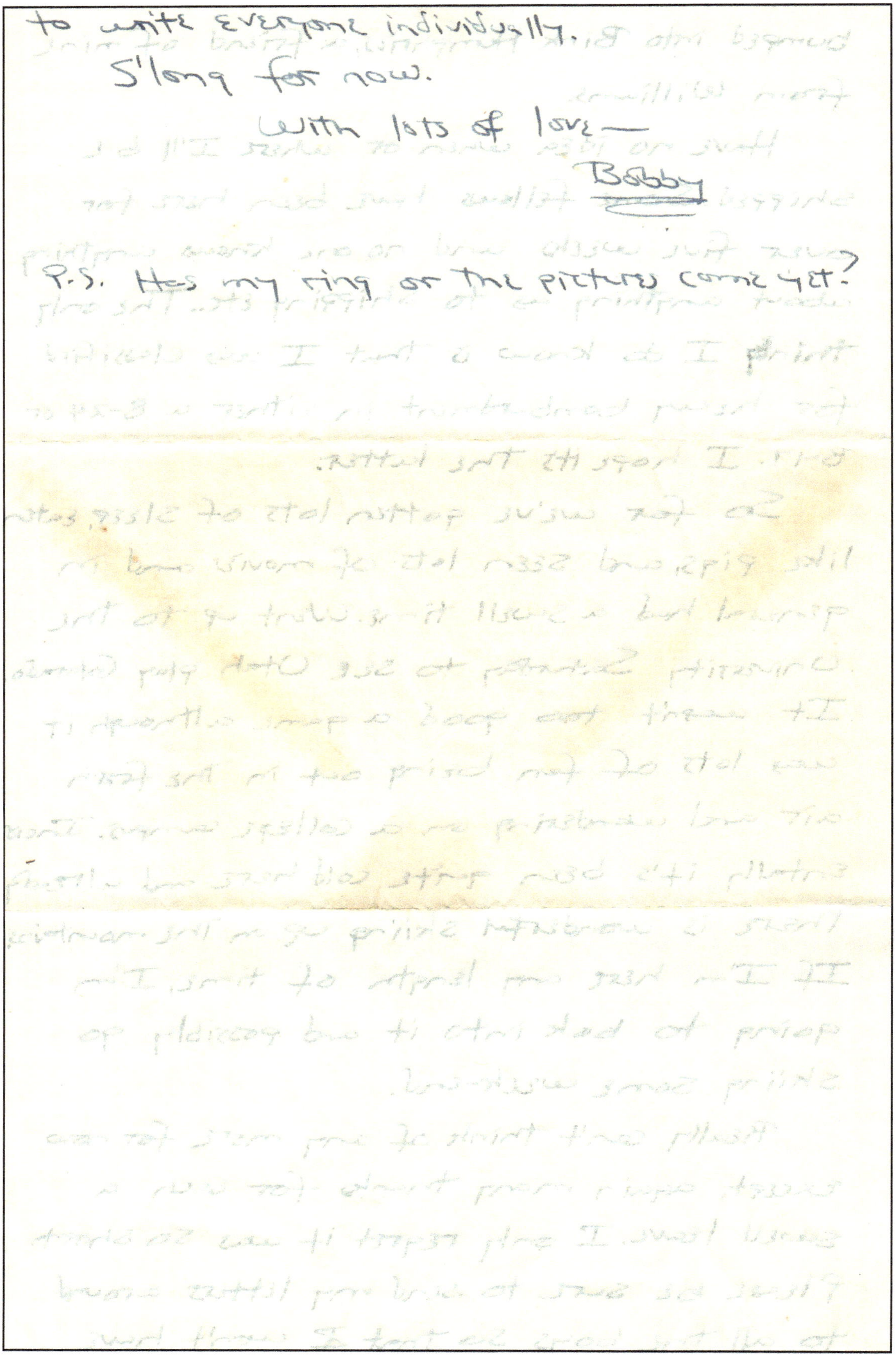
to write everyone individually.
S'long for now.
With lots of love—
Bobby
P.S. Has my ring or the pictures come yet?

NOVEMBER 7–9, 1943

15870. John Cobb Beats the Eyston Record for Speed on the Salt Flats of Great Salt Lake.
SALT
From
Great Salt Lake
UTAH
Photo by Bill

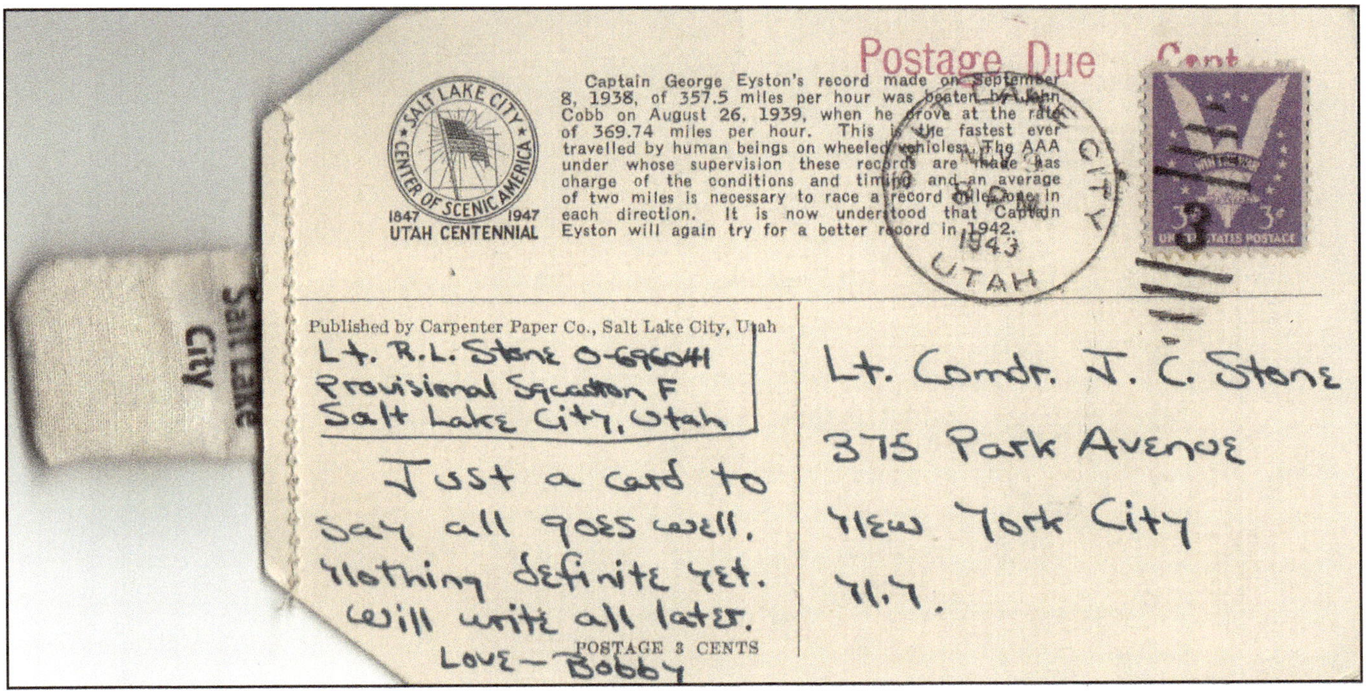
Postage Due Cent
SALT LAKE CITY
CENTER OF SCENIC AMERICA
1847 1947
UTAH CENTENNIAL
Captain George Eyston's record made on September 8, 1938, of 357.5 miles per hour was beaten by John Cobb on August 26, 1939, when he drove at the rate of 369.74 miles per hour. This is the fastest ever travelled by human beings on wheeled vehicles. The AAA under whose supervision these records are made has charge of the conditions and timing and an average of two miles is necessary to race a record mile, one in each direction. It is now understood that Captain Eyston will again try for a better record in 1942.
SALT LAKE CITY
1943
UTAH
UNITED STATES POSTAGE
3¢ 3¢
Published by Carpenter Paper Co., Salt Lake City, Utah
Lt. R.L. Stone O-696044
Provisional Squadron F
Salt Lake City, Utah
Just a card to
say all goes well.
Nothing definite yet.
Will write all later.
Love — Bobby
POSTAGE 3 CENTS
Lt. Comdr. J. C. Stone
375 Park Avenue
New York City
N.Y.
Salt Lake
City

Friday

Dear Dad + Bee—

Just a note to say that all goes well and thanks alot for your letters. I received the ring and pictures, both of which were gladly received. I returned the proofs this afternoon, so you should get them in the middle of next week.

I agreed with you on the one you selected but I didn't think that any of them were too wonderful. I guess I have no complaints, considering the subject. I would appreciate it if you'd order me one print along with yours. When you get it, you can send it on to me and I'll pay you for it. Incidentally I owe you $3.00 for my ring which is enclosed.

All hell broke loose around here when the Colonel restricted us to our area for two days. If all goes well, we ought to get out again tomorrow—I sure hope so cause this place is a real dump.

Still nothing definite about shipping although something may come up in a day or so. I'll let you know as soon as I hear anything myself.

NOVEMBER 19, 1943

Very little other news from here and it's hell trying to write on my bunk with 65 noisy Lts. sounding off playing poker, crap, writing letters, or just bulling.

S'long now.

All love —

Bobby

The Belvedere Apartment Hotel
29 SOUTH STATE STREET
SALT LAKE CITY 1, UTAH

Tuesday

Dear Dad & Bee—

Since I last wrote, life has taken on a much brighter outlook. At that time we were restricted to our area and really lived a miserable life. Starting last Saturday they again allowed us to stay off the post at night as long as we reported at 7:30 every morning for the reading of shipping orders etc.. They've called off school and so we're free almost all the time.

Rooms are so hard to get that as soon as we gave up our apartment (when we were restricted) it was taken and we couldn't get it back. There isn't a room to be had in town so two of us have taken a room with an

HOME OF RADIO STATION KUTA

NOVEMBER 23, 1943

adjoining sitting room over in the transient BOQ.[27] It's not the best but it's lots nicer than living over in the barracks where you freeze to death.

For the past few days a great many groups have shipped out. Yesterday a bunch of kids from our Childress group were alerted and they left today. There were some more read off today but they only got up as far as the m's. If I'm not read off tomorrow, I'll probably be stuck here until some time in December. They've shipped out alot of men but we've still got a large number left. You've never seen so many officers together at one time. It's really a mad-house.

Haven't done anything exciting. We do manage to have a good meal every night followed by a movie, bowling, or some such entertainment. On Thursday (if we're still here) we're going to

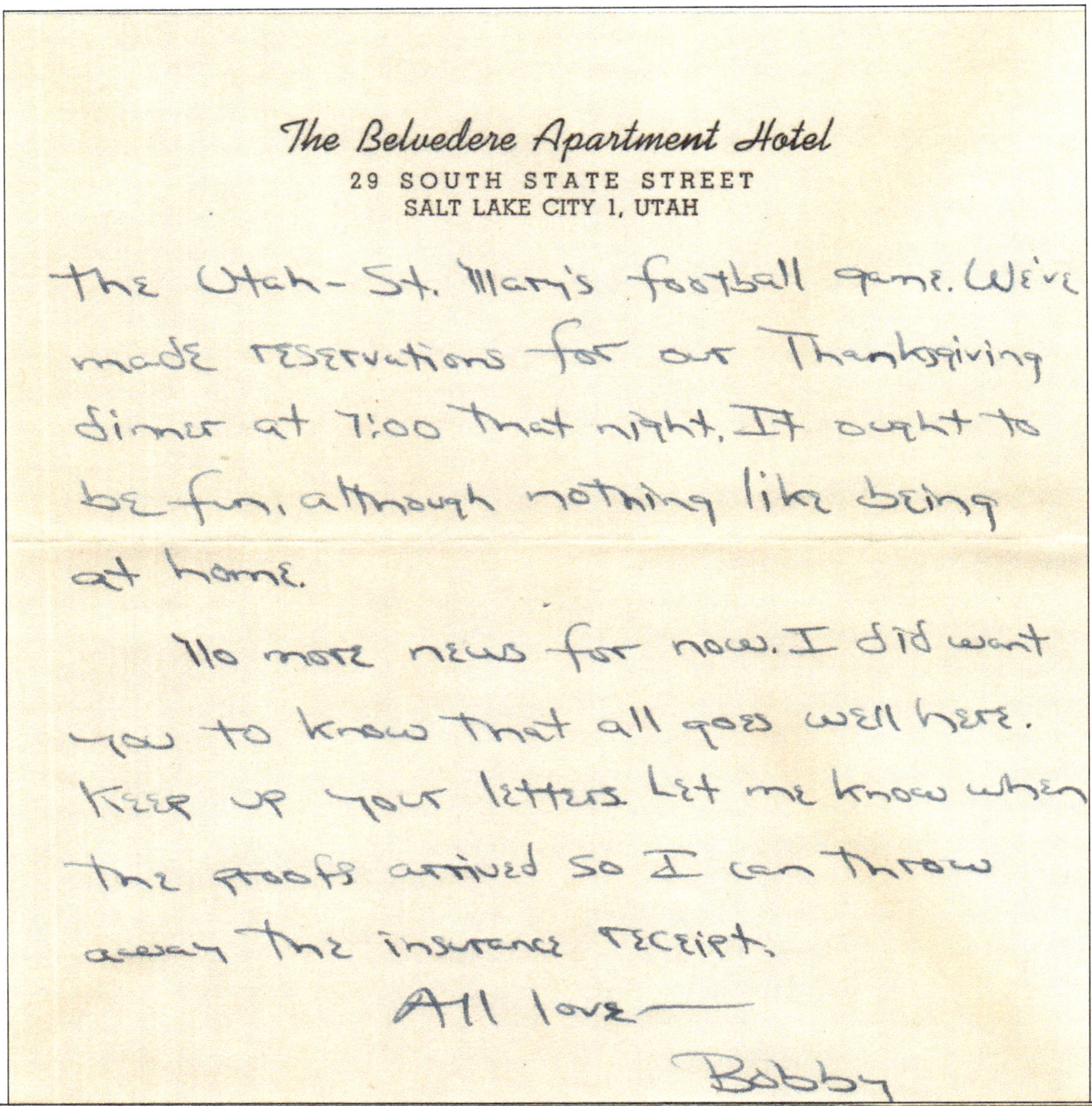

The Belvedere Apartment Hotel
29 SOUTH STATE STREET
SALT LAKE CITY 1, UTAH

the Utah-St. Mary's football game. We've made reservations for our Thanksgiving dinner at 7:00 that night. It ought to be fun, although nothing like being at home.

No more news for now. I did want you to know that all goes well here. Keep up your letters. Let me know when the proofs arrived so I can throw away the insurance receipt.

All love—

Bobby

The Belvedere
Apartment Hotel
29 South State Street
SALT LAKE CITY, UTAH

Lt. Comdr. J. C. Stone
375 Park Avenue
New York City

NOVEMBER 23-28, 1943

OFFICERS' CLUB
WENDOVER FIELD
UTAH

Sunday

Dear Dad + Bee —

As always it was swell to talk to you yesterday. As you could gather from what I said, this place is really pretty bad. Everything is definite that we are going to California. It is really an unheard-of break to be joining the movement instead of being stuck here for three months. I still can't believe that it's true.

Incidentally, we are going to March Field which is in the San Bernardino Valley, about sixty miles from Los Angeles, Hollywood, etc.. It's meant to be a darn nice field and of course lots pleasanter than being stuck here in "no-man's land."

If you write to Lt. R.L.S. 0-696041
399th Bombing Group
Squadron 607
March Field, California

I ought to get the letter. That may not

be my exact address, but I'm sure the letter will reach me. Mail will be muchly appreciated! If you write right away, the letter ought to be there when we arrive since we'll be leaving shortly.

As I said yesterday I have some swell gents in my crew. My pilot is a damn nice looking kid about 24 or so. He is an A-1 guy with a good head on his shoulders and I think he'll make an excellent leader. Incidentally he comes from Kansas and his name is "Hap Middleton". My co-pilot is also a good Joe, a little younger than Hap but equally as capable, I think. His name is Ken Githens and he comes from Portland, Oregon. From all indications we ought to hit it off just fine and we ought to make for a good crew. Our gunners, radioman, and engineer all seem like good kids although I don't know them too well. We have six inlisted men in the crew, ranging from Pfc. to Sgt. Our crew is complete except for the navigator which we don't pick up for awhile yet. More about all the boys when I get to know them

NOVEMBER 28, 1943

OFFICERS' CLUB
WENDOVER FIELD
UTAH

better. So far everything looks great!

Yesterday we went through a complete physical and got a whole series of shots and my arm felt like a pin cushion for awhile. We spent the afternoon at the sub-depot filling shortages in our flying equipment.

As soon as we hit the coast we'll be in for some very intensive training. Ground school and hours of flying will keep most of our time occupied. We've already been warned that our free time will be very little. From now on we'll be playing for keeps and so we've got alot to learn before we go over to combat. Yesterday I went through a B-24 and believe me it's quite diffent than an AT-11. Our whole crew has alot to learn.

Can't think of any more so I'll put a halt to my ramblings. I'll write again

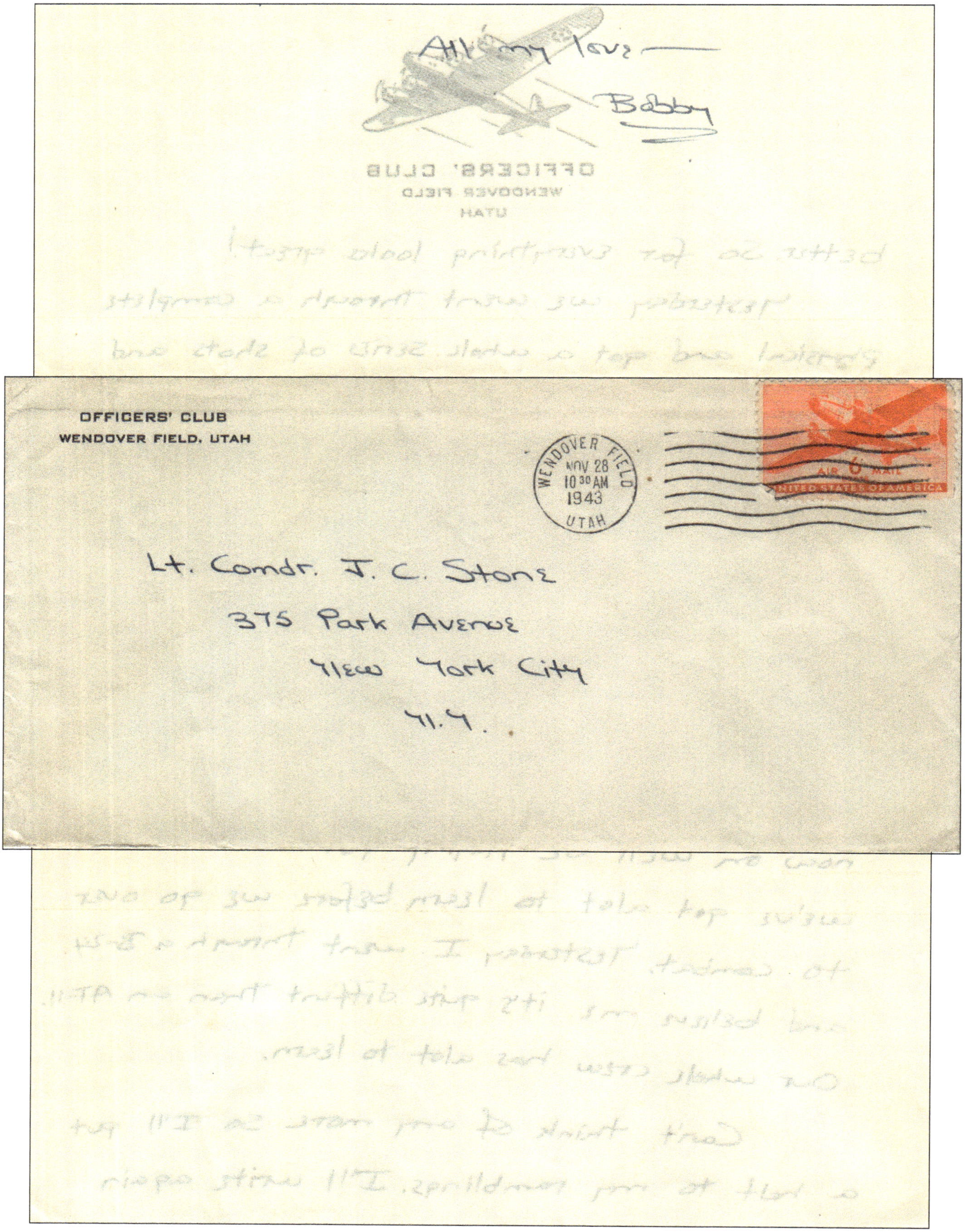

All my love —
Bobby

OFFICERS' CLUB
WENDOVER FIELD, UTAH

WENDOVER FIELD
NOV 28
10 30 AM
1943
UTAH

AIR MAIL 6
UNITED STATES OF AMERICA

Lt. Comdr. J. C. Stone
375 Park Avenue
New York City
N.Y.

NOVEMBER 28, 1943

REPLACEMENT TRAINING UNIT
MARCH & HAMMER FIELDS, CA

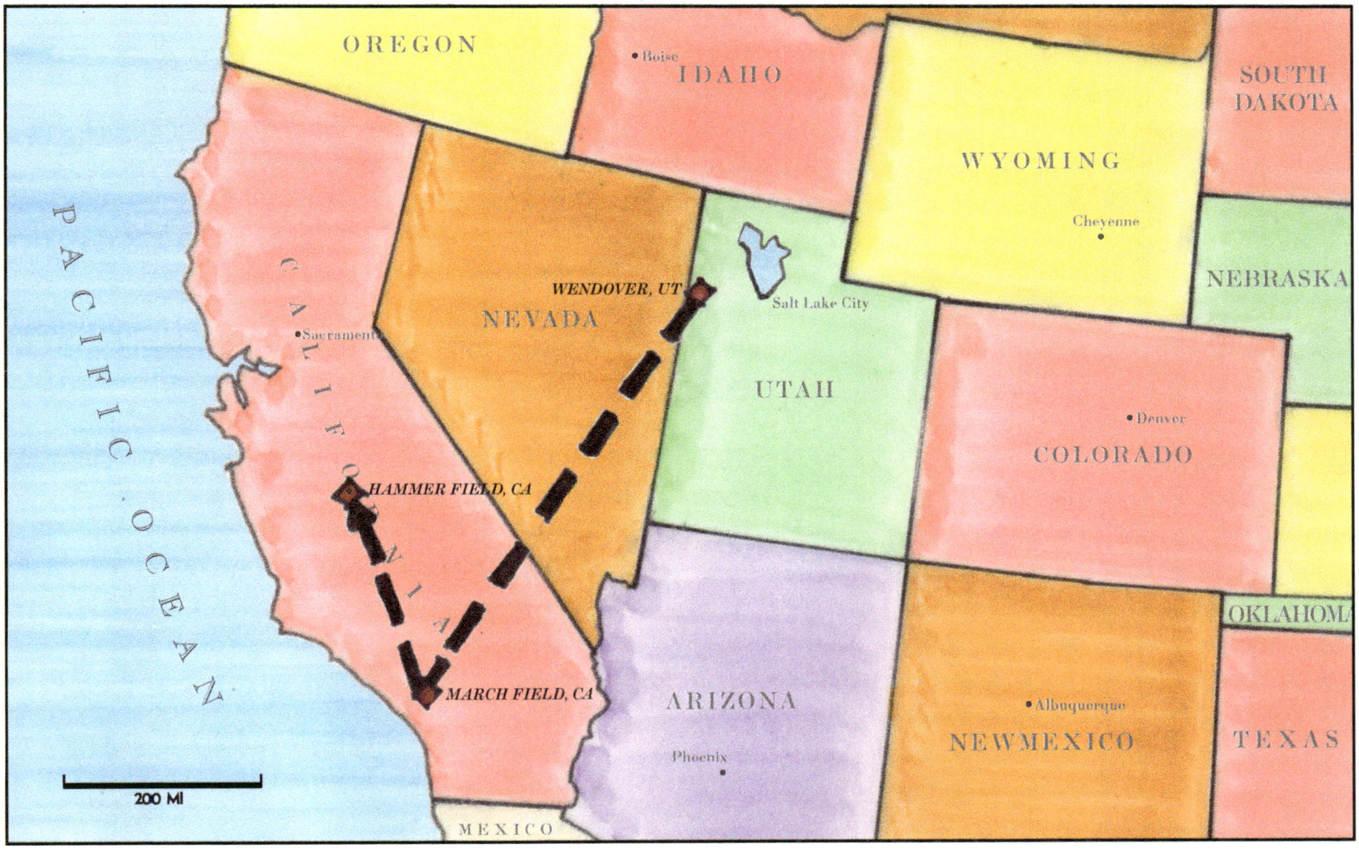

DECEMBER 1943–JUNE 1944

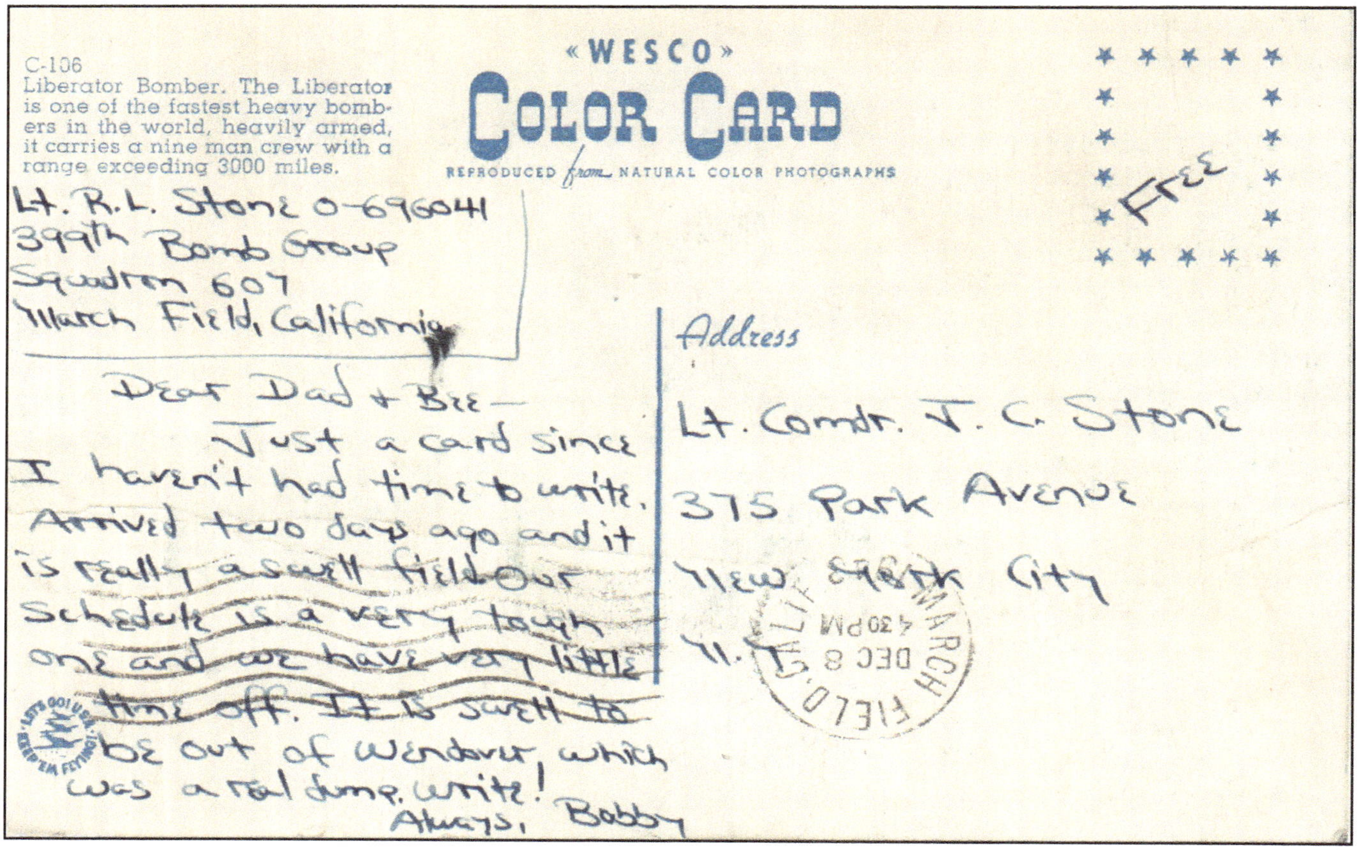
C-106
Liberator Bomber. The Liberator is one of the fastest heavy bombers in the world, heavily armed, it carries a nine man crew with a range exceeding 3000 miles.

«WESCO»
COLOR CARD
REPRODUCED *from* NATURAL COLOR PHOTOGRAPHS

FREE

Lt. R.L. Stone 0-696041
399th Bomb Group
Squadron 607
March Field, California

Dear Dad + Bee—
Just a card since I haven't had time to write. Arrived two days ago and it is really a swell field. Our schedule is a very tough one and we have very little time off. It is swell to be out of Wendover, which was a real dump. Write!
Always, Bobby

Address
Lt. Comdr. J. C. Stone
375 Park Avenue
New York City
N.Y.

MARCH FIELD, CALIF. DEC 8 4 30 PM

LET'S GO! U.S.A. KEEP 'EM FLYING!

DECEMBER 8-9, 1943

MARCH FIELD, CALIFORNIA

Thursday Nite

Dear Dad & Bee —

I hope you'll excuse my not having written for so long, but since we arrived here late Sunday night we've been extremely busy. We pulled in here after an uneventful, yet pleasant trip from Wendover, which was a real relief to be leaving behind us.

The physical setup of this field is quite nice although it's tough getting around from place to place since it's so darn big and spread out. This is a very old field and has a great many permanent buildings. Our BOQ is adequate — we live two men to a small room with a closet and a desk. It's nothing exceptional, but its definitely O.K.

Both "Hap" and Ken continue to be real swell gents. Incidentally our whole squadron was assigned navigators last night. We have a kid by the name of Kamps and as yet we've passed no judgement on him—only time will tell.

The schedule for the combat crews is no picnick out here. We're on call to go to school and fly for 24 hours a day for five days. Then on the sixth we're off for 24 hours. We have to stay on the post every night except when we have our day off. That's kinda rough on fellows like Hap and Ken whose wives arrived and are living in Riverside. Even though they only see them occasionally I still envy them.

We are working under a ground school and flying program that is designed to keep us busy all the time since they are trying to give us three phases of O.T.U.[28] in two months, when ordinarily it is supposed to take three months. Right now they plan to have us leave for combat by the second week in February—that certainly doesn't seem far off and we have so much to learn by then!

We've run into one good break here when we found the chow to be A-1. It's really a treat to eat good meals again after half-starving to death at Childress this summer. We have a choice of three places to eat here and all of them are excellent.

Can't think of anything else to write now, although it seems as if so much has happened since we arrived on Sunday. Please write often because it's quite easy to get feeling blue when you're doing combat flying five and six hours a day or nights, and mail does wonders to keep up the moral. I know I won't have a chance to answer half your letters, but I hope you'll understand and write anyway. It makes such a difference.

I must get to bed now cause sleep means so much when you're under a constant sitrain. S'long now.

Lots of love—

Bobby.

P.S. Please be sure to send my letters around to Don, Jim, etc. because I just can't possibily write them indiviually as much as I'd like to.

P.S.S. Don't remember if I told you or not, but I ran into Pete Hoyt (remember him?) the last day I was in Salt Lake City. He has his pilot's wings now and was being shipped out as a co-pilot. It was such fun seeing him again after all these months. It's almost a year ago we left for Nashville together.

Friday

Dear Dad + Bee —

I haven't much in the way of news but even so a few lines are in order to say that all goes well. Still no word as to when I'll be crewed up and be shipped out.

Just like all good things our pleasant set-up came to an abrupt end on monday. Everybody is now required to be on the post every night by one o'clock at night. They have us going to school every day from eight in the morning until five. It's horribly confused and at best, a complete farce. We don't get a darn thing out of school and so it's a complete waste of time. They make us go just to keep our day occupied. Frankly I'd rather sleep.

Comes five o'clock and we all head for town to indulge in a good meal and perhaps a movie or some such entertainment. Don't remember if I told you or not, but last Saturday we saw the Utah-Colorado football game. Not a good game, but lots of fun.

No more news now. Will write as soon as I find out about being moved out etc.

Lots of love —

Bobby

P.S. Haven't heard from you yet and I'm wondering if my ring or the pictures have arrived yet?

DECEMBER 10-15, 1943

MARCH FIELD, CALIFORNIA

Wednesday Dec. 15th

Dear Dad and Bee—

It seems like ages since I last heard from you, but I guess you've been pretty well occupied with Don being home. I too have been mighty busy with a very full schedule of ground school and flying.

The crew continues to be swell and Hap is a very able pilot. Incidentally "Whitey" has turned out to be an A-1 gent, contrary to a hasty first impression.

Our schedule here is even rougher than in the Cadets and we have even less time to ourselves. Our flying schedule is gruelling cause we're in the blue six hours a day or night, every day. That's a long time to be up there at one clip.

We've taken some rotten deals out here and as yet we haven't left the post. We were to go on a 24 hour pass starting tomorrow but this afternoon they cancelled all passes until further notice. It's really rough when you think that we'll be in combat in less than three months and there we won't have any place to go on passes. Incidentally, according to all information we'll be sent into the Pacific theater. We're in an R.T.U. (Replacement Training Unit) not O.T.U. which means that we will not be sent as a large unit but rather as single ships joining a large unit as a replacements.

Before I forget, I hope you'll understand and excuse a delay in any Xmas presents but since we won't be getting off tomorrow I won't have a chance to get anything to any of you by the 25th. I hope you'll understand but it's not my doings.

Speaking of Xmas Bee, you mentioned that I might like a "Parker 51" pen. At the time I said no but since then my pen got broken. If you can get one, I'd love a medium in black and silver. It's just a suggestion if the offer still holds good. I'd love one, cause I've had to borrow a pen ever since I broke mine.

No more now, except let's hear from you cause mail is really welcomed way out here.

Lots of love—

Bobby

DECEMBER 15-16, 1943

MARCH FIELD CALIFORNIA

December 16

Dear Dad—

It was with the greatest pleasure that I just received your long newsy letter. I wrote you last night saying I hadn't heard from you for some time, and so hence this note

I'm sorry to hear that Bee is laid up and I hope she's in A-1 shape by now. Give her my best and tell her to get well real quick like.

It sounds like Don had a swell furlough and I'll bet you loved having him home. I sure wish I could have seen him. Congratulate Barry on his going into the marines.

I was terribly sorry to hear of the death of Len's mother. I, of course, wrote him immediately. I sure hope he isn't too upset, cause I know how close he was to her.

Nothing much new—still flying and going to school for long hours. Everybody is plenty irate because we still haven't been given our pass and we're indefinitely restricted to the post. Nuff for now.

Write soon.

All love—

Bobby

DECEMBER 16–21, 1943

Tuesday

Dear Dad & Bee—

I want to thank both of you for your swell birthday letters and, Dad, for the over-generous check. Yesterday we had our first pass and the check really came in handy to provide for a good time in Hollywood. This year my birthday wasn't anything like years gone by, but instead just another day. Being away from home on such an occasion just isn't fun, and makes me wish this mess was over even more than I already do—

It was fun to get off the post and go to Hollywood where we stayed over night. Did a little drinking and saw some entertainment. 'Twas kinda fun.

You asked about our navigator, Bee. Well, he's a darn swell guy and we all like him alot.

By the way you asked about an Xmas box you'd sent and it hasn't come yet. The mails are so slow that I imagine it will come soon.

Before I forget, thanks oodles for the phone call on the 19th — 'twas so swell to talk to you on my birthday. I hope you don't mind being stuck with reversed charge calls now and again, but it gets kinda lonely stuck way out here so damn far from home.

Again a million thanks for the swell letter and the check, Dad.

All love —

Bobby

DECEMBER 21-22, 1943

Wednesday

Dear Dad—

The folder with the bonds arrived this afternoon and I want to thank you just loads. You were so darn over-generous in giving me the bonds as well as the large check. As soon as I get ahold of a folder I'll send you the bonds to deposit in my accou

This afternoon our squadron took a beating when our weekly passes were indefinitely cancelled. The way they treat the combat crews here is discouraging and somehow we always get the short end. The permanent party on this field are the only ones who get a half decent break.

Had quite a bit of excitement on Saturday night when the weather closed in and all the ships got back to the field except for nine. I didn't fly that afternoon because the bombing ranges were closed and so all bombardiers had to go to class.

When Hap called the tower they gave him instructions to go on and land at Long Beach. Well, from six until after nine we had no contact with them and they had all the radios buzzing and all the airway controls trying to reach them. It's such a helpless feeling to know that they were lost and not be able to do anything about it. Time went on and we'd given them up as lost since they only had about ten minutes gas left and we hadn't heard from them. A few minutes later a call came from Long Beach that a B-24 had just landed with only a matter of minutes gas left. They had been lost for hours, but they came out of it by the skin of their teeth.

When the call came, the Colonel (the group commander) said to me "Lt. you and I are going over to the club for a few drinks." I wasn't dressed for the club so he got off there and gave me his car to go to my BOQ where I quickly got dressed. When I met him at the club I was greeted by the Col. with a drink in each hand. I stayed there until quite late, drinking with him and several of his pals. I felt

So important to have the Colonel buying me drinks. He's a swell gent—quite young, with lot of decorations. He's a pilot back from combat.

For the past three days my crew has been grounded at Long Beach waiting for a clearance to fly back. Since we've been out here it has been very rainy with a very low ceiling and quite bad for flying. I'm very anxious to see the boys and hear all about their experiences.

Again Dad, I can't thank you enough for the bonds and check. Once more, your swell letter was appreciated more than ever before. You're a great guy, Dad.

All love—

Bobby

Designers and Illustrators Card No. A-1
PRINTED IN U.S.A.

Christmas Greetings
AND BEST WISHES
FOR A HAPPIER
NEW YEAR

*

Best o' love—

Bobby

DECEMBER 25-28, 1943

Officers' Mess
MARCH FIELD
RIVERSIDE, CALIFORNIA

Tuesday

Dear Dad & Bee—

No particular news since I wrote two days ago. Today we're supposedly on pass but I'm so tired that I'm going to stay right on the post. Think I'll get a little sun at the pool this afternoon.

This past week we've been flying all hours of the day. They are trying to get in all our flying minimums as soon as possible.

Enclosed are a few snaps that I've had for some time. They're not too good but I thought you might like having them.

Write often.

All love—

Bobby

Wednesday

Dear Dad + Bee—

First off, a million thanks for the beautiful pen that just arrived today. It's really just swell and writes so easily.

I was sorry to hear that 375 is temporarily a sick ward. I hope both of you are 100% well again.

Xmas was a fairly sad day for all of us. We were up at 5:30 in the morning and had to fly until noon. Then we went to ground school until six. It was just another day and quite unlike Christmas. Incidentally Bee, that box you said you'd sent some time ago has never arrived. The mails were all jammed up but it shouldn't have taken all that while.

Got off again on a 24 hour pass and I went in and stayed with Ronnie and Doug.[29] I had dinner there and stayed over night. They have a darling house just outside of Beverly Hills. Was fun to & see them again.

A few days ago Hap was removed as our first pilot. He took a raw deal and was sent away to another field. I'll tell you about it some time but it's too involved

DECEMBER 29, 1943

to write. We were assigned a new pilot by the name of Jim Robinson. He's a first lieutenant who was a pilot instructor here. He's a swell egg and a damn fine flyer.

Say Dad, I got a ride into LA with a Captain in the air force who said he had a good friend who used to be a governor on the exchange and is now a Lt. Comdr. in the navy. By any chance do you know a fellow by the name of Wardell?

Can't think of anything else except that we're still flying lots. We're doing high altitude bombing from 20,000 ft. It's really tiring to stay up there six hours at a clip.

I tried to reach you on Christmas day but of course the lines were so tied up that I was out of luck. Again a million thanks for the nifty pen.

Here's wishing you a very happy new year and that next year we will all be together again with this mess only a bad memory.

Lots of love —

Bobby

P.S. Please address and mail the enclosed.

At left is a group formation we flew up to Frisco In December '43 at March Field, California

SCRAPBOOK PHOTOS/DECEMBER 30, 1943

Thursday

Dear Dad + Bee—

The Xmas box arrived today and I want to thank you a million for the wonderful assortment of gifts. It was such fun opening the various packages. Every one of them was something that I can really use—a swell selection of presents, Bee. Thanks loads!

New Years Eve won't be any more than another night for us. I fly tomorrow morning, school all afternoon, and then bomb trainer from eight until eleven. Not my idea of how to spend New Years Eve.

I'd love to speak to you tomorrow night but I doubt if I'll be able to reach you cause the lines are so darn jammed with calls. If I don't, I want to wish you the best for a very happy new year. Let's hope this mess is over within the year and we can all be together again.

Again many, many thanks for the Xmas presents. Thanks loads for sending that editorial, Dad. I had such fun reading it cause it brought back so many pleasant memories of past Christmases. Happy New Year, with love—

Bobby

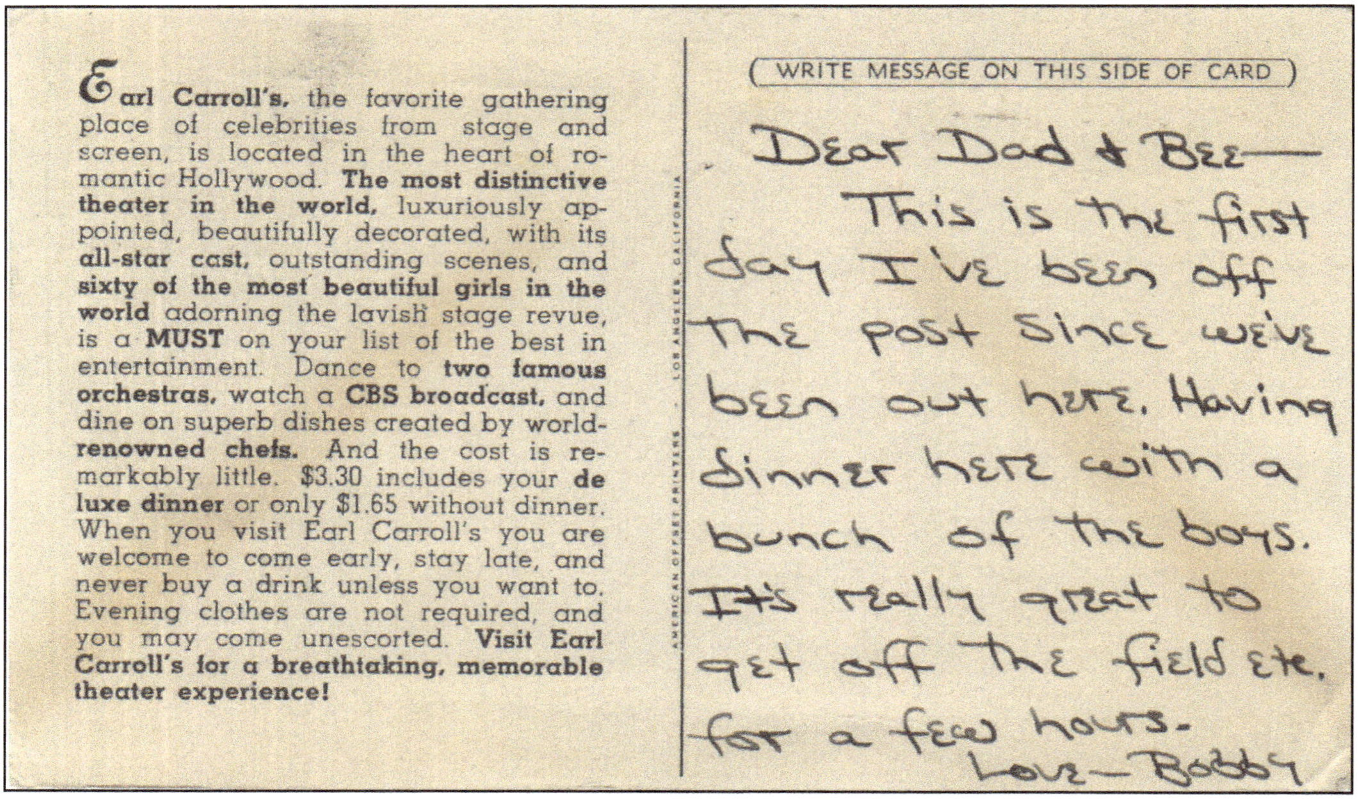
Earl Carroll's, the favorite gathering place of celebrities from stage and screen, is located in the heart of romantic Hollywood. **The most distinctive theater in the world,** luxuriously appointed, beautifully decorated, with its **all-star cast,** outstanding scenes, and **sixty of the most beautiful girls in the world** adorning the lavish stage revue, is a **MUST** on your list of the best in entertainment. Dance to **two famous orchestras,** watch a **CBS broadcast,** and dine on superb dishes created by world-**renowned chefs.** And the cost is remarkably little. $3.30 includes your **de luxe dinner** or only $1.65 without dinner. When you visit Earl Carroll's you are welcome to come early, stay late, and never buy a drink unless you want to. Evening clothes are not required, and you may come unescorted. **Visit Earl Carroll's for a breathtaking, memorable theater experience!**

AMERICAN OFFSET PRINTERS — LOS ANGELES, CALIFORNIA

(WRITE MESSAGE ON THIS SIDE OF CARD)

Dear Dad & Bee—
This is the first day I've been off the post since we've been out here. Having dinner here with a bunch of the boys. It's really great to get off the field etc. for a few hours.
Love—Bobby

DECEMBER 31, 1943-JANUARY 1, 1944

UNITED STATES AIR FORCES

Saturday Nite

Dear Dad + Bee—

As you can see we're still here at Hammer Field tonight. We took off at 3:30 this afternoon and circled the field twice and had to land again because one of our engines was still on the fritz. Consequently, we won't try to leave again until tomorrow afternoon when the ship ought to be all fixed up.

Yesterday we were flying in a big formation of the IV Bomber Command up to San Francisco and Sacramento when one of our engines failed. We had to leave the formation and head for the coast (we were flying out over the ocean) and land at the nearest airport, which turned out to be at Fresno. It's a fairly nice field located about nine miles from Fresno, which is south of Sacramento in the San Jaquin Valley.

We didn't do any celebrating for New

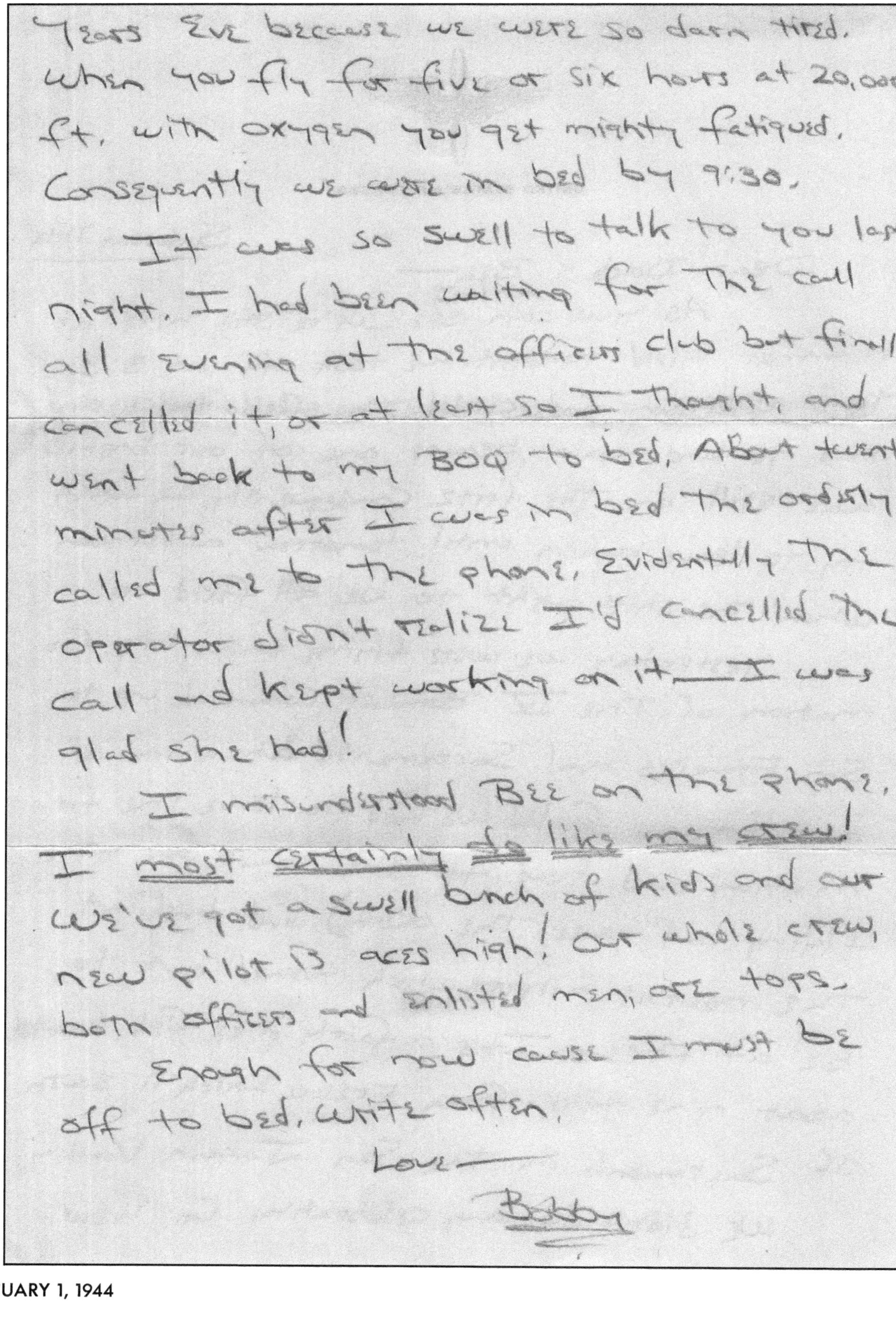

Years Eve because we were so darn tired. When you fly for five or six hours at 20,000 ft. with oxygen you get mighty fatigued. Consequently we were in bed by 9:30.

It was so swell to talk to you last night. I had been waiting for the call all evening at the officers club but finally cancelled it, or at least so I thought, and went back to my BOQ to bed. About twenty minutes after I was in bed the orderly called me to the phone. Evidently the operator didn't realize I'd cancelled the call and kept working on it — I was glad she had!

I misunderstood Bee on the phone. I <u>most</u> <u>certainly</u> <u>do</u> <u>like</u> <u>my</u> <u>crew</u>! We've got a swell bunch of kids and our new pilot is aces high! Our whole crew, both officers and enlisted men, are tops.

Enough for now cause I must be off to bed. Write often.

Love —

<u>Bobby</u>

JANUARY 1, 1944

Sunday 16

Dear Dad + Bee—

Excuse my not writing lately but for the past week or so we've been awfully busy with late hours flying. We flew until an ungodly hour last night and so we have the whole day off today. Alot of the gang took off for LA but I'm sticking by for some letter writing and some back sleep.

Before I forget, the picture arrived in good shape. Many thanks, Bee. Frankly, I don't like it too well. Think it's too stiff and kinda sedate looking—hardly like R.L.S.!

We've gotten in many hours of flying this past week because of a streak of beautiful weather. Today there isn't a cloud in the sky and it's as warm as summer time. That's the good side of the picture—prior to this we've had just day after day of rain and lots of fog when we couldn't fly at all. On the whole the weather has been very poor since we've been out here.

Can't think of any more now. The crew is still tops. Hope all goes well at home. Write often.

All love—
Bobby

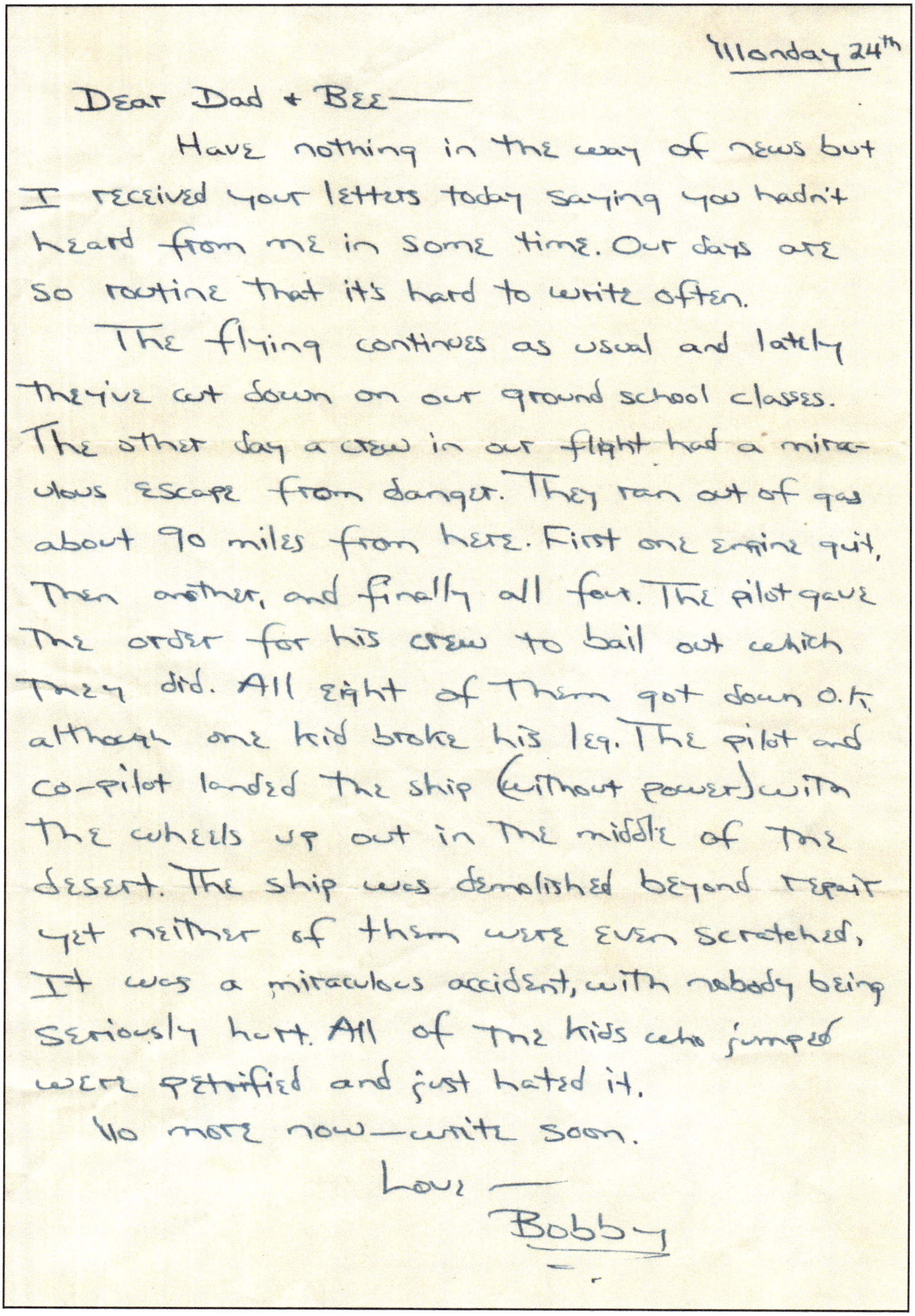

Monday 24th

Dear Dad + Bee—

Have nothing in the way of news but I received your letters today saying you hadn't heard from me in some time. Our days are so routine that it's hard to write often.

The flying continues as usual and lately they've cut down on our ground school classes. The other day a crew in our flight had a miraculous escape from danger. They ran out of gas about 90 miles from here. First one engine quit, then another, and finally all four. The pilot gave the order for his crew to bail out which they did. All eight of them got down O.K. although one kid broke his leg. The pilot and co-pilot landed the ship (without power) with the wheels up out in the middle of the desert. The ship was demolished beyond repair yet neither of them were even scratched, It was a miraculous accident, with nobody being seriously hurt. All of the kids who jumped were petrified and just hated it.

No more now—write soon.

Love—

Bobby

JANUARY 24-FEBRUARY 14, 1944

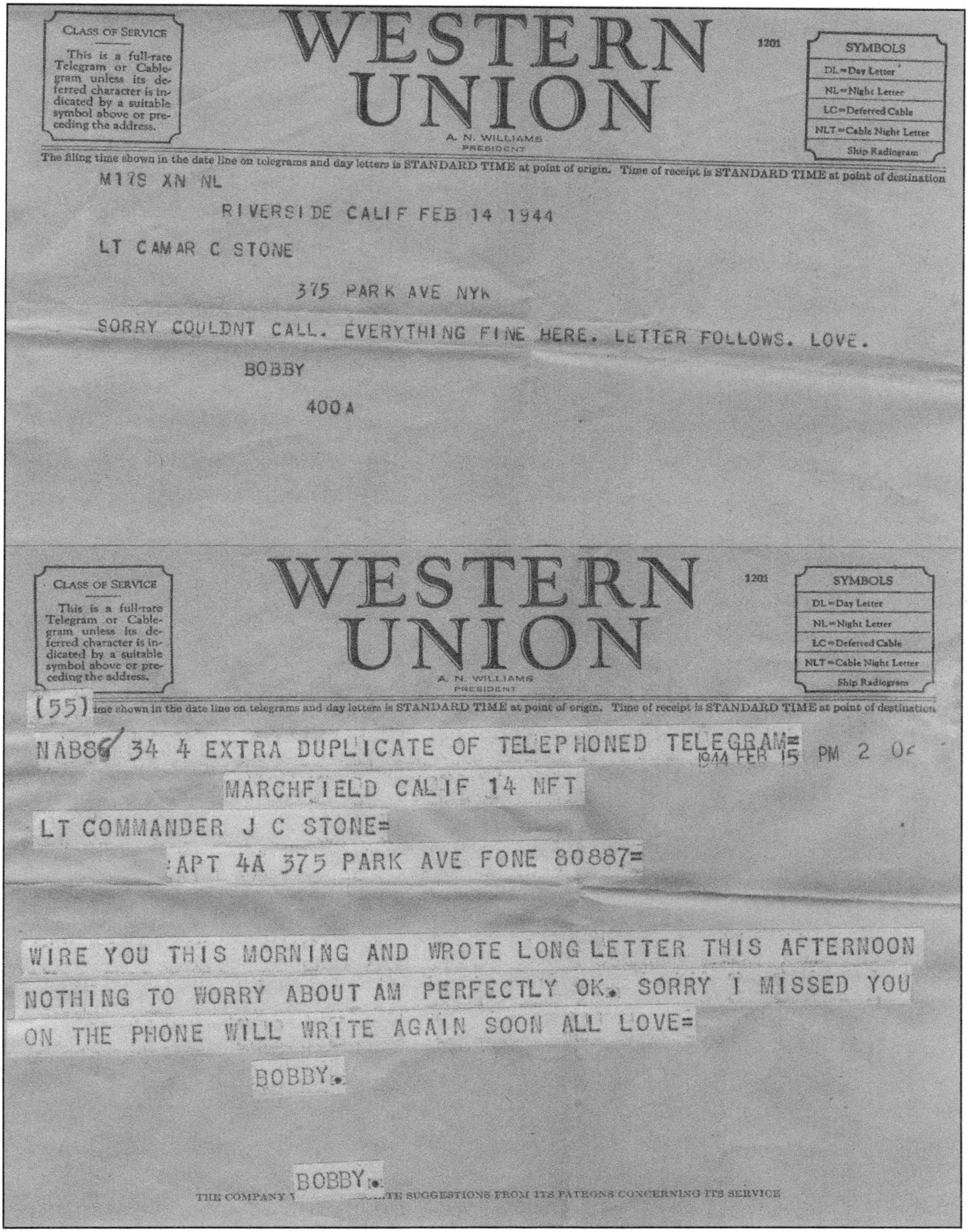

WESTERN UNION

CLASS OF SERVICE
This is a full-rate Telegram or Cablegram unless its deferred character is indicated by a suitable symbol above or preceding the address.

A. N. WILLIAMS
PRESIDENT

1201

SYMBOLS
DL=Day Letter
NL=Night Letter
LC=Deferred Cable
NLT=Cable Night Letter
Ship Radiogram

The filing time shown in the date line on telegrams and day letters is STANDARD TIME at point of origin. Time of receipt is STANDARD TIME at point of destination

M17S XN NL

RIVERSIDE CALIF FEB 14 1944

LT CAMAR C STONE

375 PARK AVE NYK

SORRY COULDNT CALL. EVERYTHING FINE HERE. LETTER FOLLOWS. LOVE.

BOBBY

400A

WESTERN UNION

CLASS OF SERVICE
This is a full-rate Telegram or Cablegram unless its deferred character is indicated by a suitable symbol above or preceding the address.

A. N. WILLIAMS
PRESIDENT

1201

SYMBOLS
DL=Day Letter
NL=Night Letter
LC=Deferred Cable
NLT=Cable Night Letter
Ship Radiogram

(55) [illegible]ime shown in the date line on telegrams and day letters is STANDARD TIME at point of origin. Time of receipt is STANDARD TIME at point of destination

NAB86 34 4 EXTRA DUPLICATE OF TELEPHONED TELEGRAM= 1944 FEB 15 PM 2 0

MARCHFIELD CALIF 14 NFT

LT COMMANDER J C STONE=

:APT 4A 375 PARK AVE FONE 80887=

WIRE YOU THIS MORNING AND WROTE LONG LETTER THIS AFTERNOON NOTHING TO WORRY ABOUT AM PERFECTLY OK. SORRY I MISSED YOU ON THE PHONE WILL WRITE AGAIN SOON ALL LOVE=

BOBBY.

BOBBY.

THE COMPANY [illegible]TE SUGGESTIONS FROM ITS PATRONS CONCERNING ITS SERVICE

MARCH & HAMMER FIELDS, CA

Monday Afternoon.

Dear Dad, Bee, Don, Jim, Barry, Ken & Bunny -[30]

I'm sorry it's been so many ages since I last wrote but it so happens that I've been here in the hospital for the last three weeks. I didn't think it would be wise to worry you until it was all over but for some time I've had trouble with my leg at high altitude when it was so terribly cold. So, after much consultation they decided to operate on my leg and remove my plate taking the chance it was the cause of my trouble.

Right now I am feeling lots better and before long I hope to be up and about again. The operation wasn't too bad but for about a week I wasn't feeling too hot. My leg was rather painful but it's coming along nicely now. The Major who operated on me is supposed to be a good orthopedic man. He, of course, knew of Gallie[31] and thinks very highly of him.

The day I was operated on, Ronnie and Doug came over to the hospital and were here when I woke up the first afternoon. It made it lots easier for me cause I wasn't feeling too marvelous. I think Ronnie is coming over again tomorrow.

The one tough thing about all this seige is the fact that I was removed from my crew when I was put in the hospital. It really breaks my heart because I had such a swell gang. The boys are swell and come up to see me all the time. They always bring my mail up here, etc. Incidentally, continue to write to the same address as always because I'll get my mail quicker than if it came directly to the hospital.

Speaking of mail, I'm afraid I owe everyone a letter but I haven't written a soul for the past three weeks or so. Please be sure that this letter gets around to all the family so they'll excuse my not writing. Hope you can make out my scrawl but I'm on my back writing since I still get dizzy when I sit up, because they've been stuffing me with sulfa pills for about a week now and they have this effect on you.

Can't think of any more now cause life is kinda dull here in the hospital. I hope this letter finds you all well and in top spirits. Please don't worry about R.L.S. because I'm feeling lots better now and ought to be up walking again before too long. I hope you received my telegram that one of the boys was sending for me this morning.

Please thank Bunny for her sweet letter that arrived this morning. Tell her that I'll write as soon as I'm up and around. Be sure you tell her cause I got a long letter from her this morning.

'Nuff for now - All love - Bobby.

P.S. When they removed my plate, they found the screws to be a little loose. Consequently, it was just as well that it came out - it makes a swell souvenir! A little black metal plate with six separate screws. Just like something a carpenter would have.
P.P.S. Got your telegram this morning, Dad, and of course you can understand why I wasn't able to call back on Sunday. Love again - Bobby.

Lt. R. L. Stone O-696041
399th Bomb Group, Squadron 607, March Field, California.

FEBRUARY 21-22, 1944

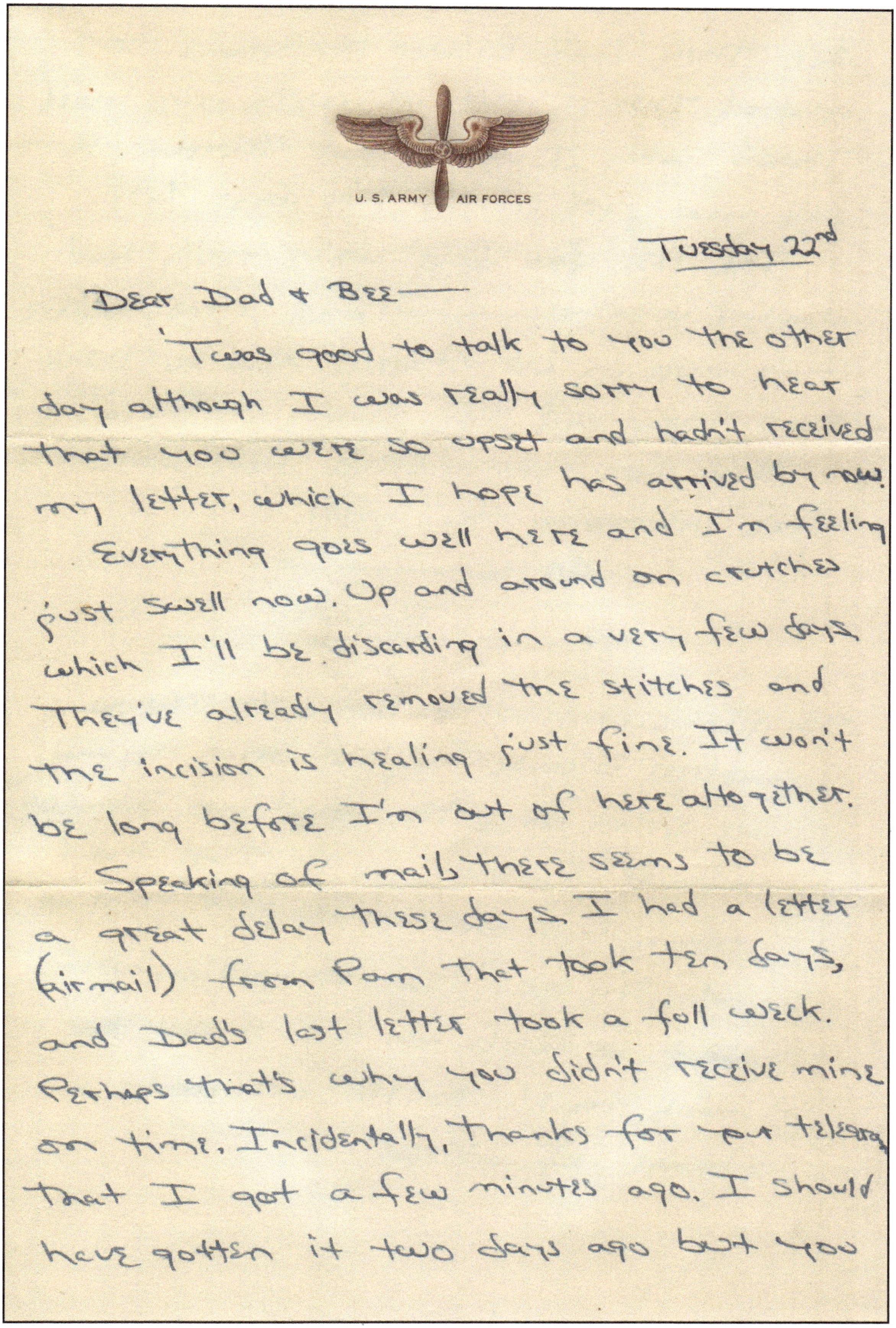

U. S. ARMY AIR FORCES

Tuesday 22nd

Dear Dad & Bee——

'Twas good to talk to you the other day although I was really sorry to hear that you were so upset and hadn't received my letter, which I hope has arrived by now.

Everything goes well here and I'm feeling just swell now. Up and around on crutches which I'll be discarding in a very few days. They've already removed the stitches and the incision is healing just fine. It won't be long before I'm out of here altogether.

Speaking of mail, there seems to be a great delay these days. I had a letter (air mail) from Pam that took ten days, and Dad's last letter took a full week. Perhaps that's why you didn't receive mine on time. Incidentally, thanks for your telegram that I got a few minutes ago. I should have gotten it two days ago but you

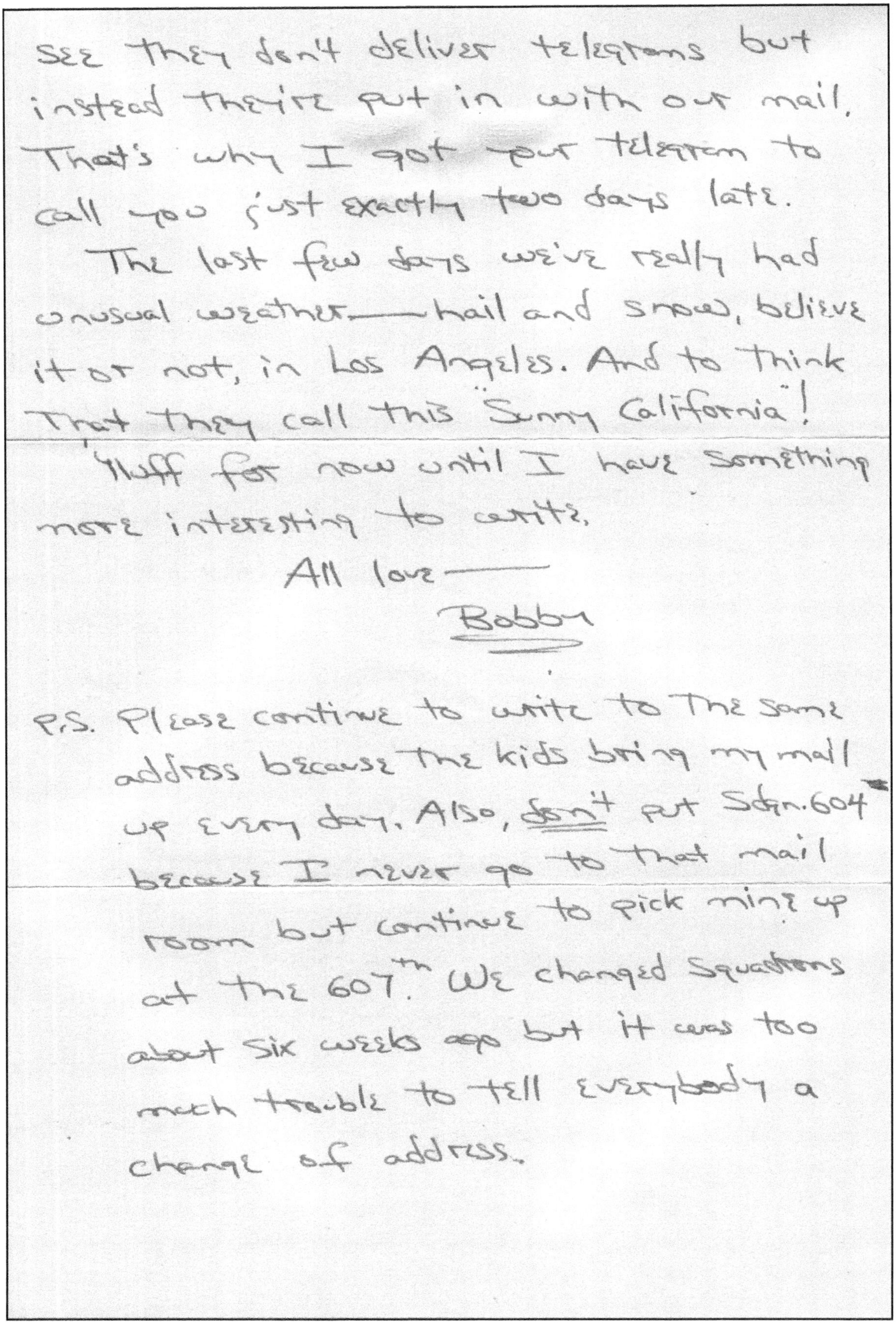

see they don't deliver telegrams but instead they're put in with our mail. That's why I got your telegram to call you just exactly two days late.

The last few days we've really had unusual weather — hail and snow, believe it or not, in Los Angeles. And to think that they call this "Sunny California"!

'Nuff for now until I have something more interesting to write.

All love —

<u>Bobby</u>

P.S. Please continue to write to the same address because the kids bring my mail up every day. Also, <u>don't</u> put Sqdn. 604 because I never go to that mail room but continue to pick mine up at the 607th. We changed Squadrons about six weeks ago but it was too much trouble to tell everybody a change of address.

FEBRUARY 22-23, 1944

U. S. ARMY AIR FORCES

Wednesday 23rd

Dear Dad & Bee——

Haven't anything particular to write but I thought a letter was in order to say that all goes well with R.L.S. I'm up and around in good shape now and ought to be off my crutches before long. I have treatments and exercises at physio-therapy twice a day and my leg is coming along just fine. I can still only flex it about 90° but that takes a little time to get full use of it again. In a few days the doctor said I could have a pass to get out of the hospital for a few hours. It will be a pleasure to get out after being cooped up for a month.

Speaking of slow mail service I got a letter from both of you and from Pam today and all of them were postmarked the 8th. From the 8th to the 23rd is mighty poor service. Thanks loads for the cute valentines that arrived this morning. You might think we were in the days of the pony-express.

No more for now except that everything is just fine here. Write often.

With all love—

Bobby

Wednesday

Dear Dad & Bee—

Very little to report from this part of the world except that R.L.S. is well on the way to leaving the hospital. Two days ago I was over at the club on pass and believe me it was good to leave the hospital for a few hours. Of course I was quite weak but that's to be expected, I guess.

Before I forget Dad, I'm wondering if your office is going to take care of my income tax report etc. as they did last year. I've done nothing about it as yet and so I'd appreciate an immediate answer so I can get to work if I have to do it. It would be swell if they'd handle it for me. Since Oct. 23rd 1943 my income has been

Base Pay	$150
Flying Pay	$75
Rental	$45
Subsistence	$21
	$291

Of course the $45 is taken out of my pay and I pay $6.60 a month for insurance.

Please be sure to let me know about this as soon as possible.

Can't think of any more for now. Write often.

All love—

Bobby

U. S. ARMY AIR FORCES

Saturday

Dear Dad & Bee——

Both packages of eats arrived much to the pleasure of Bob and numerous ward mates. Can't thank you enough for the swell selection of sweets. Really appreciated the thoughtfulness to say nothing of alot of delicious food. That was certainly a coincidence (and a lucky one for me) that both of you sent something the same day.

Everything goes well at this end and my leg is coming along just fine. Was over at the club on pass again yesterday and as always it was good to be out of here for a few hours. If all goes well, I ought to be out of here in a week or so.

I saw all of the kids in my flight yesterday and it broke my heart to see them getting ready to leave. Their orders came through and they leave tomorrow.

MARCH 4, 1944

It's really tough to be separated from all of them particularly since I've been with some of them for almost a year. There are a few of us who have been together ever since Cadet days, and it's kinda rough not to continue on with them. 'Nuff said.

I can't think of any more news since life in the hospital is extremely routine and extraordinarily dull. Again many thanks for the boxes of food and for your frequent letters—keep 'em up.

Lots of love—

Bobby

U. S. ARMY AIR FORCES

Sunday

Dear Mildred + Eddie[32] —

I hardly know where to begin what with thanks for the letters, cute card, and delicious box of sweets. Anyway, let it suffice that I really appreciate your thoughtfulness. The assortment of eats certainly hit the spot.

As you can imagine, life here in the hospital hasn't been any fun but before long I ought to be out. The toughest part of all this is the fact that I had to leave my crew. It's tough to be separated from a bunch of kids you've gotten to know and like alot.

I was certainly glad to hear that John[33] was home on furlough. I know how swell it must have been to see him again. The only trouble with a furlough is that it's always too darn short. Would that we could all come home for a permanent furlough!

MARCH 5, 1944

Again many thanks for all your thoughtfulness,
Mildred — you know how I appreciate it.

All love —

Bobby

Lt. R.L. Stone 0-696041
399th Bomb Group
Squadron 607
March Field, California

MARCH FIELD CALIF. MAR 5 11-AM 1944

Free

Mr. & Mrs. Edwin I. Hilson
927 Fifth Avenue
New York City
N.Y.

U. S. ARMY AIR FORCES

Wednesday 15th

Dear Dad & Bee —

It was really swell to talk to you all yesterday. I've tried to reach you several times but as you know, it always entails an awfully long delay.

All goes well here and I'm leaving the hospital tomorrow. It's been a long seige, a little over seven weeks, and I'm mighty glad to be getting out. My leg is in good shape, although it's still rather weak. Of course I lost a little weight but I'm sure I'll gain that back when I start living a normal life again. You never eat properly in a hospital or at least I don't.

As yet I don't know what will happen with me ~~—~~ but as soon as something develops I'll notify you. If I were lucky enough to get a leave it would be great, but unfortunately they don't give sick leaves

MARCH 15, 1944

any more. If I could get a few days you can be sure I'd be on the earliest airliner to N.Y. Excuse me while I go off on a little day-dreaming.

I was out of here for a few hours tonight and saw the Eddie Cantor broadcast at the post gym. He had Carole Landis on his program and all in all it was a swell show. We've had Jack Benny, Kay Kyser, and Bob Hope since I've been here although this is the first broadcast I've gotten to.

It really felt odd wandering around the field today. I seemed almost lost, not knowing a soul. I dread the ~~the~~ thought of starting from scratch again. It made it so much easier knowing all the kids so well.

Before I forget, please thank Bunny for her last letter and tell her I'll write as soon as I'm settled again. Please also thank O'ma for her letters and tell her why I haven't been able to write. Thanks.

No more for now except to say again 'twas swell to talk to you yesterday.

All love —

Bobby

Officers' Mess
MARCH FIELD
RIVERSIDE, CALIFORNIA

Friday 24, 1944

Dear Dad & Bee—

Just a quickee to say that all goes well with R.L.S. I've been out of the hospital for just a week and believe me it's mighty good.

Last Friday I went into LA (illegally) and spent three days with Ronnie and Doug. Had a fine time eating good food, taking it easy, and in general enjoying myself. Had quite a treat when Doug took us out to Warner's where we saw Humphrey Bogart making a new picture. It was really interesting since I'd never been on a movie lot before. Incidentally Dad, Ronnie's address is

Mrs. Douglass Drake
10531
[redacted] Rochester Avenue
West Los Angeles
California

MARCH 24, 1944

As yet they haven't decided what they are going to do with me but I think I will go into a pool and replace somebody on a crew if there is a vacancy. I'm not sure of this, but something ought to happen within the next week or so. I'm still not on flying status because I have to take my "64" which is the flying physical exam.

Can't think of any more now so I'll write again as soon as anything comes up.

Lots of love —

Bobby

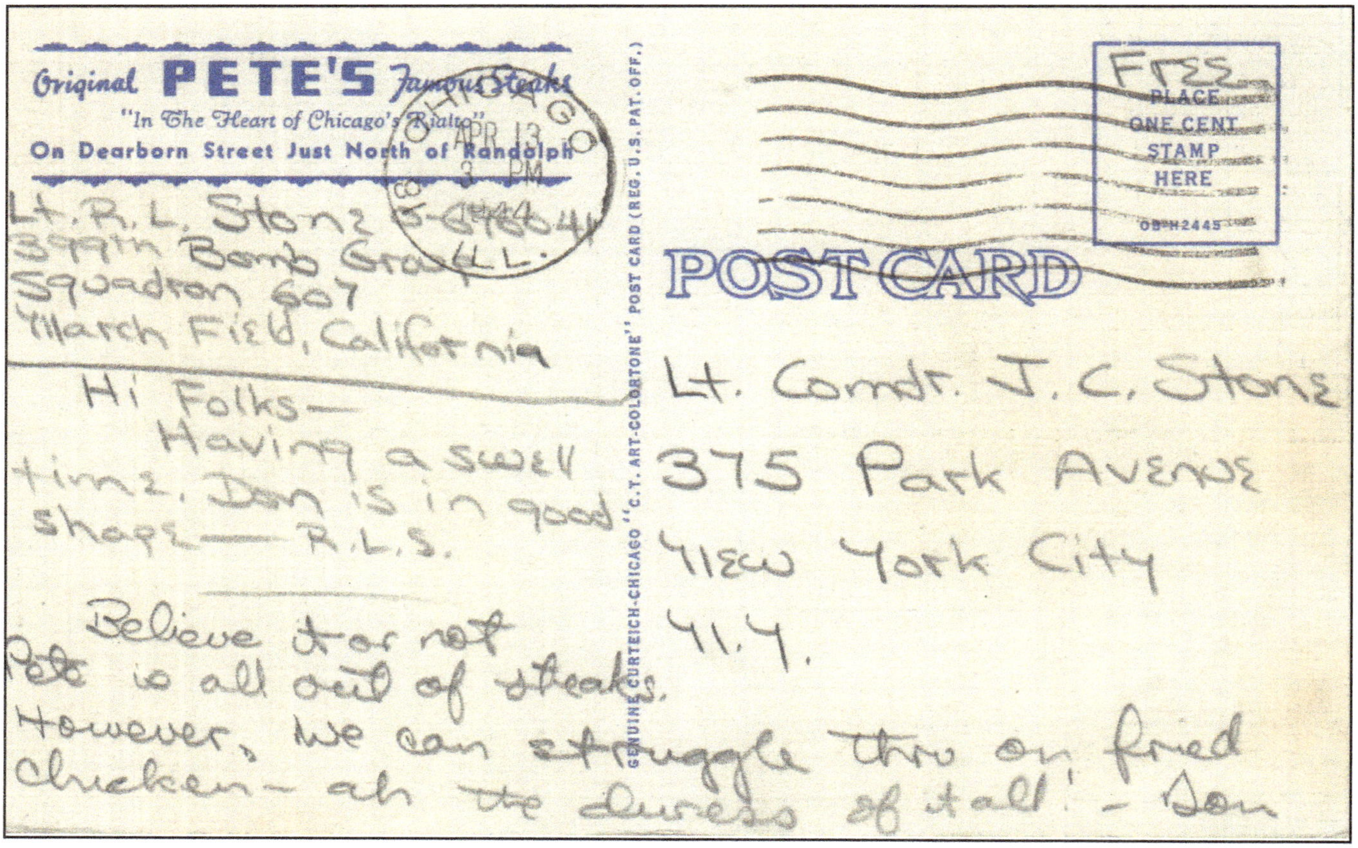

APRIL 13-15, 1944

UNITED STATES AIR FORCES

Saturday Nite

Dear Dad & Bee—

Well here I am, back at it again after two wonderful weeks at home. I never know where to begin to thank for my good time. Home is certainly a great place and I wish we could all see alot more of it than we have during the past year—these shorts stays are swell but not nearly long enough.

My visit with Don worked out perfectly. I pulled into the Station about a half hour late and much to my surprise there was Don waiting for me. He's really in good spirits and looks fine. Of course, it was swell to see him after all this time and we had a swell reunion.

We went immediately to the Blackstone where we spoke to you. Before I forget Dad, we only had one meal at the Blackstone and so we didn't bother to use the charge account. Thanks loads, anyway. Had breakfast at the

Blackstone and it was a pleasure to see Don eat. He evidently doesn't have very good food at his camp and you know how he likes his food. After breakfast we bumped into Capt. Steinback who gave us the use of his suite and wanted to meet us for cocktails.

In the morning we wandered all over Chicago and I did some shopping at Marshall Field. Went to a place called Pete's for lunch to get Don a steak and unfortunately they had none. That afternoon we went to see "A Guy Named Joe", which is tops. Got out about four o'clock and returned to the hotel to get my camera. I took a bunch of snaps of the Cpl. and I hope they come out. Don planned to take a 6:00 train so we went out to supper. Had a great big steak at the Brown Derby after which I took him to the train.

I can't thank you enough Dad, for making the arrangements with the Capt. etc. Incidentally, I wrote him today. It was

APRIL 15, 1944

swell to see Don and I'm so glad that it worked out so well. It was such fun talking over old times (and good ones they were) as well as our various army experiences etc.

After I saw Don off I had until 1:45 when my plane left. Was feeling very low with nothing to do and the thought of my leave being over still fresh in my mind. I called up a gal, a good friend of Pam's from college whom I knew through her. ~~and~~ Went up to where she was working. Pam had given me her address on a match cover saying to call her. Of course, I never thought I would at the time but I'm glad I did.

We sat around and talked for awhile and then went out to do the town. We went to more different places and I can't remember half of them. She stayed with me until about 12:00 when I went back to the Blackstone. Bumped into Capt. S. who took me in for a drink and we saw Paul Draper dance a jig. At about 12:45 the car picked me up and I ~~cast~~ off for the airport. Was lucky all the way out here and wasn't removed. All but one passenger was army or navy.

Before I forget, my address is different. There is no longer a 399th base instead it is called the 420th Base Unit. The Squadrons have been renamed and mine is now called T-1.

Lt. R.L.S.
420th Base Unit
Squadron T-1
March Field, Calif.

Please use this address from now on and tell anyone you see of the change. Haven't found out my new set-up but will very shortly. Will write all as soon as I find out anything.

Again a million thanks for a swell two weeks at home. Also Dad, 'twas really nifty of you to have given me the generous check for my plane fare — you know how much I appreciate it. You're sure a great Dad.

Please be sure to keep me posted as to your navy situation. I've got my fingers crossed that your blood pressure stays down.

Excuse my scrawl but I'm in a rush. S'long for now. All love—

Bobby

APRIL 15-17, 1944

Officers' Mess
MARCH FIELD
RIVERSIDE, CALIFORNIA

Monday 17th

Dear Dad & Bee—

Nothing new since I last wrote except my address. With the change over from the 399th to the 420th there is a terrific amount of confesion with the mail and all combat crews collect their mail at one, instead of three mail rooms as we use to. So, I got myself a box at the post office and my new address is—

Lt. R.L.S. 0-696041
Box 1416
March Field, Calif.

In the future please use this address and pass it on to the boys and anyone else who wants to write me.

Hope all goes well with you Dad, re the navy. Write me all the dope.

Love— Bobby

Officers' Mess
MARCH FIELD
RIVERSIDE, CALIFORNIA

Friday Nite

Dear Dad + Bee—

I haven't anything in the way of news but I just thought of something for you to give Don for his birthday. I remember that he was looking for a good wallet when we were in Chicago. He has one but its fairly well worn out. This is just a thought and I know you wanted a suggestion for Don's birthday. I'd have gotten him a wallet when I heard him mention it except that I'd already gotten him something.

Spent the evening with Ronnie and Doug last night. I really envy Ronnie who is flying East tomorrow night. I'd love to be making the trip with her even

APRIL 21, 1944

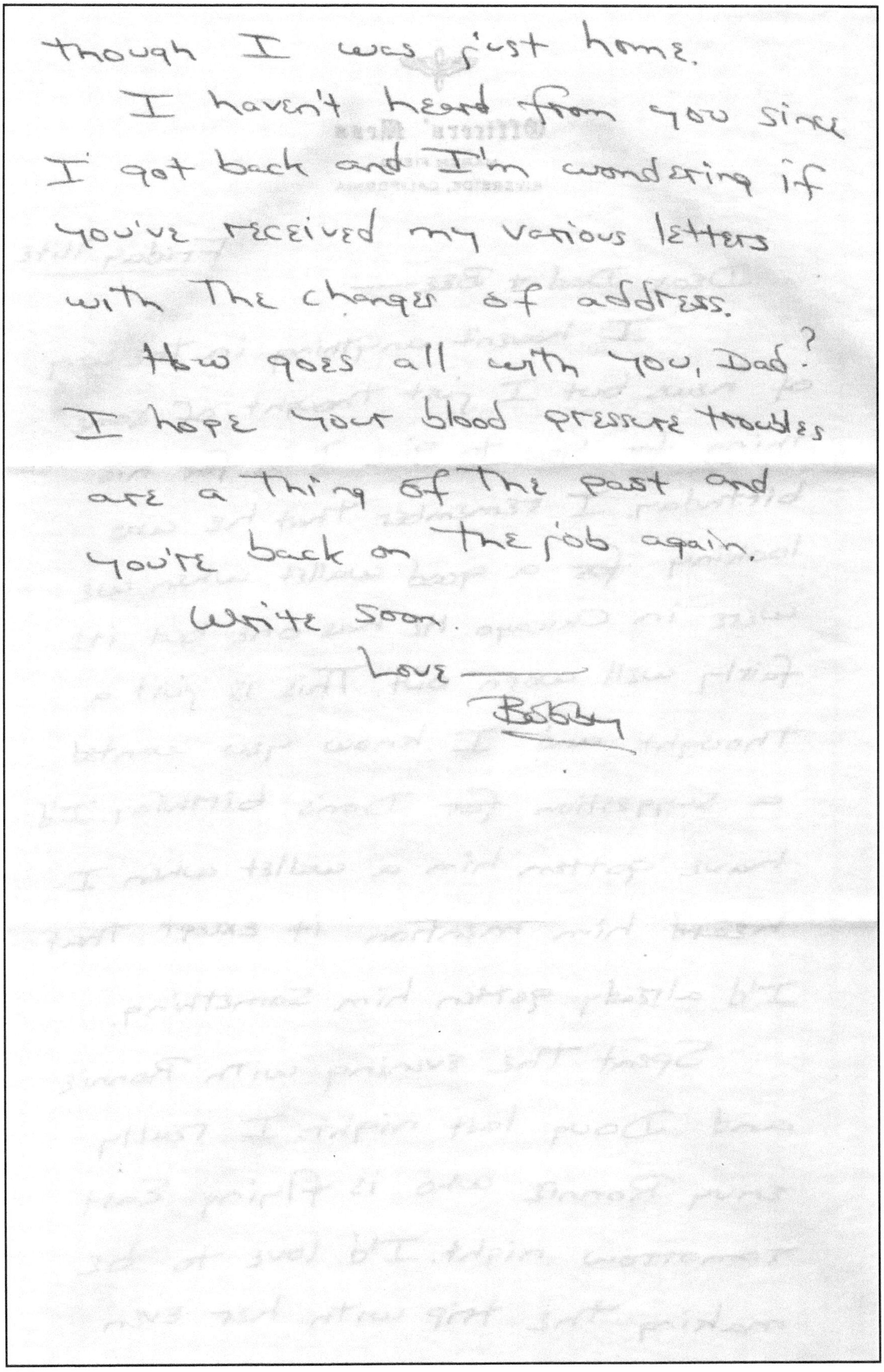

though I was just home.

I haven't heard from you since I got back and I'm wondering if you've received my various letters with the changes of address.

How goes all with you, Dad? I hope your blood pressure troubles are a thing of the past and you're back on the job again.

Write soon.

Love —

Bobby

Sunday

Dear Dad & Bee—

Just a few lines to say that I believe I'm finally on a new crew. As yet I haven't met the fellows because it just came out on orders yesterday. I'll write all details next week.

The weather out here is most summery and beautiful. I have a wonderful tan from the five or six times I've played tennis and swam. Two days ago the mercury hit a high of 97°.

The Grapevine arrived this morning and was certainly lots newsier than ever before. It always brings back many pleasant memories to receive the Grapevine. I think the list of addresses was a clever idea.

Many Thanks for your letter earlier in the week Dad, and your long message two days ago, Bee.

All love—Bobby

APRIL 30-MAY 1, 1944

Monday

Dear Dad + Bee—

Haven't much in the way of news but thought I'd write a line or two to let you know that all goes well with R.L.S.

I'm not sure but I believe I will get a new crew at the end of the week. Will let you know when it's definite.

Have had fun all week flying small twin-engine ships with the tow-target squadron. I had to get in 12 hours to collect my back flight pay and had a swell time doing it. I got about 10 hours of pilot time. We'd go up and I'd fly the whole mission while the pilot slept—good experience.

Played tennis twice and it was great to swing a racket again. They have two hard surface courts on the post. Also a swell pool. Please write often. All love—

Bobby

Tuesday

Dear Dad + Bee—

Well at long last I'm on a crew. I'm now in Squadron T-3 which is the old 607th Squadron, which is swell because I know nearly all the instructors down there. Although I don't know them too well, I think that my pilot and co-pilot are good gents. As yet, we have no navigators and I haven't met our enlisted men. You see, yesterday was the first day I started going to school and as yet I haven't flown.

Saw the Bob Hope show last night and it was a real treat. His broadcast lasted for half an hour and he carried on for an hour and a half after he went off the air. He's really a swell comedian and he's got a great show with Francis Langford, Colonna, Vera Vague, and Stan Kenton's band.

Must stop now cause I'm writing from class—most boring to have to go through this stuff for the second time.

All love—Bobby

Officers' Mess
MARCH FIELD
RIVERSIDE, CALIFORNIA

Friday

Dear Dad & Bee ——

Was so glad to receive your letter today telling of Don's whereabouts. I haven't had a word from him since I saw him in Chicago and I was wondering if he'd ever received the present I sent him on May 3rd. I guess he's been busy what with his transfer and all. The change certainly seems like a good break.

Since my last letter I've changed crews. Yesterday a pilot came in looking for a new bombardier for his crew. He had finished all the phases and would have shipped out in ten days or so but his bombardier took sick. So, he wanted me to replace him rather than take a new man with no experience in a B-24. He and his co-pilot and navigator all seemed like swell gents and so I accepted the position. We are now put back in the middle of second phase, and it means that I won't have to repeat all the boring ground school etc. They seemed very anxious that I join the crew and I'm mighty glad I did. Will write more when I get to know the fellows better.

As you may have gathered I was rather disappointed with my other crew, although I didn't know them too well. I had two flight officer pilots who were quite young and a little scatter-brained. Most of the kids who are coming in now seem to be quite immature and surprisingly young. To have gotten on my present crew would appear to be a swell break.

I was certainly glad to receive your letter re the navy and to hear that you feel as you do

MAY 12, 1944

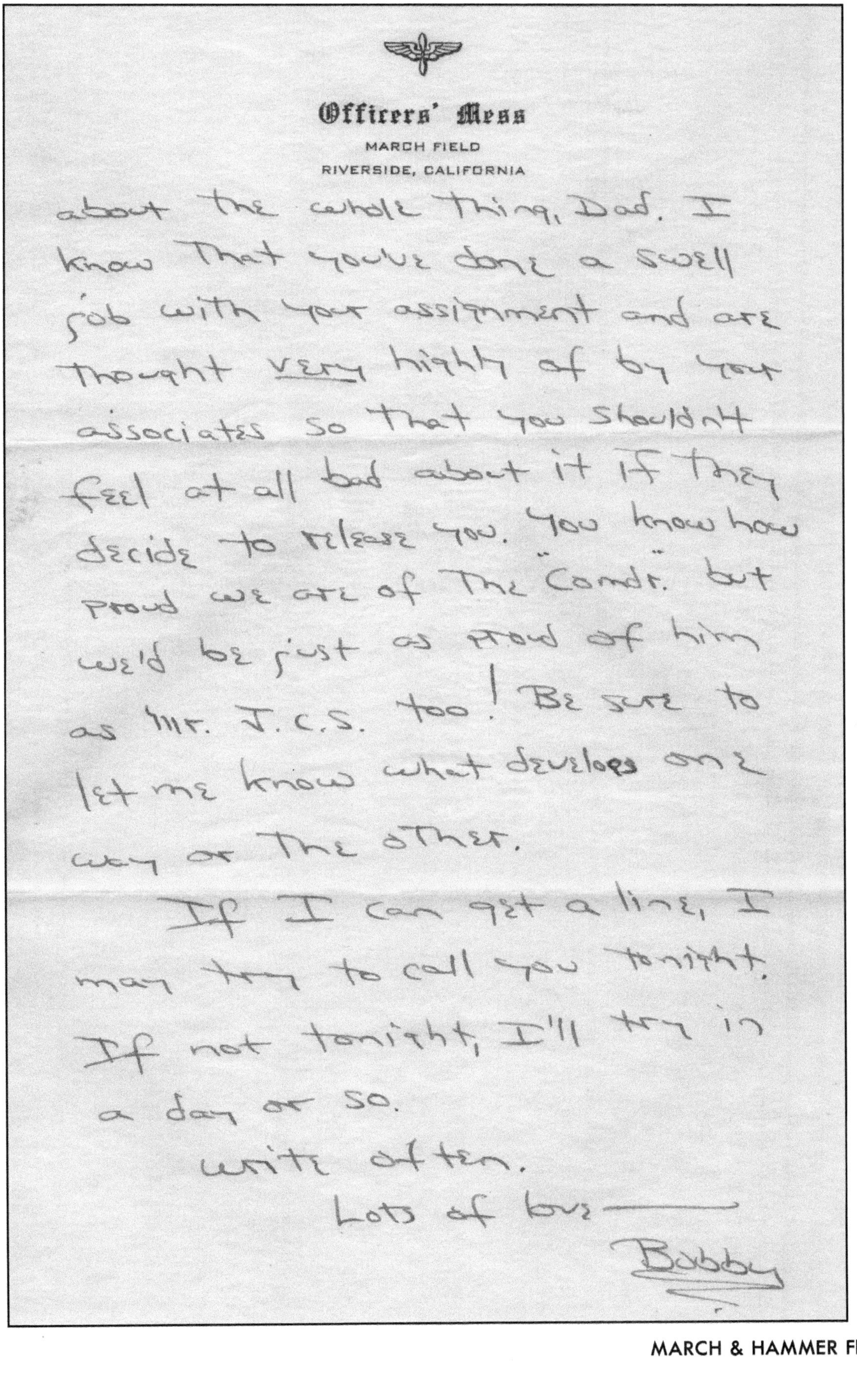
Officers' Mess
MARCH FIELD
RIVERSIDE, CALIFORNIA

about the whole thing, Dad. I know that you've done a swell job with your assignment and are thought very highly of by your associates so that you shouldn't feel at all bad about it if they decide to release you. You know how proud we are of the "Comdr." but we'd be just as proud of him as Mr. J.C.S. too! Be sure to let me know what develops one way or the other.

If I can get a line, I may try to call you tonight. If not tonight, I'll try in a day or so.

Write often.

Lots of love ——

Bobby

Officers' Mess
MARCH FIELD
RIVERSIDE, CALIFORNIA

Sunday Nite

Dear Dad + Bee—

Just a note to say that I've been trying to reach you by phone the last couple of days, but unfortunately you've been out each time. I tried again tonight but there was a five to six hour delay and so I gave up. Didn't have anything particular to say but I just thought it would be fun to talk to you again! Perhaps I can get a line through some time this week.

I received a long letter from Don today telling of his new setup etc. I think his change-over is a good break and I only hope he can stick with it for awhile and not get shifted to another outfit before he even has

MAY 14, 1944

a chance to get started. He has certainly done the rounds during his short time in the army.

No more for now cause I wrote all the news in my long letter yesterday—just wanted you to know that it was I who called, so you wouldn't worry.

All love—

Bobby

Officers' Mess
MARCH FIELD
RIVERSIDE, CALIFORNIA

Sunday

Dear Dad & Bee—

I can't tell you how happy I was to hear that you are at Alderbrook. I'm sure that the rest and relaxation are something that you've needed for a long time. Who knows, maybe a good dose of Alderbrook is just what the doctor ordered.

Nothing new here except that I'm on a really swell crew. The pilot, co-pilot, and navigator are all tops. I haven't flown with them yet because I've had a bad throat and have been grounded all week. It's lots better now and I ought to be O.K. in a few days.

I really have nothing more

MAY 21, 1944

to write but I did want you to know that all goes well with R.L.S. Have yourselves a swell time at Alderbrook and don't spare the "big ones". I surely envy you being able to remove the uniform and live like a fisherman for a couple of weeks. Have fun!

All love—

Bobby

Officers' Mess
MARCH FIELD
RIVERSIDE, CALIFORNIA

Saturday

Dear Dad + Bee ——

As usual, it was swell to talk to you the other night. I was so glad to get you after trying Alderbrook with no answer for two hours. I kept trying, thinking you might be fishing.

Your stay sounded like a huge success and I'm sure the rest did you a world of good, Dad. I'm glad for your sake that your Navy situation has come to a head because I know how restless you were with the whole thing in mid-air. It's swell that you're so philosophical about the whole thing and I'm sure that the Navy's decision is all for your own good. Now you can get a good rest without feeling

JUNE 3, 1944

that you're not doing your duty. It's not easy to have to live by the rigorous routine of the hours you did.

As I told you on the phone (and it's not for repitition) I'll be pulling out of here in around three weeks. From March you know where I go and from there it's all a guess. Once we leave March our whereabouts is supposedly secret and all mail etc. has to be sent here and forwarded on. The other crews have stayed in the country about 10 days or so after leaving here but of course that's all quite indefinite. That's all I can tell you because I don't know anything more definite right now.

Let's hear from you soon.

All love —

Bobby

U. S. ARMY AIR FORCES

Sunday

Dear Dad & Bee—

It was swell to talk to you last night and find everything ship-shape at Alderbrook. I'll call you again the latter part of next week before we leave March.

For the past week or so we've had miserable weather but none the less have flown a great deal. We've just about completed all our minimums and one or two more flights ought to finish us up.

You asked about my crew—the pilot's name is Bill Elkins and he's from Texas. The co-pilot is also from Texas and his name is Joe McGarvey. [34] Both are swell gents. The navigator is

JUNE 11, 1944

from Portland Wash. and is really tops. He's the best navigator I've ever flown with. The six enlisted men are from various and sundry places and are all pretty good men. My pilot and navigator are both married and their wives are in Riverside. Joe and I are the only single officers — damn it!

Not much more news from here cause I told you most everything last night. Please continue to write as I always love hearing from you.

All love —

Bobby

B-24 BATTLE POSITIONS

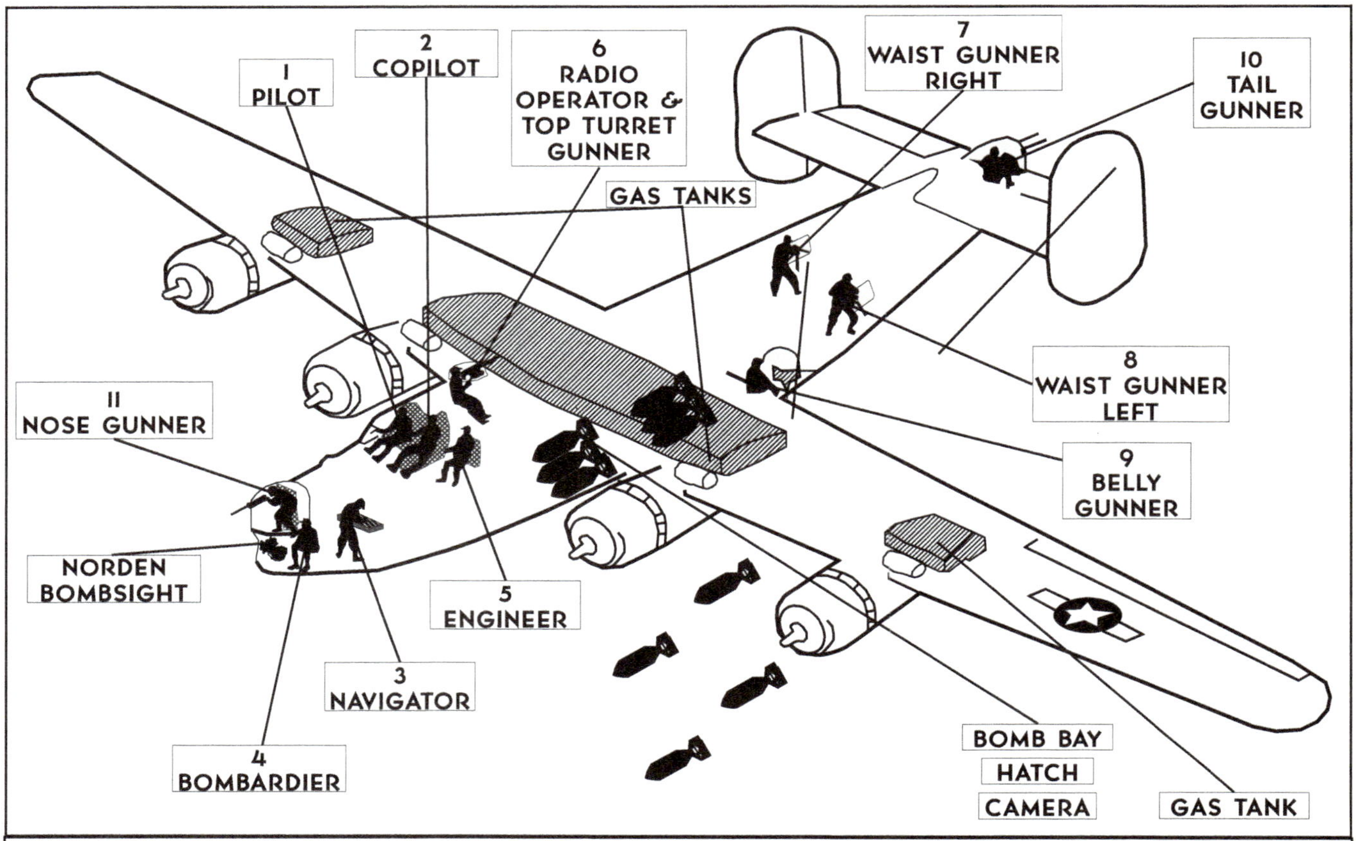

Crew

1. Bill Elkins, Pilot; 2.Co-Pilot, Bill McGarvey; 3. Otto Zach, Navigator; 4. Bob Stone, Bombardier; 5. Engineer, Sgt. Nickola; Asst. Engineer, Sgt. Freeman; 6. Radio Operator & Top Gunner, Sgt. Weaver; Asst. Radio Operator, Sgt. Rudler; 7. Right Waist Gunner; 8. Left Waist Gunner; 9. Belly Gunner; 10. Tail Gunner, Sgt. French; 11. Nose Gunner, Sgt. Fox

B-24 LIBERATOR HEAVY BOMBER

The B-24 Liberator was a heavy bomber produced from 1940 to 1945 at a cost of $297,627 which is the equivalent today of $4.77 million. Often compared with the B-17, it was a more modern design with a higher top speed, greater range, and a heavier bomb load; it was also more difficult to fly, with heavy control forces and poor formation-flying characteristics. The placement of its fuel tanks throughout the upper fuselage and its lightweight construction—designed to increase range and optimize assembly line production—made the aircraft vulnerable to battle damage; moreover, it was notorious for its tendency to catch fire. And its high fuselage-mounted "Davis Wing" also meant it was dangerous to ditch or belly land since the fuselage tended to break apart. Nevertheless, it provided excellent service in a variety of roles thanks to its large payload and long-range capabilities.[35]

B-24 DIAGRAM/SCRAPBOOK PHOTOGRAPH

1st Pilot — Bill Elkins (L)
Alias "Pop"
From Killeen, Texas

Co-Pilot — Bill McGarvey
Alias "Mac"
From Premont, Texas

Navigator — Otto B. Zach (3)
Alias — "The Russian"
From Portland, Oregon.

Radio Operator T/Sgt. Weaver
West Virginia

2) Armorer Tail Gunner S/Sgt. French
Minnesota

3) Nose Gunner S/Sgt. Fox
West Virginia

Bombardier — "Yours truly"

From Ohio

2) Engineer T/Sgt. Nickola
From N.Y.

3) Asst. Engineer S/Sgt. Freeman
From Minnesota

Three shots of ships we flew
back at March Field, California

UNITED STATES ARMY
AIR FORCES

Monday Aft

Dear Dad + Bee—

Just a note to say 'twas swell to talk to you yesterday. Had a disappointment when I couldn't get through to talk to Don. I did however, speak to Jim who was swell as ever.

Had a fine time cooking hamburgers etc. over a fire yesterday. 'Twas such fun to go on a picnic again. Played bridge last night.

This morning I did alot of errands in Beverly Hills while Ronnie was doing nursing. She'll be back in a little while. Tonight I'm going to take the Drakes out for a steak dinner and then return to March later.

As I said on the phone please

JUNE 19, 1944

continue to write to Box 1416 and it will be forwarded. As soon as I get an A.P.O. number I'll sent it to you.

If I have a chance to write or call from Frisco I will but if not please don't worry about me. I have no idea how long I'll be there or how busy I'll be so don't expect to hear from — if I possibly can I'll contact you.

All love —

Bobby

BOB'S ST. FRANCIS MEDAL

During this training period at March Field, Bob and a fellow cadet drove to the Mission Inn in Riverside, California where a chapel had been dedicated in 1933 as the International Shrine of the Birdmen. There was a sterling silver medal that was made to commemorate the event and it became a tradition that aviators went into combat with one of these medals in their pocket. Bob's was worn smooth by his constant touch for reassurance on all his plane flights even after the war.

When asked if he had a "special routine" before he embarked on a flight, he said "the only special routine I had before each mission was that I wore exactly the same clothing as I had on the mission before and always carried a silver coin given to me by a fellow flyer, which was a St. Francis medal. St. Francis of Assisi was the patron saint of the birds and protects the men who fly. Sadly, the man who gave me this coin, which I have carried in my pocket every day since I got it, was killed when his plane exploded leaving Florida for combat missions in England. He was 21 years old—the same age that I was then. I also carried—and still do today—the St. Christopher medal, given to me by my brother Don for protection. However, because I am superstitious, I always said goodbye to the ground crew chief when I climbed on the plane for a mission and said, 'I'll see you tonight, FOR SURE!'"

Front and back of Bob's St. Francis Medal worn smooth.

Design of the original St. Francis Medal.

MARCH FIELD, CA–SAN FRANCISCO, CA–KLAMATH FALLS, OR–SEATTLE, WA

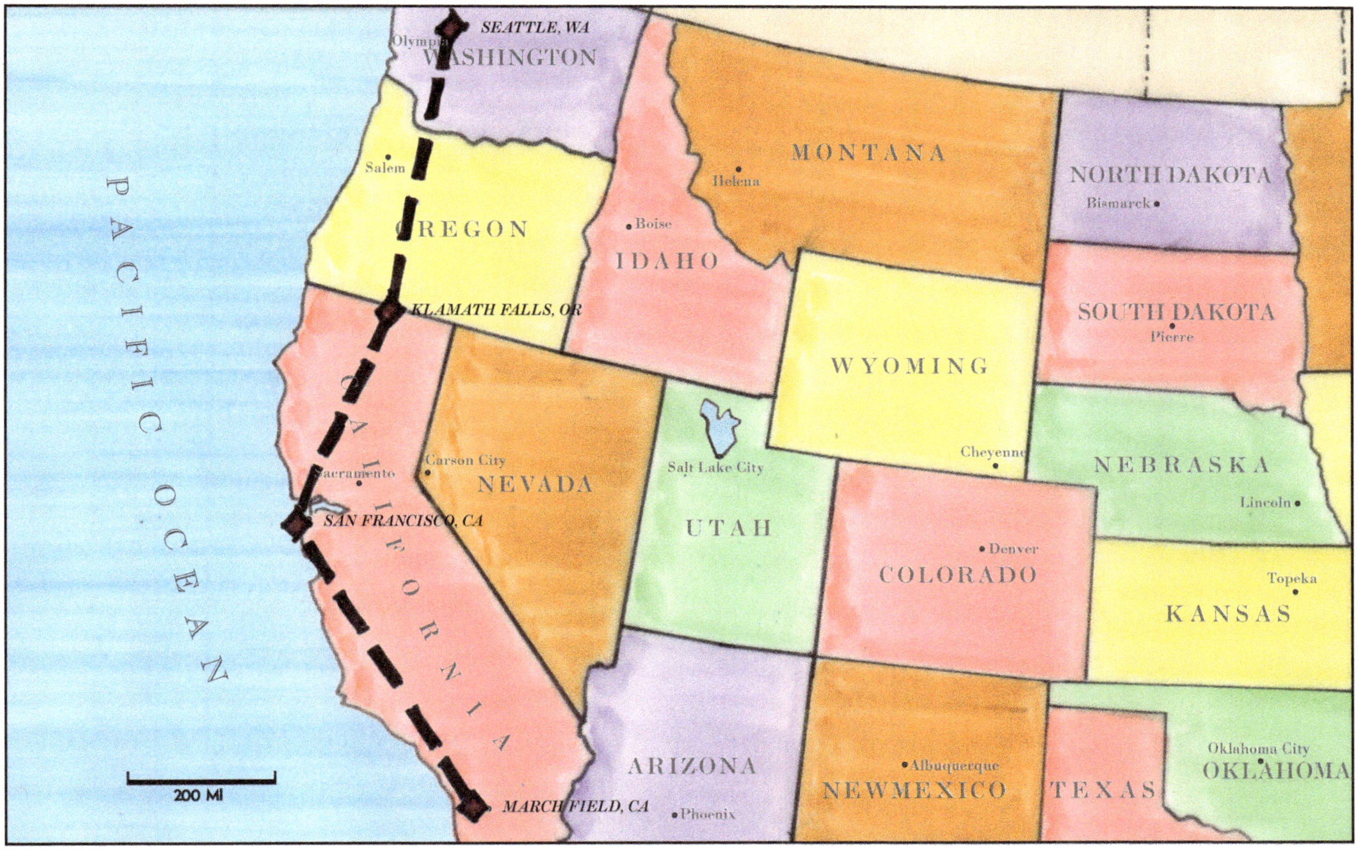

JUNE–JULY 1944

Dear Dad & Bee—

I haven't much time to write this morning because things are really buzzin'. Enclosed are a couple of insured package slips and an express receipt. At the last minute we had to get rid of some clothes etc. That I shipped homeward. I also sent some letters etc. That I'd like you to put in my closet for me. I sent some papers home that I think I should have destroyed so please be sure that nobody fools with them. They are mainly notes from bombardier school that I want to keep.

Wish I could tell you more about our setup but as yet we're still in a state of confusion and rumor ourselves.

Must run now but will write as soon as I have a chance. I hope all of you will do likewise.

Love—

Bobby

JUNE 28, 1944

Wednesday

Dear Eddie—

I returned to March yesterday, after being grounded at Fresno for four days, and was so pleased to find your letter awaiting me.

I would really love to get in to see you and I've already tried to arrange something. As it now stands, I will call you at the Ambassador sometime on the 7th and find out when you can see me. I imagine most of your time will be taken but if you could squeeze a meal in sometime I'd certainly enjoy seeing you. If I don't find you in when I call, I'll leave word where you can call me at your convenience.

I hope this isn't too involved and I can get in to see you, Eddie. It would be swell.

Always—

Bobby

CABLE ADDRESS
SICNARF

HOTEL ST. FRANCIS
ONE OF THE WORLD'S GREAT HOTELS
SAN FRANCISCO ~ CALIFORNIA

DAN E. LONDON
GENERAL MANAGER

Sunday

Dear Bee——

I just mailed a long letter to all of you and just now remembered I'd forgotten to tell you something. I have sent several packages home to Lt. R.L.S. and they are things I'd like you to put away for me. The clothes had better be camphored and the junk put in my closet. Thanks in advance.

Love——

Bobby

Friday

Dear Eddie—

I was so disappointed when I received your telegram this morning. I can't tell you how much I was looking forward to seeing you, Eddie. It would have been such fun. If ever again you're out this way again, please be sure to let me know.

I wrote you at the Ambassador when I received your letter and I imagine thats been forwarded to you. Before I got your telegram this morning, I called the hotel and they rang your room. Somebody answered and said that you hadn't made the trip. It was about nine o'clock but the person sounded as if I'd awakened him so you'd better explain to him (whoever it was) that it was just one of your ruffian nephews calling.

My best to the family.

Always—

Bobby

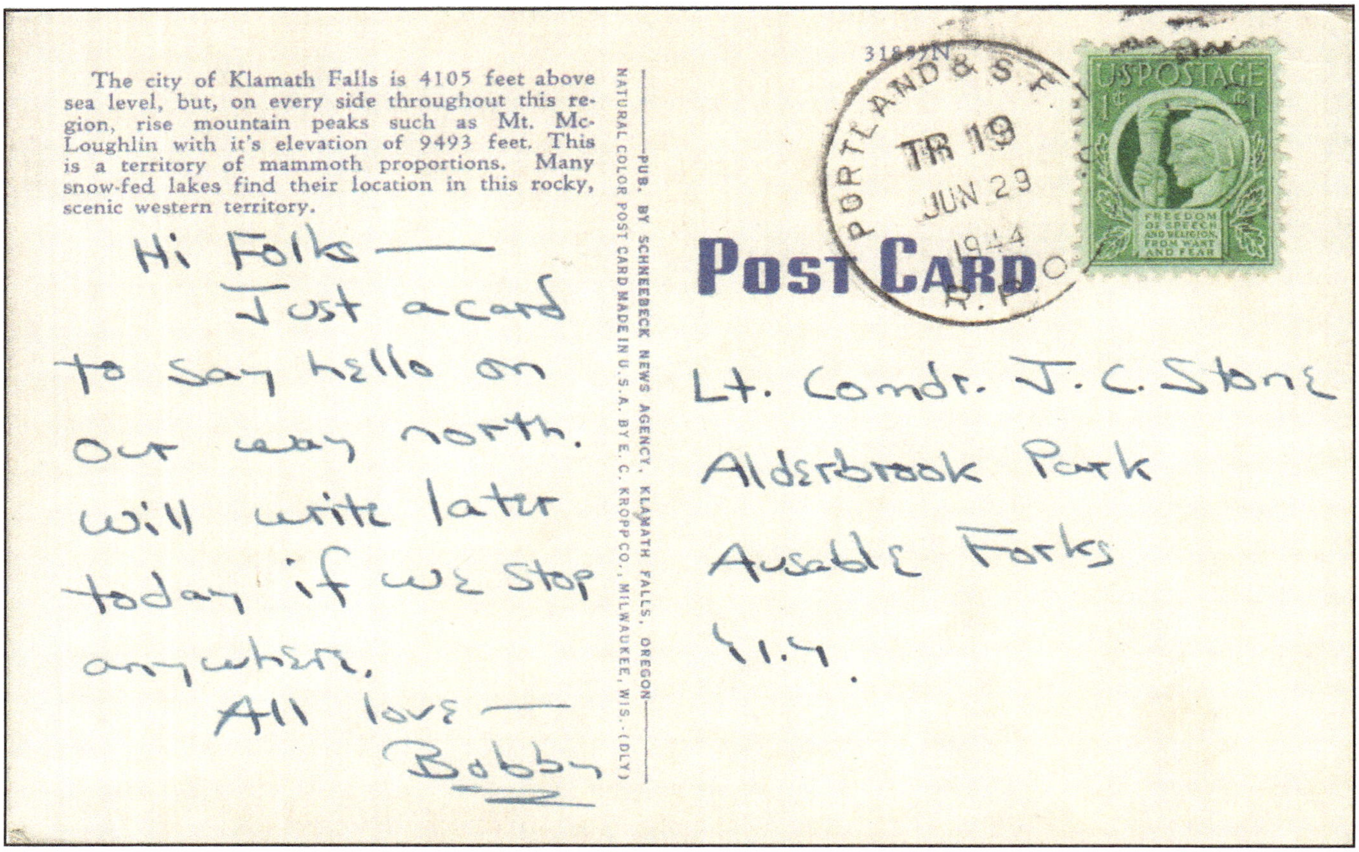
The city of Klamath Falls is 4105 feet above sea level, but, on every side throughout this region, rise mountain peaks such as Mt. McLoughlin with it's elevation of 9493 feet. This is a territory of mammoth proportions. Many snow-fed lakes find their location in this rocky, scenic western territory.

PUB. BY SCHNEEBECK NEWS AGENCY, KLAMATH FALLS, OREGON
NATURAL COLOR POST CARD MADE IN U.S.A. BY E. C. KROPP CO., MILWAUKEE, WIS. (DLY)

PORTLAND & S.F. R.P.O.
TR 19
JUN 29
1944

US POSTAGE 1¢
FREEDOM OF SPEECH AND RELIGION, FROM WANT AND FEAR

POST CARD

Hi Folks—
Just a card to say hello on our way north. Will write later today if we stop anywhere.
All love—
Bobby

Lt. Comdr. J. C. Stone
Alderbrook Park
Ausable Forks
N.Y.

JUNE 29-30, 1944

NEW WASHINGTON HOTEL
SEATTLE

Friday Nite

Dear Dad + Bee——

'Twas swell to talk to you tonight for the last time for quite awhile. I never thought I'd be able to call again after we left Frisco but luckily I was.

Had a swell train trip (though slow) up here and we really traveled in style. The officers had drawing rooms, of all things! It really made the trip a real pleasure.

They let us out tonight for the last time before we "sail the ocean blue." The officers are supposed to have staterooms but I'll bet it won't be anything like our trip on the Georgic or Lafayette!

HOST TO THOUSANDS OF DISTINGUISHED GUESTS

I haven't received any mail at my new address but I hope I'll find some waiting at our destination. I'll write again as soon as I have a chance and have anything to write.

Best love to you—

Bobby

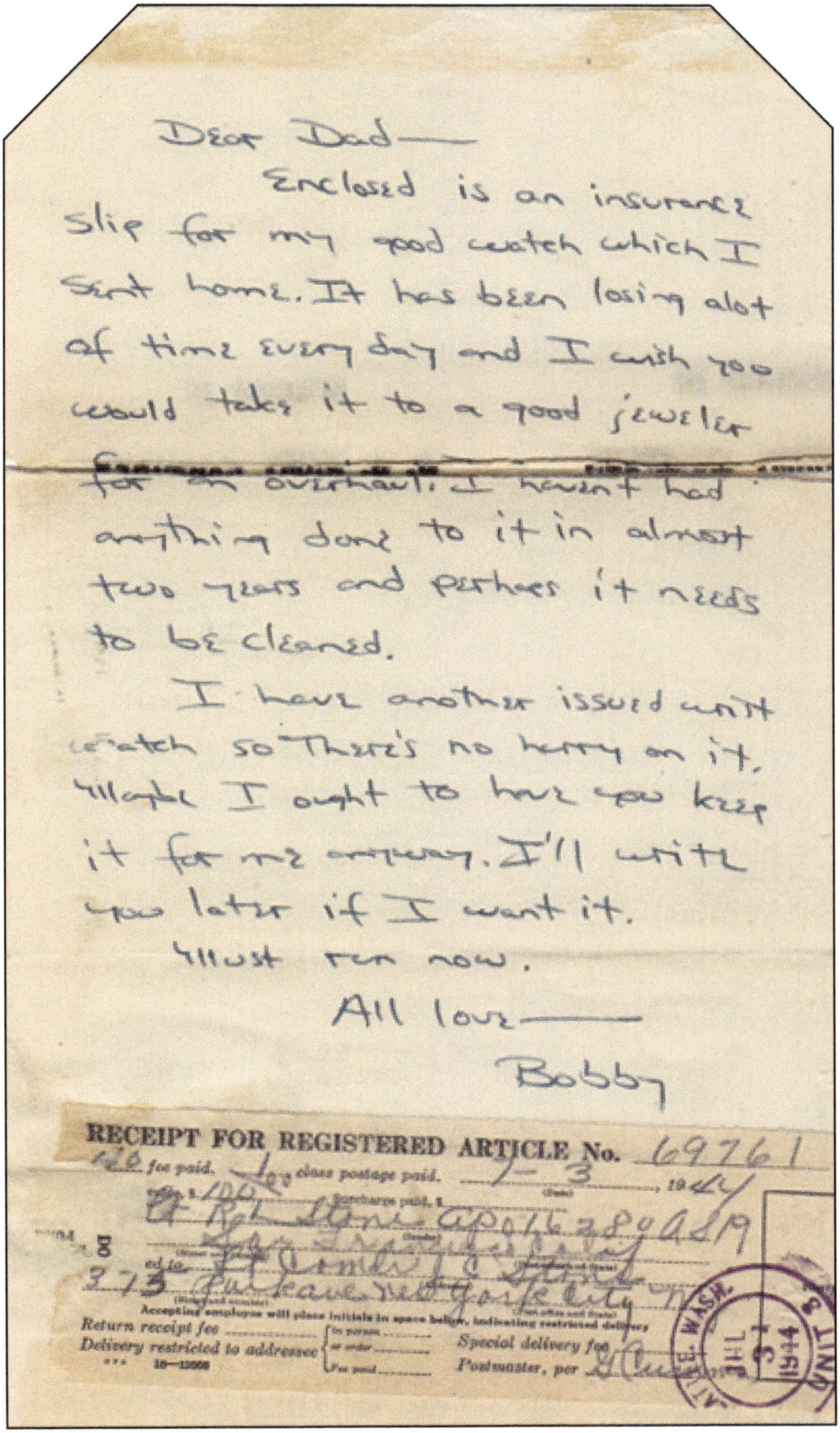

Dear Dad—

Enclosed is an insurance slip for my good watch which I sent home. It has been losing alot of time every day and I wish you would take it to a good jeweler for an overhaul. I haven't had anything done to it in almost two years and perhaps it needs to be cleaned.

I have another issued wrist watch so there's no hurry on it. Maybe I ought to have you keep it for me anyway. I'll write you later if I want it.

Must run now.

All love—

Bobby

RECEIPT FOR REGISTERED ARTICLE No. 69761

fee paid. class postage paid. 7-3, 1944 (Date)

Surcharge paid, $

Accepting employee will place initials in space below, indicating restricted delivery

Return receipt fee

Delivery restricted to addressee { In person / or order / Fee paid

Special delivery fee

Postmaster, per

UNITED STATES AIR FORCES

Dear Dad—

I just want to write you a few lines to wish you the happiest of birthdays and to let you know that I'm thinking of you on July 15th and only wish that all of us could be with you to help celebrate your 50th.

You're a swell gent Dad, and you make a mighty tough example for your sons to live up to. I only hope that on my 50th birthday I have as many friends and have made as great a success out of my life as you have.

This damn war sure makes it tough for all of us and particularly on special occasions. Let it suffice that I'll be with you in spirit to wish the greatest Dad a fellow ever had, a million happy returns on the 15th.

With loads of love—

Bobby

JULY 4, 1944 BUT "DO NOT OPEN UNTIL JULY 15, 1944"

7th AIR FORCE GUNNERY SCHOOL OAHU, HI

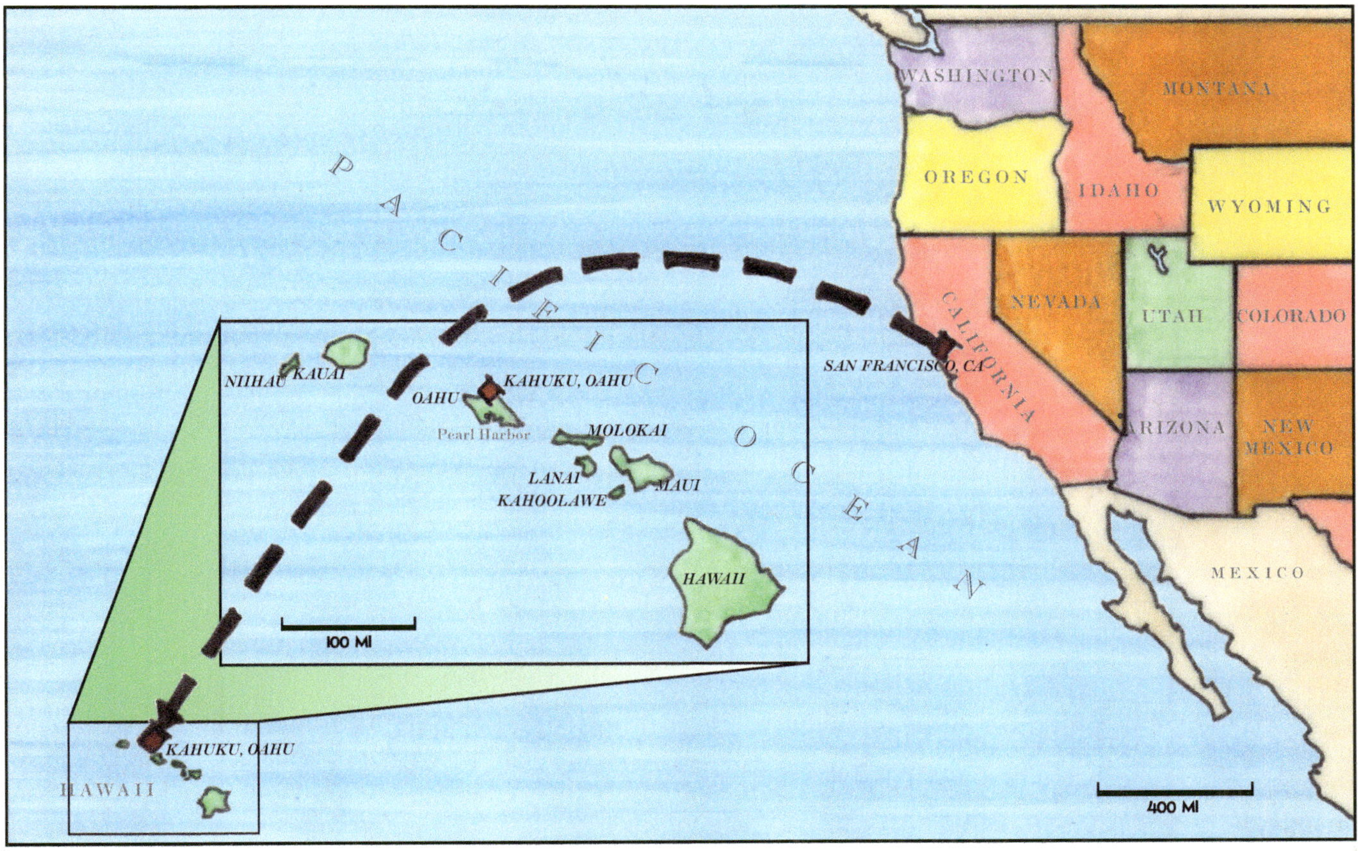

JULY 1944–OCTOBER 1944

UNITED STATES AIR FORCES

Somewhere at Sea

Dear Dad, Bee, Don, Jim, Barry + Ken—

This is going to be a tough one to write due to the rigid restrictions on what we may say. None the less I want to have a letter to mail as soon as we hit our destination to let you know that I am well and fine.

Our accomodations on the ship aren't too good due to a great overcrowding. Most of the officers have small staterooms that are adequate. The poor enlisted men are jammed into the hold like sardines.

On shipboard we eat only twice a day. Once in the morning and then again late in the afternoon. The chow is quite well prepared and our extreme hunger makes it exceptionally tasty.

Our first day at sea was really rugged. About 75% of the passengers were horribly sick. The crew said that it was the toughest day they'd had since they'd been making trips across. It was really hell for the first day at sea. Luckily enough I was able to keep down my food although on several occasions it was dubious. The following day the sea was smooth again and everyone felt lots better. We saw faces on deck that we didn't know were on board until then.

Life on shipboard hasn't been too dull although this hasn't been a pleasure cruise. During the daytime we spend most of our time up on the hurricane deck enjoying the sun or else down in the mess hall playing poker. There is a tremendous amount of gambling on the boat because of no other entertainment.

So far on shipboard we have had very few duties. In fact the only work I've done so far is censor our enlisted men's mail. We have to censor all of their mail before we hit port and believe me they've written alot.

I'm running low on news so I'll close here by saying that I hope I have some mail waiting for me upon my arrival. I got two letters from you and one from Pam before I left the coast—they came to my APO number. By the way, many thanks for the check treating me to a last fling in L.A., Dad.

Speaking of mail, please write straight mail as much as possible because I really prefer that to V-mail. If regular mail takes too long in reaching me, I'll let you know and you can start using V-mail. Please be sure that all my letters make the rounds, Dad, because I doubt if I'll be able to write everyone individually. Be sure, however, to tell everyone that I really will appreciate alot of mail.

My very best to everyone and my love to you all.

Bobby

P.S. Say hello to the Hilsons for me.

To: Lt. Comdr. J. C. Stone
375 Park Avenue
New York City
N.Y.

FROM
Lt. R.L. Stone 0-596041
APO 16280 (AS) 19
San Francisco, Cal.

(CENSOR'S STAMP)

SEE INSTRUCTION NO. 2

(Sender's complete address above)

Somewhere at Sea

Dear All— [36]

I just finished a long letter to you but I thought I'd send one V-mail just in case the straight mail is slow in arriving. Let me know which arrives first.

The trip so far has been rather dull, but then it's not intended to be a Cook's tour. Most of our time is either spent on deck or else playing cards.

As yet our final destination is still a question mark and only time will tell. Here's hoping when we arrive I'll find some mail from the various Stones waiting for me. I received some mail from you before I left the coast—it was mailed to my APO number.

Hope you receive my long newsy letter before too long. Until then, my love to you all—Bobby

HAVE YOU FILLED IN COMPLETE ADDRESS AT TOP?

V-—MAIL

HAVE YOU FILLED IN COMPLETE ADDRESS AT TOP?

OAHU, HI

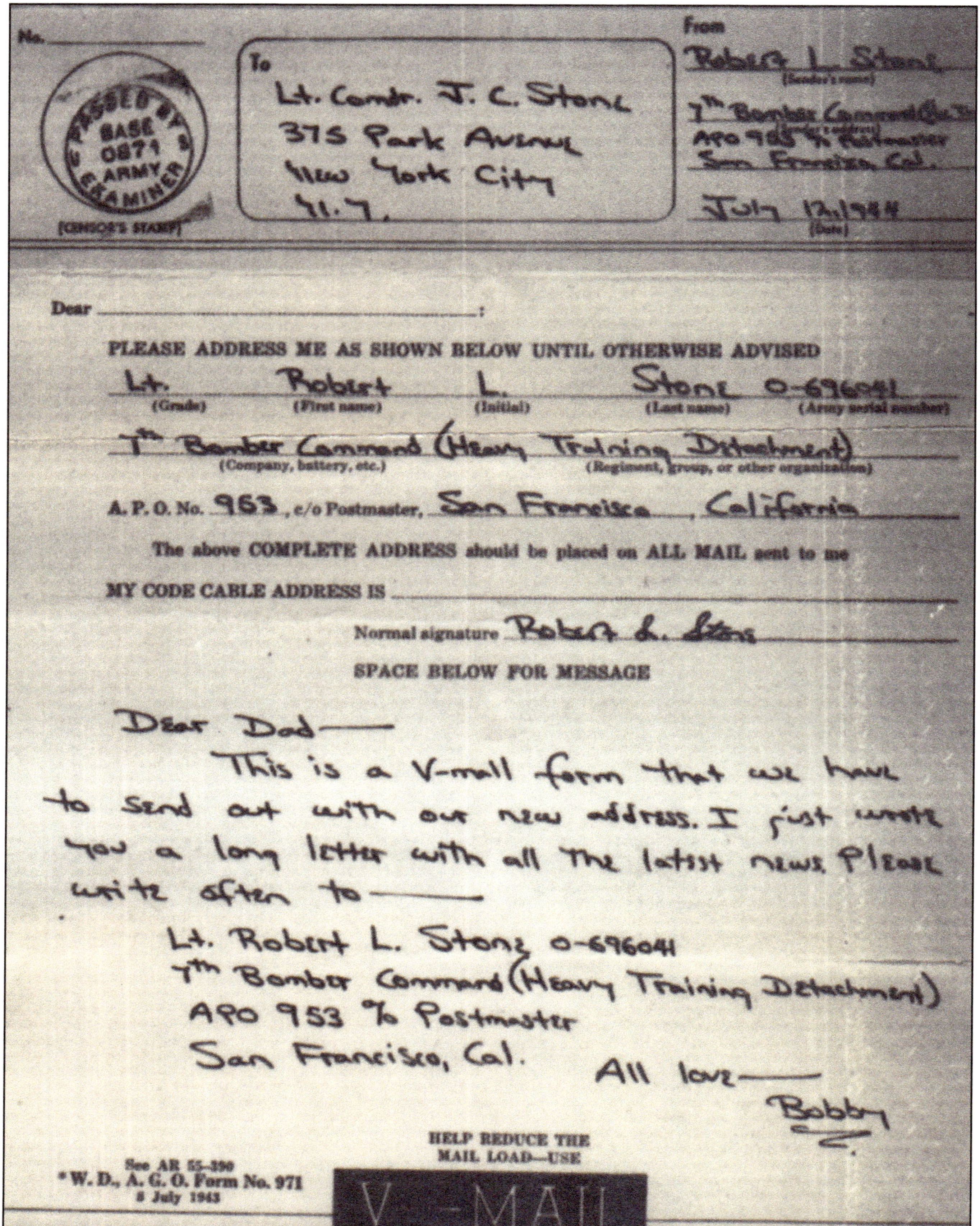
No. ______

PASSED BY BASE 0871 ARMY EXAMINER
(CENSOR'S STAMP)

To
Lt. Comdr. J. C. Stone
375 Park Avenue
New York City
N.Y.

From
Robert L. Stone
(Sender's name)
7th Bomber Command (He...
(Sender's address)
APO 953 % Postmaster
San Francisco, Cal.
July 12, 1944
(Date)

Dear ______:

PLEASE ADDRESS ME AS SHOWN BELOW UNTIL OTHERWISE ADVISED

Lt. (Grade) Robert (First name) L. (Initial) Stone (Last name) 0-696041 (Army serial number)

7th Bomber Command (Company, battery, etc.) (Heavy Training Detachment) (Regiment, group, or other organization)

A. P. O. No. 953, c/o Postmaster, San Francisco, California

The above COMPLETE ADDRESS should be placed on ALL MAIL sent to me

MY CODE CABLE ADDRESS IS ______

Normal signature Robert L. Stone

SPACE BELOW FOR MESSAGE

Dear Dad—

This is a V-mail form that we have to send out with our new address. I just wrote you a long letter with all the latest news. Please write often to—

Lt. Robert L. Stone 0-696041
7th Bomber Command (Heavy Training Detachment)
APO 953 % Postmaster
San Francisco, Cal.

All love—
Bobby

See AR 55-390
*W. D., A. G. O. Form No. 971
8 July 1943

HELP REDUCE THE MAIL LOAD—USE
V-MAIL

JULY 12-13, 1944

UNITED STATES AIR FORCES

Thursday July 13th

Dearest All——

At long last we arrived at our new home. We were greeted by a lovely sight as our ship steamed into the beautiful Hawaiian Islands. The blue water and sandy beaches made us a royal welcome.

We stayed on ship board the first night and didn't debark until the next morning at which time we were met by trucks. They took us to our base which is a small landing strip.

To one side of us are mountains and jungle and on the other is the ocean. We live in tents and have to use mosquito nets at night because of the insects etc. Everything at the base is quite crude and life is rather on the rugged side.

For awhile we will be flying training and patrol missions before going "down under". I'm not completely sure of the nature of our work but for awhile I believe it will

OAHU, HI

consist of training.

Everything military here on the islands is extremely hush-hush and so it's very hard to write a good letter. Anything much pertaining to our base and flying etc. is out.

Was in Honolulu yesterday and it's not much of a place. It's full of navy. All of the stores are full of junk for the American soldiers to buy. It's almost like Playland. Got a look at famous Pearl Harbor although you can't get inside to look around. The islands are really beautiful with their volcanic peaks jutting up into the blue skies. Parts of the island (where we're based) are really kinda wild and woolly — nothing like the beautiful Hawaii that you see on posters and in the movies.

I hope by now that you've received the letters I wrote on the boat. As yet I haven't received any mail over here and I'm looking forward to my first letter. Incidentally, they say that air-mail comes lots faster than V-mail so please use that. From now on our time off will be quite scarce so you'll have to bear with me if I can't write often. I definitely won't be able to write anyone but you and Pam. Please tell all my friends to write

JULY 13, 1944

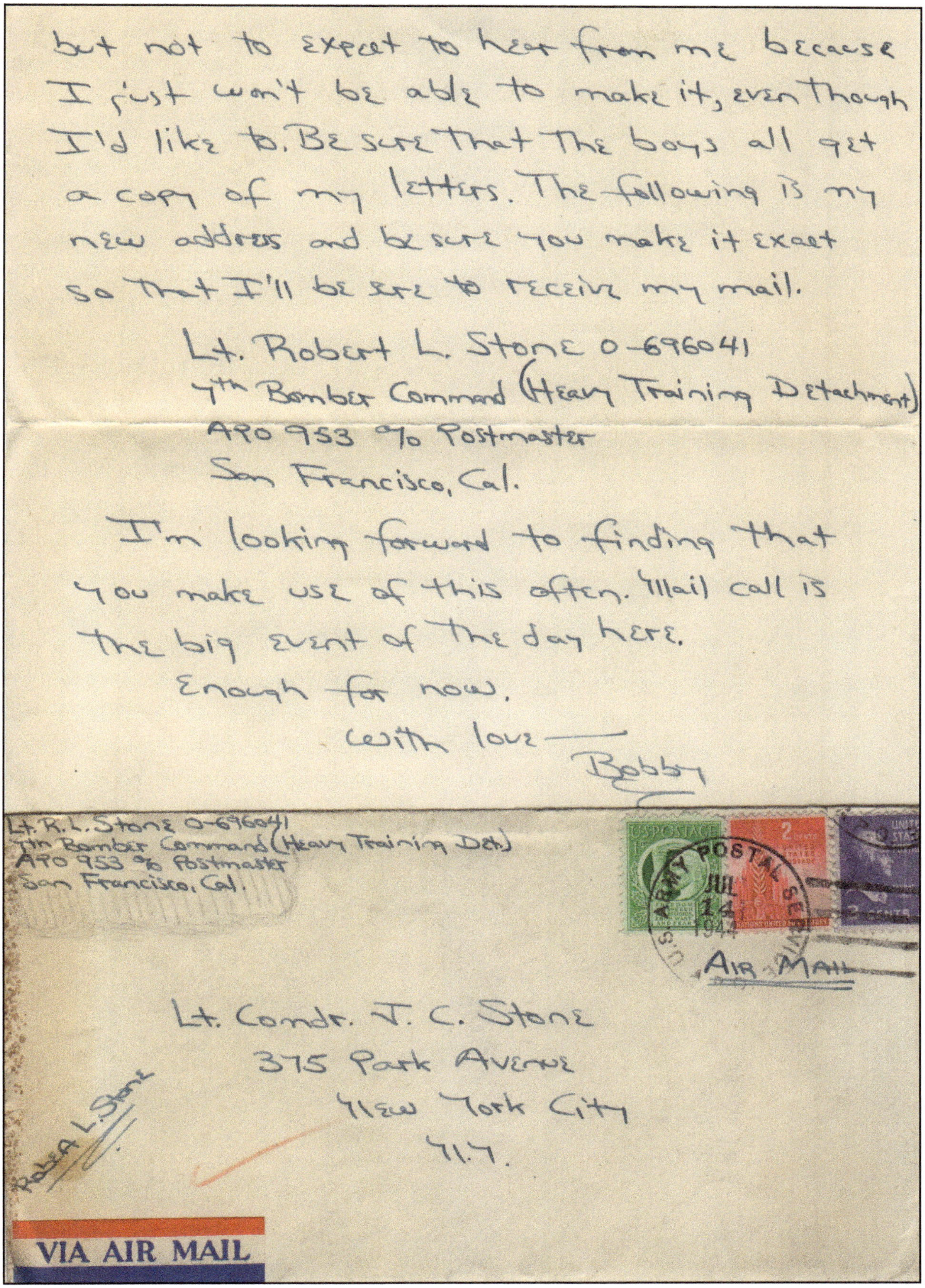

but not to expect to hear from me because I just won't be able to make it, even though I'd like to. Be sure that the boys all get a copy of my letters. The following is my new address and be sure you make it exact so that I'll be sure to receive my mail.

Lt. Robert L. Stone 0-696041
7th Bomber Command (Heavy Training Detachment)
APO 953 % Postmaster
San Francisco, Cal.

I'm looking forward to finding that you make use of this often. Mail call is the big event of the day here.

Enough for now.

With love —
Bobby

Lt. R. L. Stone 0-696041
7th Bomber Command (Heavy Training Det.)
APO 953 % Postmaster
San Francisco, Cal.

ARMY POSTAL
JUL 14 1944

AIR MAIL

Lt. Comdr. J. C. Stone
375 Park Avenue
New York City
N.Y.

Robert L. Stone

VIA AIR MAIL

OAHU, HI

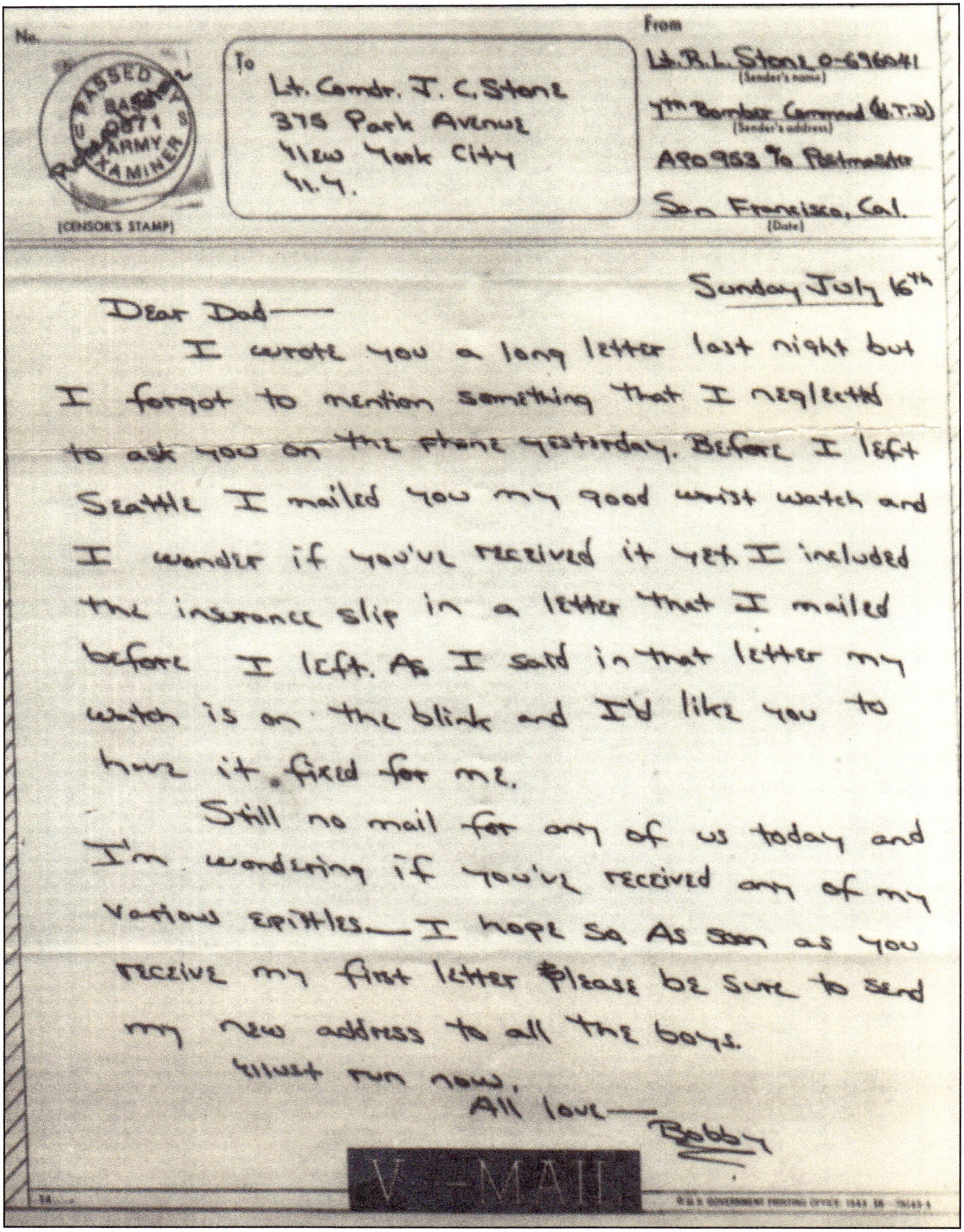

No.

PASSED BY ARMY EXAMINER 0871

(CENSOR'S STAMP)

To
Lt. Comdr. J. C. Stone
375 Park Avenue
New York City
N.Y.

From
Lt. R. L. Stone 0-696041
(Sender's name)
7th Bomber Command (A.T.D.)
(Sender's address)
APO 953 % Postmaster
San Francisco, Cal.
(Date)

Sunday July 16th

Dear Dad—

I wrote you a long letter last night but I forgot to mention something that I neglected to ask you on the phone yesterday. Before I left Seattle I mailed you my good wrist watch and I wonder if you've received it yet. I included the insurance slip in a letter that I mailed before I left. As I said in that letter my watch is on the blink and I'd like you to have it fixed for me.

Still no mail for any of us today and I'm wondering if you've received any of my various epistles— I hope so. As soon as you receive my first letter please be sure to send my new address to all the boys.

Must run now.

All love—
Bobby

V-MAIL

JULY 16-20, 1944

UNITED STATES AIR FORCES

Thursday July 20th

Dear Dad, Bee, Don, & Jim——

I haven't any particular news to write but I do have a few spare minutes just to say that all goes well at Pineapple Paradise.

We've flown several times since I last wrote, getting our bearings around the Islands. This morning we went on a three hour bombing mission on one of the small islands. As yet we haven't flown any real long missions but before long I guess we'll be making some lengthy hauls.

Life here at the base isn't too bad but there isn't a darn thing to do in the way of entertainment. We have a crude officers club where you can get all kinds of mixed drinks. There is quite a bit of gambling due to the lack of other 'diversion. Our main complaint here is the food which is pretty poor. Even in Honolulu there aren't very good places to eat although the food is a real treat after eating at the base. We're supposed to get a pass once every two weeks and I imagine we'll spend most of them at the beach at Waikiki. I was so lucky that our first pass came on the 14th and 15th so I was able to call you.

Still no mail for any of us so you can imagine what a disheartened bunch we are. I'm afraid that the APO we got at Seattle (16280 AS(19)) is no darn good or else they've held up all our mail. I hope by now ~~they've~~ that you've received my new address from here. Did you get two letters from me written from "Somewhere at sea."

Yesterday we got our tent fixed up with home-made tables and improvised chairs. I never was much as a carpenter but I surprised myself by turning out a mighty fine table.

Can't think of anything else so I'll close here. Please be sure to write often and maybe eventually one of them will catch up to me.

All love—

Bobby

2) My bed and table inside the tent at Kahuku.

July 22nd

Dear Dad & Bee—

Yesterday was a big occasion for us when our first batch of mail came through. Everybody was jubilant with a stack of fifteen to twenty-five letters. I guess they must have held up all mail coming to that temporary APO number. Many thanks for your various letters. I hope you keep 'em ~~s~~ coming.

Was quite upset when I didn't have any mail from Pam in my array of eighteen letters but realized ~~what~~ why when Ronnie's letter explained that Pam had had a brain concussion. When I spoke to Pam from Seattle she casually mentioned she was in the hospital but didn't say what was wrong. I naturally thought nothing much of it and let it go at that. I never thought to ask you when I had you on the phone a few days ago.

I was kinda worried so I decided to call her which I did this morning. She sounded in good spirits and said she was lots better. Please write me how she's coming along until she's able to write herself.

No more now but I did want you to know I'd received your first letters.

All love—Bobby

UNITED STATES ARMY
AIR FORCES

Monday 24th

Dear Dad & Bee —

I haven't any particular news since my last letter but today my crew is on pass and so I thought I'd scratch off a few lines. Your letters have been coming through alright but as yet I haven't received any to my new APO and I'm wondering if you've received my various letters. Many thanks for your long newsy letter Bee, that arrived two days ago. Please keep me posted on how Pam is coming along until she can write. I worry so when I don't hear from her but I realize that she isn't allowed to do much yet.

We've flown quite a bit of late and two days ago we led a group formation of some twenty planes. It simulated a regular bombing mission because we flew out to a small Island dropped our bombs and returned. We went through all the steps of a regular combat attack. We're getting some excellent training here — far better ~~that~~ than in the States.

JULY 24, 1944

Before I forget, how about sending me Ken's address? You might also send him mine in case he ever gets in this way. With so many ships stopping by here I always keep my eyes open with the thought of possibly bumping into him.

This afternoon I plan to head for the beach and try to pick up a little sun tan. In-spite of the tropical weather I still have a night club palor since we don't have too much of a chance to sunbathe.

Keep up your letters.

With love —

Bobby

Native surfboarder at Waikiki. Took a try at it and 'taint easy! (2)

UNITED STATES ARMY
AIR FORCES

Saturday July 29th

Dear Dad & Bee—

The last few days the mail has been coming through a little better and I just received a letter from Dad yesterday. All of my mail takes about ten days from the East Coast. I'm wondering if my letters have been coming through alright since you haven't used my new APO as yet.

Yesterday I sent home a package with two woolen sweaters and some woolen socks, neither of which I have any use for out here. Please put the sweaters away carefully because they are two of my favorites, that Pam made for me. Also, be sure to let me know when and in what condition they arrive since I have the insurance slip.

The last few days we've all been adither putting on an air-show for some unknown 37
dignitary—everyone suspects that it's Roosevelt although none of us have seen him. We really put on an aerial spectale for whomever it is.

For the past week or so we've managed to find our way to the beach sometime

JULY 29, 1944

every day.
or other, Slowly but surely I'm taking on the hue of a native.

Had my first letter from Pam yesterday which she dictated to a friend of hers. 'Twas swell to hear from her even though kinda second-hand. I hope by now she is able to write herself because I sure miss not hearing from her. Mail call is a big occasion here and it sure is a disappointment not to receive a few letters.

Cela suffit until another day.

My love to you all——

Bobby

LEFT to RIGHT: General Douglas MacArthur, President Franklin Delano Roosevelt and Admiral Chester William Nimitz aboard the USS Baltimore in July 1944 at Pearl Harbor, Hawaii.

UNITED STATES ARMY
AIR FORCES

Wednesday Aug. 2nd

Dear Folks ——

Have time for a few lines to say that everything is fine with R.L.S. At the moment we are attending the 7th Air Force Gunnery School. It's a darn good course of ground school, range, and flying that lasts about a month. We go to school for the first two weeks from 7:45 until 5:00 with only an hour out for lunch. Ten classes a day is really alot, particularly when it's as hot as it is here. The classes aren't too interesting but they are most essential. The school is good cheap life insurance.

Last Sunday we had an outing into Honolulu to see the 7th AAF ball team play. When we left after two and a half innings the score was 13-1. The fliers have Joe DiMag Joe Gordon, and a number of other big time ball players — They're just like a pro team.

My mail has been bawled up since we moved but I hope it will straighten out in a day or so. Continue to write to APO 953 and I'll get my mail eventually. Write often.

All love — Bobby

HALEKAI CLUB FOR ARMY OFFICERS
RECREATION SECTION
SPECIAL SERVICE OFFICE
CENTRAL PACIFIC BASE COMMAND

Sunday Aug 6th

Dear Dad + Bee

Our first week of classes is over and today is our day-off, and so we're down here on the beach enjoying a little sun and relaxation. As I look out on the beach it's hard to believe that there's a war on—there are people swimming, surf-boarding, and sailing.

This is really a lovely officers club located on the beach just beyond the Royal Hawaiian. They have swimming and sunbathing facilities, a writing room, and an attractive snack bar. There's a college resigter book here and I ran across several boys name's that I knew. Harvey Daniels' name was under the Dartmouth group.

Many thanks for your long newsy letter, Bee. It's one of the first I received with my new APO address. Haven't heard from Dad for awhile but I guess that's because he's still fishing. Our mail service here is terrible.

The letters chase around the island for awhile until they locate us.

Can't think of anything else, and besides it's time to be getting back. Please write often because mail is really a welcome treat.

All love——
Bobby

P.S. Please see if you can get some 620 film to send me. I believe if you take this letter to Eastman Kodak (near the station) they'll give you a few rolls to ~~see~~ send me.

Love again——
Bobby

NEW YORK, N.Y. PARCEL POST (GENERAL ANNEX)
SEP 9 1944

UNITED STATES ARMY
AIR FORCES

Thursday Aug. 10th

Dear Dad & Bee ——

There's little news from these parts but a few lines are in order to say that all goes well with your wayward son. I'm still at the The 7th AAF Gunnery School going to school for ten periods a day. Next week we go out on the range and then on the last week we do air to air firing. The work at school is well worth while although it tends to be dull at times.

Life here is quite a treat in comparison to the base. We're living in barracks and have excellent chow. We have a beautiful officers club where they have a movie (out in the open air) almost every night. It's really a pleasure to live like a human being for awhile.

I was so glad to receive your long letter from Canada, Dad. It sounds as though you had some darn good fishing and I'm sure the relaxation did you a world of good. Incidentally the mail comes through most irradically and almost always takes sixteen days or more. I hope my letters got through better than that.

Many thanks for giving me the name of Mr. Kellett at Dean Witter + Co. I most certainly will look him up the next time I go into town. You beat me to the punch by sending me a contact here because I was going to write you about it and already I'd looked in the phone directory to try to find a branch office of one of the N.Y. firms — however to no avail. Getting money takes a long time here unless you know someone with an account in a Hawaiian bank. Otherwise your check must be sent to the Mainland and then back.

I'm sure you've read in the papers about Roosevelt's visit here two weeks ago. We put on a big air show for him but at the time couldn't mention it in letters. As you can imagine the islands were in a state of excitement for a week or so.

Must be off to bed now. Please write often because I so love hearing some word from home. The mail situation is terrible so please be sure that I get some when it does find its way through.

My love to you —

Bobby

UNITED STATES ARMY
AIR FORCES

Thursday 17th

Dear All ———

There isn't much in the way of news from these parts because our life at the Gunnery School is very routine. We finished our two weeks of class work and have been out on the range all week. We've really gotten alot of valuable training here. Next week we wind up the course with air to air firing.

It's really a pleasure to be here, living like a king compared to our former mosquitos' paradise. The officers club is as nice as any in the states and we eat royally. We're making the most of it since another month will doubtless find us on some small island in the large Pacific. Kinda looks like the Bonins are next on the list!

A friend of mine just brought in some mail among it your letter, Bee. I am certainly sorry to hear of the tragedy. Although I only met him once, Seymour seemed like a great guy and I know how fond you all were of him.

It's odd how the mail comes through. Yesterday I received a letter from Dad postmarked

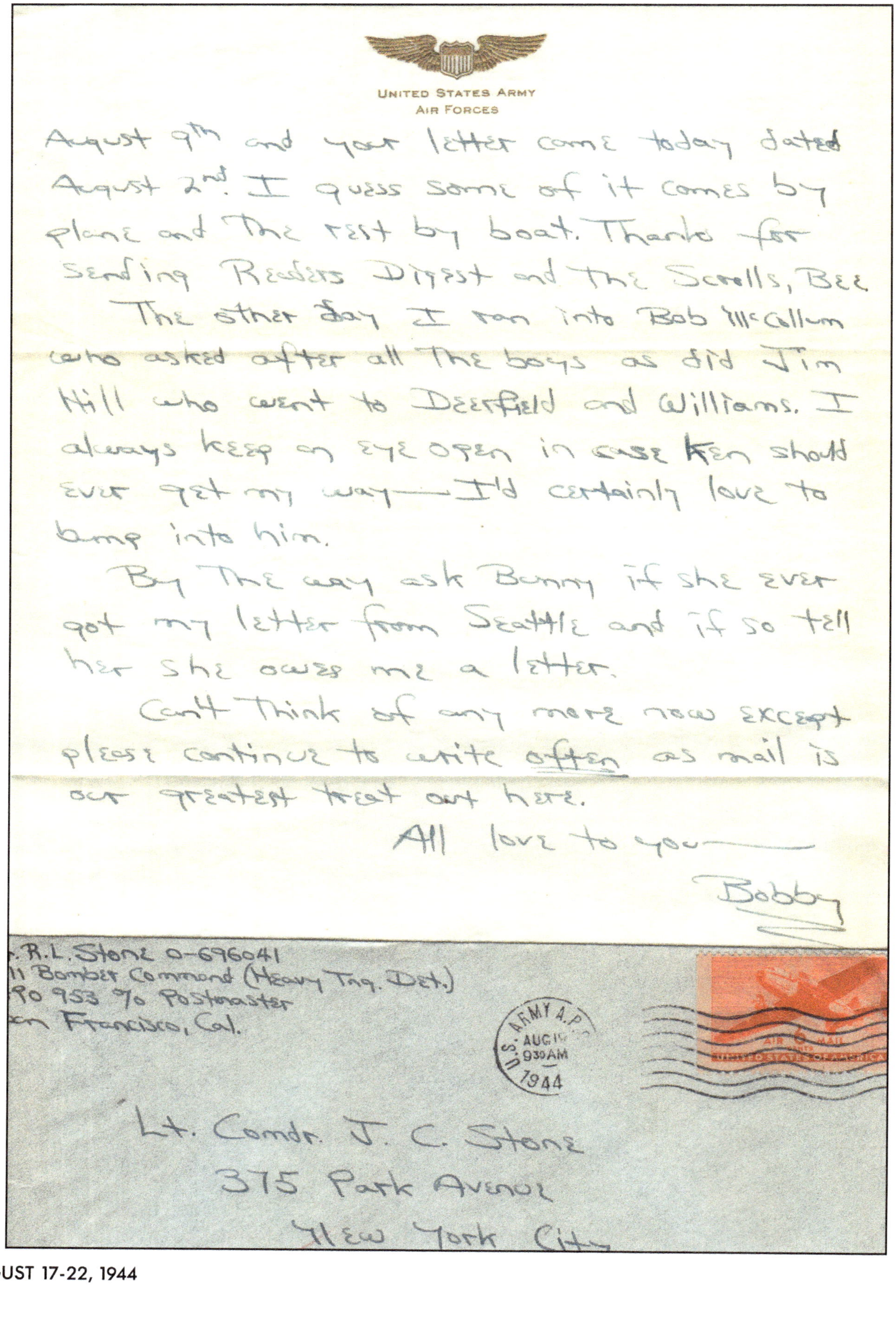

UNITED STATES ARMY
AIR FORCES

August 9th and your letter came today dated August 2nd. I guess some of it comes by plane and the rest by boat. Thanks for sending Readers Digest and the Scrolls, Bee.

The other day I ran into Bob McCallum who asked after all the boys as did Jim Hill who went to Deerfield and Williams. I always keep an eye open in case Ken should ever get my way—I'd certainly love to bump into him.

By the way ask Bunny if she ever got my letter from Seattle and if so tell her she owes me a letter.

Can't think of any more now except please continue to write often as mail is our greatest treat out here.

All love to you—

Bobby

.R.L. Stone 0-696041
11 Bomber Command (Heavy Tng. Det.)
PO 953 % Postmaster
n Francisco, Cal.

U.S. ARMY A.P. AUG 19 930AM 1944

AIR 6 MAIL
UNITED STATES OF AMERICA

Lt. Comdr. J. C. Stone
375 Park Avenue
New York City

AUGUST 17-22, 1944

UNITED STATES ARMY
AIR FORCES

Tuesday Aug. 22nd

Dear Folks——

The last few days have brought in alot of mail and a good share of it from all of you——many thanks and be sure to keep your pens in action.

At the end of the week we'll be finished with Gunnery School and then back to "mosquito's paradise." This week we are doing air to air firing every day to finish up the course. I kinda hate to leave here since it's been a pleasure to have lived like a human being for a few weeks, eating three good meals today.

I continue to bump into kids from college or else former army acquaintances. It certainly is a small world even way out here. Had a letter from my best friend from Childress and he just completed his 50th mission in Italy and he's ready to come home. He's really seen alot of hell but he made the grade. If it hadn't been for my leg I'd be with him now and finished up myself if I'd fared as well.

Was in town today doing a little shopping and a few odds and ends. We had the day

OAHU, HI

UNITED STATES ARMY
AIR FORCES

off today since we flew all day yesterday. I came back early this afternoon because there isn't a darn thing to do in town. Honolulu certainly ranks high among the biggest dumps I've ever visited.

Must run now but I hope this letter finds you all fine and in good spirits. Write often!

All love —

Bobby

Oahu, Hawaii
September 1, 1944

Dear Dad, Bee, Don, Jim, Barry, & Ken ——

I hope you'll all excuse the lapse with no mail from these parts but life has taken up a speedier tempo of late. Gunnery school is over and I'm now the proud possessor of a very impressive diploma. At the moment we're back in our tents at this mosquito ridden paradise

Our daily (and nightly) schedule is a mighty full one right now. We're flying all the time and have a few classes between times. We've been concentrating on bombing and long navigation missions, and we're just about ready to try our luck with the Nips.[38] In fact by the time you answer this letter I doubt if I'll still be here in Hawaii. I can't tell you much about my future destinations but you can best follow my whereabouts by reading the activities of the 7th AAF Liberators in the daily papers.

Incidentally that stuff about the B-29's is completely false. I never even mentioned to Ronnie anything about our flying and I have no idea where she got the notion

about my changing to B29's—not that I wouldn't like to!

Yesterday I made several phone calls in Honolulu to try to locate Barry but it was to no avail. I'm afraid he'll have to contact me through my mailing address. It certainly would be swell if we could get together.

That was certainly swell about Tommy getting his promotion. Tell his Dad I had written him before I heard from you and I'm writing him again today to congratulate him—in his last letter he was still a first. Out here promotions seem to be unheard of, and to think I'll be in grade for a full year next month. The air force has certainly backtracked from their policy of two or three years ago.

That's about all for now except to say that your letters are coming through fine and I hope you'll all keep writing <u>often</u>.

Love to you all—

Bobby

Oahu, Hawaii
September 8, 1944

Dear All——

Since my last letter I've been quite well occupied with a big dose of flying. We flew down to Johnston Island and to Midway. The former was a flight of over eleven hours. Believe me that's a long time to be up in a B-24, which was not designed for comfort. Both missions were mainly for the navigator, although we did drop a few bombs on the way back. The navigator really did a swell job and got us through in fine shape.

Many thanks for all your various letters—it's certainly great to hear from you often. Please keep your pens at work because ~~I~~ it's your letters that keep the old morale from hitting rock bottom. You surely are a regular Walter Winchell, Bee. I was kinda surprised to hear about Delia's engagement. Was glad to receive the letters from both of the Jacks. I intend to write them if I can ever find a minute or two.

As yet I haven't had a chance to see Mr. Kellet, Dad, although I intend to if I ever get back to town before we leave. From now on we'll be fairly busy flying, I imagine.

The mosquitos are driving me mad so I'll have to stop now. Just about sundown they come out in squadrons and really go after us.

S'long to you all for now—I'll try to find something of interest to write at the beginning of the week.

All love—

Bobby

1.) Tent row at Kahuku

UNITED STATES ARMY
AIR FORCES

Oahu, Hawaii
September 14th

Dear Dad—

I was so very glad to receive the news of Don's promotion. He's really got what it takes and actually deserves alot more than just three stripes, and my hat's off to him! I got the good news directly from him a few days ago myself.

In his letter Don mentioned something about the possibility of going to O.C.S.,[39] but he didn't sound as though he was going to do anything about it. He seems very anxious to get overseas. I wish he wouldn't be in such a rush and would go to O.C.S. if he has an opportunity. I know he has the stuff to get through in a walk, judging by some of the punks you meet with commissions. I wrote Don and told him my feelings and I just wonder what you think about it, and if he said anything to you about it.

Our going down under has been delayed a little because of a few training missions we have yet to fly. Of late our planes have been out of commission and so we haven't done much flying for the last ten days or so.

Before I forget, yesterday I mailed you a folder containing my commission paper, my discharge, and my diploma from Gunnery School. They are things that I have no use for right now and they'd only be ruined if I kept them. Be sure to let me know when they arrive.

Just got back from a couple of days in Honolulu. As usual there wasn't anything much to do but it was a pleasant change from the air base. The room we had at the officers club in town was occupied by Jack Benny [40] the day we left. He's been on a tour in the Pacific area this last summer.

Well Dad, I guess that's about all for now.

All love—

Bobby

Lt. R.L. Stone 0-696041
VII Bomber Command (Trng. Det. Heavy)
APO 953 % Postmaster
San Francisco, Cal.

U.S. ARMY POSTAL SERVICE
SEP 15 1944

Mr. J. C. Stone
11 Wall Street
New York City
N.Y.

Robert Stone

AIR MAIL

SEPTEMBER 14-16, 1944

Oahu, Hawaii
September 16th

Dear Dad + Bee——

Still very little flying due to a scarcity of planes in commission, but starting next week we'll be back at it again thick and heavy. I hope we finish up here before long because everyone has become restless and quite irritable just waiting around. All of us were very eager when we first arrived, but when we didn't go "down under" we became lazy and indifferent. Now we want to go down and get our missions in and come home if we're that fortunate.

Before I forget, I mailed home a foot locker today with my blouse, pinks, raincoat, green shirt, a few odds and ends, and some pictures and papers of mine. Please put the clothes away and put the package of papers etc. in my closet. There's a picture of Pam wrapped up in a towel so it won't break, that I'd like you to put up on my dresser. I have a couple of her in a leather frame, and I was afraid this one would break if I lugged it around with me. I'm sending all these things home because they'd only be excess baggage where we'll be, and so I want to get rid of them. Be sure to let me know when it arrives, probably in a month or so.

Yesterday we had a series of lectures and demonstration

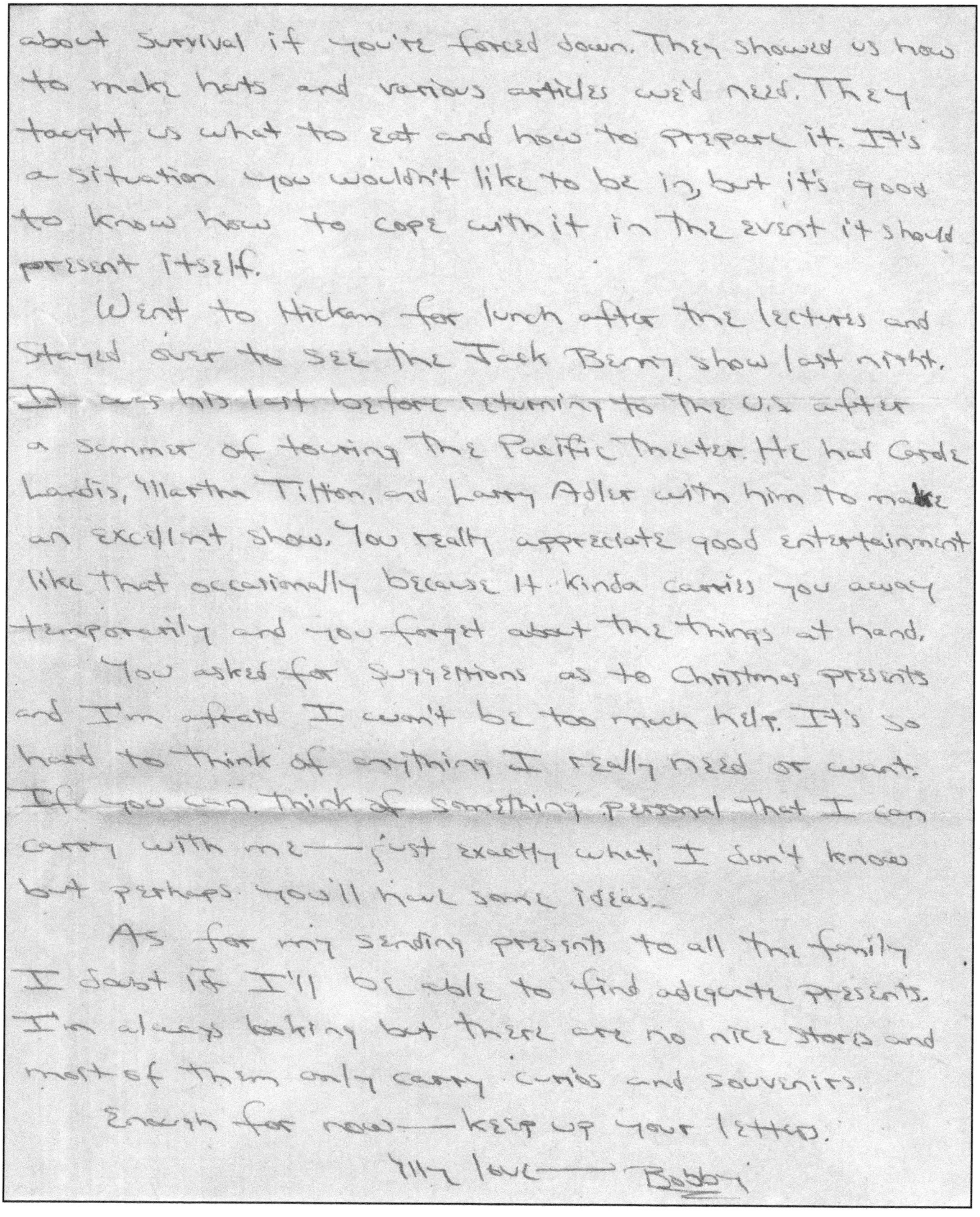

about survival if you're forced down. They showed us how to make huts and various articles we'd need. They taught us what to eat and how to prepare it. It's a situation you wouldn't like to be in, but it's good to know how to cope with it in the event it should present itself.

Went to Hickam for lunch after the lectures and stayed over to see the Jack Benny show last night. It was his last before returning to the U.S. after a summer of touring the Pacific theater. He had Carole Landis, Martha Tilton, and Larry Adler with him to make an excellent show. You really appreciate good entertainment like that occasionally because it kinda carries you away temporarily and you forget about the things at hand.

You asked for suggestions as to Christmas presents and I'm afraid I won't be too much help. It's so hard to think of anything I really need or want. If you can think of something personal that I can carry with me—just exactly what, I don't know but perhaps you'll have some ideas.

As for my sending presents to all the family I doubt if I'll be able to find adequate presents. I'm always looking but there are no nice stores and most of them only carry curios and souvenirs.

Enough for now—keep up your letters.

My love— Bobby

22 SEPT.

ARMY - NAVY
BASEBALL

FURLONG FIELD

(OFFICERS)

22 SEPT.

First game of Army-Navy
World Series.
Johnny Beazley vs. Virgil Trucks

Admiral Nimitz throws in the
first ball after making a
short speech—quite impressive!

ARMY—0

VS.

NAVY—5

**DiMaggio, Beazley, Rizzuto, McCoskey
And Other Major League Stars To Play
In Biggest Baseball Classic Of The Year**

FURLONG FIELD, CHA3 ★ FRIDAY, SEPT. 22, 1944

Oahu, Hawaii
September 23rd

Dear Dad + Bee——

Many thanks for all your various letters which have been coming through quite rapidly of late. Your last letter only took six days, Dad. On the other side of the ledger however, I've gotten some that have taken over a month so I guess it's all just luck.

That certainly was something about Toni being caught thieving. I never did think she was all there. The oddest coincidence was that the afternoon I received your letter with the clipping I spotted the enclosed out of Yank magazine. Also out of Yank is the clipping of Lt. Shepard Shedden whom I believe is the son of one of your friends, Dad. I remembered that name and it struck a familiar note, am I not right that you know his dad?

Before I forget my July bank statement just arrived from N.Y. and you have a check for $12 outstanding. I'm wondering if you ever received that letter. I mailed it to pay for Pam's flowers you ordered and asked you to send her some more and enclosed a card. Please be sure to let me know if you received that letter and if so please cash the check because it's bawling up my bank book.

SEPTEMBER 23, 1944

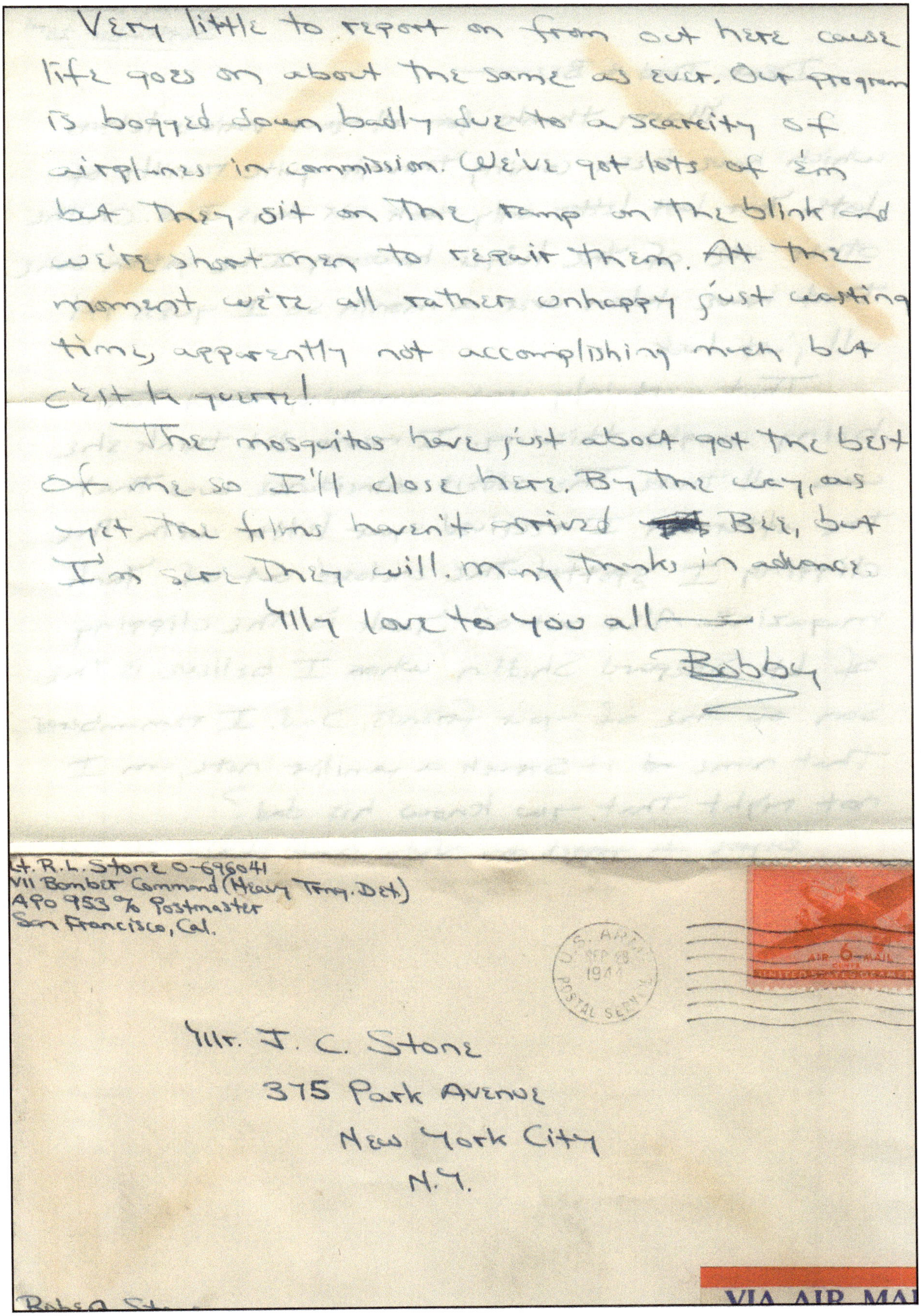

Very little to report on from out here cause life goes on about the same as ever. Our program is bogged down badly due to a scarcity of airplanes in commission. We've got lots of 'em but they sit on the ramp on the blink and we're short men to repair them. At the moment we're all rather unhappy just wasting time, apparently not accomplishing much but C'est la guerre!

The mosquitos have just about got the best of me so I'll close here. By the way, as yet the films haven't arrived Bee, but I'm sure they will. Many thanks in advance.

My love to you all—

Bobby

Lt. R.L. Stone O-696041
VII Bomber Command (Heavy Trng. Det.)
APO 953 % Postmaster
San Francisco, Cal.

U.S. ARMY
SEP 28
1944
POSTAL SERVICE

AIR 6¢ MAIL

Mr. J. C. Stone
375 Park Avenue
New York City
N.Y.

VIA AIR MA

OAHU, HI

HEADQUARTERS 11TH BOMBARDMENT GROUP (H)
Office of the Commanding Officer
APO # 241

25 September 1944

To those young men with silver wings who have recently joined the 11th Bombardment Group, greetings:

We welcome you to one of the three oldest bombardment groups in the Army Air Forces (from a World War II combat standpoint). We are glad to have you here. We need you. We know that you come to us physically fit and well supplied with the old grey matter. Being young Americans of high caliber your courage is unquestioned. You can take justifiable pride in being a part of this organization. This Group was organized 1 February 1940 as Headquarters and Headquarters Squadron, 11th Bombardment Group (M), 18th Wing, Hawaiian Air Force, and in December 1940 was redesignated as a heavy bombardment group. Based at Hickam Field December 7, 1941, the 11th Group sustained heavy casualties among its ground and flight personnel. In June 1942, elements of the 11th Group formed a part of the aerial vanguard in the battle of Midway, the turning point in the Pacific War. From July until November 1942, the 11th was based in the Solomons and operated under extremely adverse conditions with such high efficiency and spirit that it was awarded a Presidential Citation. One of the outstanding accomplishments was its part in the battle of Guadalcanal. On 17 April 1943, the 11th Group became a part of the 7th AAF, and during October began its part in the Gilbert-Marshall-Caroline campaign. It has since moved from Funafuti to Tarawa, and on 31 March 1944 to Kwajalein. We will shortly be on the move again - closer than ever to the heart of the Japanese Empire.

You come to us well trained for the task at hand, yet, unless you have had previous combat experience, there will be many little things for you to learn, and it is with that in mind that this is being written. You will not be cross-examined on its contents. But if you are with us in wanting to get this war over with as soon as possible, and with as few casualties as possible, read on:

1. <u>KNOW YOUR AIRPLANE</u>

a. Read about it -- Talk about it -- Think about it. You can never know too much about it. Ask yourself the following questions, and if you don't know the answers, go after them. These are only samples of many similar questions that could be asked.

b. What would you do if you lost two engines over enemy territory? What would you do if about half your control cables were shot out in the bomb bay? At least some of the pilots to whom these things have happened have come back to tell about it. Would you know how to lower the landing gear if your hydraulic system was shot out? Are you sure your engineer would know? If one of your main fuel lines was cut by flak and you needed the gas in that system for your other engines, would your engineer know how to get it for you? Above the center section is a pump that transfers the fuel from your wing tip tanks. If this pump stuck or shorted out, could you, or couldn't you, use that fuel? We all hope that none of these things ever happen to you, but we can't guarantee it, and out there you're on your own, you and your crew.

- 1 -

SEPTEMBER 25, 1944

2. <u>SPARE THE HORSES</u>

a. Now, about those engines: The book says that you may use so many rev's and so many inches going up, coming down, here, there, etc., but Old Man Past Experience says they will take you farther (and bring you back) if you baby them along whenever possible. Of course, if you ever need them to get away from Tojo quickly, push them against the peg, and God be with you.

3. <u>WHO AND WHAT IS A CREW CHIEF</u>?

a. He is the key man in the little organization that cares for your plane. Get acquainted with him. He is as interested in your success as you are. When you return from a flight and have found anything wrong, be sure he has a full report of the trouble. He will do his best to have it right next time. Many an airplane has taken off with some previous malfunction uncorrected because no one wrote it upon the Form 1, or because the engineer forgot to tell the crew chief.

b. The Form 1, by the way, is the crew chief's report to you on the condition of the airplane, and, when you get back, it is your report to him on the same subject. Incidentally, the crew chief often works while we sleep and while we rest, and will miss a meal or a night's rest to have her ready for you on time. Why not drop down once in a while and see what he does to the old jalopy when it is back in camp? You might both profit from such a visit.

Always remember that the goal of the 11th Bombardment Group is: TO DROP ALL OUR BOMBS ON THE ASSIGNED TARGET WITH A MINIMUM LOSS OF OUR AIRCRAFT AND COMBAT CREWS.

HAPPY LANDINGS!

R. L. Waldron

R. L. WALDRON
Colonel, Air Corps
Commanding

- 2 -

Welcome to new recruits, September 25, 1944.

"Bolivar Jr" B-24M-20-CO Liberator, 431st BS, 11th BG, 7th AF Agana Airfield, Guam, Marianas Island.

A B-24 Liberator plane dropping bombs over Germany.

Oahu, Hawaii
September 30th

Dear Dad + Bee——

Finally we finished up our training missions when we flew our last this week. By the time you get this letter I'll almost certainly be on my way to destination unknown. As I've said before you can follow my whereabouts by watching the doings of the 7th AAF Liberators in the daily papers. Incidentally, enclosed is a clipping from a local paper that I thought might interest you. It gives some idea of the type of flying etc we're up against out here. It won't be any tea party but we're all pretty anxious to get going and take a crack at the Nips. From now on you'll have to cross your fingers for me to get my thirty-five missions completed. Would that it were as easily done as said!

I was terribly upset last week when I received the Grapevine and a clipping from Pam with the news of the death of Jimmy Levy. I don't recall if you ever met him, but he went on one of the skiing trips to Conway with Pam et moi. We were quite close and he was really a great guy. Somehow I didn't think he'd lose out in the war but the odds were against him and he was shot down over Elba. A really swell kid I'll never forget. It

OAHU, HI

always seems that's it's the best who have to pay the price of war while the no-goods get by untouched. I don't mean to seem bitter but Jimmy's death really hit me a low blow.

I wasn't too surprised but yet very happy to hear of Timmy's engagement. Delia's wedding sounded swell and I'm sure she made a lovely bride. (Just entre nous, I can't picture she and George hitting it off but maybe she's changed alot.) I hate to hear of everybody getting hitched up because there won't be anybody left for the poor fools who are off at the wars. All I've got to hear is that a certain person is engaged, and I believe I'd settle over here on some small island. Enough said!

I was certainly glad to hear that Don got home for a few days. From what I gather, he must have had a fine time while in town. The St Regis and Stork club sounded rather gay. What I wouldn't give for a night of that now! By the way, be sure to tell Eddie Hilson that I think he's a "stinker" for stealing away my gal when I'm away and can't defend myself. Be sure to kid him along for me.

Many thanks for all your letters which have been coming through quite regularly of late. Please be sure to keep writing regularly because mail will mean more than ever once we get down under. As soon as I have a new address I'll write you but until then continue to use my present address. I doubt if I'll have a chance to write much more before we pull out because we'll be kinda busy, so don't expect to hear from me for awhile. Incidentally Dad, you wondered about the dates on my letters. I believe that the postmark is put on in Frisco since that's where we pay postage from. Mail from here to the mainland is send on a basis as of Frisco to where it's going—that is packages go to Frisco for nothing, and you're charged rates from there to where it's going. I think that explains it because the dates that I put inside the letter is always accurate when I write it. Incidentally Bee, the film hasn't arrived yet but I'm sure it will after awhile because most packages go by boat. I'll let you know as soon they do arrive.

Well all, I guess that's about it for now. Please be sure to send my letters around to all the boys from now on because I doubt if I'll have too much time to write from here on — bear with me and I'll write as often as possible.

My love to you all —

Bobby

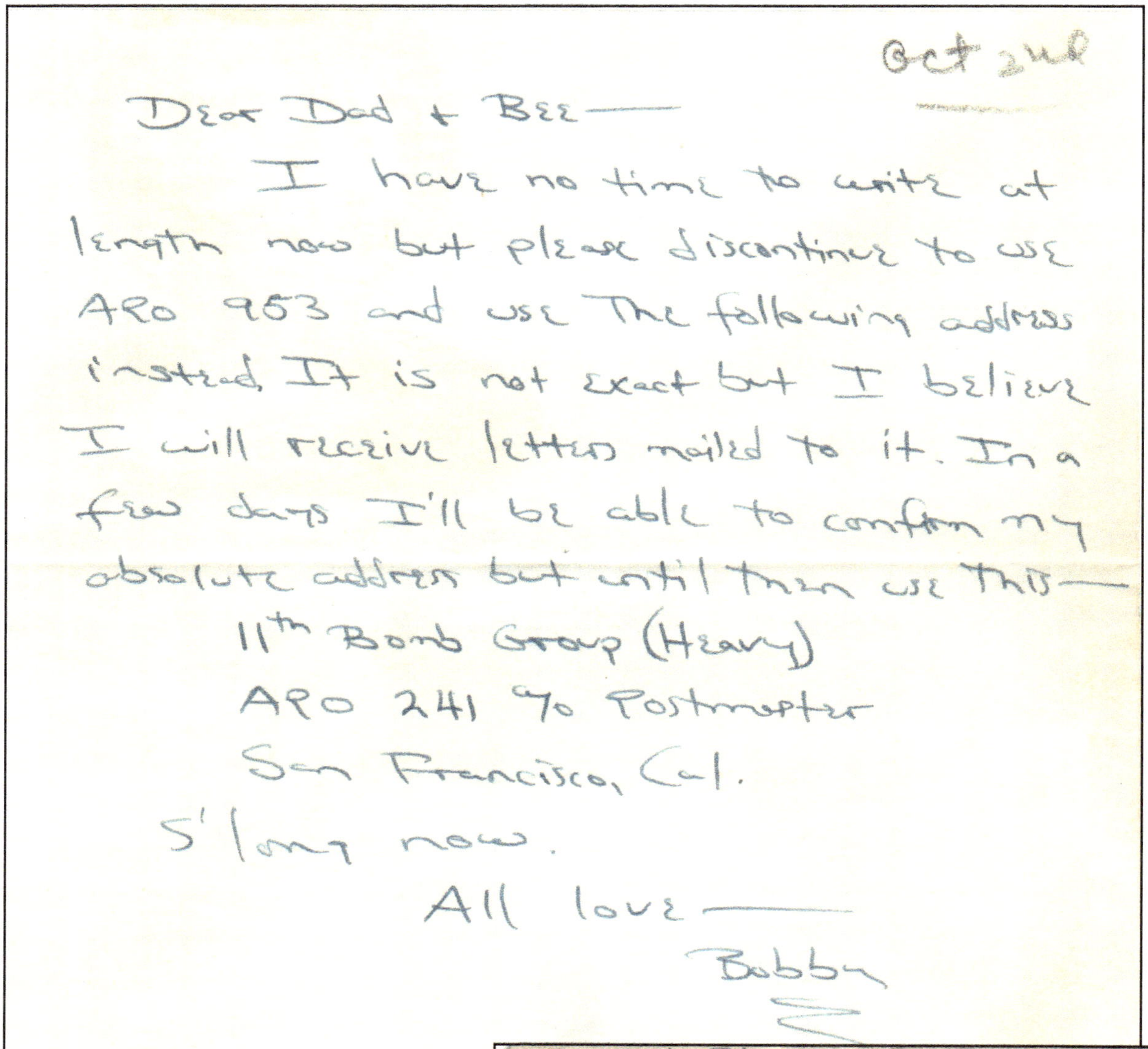

Oct 2nd

Dear Dad + Bee—

I have no time to write at length now but please discontinue to use APO 953 and use the following address instead. It is not exact but I believe I will receive letters mailed to it. In a few days I'll be able to confirm my absolute address but until then use this—

11th Bomb Group (Heavy)
APO 241 % Postmaster
San Francisco, Cal.

S'long now.

All love—

Bobby

Lt. Robert L. Stone 0-696041
VII Bomber Command (Tng. Det. Heavy)
APO 953 % Postmaster
San Francisco, Cal.

Mr. J. C. Stone
375 Park Avenue
New York City (22)
N.Y.

Robert Stone

OCTOBER 2, 1944/SCRAPBOOK PHOTOGRAPHS

HAWAII IN THE 1940's

The Royal Hawaiian Hotel (1)
Occupied by the Navy

When Bob finished his training on the U.S. Mainland he was assigned with his crew to the Pacific area for combat duty and flew from a "secret" airbase called "Kahuka" on Oahu—far from Diamond Head and Honolulu. During this final stage of training they dropped bombs to practice on targets in the ocean and on Enewetak Atoll.

When Bob was at Hertz in the 1970's the company was a sponsor of the Hawaian Open Golf Tournament and Bob made his first trip back since the war. I still remember his amazement as he looked out the window of the plane at the strip of tall hotels lining Waikiki Beach as his memories were reflected in these photos from his scrapbook. One day we hired a driver who knew about the "secret" airstrip as Bob knew he could never find it on his own. It was totally overgrown with weeds and we were told that it had been used as a drag strip before it became totally useless from decay and disuse. In remembering this vision now it reminds me of scenes from the 1949 movie "Twelve O'Clock High" when actor Dean Jagger returns to an abandoned airfield in England and relives events from WWII. Bob and I watched this movie together many times and I now wonder what memories this triggered in him when he returned to Kahuka—I just remember him saying that it did not look like anything he remembered and the missions from this field were only practice runs and not the real thing so maybe the memories were not indelible.

Surfboarders at Waikiki
with Diamond Head in the
background (3)

Looking down on Pali Road (3)

neapple Field, Maui (1.)

Halemaumau, Hawaii Nat'l. Park
Hilo, Hawaii

Hanalei Valley, Kauai (1)

Kau Kau Korner (1)

"Kau Kau Korner"
(Crossroads of the Pacific)

The Kau Kau Korner was a 24-hour drive-in at the intersection of Kalakaua Avenue and Kapiolani Blvd. at the entrance to Waikiki. This art deco structure existed from the early 1940s until 1960. Its well-known sign was a landmark for tourists.

AWAITING FIRST MISSION
MARSHALL ISLANDS

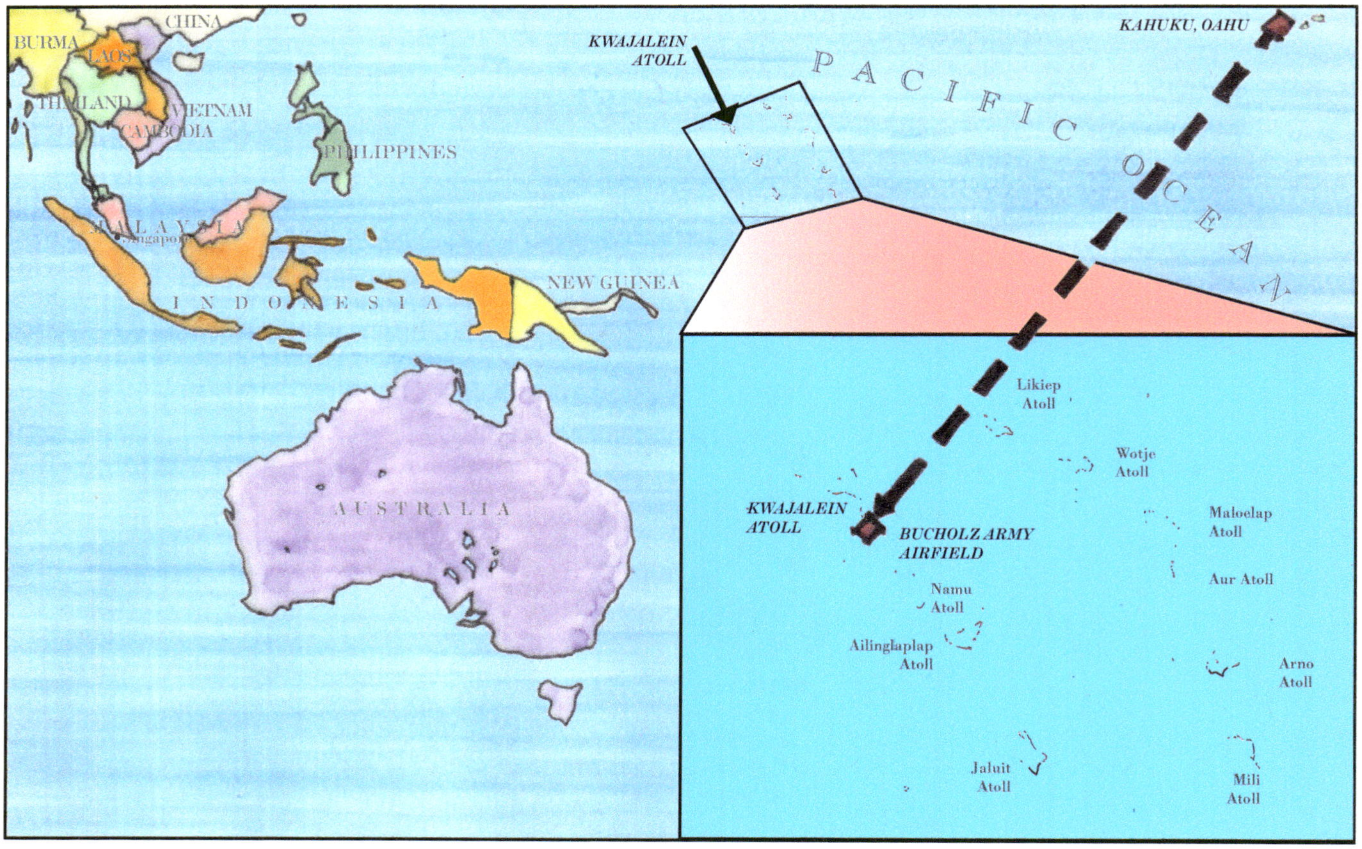

OCTOBER 1944

1) Headquarters at Kwajalien
largest atoll in the Marshalls
Arrived on October 7, 1944

2) Water tank riddled by
U.S. bombardment when
island was in Jap hands.

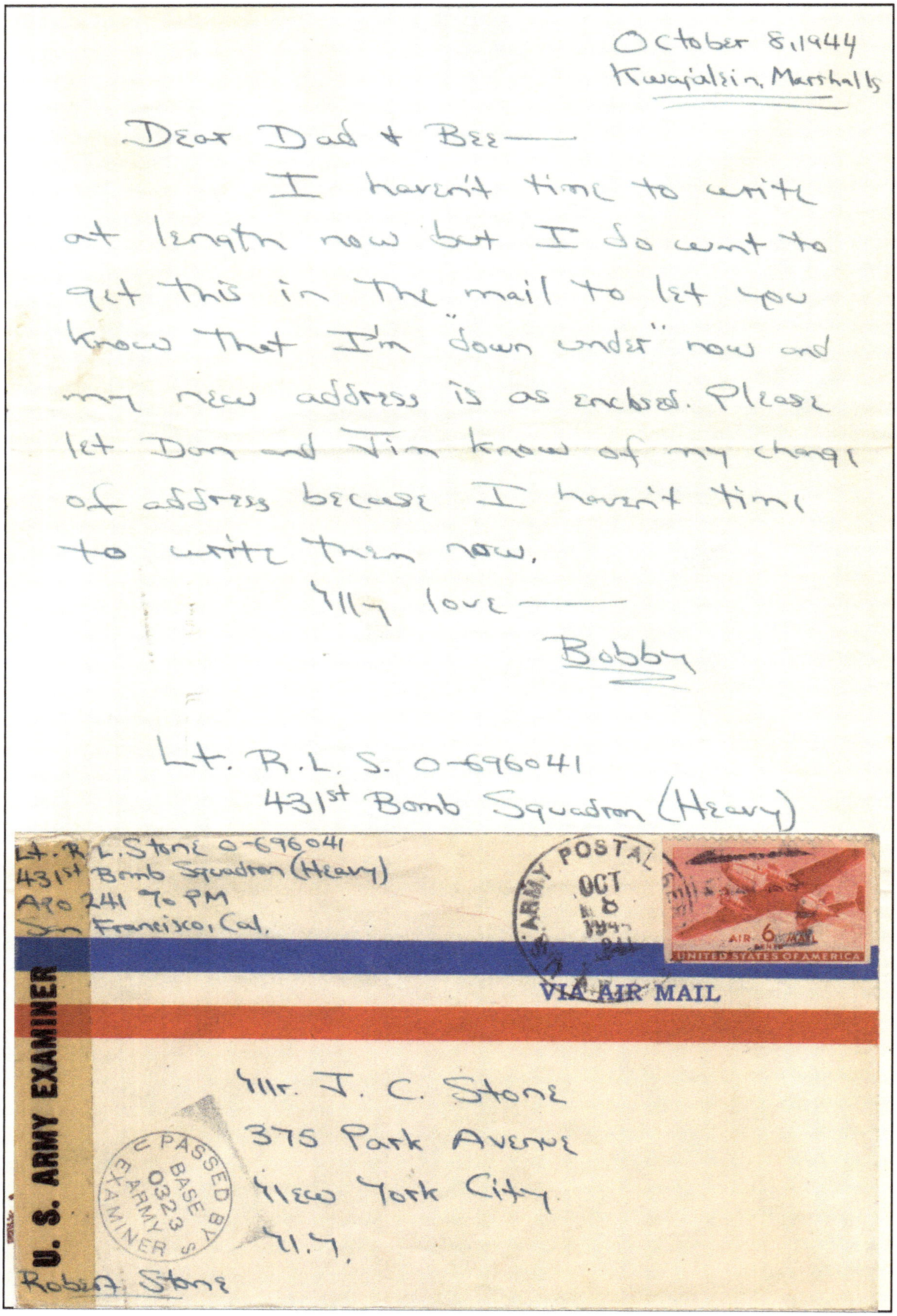

October 8, 1944
Kwajalein, Marshalls

Dear Dad & Bee—

I haven't time to write at length now but I do want to get this in the mail to let you know that I'm "down under" now and my new address is as enclosed. Please let Don and Jim know of my change of address because I haven't time to write them now.

My love—

Bobby

Lt. R. L. S. 0-696041
431st Bomb Squadron (Heavy)

Lt. R. L. Stone 0-696041
431st Bomb Squadron (Heavy)
APO 241 % PM
San Francisco, Cal.

U.S. ARMY POSTAL
OCT 8 1944

AIR 6 MAIL
UNITED STATES OF AMERICA

VIA AIR MAIL

U. S. ARMY EXAMINER

PASSED BY BASE ARMY EXAMINER 0323

Mr. J. C. Stone
375 Park Avenue
New York City
N.Y.

Robert Stone

OCTOBER 8, 1944

Kwajalien, Marshalls

October 8, 1944

Dear Dad, Bee, Don, Jim, et al—

Well at long last we're down under after spending three months on Oahu. We came down by A.T.C.[41] Stopping off at a small navy base overnight. Surprisingly enough we're allowed to tell the name of our base here. I won't try to tell you too much about this atoll because there's not much here to tell about. The island took such a pounding from the U.S. airforce that there isn't a live tree on the island. The place is absolutely flat and completely devoid of any plant life. All of the buildings on the island are very crude and kinda makeshift.

The fellows down here are really good gents. We arrived yesterday afternoon and by supper we had met most of the boys in our squadron. They are all very friendly and have done everything possible to make us feel at home and a part of the outfit. Some of them are old veterans finishing up their last few missions while others are have only been out here a short while. The way it is now you have to fly thirty-five missions before returning to the States. Usually it takes around six or eight months to finish up. After each fifteen missions you're sent on a rest leave for ten days on Oahu.

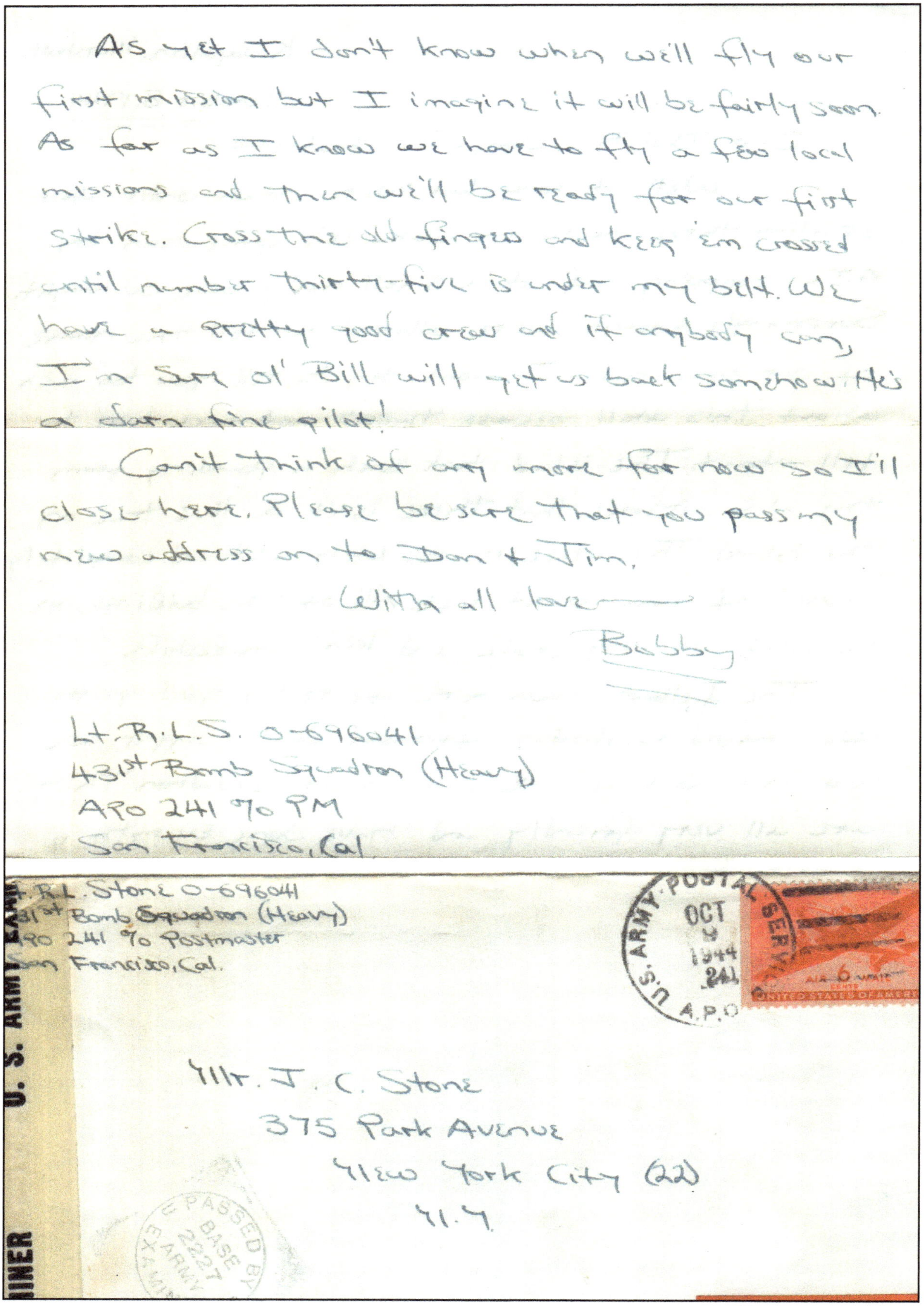

As yet I don't know when we'll fly our first mission but I imagine it will be fairly soon. As far as I know we have to fly a few local missions and then we'll be ready for our first strike. Cross the old fingers and keep 'em crossed until number thirty-five is under my belt. We have a pretty good crew and if anybody can, I'm sure ol' Bill will get us back somehow. He's a darn fine pilot!

Can't think of any more for now so I'll close here. Please be sure that you pass my new address on to Don & Jim.

With all love—

Bobby

Lt. R.L.S. 0-696041
431st Bomb Squadron (Heavy)
APO 241 % PM
San Francisco, Cal

OCTOBER 8, 1944/THE BATTLE OF KWAJALEIN

1) Jap grave with estimated dead of 300.

THE BATTLE OF KWAJALEIN

These gravesites are believed to be from the Battle of Kwajalein, a four-day battle, which started on January 31, 1944 and ended with the Allies capturing the islands on February 3, 1944. In Bob's letter dated October 8, 1944 (on previous pages) he explains "I won't try to tell you about this atoll because there's not much here to tell about. The island took such a pounding from the U.S. Air Force that there isn't a live tree on the island. The place is absolutely flat and completely devoid of any plant life."

In October of 1944—about eight months after the battle—Bob was stationed at the Kwajalein Atoll, one of 24 coral atolls (composed of 1,156 islands and inlets) which make up the Marshall Islands in the Pacific Ocean.

In the Battle of Kwajalein, the Allies captured the three major islands of the atoll: Kwajalein, Roi and Namur. The battle was won using B-24 Liberators, Navy ships, the 4th Marine Division and the Army's 7th Infantry Division. The Japanese were just outnumbered and under prepared.

It is estimated that 7,870 Japanese soldiers were either killed or wounded during the battle, and 105 were captured. The Allies losses were estimated at 372 killed and 1,592 wounded.

This battle was a very important step in penetrating the outer-ring of Japan's defenses.

After the seizure of the islands, the United States converted the former Japanese naval base into a major American base and staging area for further campaigns against the Japanese. It is now known as Bucholz Army Airfield. [42]

2) Another Jap site with estimated dead of 500.

October 10th, 1944

Dear Dad + Bee—

There's very little in the way of news from down here but a few lines are in order to say that all goes well with R.L.S.

The last few days were kinda dull around here because most of the boys were away on a raid. We didn't go with them so we still have our first mission to look forward to. It's hard to believe that after all this time we're actually going to fly in the real thing. Ugh, what a thought!

Today I walked around the atoll taking a few pictures for my scrap book. There are still a bunch of Jap installations with gaping holes in them from U.S. gun fire. Actually there's very little

OCTOBER 10, 1944

on the island worthy of a picture. It's just a flat coral atoll with no plant life of any sort, any more.

The two big gripes here are the food and the weather. Of course, we eat rations which aren't the most appetizing food in the world. The weather is terribly hot and very sultry. Most of the boys wear short pants and half-sleeved shirts. Even so it's unbearably unpleasant because you're constantly perspiring, even right after showering.

As yet I haven't heard from you down here but I imagine I will in a day or so. Some mail has been forwarded from APO 953 but none from any of you. Write often.

Love —

Bobby

Kwajalien, the Marshalls
October 15th, 1944

Dear Dad + Bee—

There's very little to relate since we're still sweating out our first mission. By the time you receive this letter we should have had our first taste of combat.

The other night we had some entertainment when Betty Hutton put on a show for us. Unfortunately the program was cut short when she became sick. I think that it was a combination of her wild antics ~~&~~ and the heat—they just didn't mix.

The weather down here is really getting me. It's so sweltering during the day time that we go around with very little clothing on but none the less perspire continually. It's a sultry heat that's very unpleasant, and tends to make you feel uncomfortable.

OCTOBER 15, 1944

As yet I haven't received mail from any of you. I did get one letter from Pam that was forwarded from APO 953. Perhaps some mail will be coming along from you in a day or so. I hope so because mail call is the big occasion of the day down here.

All of the boys are down in the mouth right now since an order came through requiring forty missions. It always used to be thirty and then became thirty five and now forty. Some of the boys were almost finished and would have been home by Christmas until the new order came through. Now it will take about a year to finish up and that's not a very comforting thought. Oh well, C'est la guerre.

Write often,

All love —

Bobby

40 COMBAT MISSIONS
MARIANA ISLANDS

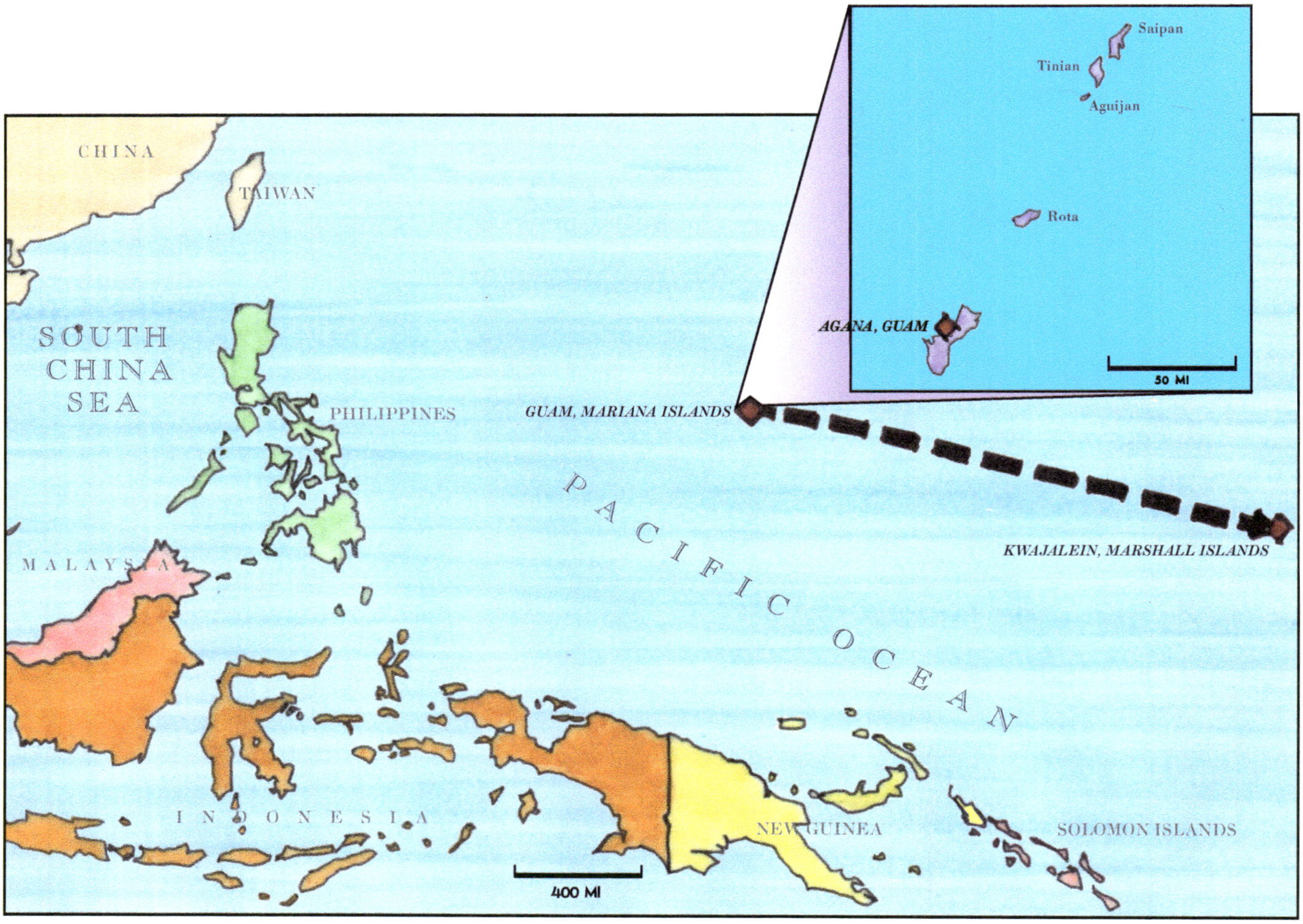

OCTOBER 1944–MAY 1945

1) Shore-line of Guam.

2) Another view of the picturesque coast-line.

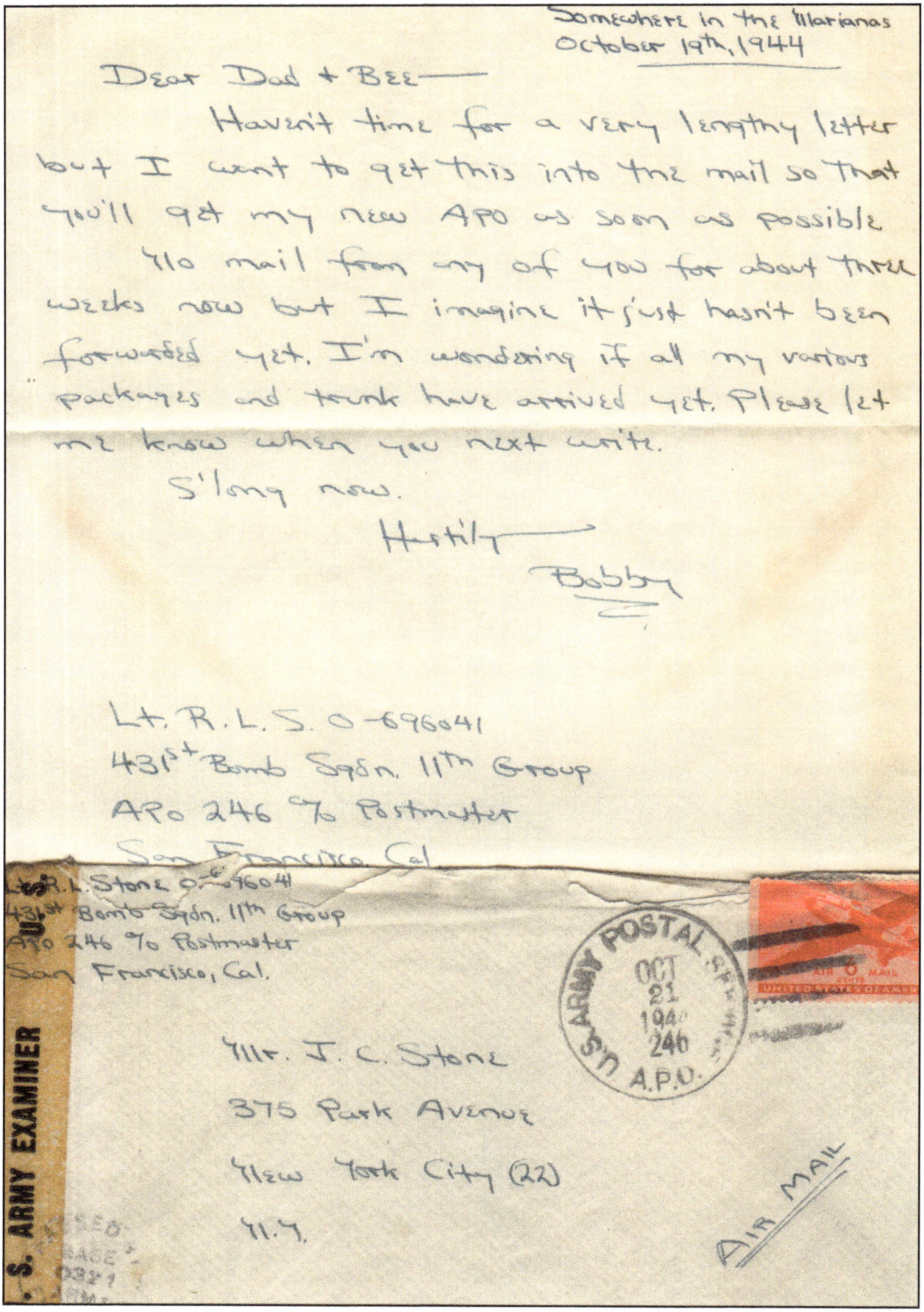

Somewhere in the Marianas
October 19th, 1944

Dear Dad + Bee—

Haven't time for a very lengthy letter but I want to get this into the mail so that you'll get my new APO as soon as possible.

No mail from any of you for about three weeks now but I imagine it just hasn't been forwarded yet. I'm wondering if all my various packages and trunk have arrived yet. Please let me know when you next write.

S'long now.

Hastily—

Bobby

Lt. R. L. S. O-696041
431st Bomb Sqdn. 11th Group
APO 246 c/o Postmaster
San Francisco, Cal

Lt. R. L. Stone O-696041
431st Bomb Sqdn. 11th Group
APO 246 c/o Postmaster
San Francisco, Cal.

U.S. ARMY POSTAL SERVICE
OCT 21 1944
246
A.P.O.

AIR 6 MAIL CENTS
UNITED STATES OF AMERICA

U.S. ARMY EXAMINER

Mr. J. C. Stone
375 Park Avenue
New York City (22)
N.Y.

AIR MAIL

OCTOBER 19-21, 1944

Somewhere in the Marianas

October 21, 1944

Dear Dad + Bee——

Finally I have some time to write, and bring you up to date on my new set-up, that is as much as possible.

As you can see I am now up somewhere in the Marianas. As yet the disclosure of the name of our island is strictly taboo so that's that. Needless to say life here is very rugged—just like you see in the movies. We are living in tents which we've tried to set up but they don't make very good quarters. The first night we had no mosquito nets and we were almost carried away. We spent most of the day yesterday digging up the roots and grass in our tents, and that plus the aid of our nets (we procured from the navy) made for lots better sleeping last night.

For the moment there isn't much more that I can write about this place. Until we get everything running smoothly it will be a fairly rough existance. At the present we are eating rations and frankly there's nothing less palatable. In fact, on most of the islands the big gripe is nearly always the food. Oh well, when you can't get fresh things that's the best you can do—eat rations. All of the boys are getting pretty tired of eating coconuts. You see our tents are in a big grove of them and you can just step outside

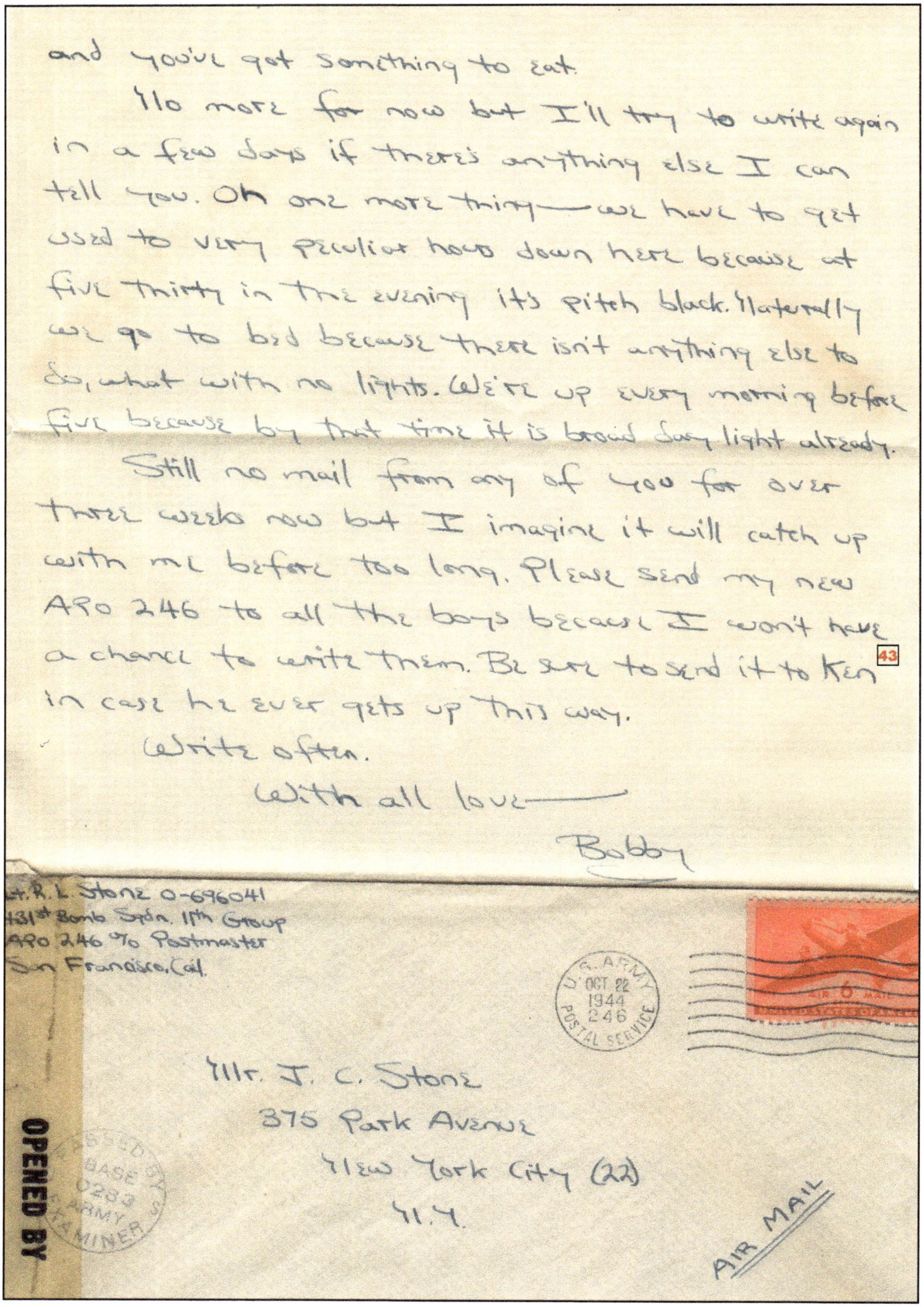

and you've got something to eat.

No more for now but I'll try to write again in a few days if there's anything else I can tell you. Oh one more thing—we have to get used to very peculiar hours down here because at five thirty in the evening it's pitch black. Naturally we go to bed because there isn't anything else to do, what with no lights. We're up every morning before five because by that time it is broad day light already.

Still no mail from any of you for over three weeks now but I imagine it will catch up with me before too long. Please send my new APO 246 to all the boys because I won't have a chance to write them. Be sure to send it to Ken in case he ever gets up this way. 43

Write often.

With all love—

Bobby

Lt. R. L. Stone 0-696041
431st Bomb. Sqdn. 11th Group
APO 246 % Postmaster
San Francisco, Cal.

U.S. ARMY OCT 22 1944 246 POSTAL SERVICE

Mr. J. C. Stone
375 Park Avenue
New York City (22)
N.Y.

OPENED BY

PASSED BY BASE 0283 ARMY EXAMINER

AIR MAIL

OCTOBER 21, 1944 SCRAPBOOK PHOTOGRAPHS

1) Some typical thicket country, of which there is alot on Guam

2) A church in Agana that was demolished by Yank bombs before the invasion.

1) The airfield on Yap Island. Our target on our first missio flown off of Guam.

The Marianas
October 25, 1944

Dear Dad + Bee——

Just a few lines from your Pacific reporter to say that all goes well with R.L.S. We finally flew our first mission and I only hope that the next thirty-nine work out as successfully. It's no tea party out here but with a bit of luck I ought to get by alright.

The last couple of days we have been busy trying to make our tents and our area more liveable. We've made some crude tables, shelves, and racks from a bunch of old bomb cases. Everything is still in a state of being organized and so there's still lots to be done before things are running smoothly. After living down here I doubt if I'll ever want to go on another camping trip — I'll have had just about enough outdoor life!

I was awfully glad to receive a letter from you Bee, that was written on the 10th to APO 241 and forwarded on. That's the first mail I've had from home in nearly a month. I'm sure you've all written but somehow none of your letter have caught up to me yet. I imagine after awhile I'll get a whole bunch of letters all at once. Many thanks for the set of pictures. They certainly were good ones. I'm certainly glad that my trunk arrived in good

OCTOBER 25, 1944

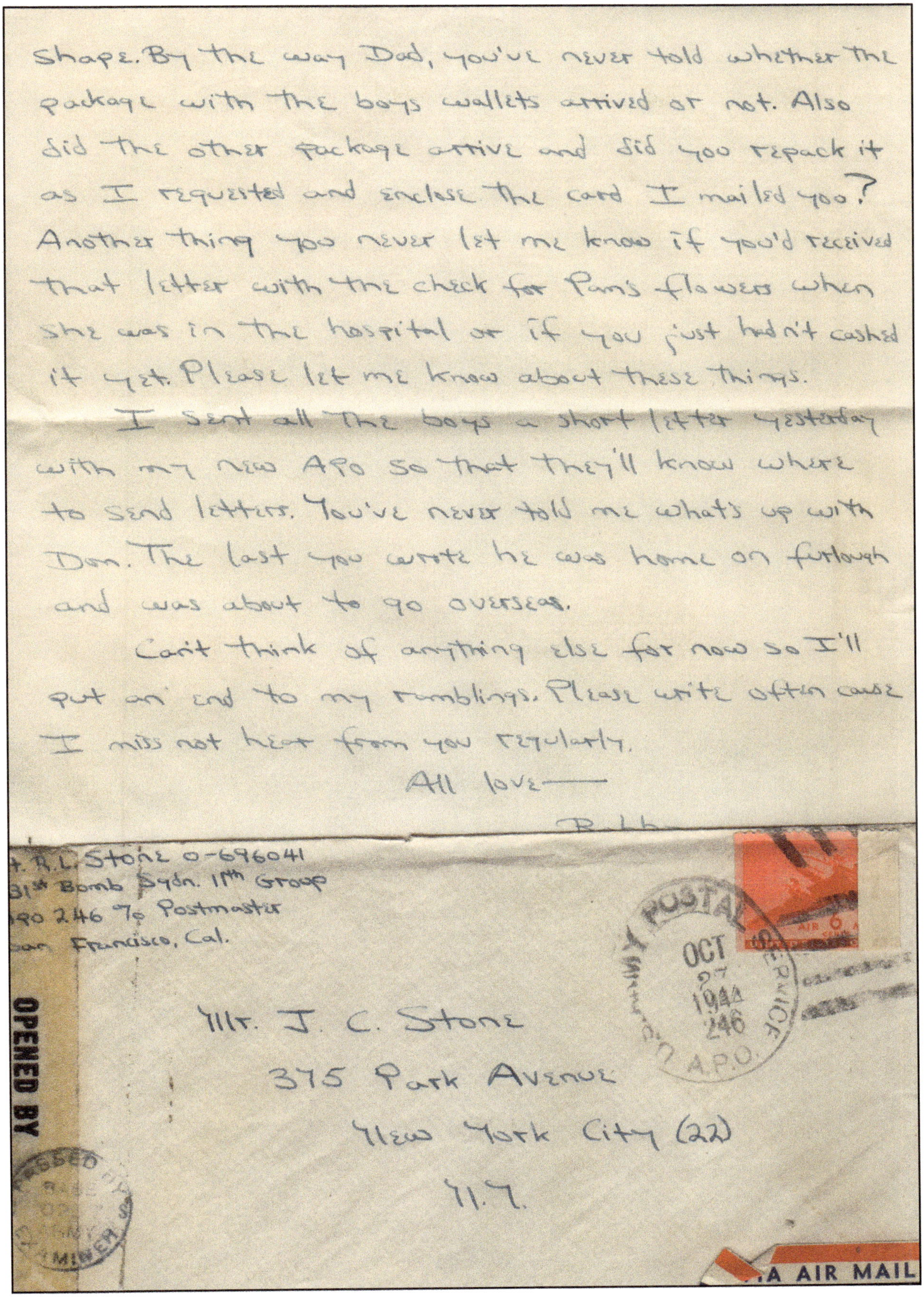

shape. By the way Dad, you've never told whether the package with the boys wallets arrived or not. Also did the other package arrive and did you repack it as I requested and enclose the card I mailed you? Another thing you never let me know if you'd received that letter with the check for Pam's flowers when she was in the hospital or if you just hadn't cashed it yet. Please let me know about these things.

I sent all the boys a short letter yesterday with my new APO so that they'll know where to send letters. You've never told me what's up with Don. The last you wrote he was home on furlough and was about to go overseas.

Can't think of anything else for now so I'll put an end to my ramblings. Please write often cause I miss not hear from you regularly.

All love—

Bob

t. R.L. Stone O-696041
31st Bomb Sqdn. 11th Group
PO 246 % Postmaster
an Francisco, Cal.

POSTAL SERVICE
OCT 27 1944 246
A.P.O.

AIR 6

OPENED BY

PASSED BY EXAMINER

Mr. J. C. Stone
375 Park Avenue
New York City (22)
N.Y.

VIA AIR MAIL

The Marianas

October 30, 1944

Dear Dad + Bee—

Yesterday a big batch of back mail caught up with me and I became the proud possessor of nineteen letters—six of them were from your way so I guess a few lines are in order. Now you can understand why I hadn't heard from you for about three weeks—one letter was dated September.

I'm glad to hear that all my various packages arrived alright. As far as the trunk goes I didn't have anything in the top so it's o.k. too. I was there when the censor put his seal on because I went through it with him.

Life here continues about the same as ever. Our tents are becoming more and more liveable as we construct new articles of furniture. The last few days we've had a bit of rain and consequently our tent is a mess—you get out of bed into the mud. I never was cut out for this camping life but I'm certainly getting a dose of it now.

Our chow continues to be C rations and frankly I'd like to meet the guy who first invented them. Yesterday we got our first ration of warm coke and beer. I never thought I'd be able to drink warm beer but strangely enough I am!

OCTOBER 30, 1944

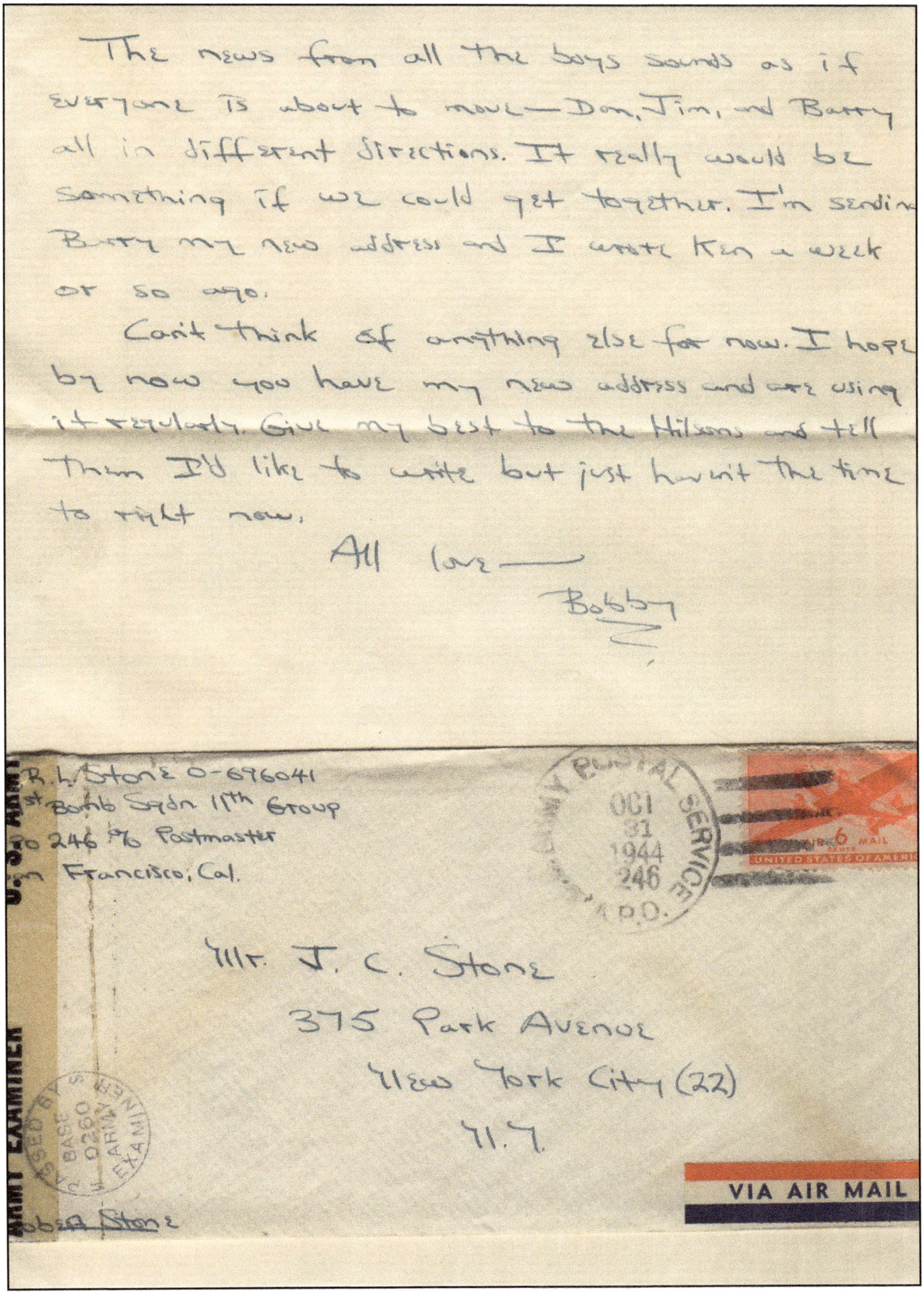

The news from all the boys sounds as if everyone is about to move—Don, Jim, and Barry all in different directions. It really would be something if we could get together. I'm sendin Barry my new address and I wrote Ken a week or so ago.

Can't think of anything else for now. I hope by now you have my new address and are using it regularly. Give my best to the Hilsons and tell them I'd like to write but just haven't the time to right now.

All love—

Bobby

R. L. Stone O-696041
st Bomb Sqdn. 11th Group
o 246 % Postmaster
n Francisco, Cal.

ARMY POSTAL SERVICE
OCT 31 1944
246
A.P.O.

AIR 6 MAIL
UNITED STATES OF AMERICA

Mr. J. C. Stone
375 Park Avenue
New York City (22)
N.Y.

U. S. ARMY
ARMY EXAMINER

PASSED BY
BASE 0260
ARMY EXAMINER

obert Stone

VIA AIR MAIL

The Marianas
November 4th

Dear Dad + Bee——

For a change I have some news that I'm sure you'll be interested to hear —— yesterday after much searching I ran into Barry's[44] outfit and believe it or not he's stationed only a few miles away. Of all the islands in the blue Pacific we ended up a few miles apart —— if that doesn't prove it's a small world, I'll eat my hat.

Barry seemed in the best of spirits and none the worse for the life he's leading out here. I met all his tentmates who seem to be good gents, all of them quite typical of the young kids in the marines. They all complain of the rotten deal that the marines get but none of them would swap places with anyone. If all goes well and I'm not out on a strike, Barry plans to come over to visit me, in a day or so. You should be at ease about the old marine Bee, because he really never seemed in better shape both physically and mentally. Frankly I think the life is doing him a world of good!

We got another strike under our belt since I last wrote you. It was a lots tougher mission than our first but everything worked out alright. Just keep the old fingers crossed for me and who knows I'll probably get through this mess alright.

NOVEMBER 4, 1944

Conditions here at the camp are getting better every day as the site becomes more and more built up. Our mess hall is lots better now although the rations still don't pass for food, in my opinion.

What's the latest news from Don? I haven't heard from him since I was back at APO 953. I'm wondering if he's left for overseas yet.

That's about all for now — write often!

All love —

Bobby

The Marianas

October 5th, 1944 [45]

Dear Dad & Bee—

Even though I wrote you a long letter a day or so ago I thought I'd write a line or two to say that I had Barry over for lunch today. He came over with a couple of friends and I took them to the best chow we've had since we've been down here—believe me they really ate heartily as if they hadn't had a bite to eat in ages. Frankly I haven't eaten that well in a long time myself.

This afternoon I took them all down to the line and we went through a ship and I showed them all around. Then later on I drove them back to their camp which is only about twenty minutes away.

As I said the other day, Barry is in swell shape and it was fun having him over today. Some time when we're not flying a strike I'm going to try to take him up on a local test hop, if I possibly can.

Must run now.

With all love—

Bobby

The Marianas
November 6th

Dear Mildred + Eddie—

For some time now I've intended to write you but somehow I just haven't gotten to it until today. It always seems that we're busy (usually fixing up some contraption in our tent) even when we're not out on a mission.

As always it was swell to receive your letter, Mildred. It certainly was a crime about Wilkie[46] and I'm sure it cut deeply with you because of your close association with him. His loss is one that will be felt by the entire nation because I believe he was a great man.

As you probably know I'm up here in the Marianas flying my missions. I've already flown a couple of missions and so far it hasn't been too rough and I only hope the rest of my missions come out as luckily.

Our conditions out here aren't too good but they are improving as we get more organized. Life in a tent and eating C rations doesn't appeal to me somehow. I don't believe I'll ever go on a camping trip again.

A couple of days ago I searched around the island and tracked down Barry's outfit. Yes believe it or not, he's stationed not ten miles away from me. Isn't that a coincidence that out of all the islands in the Pacific we should end up in the same place!

A few days ago I received that long letter from John because it was sent to my old A.P.O. He certainly writes an interesting and extremely clever letter. I'd like to write him but I just haven't time now so please give him my best when you next write him.

I must run along now and put an end to my rambling. I know this is a dull letter but I did want you to know I'd received your letters and appreciated hearing from you.

My best to you all.

Fondly—

Bobby

The Marianas
November 14th

Dear Dad + Bee—

Been rather busy all week and this is the first time I've had a chance to dash off a few lines. Everything is about the same as ever out here and life goes on as usual. I've now got in four missions which is only a step in the right direction—forty! As each mission comes up the great tenseness and anxiety gets less as you become more accustomed to what happens. I guess you're always scared of the flak bursting around your ship and the attacking fighters but still you learn to keep calm enough to perform your duties.

The mail is coming in lots better now and I've already received mail to APO 246. Some letters came through in eight and some in eleven days. It certainly must have been swell to have both Don and Jim home for a few days. Be sure to keep me posted as to their new addresses and whereabouts when you receive them.

On Sunday when I came back from Church Barry and two of his tentmates were waiting for me I took them all to a delicious Sunday dinner—we really had a super special meal. As I said in my last letter, he's in fine spirits. I still can't get over the fact that we should end up so close together out here—it's almost incredible.

You've asked several times if I'd seen Jack Naylor and as yet I haven't. I've had numerous opportunities to call on him but somehow I just haven't gotten around to looking him up. Perhaps I'll give him a buzz the next time I'm up his way.

As yet the Xmas box you sent has not arrived but I'm almost certain that it will be forwarded on eventually. I still haven't gotten the film that you sent Bee, but I'm hoping it will catch up to me sometime — I sure hope so! Speaking of Xmas Dad, please be sure to mail Don + Jim's gifts in plenty of time to their new addresses.

Guess that's about all for now cause there's so little to tell you about our existance out here. Our strikes of course can't be discussed so we're kinda limited on what we can write.

Let's hear from you often.

All love —

Bobby

NOVEMBER 14-17, 1944/NEWSPAPER CLIPPINGS

THE NEW YORK TIMES, F[R]IDA

Global Bombing: Allies Blasting the

AY, NOVEMBER 17, 1944.

Enemy in Three Theatres of War

"Like a fish in a rain barrel" is the description applied by United States Army Seventh Air For
mbardiers to this raid on Iwo Island, wherein they picked off Japanese planes parked on the airst
and is only 650 miles from Tokyo.

OVER HAHA JIMA, one of the northernmost of the Jap bases much bombed by the 7th AAF from the Marianas, soars a flight of Liberators. The two B-24's are "Madame Pele" (left) and "Hellcat Belle."

F ★ 8 *November 28, 1944*

Good shot of our formation leaving Haha Jima after a raid on shipping in the harbor.

Hellcat Belle pictured at left, which we stripped a few missions later on.

The Marianas

December 7th, 1944 [47]

Dear Dad + Bee—

I'm afraid I've sadly neglected my correspondence again but we've been fairly busy. Our missions are coming along fairly well and so far we've flown ten. Your mail is very slow in coming through and lately your letters have taken almost four weeks. I only hope mine aren't as badly delayed.

So far only one Christmas package has arrived but I still have my fingers crossed that the others will show up eventually. The box from Robert Day Dean's [48] arrived in fine shape Dad, and I want to thank you for the delicious sweets. Nothing was spoiled and it was a real treat to feast on some good cookies and candies, after always eating C-rations.

As you can see by the enclosed check I am taking your advice about the war bond—as a matter of fact I've had it on my mind to do something along that line for quite some time. I trust that you will take care of putting it in a vault for me so that I will have it when I get home. As long as the bonds are redeemable for ready cash whenever you want, I think it's a swell investment. It might as well be put to good use now as long as I can get ahold of the money whenever I need it in the future

Life out here continues the same as ever. Our living conditions have improved a great deal and our chow isn't too bad. Occasionally we even get a fresh meal. Everything considered, it's not too bad. Between raids is the worst because you have a chance for boredom and loneliness to set in. As long as you're busy it isn't too bad but when you're idle it's demoralizing.

I haven't seen Barry for quite some time because I've been away on missions the last two times he came over. If all goes well, I may see him this coming Sunday.

Guess that's about it for now. Let's hear from you as often as possible because your letters are always welcome.

My love to you——

Bobby

The Marianas
December 12th, 1944

Dear Dad & Bee—

It seems as though I just wrote you a few days ago but here I am with time on my hands between missions, so I'll scratch off a few lines. You've been swell about writing and your letters have been coming through quite regularly. All incoming mail takes anywhere from two weeks to a little over a month.

I finally heard from Jim who seems to be working quite hard at Parris Island. I certainly hope he makes the grade after setting his heart on it so. I'm anxious to hear from Don and find out where destiny carried him. Today I received a swell letter from Ken telling of some of his recent experiences. It doesn't look like he'll be around these immediate parts but perhaps some day we'll cross paths. I haven't seen Barry for almost a month now because each time he's come around I've been away on a raid.

To answer a couple of questions Dad, I didn't get in to see Mr. Kellett while I was on Oahu. Perhaps I will when we go back to Oahu on rest leave. I certainly will keep my eyes open for Comdr. Bird and Lt. Comdr. Doyle. I don't know how I'll ever hear of him pulling in but if so I'll certainly look him up.

Oh incidentally, Don's new APO (316) is the same as that of a nurse friend of one of the boys in our squadron, and she is stationed in England. I have no idea if that means Don's APO spots him in the land of John Bull but its a thought.

The various clippings you've sent have certainly been interesting, Dad. Please keep it up because its fun to read what's going on in the diffent places. The news, that is from the papers, we get out here is practically nil. Occasionally someone will get a few papers from home and of course they do the rounds. The clippings you've sent, I put up on our bulletin board for all the gang to read.

Several days ago I enclosed a check for $150— to purchase a war bond as you suggested, so please be certain to notify me of its arrival. I believe that all the mail gets through alright if you only wait long enough.

I'm afraid I've exhausted all inspiration so I'll put a halt to my idle banter. Incidentally I now have twelve missions to my credit.

Write often.

Love—

Bobby

DECEMBER 12, 1944/SCRAPBOOK PHOTOGRAPHS

1.) Sinajana, the native village, where we had our laundry done

2.) Native house along the run to the airfield.

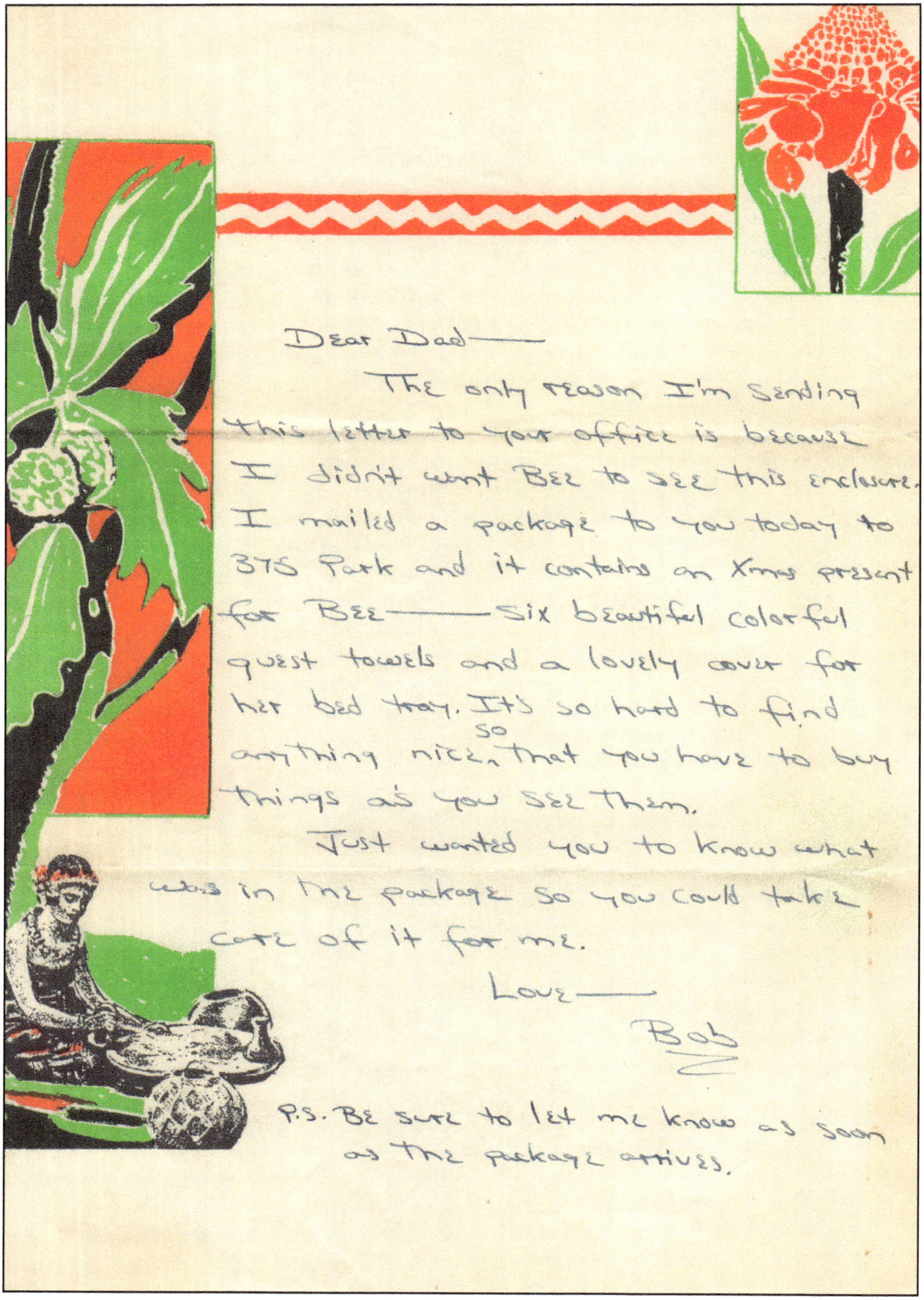

Dear Dad—

The only reason I'm sending this letter to your office is because I didn't want Bee to see this enclosure. I mailed a package to you today to 375 Park and it contains an Xmas present for Bee—six beautiful colorful guest towels and a lovely cover for her bed tray. It's so hard to find anything so nice, that you have to buy things as you see them.

Just wanted you to know what was in the package so you could take care of it for me.

Love—

Bob

P.S. Be sure to let me know as soon as the package arrives.

DECEMBER 17, 1944

The Marianas

December 17th, 1944

Dear Aunt Jane[49]—

I can't tell you how pleased I was to have received the delicious assortment of Christmas packages. It was such fun opening all the beautifully wrapped packages and most welcome were all the contents which certainly hit the spot—I've always liked little snacks and out here they're even more enjoyed. Many thanks also for the reading material which is quite scarce out this way. Really Jane, it was too sweet of you to have taken the time and effort to put up such a swell bunch of Christmas packages and I truly appreciated it.

I imagine that you've learned of most of my activities from the folks. I have already flown twelve missions on my way toward our goal of forty. It's a long, hard pull. Conditions out here aren't too good but they are improving all the time. We are living in tents and when it rains its like living in a mud hole. Supposedly this is the dry season but you couldn't prove it by me.

I suppose that Dad told you I ran into Barry quite some time ago and have see him several times since then. He's in great shape and seems to be getting along fine.

MARIANA ISLANDS

Well June, I guess that's about all from these parts but again I want to thank you a million for the assortment of Christmas packages. It was just like opening a batch of presents from Santa when we were kids.

My best to Henry.

Love—

Bobby

The Marianas

December 19th, 1944 [50]

Dear Dad—

Well here 'tis another year and December 19th has rolled around again but somehow this year it has less meaning than years in the past—right now it's just another day nearer to returning home. I don't know how you timed it so perfectly, but your letter arrived yesterday. I want to thank you for your swell birthday letter Dad, and also for the overgenerous present of war bonds you got for me. I too hope and pray that it won't be too long before I'm home and we can catch up on alot of lost time together. I hate to think that I'm spending these years away from home but that's the way it goes. You're a swell gent Dad, and I wish there was some way I could express my love and admiration ~~of~~ for you—perhaps I can when this whole mess is over.

Everything is about the same as ever out this way. I still only have twelve missions due to the fact I haven't flown lately because of a sore wisdom tooth. It's all fixed up now and I'll be back up there again on the next raid.

I saw Berry again a few days ago and he's in fine shape. I believe he'll be over again tomorrow or the next day.

Before I forget, please tell Bee that as yet I haven't gotten the letters she thought she'd sent to APO 244 in error. If she did, they will be forwarded to me eventually. The box of cookies you sent arrived in good shape. Many thanks for the sweets that R.L.S. and many other hungry birdmen enjoyed. As yet the packages sent to APO 753 haven't arrived but I still have hopes. I have received quite a number of packages sent to APO 241 and forwarded alright. All packages seem to take about two months. Mail generally takes from a little over two weeks to a month. Speaking of mail wasn't that funny I should have written that I had a friend writing to APO 316 and it was in England and a few days later I got your letter saying that Don was somewhere in England.

I've just about exhausted all the recent news from out here. You read alot more in the papers than we're allowed to write in letters. Please continue to send the various clippings as you spot them in the papers re the 7th AAF Liberators in the Pacific area.

Again many thanks for your swell birthday letter and the war bonds, Dad.

With all love—

Bobby

The Marianas
December 25th, 1944

Dear Dad + Bee——

Well here tis the 25th but somehow it doesn't seem any different than any other day of the week. Sure we had a delicious turkey dinner but aside from that there was none of the usual Christmas Spirit. One day is like the next out here and you lose all track of day and date. The only thing we keep track of is how many missions we can get in during a month. I'm afraid that all the tradition of the various holidays will be lost until the war is over. After all, I guess that is the most important thing right now.

Bee, I want to thank you for your swell birthday letter which arrived a couple of days ago. It would have arrived on my birthday were the mail not so darn slow. Almost all letters take about three weeks and sometimes longer.

Everything is about the same out this way. Slowly but surely we're getting on with our missions but it's still a long way to go to reach the forty mark, and there's always the chance that they may raise it. Formerly it was only thirty missions and raised to thirty-five and while we were back at Kwajalien it was boosted to a mere forty — what next?

Finally things are shaping up in the squadron to make conditions a bit more bearable. All of the boys have wooden floors and frames in their tents now. The squadron built a club for the enlist ed men where they can get beer and coke. I believe they are under way to build us an officers club. We certainly need a place to drink beer and work off steam because it's fairly dull to spend all your time in a tent.

I don't recall if I told you or not but I saw Butty a few days ago and he was in best of shape. I believe he may be over tomorrow again. For Christmas I dug up an extra case of beer for him to celebrate.

As usual I'm lacking any further inspir-ation toward writing an interesting letter. There's so little to write when you live as routine a life as we do — enough for now.

Love —

Bobby

The Marianas
December 31st, 1944

Dear Dad + Bee ——

Well here's your Pacific correspondent back at it again to bring you up to date on the latest from out this way. Christmas and now New Years Eve is going by the boards and we're about to launch on a new year, which I hope and pray will bring us all together again and put an end to this damn war. Out here among the palm trees holidays don't mean much and so our New Years celebration merely consisted of a few warm beers and some native coconut whiskey, which is dynamite! I hope you had a pleasant visit at Williamstown over the 25th and that your Christmas was as much of a festive occasion as possible under the circumstances. Did you stay up there for New Years too?

To start off 1945 I have fifteen raids to my credit and our slogan is "twenty-five in forty-five!" It will be a long haul to complete twenty-five more missions, but as time passes the missions add up. Recently we ran into some fairly tough opposition and had a couple of close calls —— a wing and a [51] prayer really hits it on the head, but as long as you make it back that's all that matters.

To answer a couple of your questions, Dad—
Up until our ninth mission we flew a different ship each time. Since then, we were assigned a ship that belonged to a crew that finished up its missions and went home. They had the name "Flying Jenny" painted on and so we had to leave it. The name is quite appropriate because it's a fairly old jalopy but somehow it seems to get us there and back.

Barry was down here a few days ago waiting for me when I got back from a mission. We had dinner here and I drove him back to his camp. He's fine as ever and seems enthusiastic about his new work. When we get together again I'll try to have a picture taken of us to send you. It's kinda hard though because you're not allowed to have cameras or take any pictures on the Island, but I'll see if I can arrange something.

Say Dad, I want to thank you for the various clippings you've sent me. Please continue to send any clippings of the 7th AAF because it's fun to see what they write about the work we're doing. Thanks also for passing on the mail from the various boys as they come to you. You're a regular clearing house!

Still the package Bee sent to APO 953 has not arrived but there's still a chance that it may come through. It's such a shame because you mailed it so very early. I did receive the box from Robert Day Dennis and the box of cookies from 375, both of which I thanked you for long ago. Of course, they were mailed to APO 241 and got through alright.

Many thanks for all of your various letters which help to make life more bearable out here. You'd be surprised what a lift it is to come back from a raid cold, hungry, and possibly a bit banged up, and dead tired and have a few letters from your family, friends, and loved ones waiting for you. It really makes a difference.

Must run now to go get our ship loaded up. A very, very happy new year to you all.

love ——

Bobby

D. Mesmith flew 40 in the Jenny and she was willed to us—what a collection of nuts and bolts!!

The Marianas
January 3rd, 1945

Dear Dad & Bee—

Haven't much of anything to write, but I received a package from you and a letter from Bee this morning. Many thanks for the various canned eats (lobster, tongue, & sausage) which arrived in perfect shape. The cake was delicious and fresh as could be, packed in a can. All your selections will really hit the spot and are muchly appreciated. Thanks loads!

I was glad to receive the announcement and clipping of Timmy's wedding, Bee. Thanks for sending them along. You asked about Barry and he is perfectly fine. He came over this afternoon and I just returned from taking him back. Frankly I didn't even know he'd had tropical fever and if he did, it didn't do him any harm because he was in the best of shape today. He gets off every Wednesday and generally stops over to see me unless I'm off on a raid. Ordinarily I take him to supper, although I didn't today because we're eating with another squadron while our mess-hall is being rebuilt—next time he's over ours will be finished up. Actually it's no treat for him to eat with us because C-rations taste the same wherever you eat them, and that's all we've had on the menu of late.

Guess that's about all for now. I didn't have much to say, but I did want you to know that the food had arrived and that I'd seen Barry this afternoon. S'long for awhile.

All love —

Bobby

The Marianas
January 7th, 1945

Dear Dad & Bee——

I was sorry to receive your letter saying that Bee was ill over Christmas. It was a shame that you couldn't get up to Williamstown over the holidays. I hope that you're feeling fine again, Bee.

In your last letter you said you thought Don was in Belgium.[52] I think you're wrong and he's still in England, because I receive that same Christmas card—it was a picture of a Cathedral in Bruges, Belgium. I imagine he just happened to get ahold of them but I doubt if it had anything to do with his present location.

Many thanks for sending along "Is There a Santa."[53] I too hope that next Christmas you will be reading it to us in person. You asked about the "Pacific Strategic Air Force" that it spoke about in the paper—I believe that is a new command (in name only) but the missions that you read about are the ones we fly. Any time you read about Liberators raiding the Bonins and Volcano Is. you can be sure it's one of our outfits. Please continue to send along any clippings you see, pertaining to the raids we're on. It's interesting to see what they cook up for the public as opposed to what actually happened.

I'm afraid I didn't have much news after writing a couple of days ago but I did want to say I'm sorry to hear that you've been ill, Bee. I trust by now that you're fine again.

Best love—

Bobby

Lt. R.L. Stone O-696041
431st Bomb Squadron 11th Group
APO 246 c/o Postmaster
San Francisco, Cal.

air mail

U.S. ARMY JAN 7 1945 246 POSTAL SERVICE

AIR 6 MAIL
UNITED STATES OF AMERICA

Mr. J. C. Stone
375 Park Avenue
New York City (22)
N.Y.

Robert Stone

The Marianas
January 10th, 1945

Dear Mildred + Eddie——

Due to my changes of address, it took until today for the Pony Express to catch up to me with your Christmas present. Many thanks for the assortment of eats, which I can assure you will all be hungrily devoured. Our food situation still doesn't compare to the meals at the Waldorf, and so a few canned treats certainly hit the spot. As always, your thoughtfulness is greatly appreciated.

I trust that the family have kept you fairly up to date on my recent doings. Life goes on about the same as always. Christmas and New Year came and went the same as any other day, except for a turkey dinner. Out here, one day is the same as the next and holidays don't mean very much.

At present, we now have seventeen missions to our credit with a mere twenty-three yet to fly. It's a long, hard pull and will take alot of good luck for us to finish up all our raids. Lately the missions have come fairly regularly, and we've put in alot of flying time. Frankly the sooner we complete our missions the better I'll like it—this business of combat flying isn't my idea of a very practical career!

JANUARY 10, 1945

Before too long our crew ought to be going back on rest leave to Honolulu. After about three months of combat flying they send you back for a ten day rest leave. It will be a real treat to enjoy a few good meals and live like a human being again for awhile — I doubt if I'll know how to act!

I certainly hope that you had as merry a Christmas as possible and will have a very happy new year. Let's hope that it is a year in which we will all return home again.

My very best to both of you and to John and Mary.

Fondly —

Bobby

P.S. Mary thanks for the exceptionally vivid (or should I say lurid) Christmas card!

FEB 20 1945 PARCEL POST

The Marianas
January 12, 1945

Dear Dad & Bee—

Yes Bee, your wonderful Christmas box finally arrived a bit late but in perfect shape. Many, many thanks for all the various packages. It was such fun opening each individual gift—the shorts, bingo game, writing paper, and especially the cute picture frame and pictures were truly appreciated. Many thanks for all the beautifully wrapped packages, Bee. 'Twas too bad they were late but better late than never as they say, and frankly our mail service out here is hardly the best.

I hope this letter finds you up and at 'em again after your illness. It was such a shame that it spoiled your Christmas for you.

All's well out here and we now ~~hope~~ have eighteen missions to our credit. We're hoping to get in twenty-five by the time we go on rest leave so that we'll only have fifteen

JANUARY 12, 1945

to go when we get back from Oahu. There are two crews to go on rest before our turn comes up but we ought to go sometime in February, if all goes per schedule.

You mentioned again that you thought Don was in Belgium, but as I said in my last letter I believe he's still in England. I too received his Christmas card with a picture of the Cathedral at Bruges, Belgium.

I received a letter from Jim thanking for my wallet. Thanks for sending it along Dad, as well as attending to wrapping Bee's gifts.

Please continue to send along the clippings as you have been doing, Dad. It's fun to read about the missions we are flying.

Missed Barry a couple of days ago when I was away on a raid. He left a note saying that we'd tried to get together again sometime next week when I'm not flying.

Between raids we've been busy working on the officers club we're building. Everybody pitches in when we're not busy and before long we ought to have a nifty club. Little by little this place is becoming more and more livable — things have really changed from the day we arrived three months ago. There are a great many places on the island that have completely changed face and are now unrecognizable from a two months ago.

Guess that'll have to do for now. Again many thanks for all the effort you put into my Christmas package, Bee.

Best love —

Bobby

1) The roof goes up on the new officers' club.

2) Zimmy at work on the framework.

JANUARY 12-15, 1945

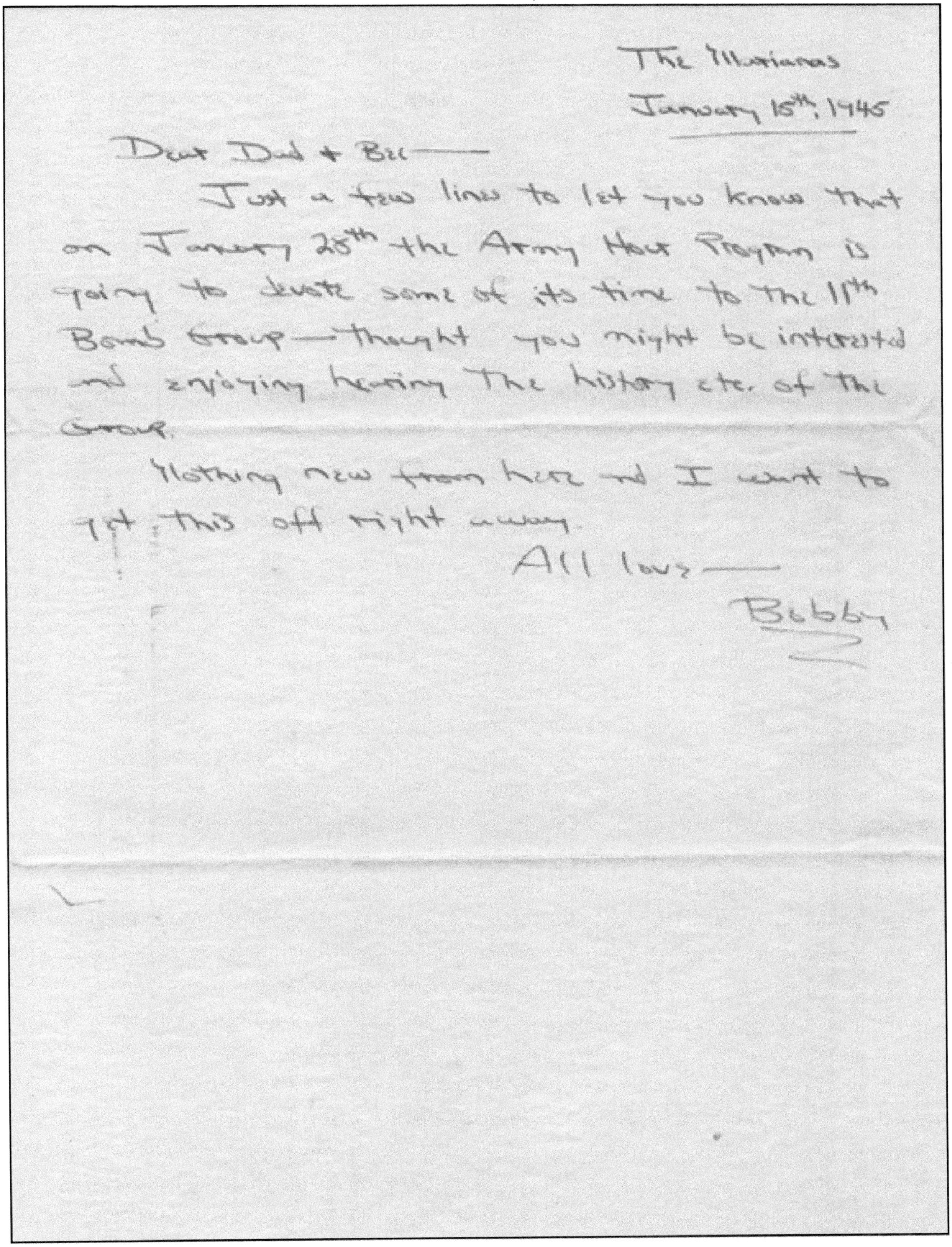

The Marianas
January 15th, 1945

Dear Dad + Bee —

Just a few lines to let you know that on January 28th the Army Hour Program is going to devote some of its time to the 11th Bomb Group — thought you might be interested and enjoying hearing the history etc. of the Group.

Nothing new from here and I want to get this off right away.

All love —

Bobby

MARIANA ISLANDS

In Flight
Feb. 9th, 1945 [54]

Dear Dad + Bee—

This morning brought to a close a very pleasant and relaxing rest leave on Oahu and Kauai. It seems like only yesterday we were on our way up, and here we are heading back to combat again. Luckily we don't have to fly a ship back but are traveling as passengers on an ATC ship.

I hardly know where to begin, what with all that's happened since I last wrote. We never expected to be up on rest leave so soon, but one night we landed from a mission and were told to be ready to leave the next morning. Needless to say, we wasted no time in packing and making ready to go. Actually our rest came at a very opportune moment because our next to last mission was a real tough one and all of us were pretty badly scared. [55] We were all too jumpy to fly for awhile so a rest leave was quite welcome. Incidentally, we now have twenty-two missions to our credit which leaves us eighteen to go. It's been a long nervewracking pull, and we've still got alot in front of us. At least we've gotten over the half way mark, none the worse for it (considering everything).

Upon checking in on Oahu, we went to one of the rest camps for combat crews out at Waikiki. For the first few days I had a

Page 23

number of things to do in Honolulu. There are always a bunch of little things you find you need "down under" and of course there's no place to buy them. Arranged for a couple of phone calls which always involve red tape, censorship, and lots of time. I can't tell you how good it was to talk to you and hear your voices again. Trans-pacific calls are always a real thrill for me — a treat that I'd like to enjoy more often! 'Twas swell talking to Bunny.

I went in and had a swell talk with Mr. Kellett, Dad. He's an awfully attractive gent and I was glad to have met him. The day I went in he invited me to his club for lunch, and I met all of his friends. They have a gang that eat together every day similar to your crowd at the Luncheon Club. It was very pleasant meeting Mr. Kellett because he's an A-1 fellow.

When we arrived at the rest camp, most of us turned in our names to go and stay on a ranch if an invitation came through. They make all arrangements for you to go over to the other islands and visit with different families. Bill and I went over to some people on Kauai. Their name was Hansen, and they ran a large sugar plantation. Never have I been treated so royally or enjoyed myself more. They were the nicest people you'd ever want to meet, and they opened their home to us as if we

page 3

had been life-long friends. They had nothing planned for us but wanted us to do whatever our fancy desired. The food was really a treat—we had all the fresh meat, vegetables, milk, butter, and eggs we could eat. There's no rationing on the islands and what with their farm on the plantation we absolutely ate like kings. During my stay, I put on eight pounds. A couple of days we went to the beach, drove all around the island, went around the plantation with Mr. Hansen, and in general took it easy. Every morning we slept as late as we wanted (they insisted we did) and then had breakfast. During the day we did just whatever we wanted and Mr. + Mrs. Hansen were always agreeable to anything. One night we all went up to their mountain home (something like Alderbrook) and cooked supper. A couple of meals we were all invited to friends of theirs. One day we went to a real Hawaiian feast where they ate raw fish and various other strange foods.

I can't adequately describe the Hansens and expect to do them justice. He was about forty and was born on Kauai. Had gone to college in the States and came back to Kauai to run the plantation. (The Hansens and all their friends are quite well to-do financially.) He was an all-around guy with a swell sense of humor. Mrs. Hansen is also around forty but looks nearer thirty. She's a very attractive gal

page 4

with all kinds of pep—really a swell person.
x Together they made ideal hosts and did everything possible to make our stay a pleasant one, and believe me they succeeded! We couldn't have had a better or more restful time. Nothing was too much for them to do for us. We ate like kings and drank nothing but the best Scotch—Canadian Club if you please! All in all, it was a real treat to visit the Hansens and happily enough they were very fond of us. In fact, they insist that we come back when we finish up our missions. Will certainly do it, if we possibly can.

I was certainly glad to hear that you got away to Virginia for a few days rest and relaxation. It must have been fun to have a little vacation.

In answer to a couple of questions in your letters, before I came on rest leave. My wisdom tooth is alright and it hasn't bothered me for quite awhile. You asked what happens if a man on a crew is sick for a mission or so. Well, anyone from a crew not flying on that mission can take his place as well as some extras who are around. The boys are anxious to go because they get in another mission that way.

It seems that I've been rambling on altogether too long so I'm going to put an end to it now. I did have alot to write as I've

page 5

been putting it off regularly for the last couple of weeks. I hope you can make out my scrawl which is quite messy, since we occasionally hit rough air. This letter ought to make fairly good time because I'm going to mail it at the first stop instead of taking it all the way "down under."

My very best to everybody, and I'll try to write again in a few days, when I have a little time.

All love—

Bobby

P.S. I really dread the thought of returning to eat C-rations and live like a primitive man again. The good food and a few conveniences of civilization are really a treat to come back to. Imagine shaving with hot water!! Rest leaves are a mighty fine institution!!!

FEBRUARY 9, 1945/DISTINGUISHED FLYING CROSS

General Orders No. 67 classified SECRET and distributed to those concerned.

GENERAL ORDERS)
:
NUMBER - 68)

HEADQUARTERS SEVENTH AIR FORCE.
APO #244, 5 June 1945

* -E-X-T-R-A-C-T- *
SECTION
* * *

AWARD OF DISTINGUISHED FLYING CROSS.................................II

* * *

SECTION II

AWARD OF DISTINGUISHED FLYING CROSS: - By direction of the President, under the provisions of the Act of Congress approved 2 July 1926 (Bull. No. 8, W.D., 1926) and pursuant to authority contained in paragraph 14, AR 600-45, 22 September 1943 and Ltr Hq AAFPOA, 18 October 1944, the Distinguished Flying Cross is awarded by the Commanding General, Seventh Air Force, to the following named officers and enlisted men, Air Corps, United States Army, for services set forth in the following citations:

* * * * * * * *

4. For extraordinary heroism in aerial flight against the heavily defended enemy base of Iwo Jima on 21 January 1945. During this mission, each as a crew member of a heavy bombardment type aircraft, assisted in destroying vital enemy ground installations. While over the target fighter interceptors were encountered and evasive action had to be taken to escape the fire of the fighters. Despite these hazards, the weather conditions encountered and the intense anit-aircraft fire, the mission was so successful that 100% of the bombs were dropped on the target area. The cool courage in the face of great danger, the high degree of professional skill and devotion to duty displayed by each exemplifies the highest tradition of the Army Air Forces:

* * * * * * *

1ST LT ROBERT L STONE 0696041 1ST LT CHARLES G SWAN JR 0704327

* * * * * * *

BY COMMAND OF MAJOR GENERAL DOUGLASS:

WILLIAM J. FLOOD,
Brigadier General, General Staff Corps
Chief of Staff

OFFICIAL:
/s/ R. J. Erickson
R. J. ERICKSON
Colonel, Adjutant General's Department,
Adjutant General

A TRUE EXTRACT COPY:
Charles G. Swan, Jr.
CHARLES G. SWAN JR.
1st Lt., Air Corps

Distinguished Flying Cross medal was awarded to Bob for the "scary" mission on January 21, 1945 that Bob refers to in his letter of February 9, 1945.

2) R.L.S. on rest leave.

3) Nettie and Hans Hansen— two perfectly swell hosts!

4) Hans on the porch of their Mt. home—kinda like Alderbrook.

SCRAPBOOK PHOTOGRAPHS

2) Close-up of R.L.S.

3) R.L.S. and Grandma Hettlehn

1) The Hansens' home at Kekaha on the island of Kauai, T.H.

Sugar Cane Field (2)

The Marianas
February 14th, 1945

Dear Dad & Bee—

Well here I am back at the grind of sweating out missions, and it seems like only yesterday that we left. I hope by now you've received my lengthy letter telling all about rest leave. It's really an effort getting used to C-rations, mosquito nets, and a hundred and one other inconveniences again.

On arriving back here we were all greeted by stacks of mail that had piled up during our absence. You've all been swell about writing often, particularly you Dad. By the way, many thanks for the box of cookies and the packages of canned things that were waiting for me. Any canned things like sardines, chicken, anchovies, tuna, etc. etc. are always appreciated and never spoil in shipping. I was lucky enough to procure a small hot plate so we can always heat up anything that has to be cooked.

Your Valentines arrived and were duly appreciated. You asked if I wanted you to continue to forward on clippings Dad, and I most certainly do. Thanks for all those you've sent as well as the boys' letters you've passed along. You have a bigger job than a clearing house on Wall Street.

FEBRUARY 14, 1945

As you doubtless know, the enclosed is a picture of our crew—not a very good one, but I thought you'd like to have it. Censorship regulations won't permit you to put names on the picture so you'll have to guess who each fellow is.

Since we've been back, we've already flown our first mission which brings our total up to twenty-three. It's almost like being a new crew again to fly missions. You sweat everything out like on our first few missions and often wonder if you remember what to do and when.

Say Dad, I want to thank you ever so much for your thoughtfulness for a check that I never received. When I went in to see Mr. Kellett it apparently hadn't arrived and so he made no mention of it. In fact, I didn't quite understand that you were refering to on the phone. However, when I got back and received your letters it clarified everything. Even though I didn't get it many thanks for being so thoughtful, Dad.

Guess that just about covers everything for now. I'll try to write in a few days after I get caught up on a few things. Please continue to write often as you have all along,

Best love—Bobby

1.) Meyers donation to the Nips
on Valentines day.

2.) Some of the boys loading
hundred pounders.

PUBLIC RELATIONS
SEVENTH AIR FORCE

DATE MAILED: 17 Feb. '45

FOR RELEASE: Immediate

PASSED FOR PUBLICATION
U.S. ARMY PRESS CENSOR
Signature Date 2/16

61618

ARMY AIR FORCES, PACIFIC HEADQUARTERS --- In what Second Lieutenant Robert L. Stone, Scarsdale, New York, bombardier of the 7th AAF Liberator, Flying Jenny, termed "the best raid from the standpoint of results", Jap installations on Iwo Jima Island took a thorough pasting.

The Flying Jenny, member of a squadron of 7th AAF Liberators, first flew over the island and dropped bombs on airfield installations, airplane dispersal areas and gun positions, causing explosions and large fires.

"We sort of paved the way," said Lieutenant Stone. "The bombs we dropped created plenty of destruction, wrecking Jap olanes parked on the ground and setting them afire."

After Lieutenant Stone's squadron hit the target area along came B-29 Superforts to drop more bombs. Later another squadron of 7th AAF Liberators, excorted by 7th AAF P-28 Lightning fighter planes, continued the attack. Then, in the afternoon warships stood off shore and poured shells onto the installations.

"We've been pounding Iwo Jima to prevent the Japs from sending out planes to raid the Superfort base on Saipan," Lieutenant Stone explained. "We've kept the runways so punched full of holes that the Japs are unable to send up planes to threaten B-29 operations.

On another mission to Iwo Jima the Flying Jenny became separated from the formation in an overcast. It was so cold that ice formed on the plane. The Fly'ng Jenny, on emerging from the overcast, was attacked by Jap fighters, escaped and dropped its bombs on the island and returned to base.

"It was about 14 below," Lieutenant Stone declared. "We picked up sheets of ice on the leading edges of the wings and the cowlings. The nose was iced up so that the gunner couldn't see out of it. We broke out of the overcast and there were three Jap fighters sitting and waiting for us.

"Each made a pass atus but did no damage. We dived back into the overcast to escape the fighters, and three or four minutes later popped out of it to find

(more)

1 add

the island right below us. We dropped the bombs and headed back to base."

Lieutenant Stone, whose parents, Mr. and Mrs. J. C. Stone, reside at 35 Cushman Road, Scarsdale, was graduated from Deerfield Academy in 1940 and attended Williams College. He has flown/22 combat missions to Yap, Haha Jima, Chichi Jima, in addition to Iwo Jima.

21245LEBAMvt - 30 -

PASSED FOR PUBLICATION
U.S. ARMY PRESS CENSOR
Signature Date
61618

Press Release from 7th Air Force Public Relations Department. Article in the Scarsdale Inquirer on p. 340.

U.S. ARMY AIR FORCES PRESS RELEASE/FEBRUARY 20, 1945

The Marianas

56

February 20th, 1945

Dear Dad & Bee—

Just a line or two to say that all's well out here and we've got a couple more missions to our credit—we now have twenty-five. You asked if we all have the same number on the crew and in general we do except for two of the boys who have one extra. Ordinarily we've flown as a complete crew but once or twice when the crew hasn't gone on a raid one man might fly with another crew.

Speaking of the crew I'm certain I told you all their names and where their homes are, way back when I was at March Field. If you think back I'm sure you'll recall it. There isn't much likelihood that their families would be in the East inasmuch as Bill and Mac live in Texas and our navigator is from Oregon. If ever they were to come East I'd certainly notify you. We've really got an A-1 crew as proven by several close calls that we've pulled through together. It's a real test of a crew when the chips are down as they have been for us on several occasions.

A few days ago we finished up our officers club and we plan to have a gala opening in a few days. It really turned out to be a swell job and it really looks professional. I'll let you know how the blow-out turns out in a few days.

Chow time, so I'll put an end to my scrawling. Keep your letters coming as always and I'll try to write soon again myself.

Love—

Bobby

The Marianas
February 22nd, 1945

Dear Dad & Bee—

I've had several letters from you in the last few days. I was glad to hear that my long letter, telling about rest leave, had arrived. Our hosts full name and address is as follows—

Mr. & Mrs Hans Hansen
Kekaha Plantation
Kauai, T.H.

I think it would be awfully nice if you were to send them a trifle with a note of appreciation for having R.L.S. as a guest at their home. I, of course, wrote them and thanked as well as sending them something from Honolulu before I left.

Incidentally, the explanation of the different dates on my letter written in flight is the fact that we crossed the date line when I mailed it. Guess it was one of the speediest letters I've ever sent you.

MARIANA ISLANDS

KDK 3/2/45

I wonder if you'd be able to send me a few rolls of 620 film. I'm just about out and have no mean of getting any here or on Oahu. Speaking of pictures I don't believe I'll be able to send you any of Barry and me. I'd always planned to take some but never got around to it.

Enclosed are a couple of snaps (poor ones) that I thought you might like to have. One was taken on rest leave and the other when I was up on Oahu before. In fact, I don't know but I may have sent you a copy before

I imagine you're as much up on the big happenings out this way as we are right in the thick of it, judging from the newscasts coming from San Francisco. Everything is happening very fast and the old U.S. is getting in a few good licks after a long period of just holding their own.

I'm so glad that you got such a kick out of my two phone calls. You

FEBRUARY 22, 1945

can be sure it was a real thrill for me too. It was swell of you to have tried to get Pam for the second time I called you, and it was just unfortunate that I had to change the date. 'Twas fun to talk to Bunny, anyway.

That's all for now but I'll write again in a few days. By the time this arrives you should have received the crew picture I sent you. I hope so, anyway.

All love—

Bobby

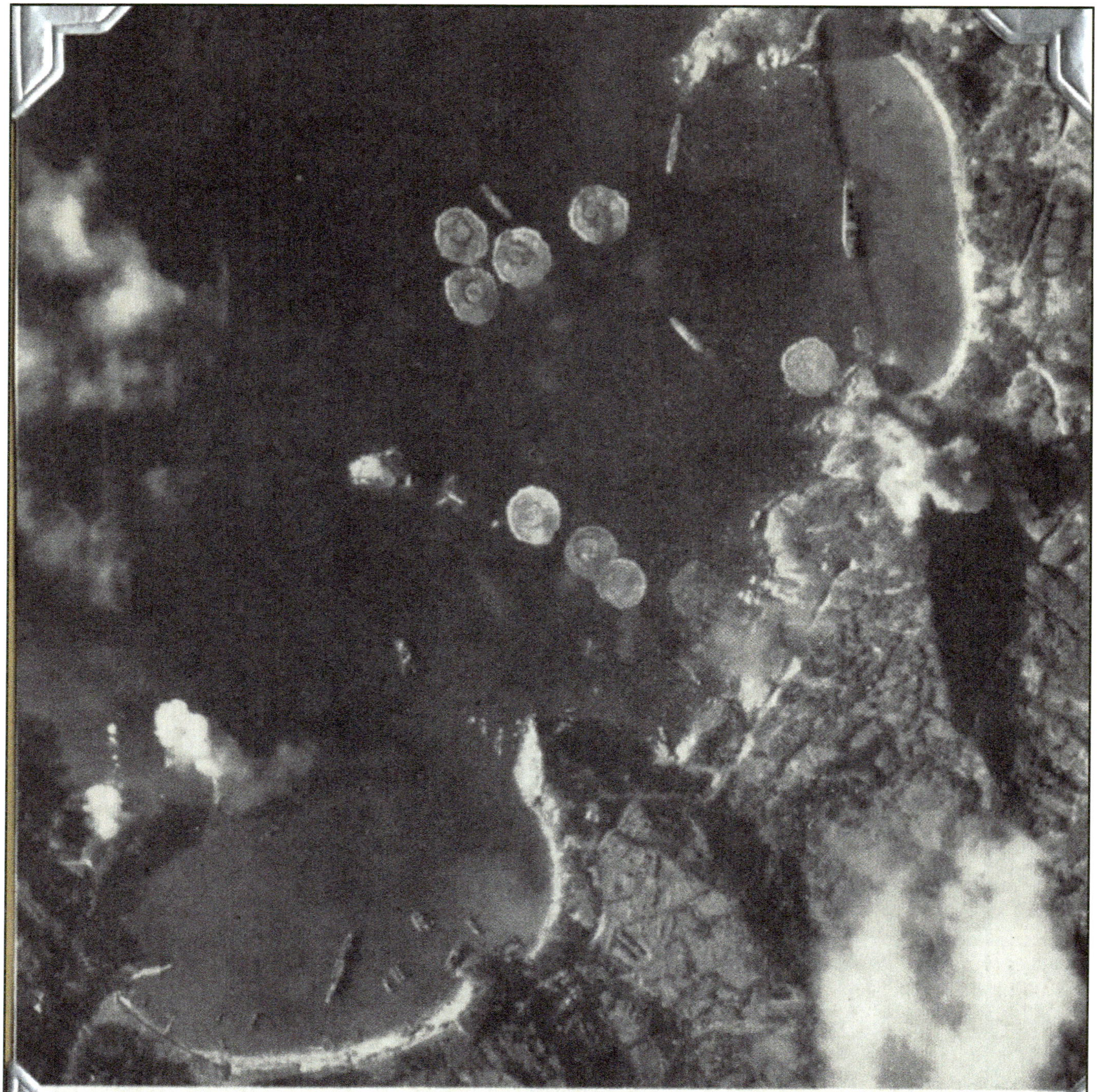

SHIPPING STRIKE over the Japanese harbor at Chichi Jima brings sev
its and near misses along waterfront. Note blasted ship (

1) One of our many thirteen hours flights up to Chichi Jima to hit shipping. No fighters but very heavy flak.

NEWSPAPER CLIPPINGS

2) The runway at Iwo takes another pounding. Good picture of those damn phos bombs — beautiful but mighty treacherous!

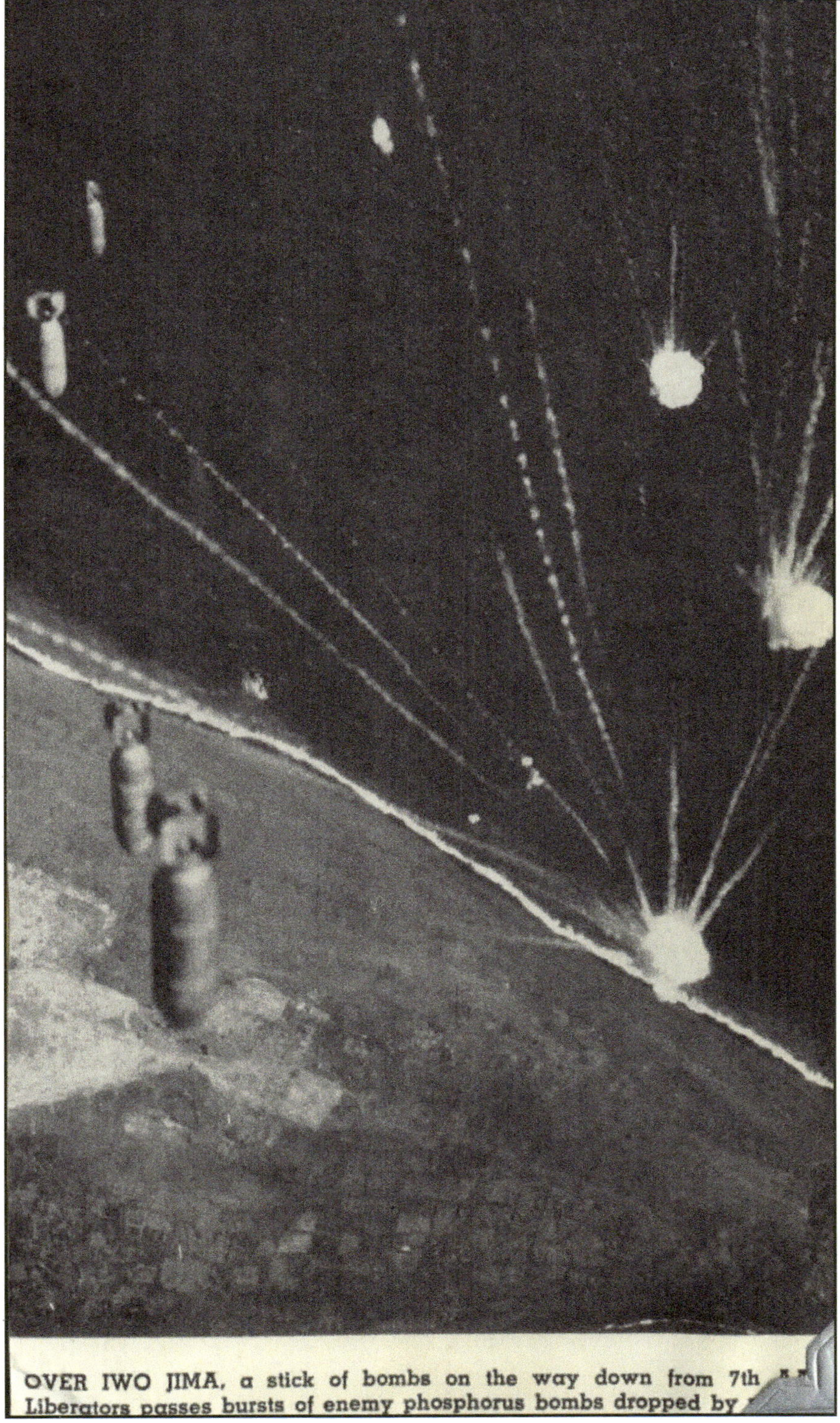
OVER IWO JIMA, a stick of bombs on the way down from 7th … Liberators passes bursts of enemy phosphorus bombs dropped by …

This is a fuze pin, which is a safety device composed of a metal cotter pin with a warning tag that was used on bombs dropped by B-24 aircraft. Usually, it was the job of the radio operator to pull the pin between the fuze and the bomb.

THE SCARSDALE INQUIRER,

SCARSDALE, NEW YORK, FRIDAY, MARCH 2, 1945

Jap installations on Iwo Jima Island took a thorough pasting recently in what **2nd Lt. Robert L. Stone**, bombardier of the 7th AAF Liberator, Flying Jenny, termed "the best raid from the standpoint of results."

The Flying Jenny, member of a squadron of 7th AAF Liberators, first flew over the island and dropped bombs on airfield installations, airplane dispersal areas and gun positions, causing explosions and large fires. "We sort of paved the way," said Lt. Stone. "The bombs we dropped created plenty of destruction, wrecking Jap planes parked on the ground and setting them afire."

B-29 Superforts followed Lt. Stone's squadron to drop more bombs on the target, and later another squadron of Liberators escorted by P-28 Lightning fighter planes, continued the attack. All afternoon warships stood off shore and poured shells onto the installations.

"We've been pounding Iwo Jima to prevent the Japs from sending out planes to raid the Superfort base on Saipan," Lt. Stone explained. "We've kept the runways so punched full of holes that the Japs are unable to send up planes to threaten B-29 operations."

On another mission to Iwo Jima, the Flying Jenny became separated from the formation in an overcast. It was so cold that ice formed on the plane. "It was fourteen below," declared Lt. Stone. "We picked up sheets of ice on the leading edges of the wings and the cowlings. The nose was iced up so that the gunner couldn't see out of it. We broke out of the overcast and there were three Jap fighters sitting waiting for us."

"Each made a pass but did no damage. We dived back into the overcast to escape the fighters, and three or four minutes later popped out of it to find the island right below us. We dropped our bombs and headed back to base."

Lt. Stone, son of Mr. and Mrs. J. C. Stone of 35 Cushman Road, was graduated from Deerfield Academy in 1940, and attended Williams College. He has flown twenty-two combat missions to Yap, Haha Jima, Chichi Jima, in addition to Iwo Jima.

2) Temms serving the boys with black death at our club opening.

3) "Pop" and some of the boys indulging in a game of skill.

The Marianas
March 29th, 1945

Dear Eddie—

'Twas good to hear from you via your official report, which I received a few days ago. All's well out this way and slowly but surely we're making it more and more unpleasant for the Nips.

Our missions have been coming along same as ever and I'm now down to where I can count them (that is those left to fly) on one hand. Am now at the thirty-five mark, sweating out those last five raids as if they were fifty-five. As you near the end, the strain and tension plays hell with you mentally. Every little thing is magnified way out of proportion, and it's just as if we were a new crew flying our first few missions over again.

The big news from out here is that Barry is back from the Iwo campaign and is headed for the States to enter the V-12 college program. His luck in returning to the states is fantastic because he's only been oversea a very short while.

The rainy season in the Marianas has started with a gusto and it's not uncommon to ten or twelve downpours a day. When it rains here it does it with a vengeance, and so we wallow around in nothing but mud. How it burns me

MARCH 29, 1945

when people write how lucky I am being in the "Sunny" Pacific! You can have it all, any time!!

That just about covers it for now. Give my best to Dotsie and the boys.

Fondly—

Bobby

P.S. I was just away from my tent at a squadron meeting and I was called out to see some Captain. He gave me a box with a note on it from Mr. Peterson. It seems he thought I was on another island and so he didn't get to see me. However, I want to thank you a million for the chocolates and the enclosed note. What a thrill it would have been had you delivered them in person! 'Twas awfully thoughtful of you to have sent the candies, Eddy.

It was a coincidence that I had written you this morning and hadn't mailed the letter, and this afternoon the package arrived. Again many thanks,

Bobby

2) Barry, after he returned from
The Iwo campaign.

SCRAPBOOK PHOTOGRAPH/APRIL 18, 1945

The Marianas
April 18th, 1945

Dear Dad & Bee—

No, as yet I still haven't flown my all-important fortieth mission but am still sweating it out. Thought I'd drop you a line however, to say that after eighteen short months (twenty-three if you count time and a half for overseas) my promotion came through and I'm now a 1st. Promotions are a sore point with all of us because they are so slow out here and back in the States all the ground officers behind desks get their promotions in no time. Oh well enough griping because it finally came through and I ought to be happy about it. My gold bar was turning silver after aging all this time!

Every day we seem to get in a few new crews and the squadron is overrun with strange faces and newly pressed khakis. Some of the boys were actually in the States two weeks ago.

No more for now but I hope in my next letter I can write that I've flown my fortieth.

Love—
Bobby

MARIANA ISLANDS

The Marianas

April 22, 1945

Dear Dad & Bee—

Today you are receiving the letter that I have dreamed of writing for the last six months. Yes, we finally flew our fortieth mission! It has been a long and trying tour of duty filled with a number of black hours and narrow escapes. All the way through we were lucky to have God on our side to pull us through when there seemed to be no chance of making it. All of us have a feeling of free men again with a great pressure having been removed. It's a mighty good feeling.

As far as coming home is concerned, it will be a little time yet before we leave here and we'll probably be up on Oahu for awhile. So, don't count the days but it shouldn't be too long before I'll be calling you from Oahu.

My joy over finishing was spoiled a couple of days ago when I had a letter returned from one of my best friends with the word "missing" on the outside. It was a letter to Bill Straby [57] who was flying a B-17 in Italy. I wrote his commanding officer to see if possibly it couldn't have been a mistake. Why it is that the best always have to pay the price is beyond me. Incidentally the bombardier on his crew was Al Swain, a classmate of his and mine at Williams. The fellow on Ken's ship is his older brother, Bob Swain. Both of them are darn nice kids. Al was a very good friend of mine at college. Don't say anything about Bill being missing until I can confirm it by a letter from his C.O. I'm hoping against hope that my returned letter was in error.

I'm glad to hear that the ashtrays arrived alright, Dad, because since then they have made a rule forbidding the mailing of that type of souvenir. Speaking of sending things, I received another box of eats yesterday. Many thanks for the always welcome tuna, chicken, and other canned treats. Incidentally the box with the film and "bayrum" has not arrived yet, but I suspect it's on the way. The papers you sent arrived yesterday Dad, in perfect tact.

Enclosed is a clipping that I found in the American magazine, that I know you'll be interested in. By now I imagine that Barry is either home or at least you've heard from him. Tell him I'm having a heck of a time trying to get his title sent home but that I think I'll be able to swing it.

I'm certainly glad to hear that you're up in the country getting some enjoyment out of the pool. In the next couple of weeks I'm going to attempt to get rid of my night club palor and pick up a little sun. Nobody would believe I've been out in the Pacific for almost a year because I'm white as a sheet. It's only after the fortieth that the boys sit around in the sun concentrating on a sun tan.

Guess that's about al for now. Keep up your swell letters and I'll write when anything new comes up.

Best love—

Bobby

APRIL 22, 1945

The Marianas
April 22nd, 1945

Dear Bunny—

Just a couple of lines to let you know that I've finally flown my fortieth mission. It's been a rough grind all the way and a real relief to have it all over with. We had a number of close scrapes but came out on top every time—thank God! Frankly, it's all been like a bad dream and it's great to wake up.

It will still be awhile before I get to the States but time doesn't bother me now as long as I don't have to sweat out any more raids.

A few weeks ago my promotion finally came through. I've been in grade for one heck of a long time now and its about time I made 1st Lt. Promotion are a sore point out here because they are so slow coming through when back stateside all those behind desks get regular promotions. C'est la guerre!

That's about all for now Bunny, but I thought you'd like to know that I'd finally flown my long dreamt of fortieth. Say hello to Ken the next time you write.

Love—
Bobby

"Pop" Elkins Crew

Standing l. to r.—
"Pop"
Mac
Zack
R.L.S.
Nick

Kneeling l. to r.—
Fox
Woody
Rudler
Freeman
Weaver
French

SCRAPBOOK PICTURE/CENSORED INFORMATION

CENSORED INFORMATION

On the following pages is a copy of the map that Bob kept with him overseas to chart his various missions. The map was approximately 3' x 4' so in reducing it for this book his writing is very small, but legible. If you use this map with the log of his combat missions on the pages following you can see where he flew and on what dates. This map and log show all the locations, i.e. censored information Bob could not mention in his letters.

Finally he was assigned to his first combat base on Kwajalein. The missions he flew from there involved "staging" to a very small atoll called Eniwetok where they refueled and proceeded on their missions, primarily over Truk, where a very large part of the Japanese navy was berthed.

When the Marines invaded and secured Guam, they built a runway for his bomber group to move to for the remainder of their missions. Guam was closer to Iwo Jima, which became their main objective and almost daily target. These missions were to keep the airfield destroyed and unusable because the Japanese would rebuild it as quickly as we bombed it. Iwo was nearer Japan and there was concern that the Japanese would use it to attack a number of the islands that the US had recaptured and controlled i.e. Guam, Tinian, and Saipan, and later on possibly the Hawaiian Islands again.

The bulk of his combat missions, flown in 1944 and 1945, included missions over Chi Chi Jima, Yap, Iwo Jima, Truk, and Marcus Island. The greatest number of missions was flown over Iwo Jima in February and March of 1945.

Because of their greater range, the B-24's flew basically in the Pacific Theater where the flights ranged from 12-14 hours over water. The larger B-29 flew from Tinian to Hiroshima with the first atomic bomb on August 6, 1945, and three days later dropped the second bomb on Nagasaki and ended the war in the Pacific.

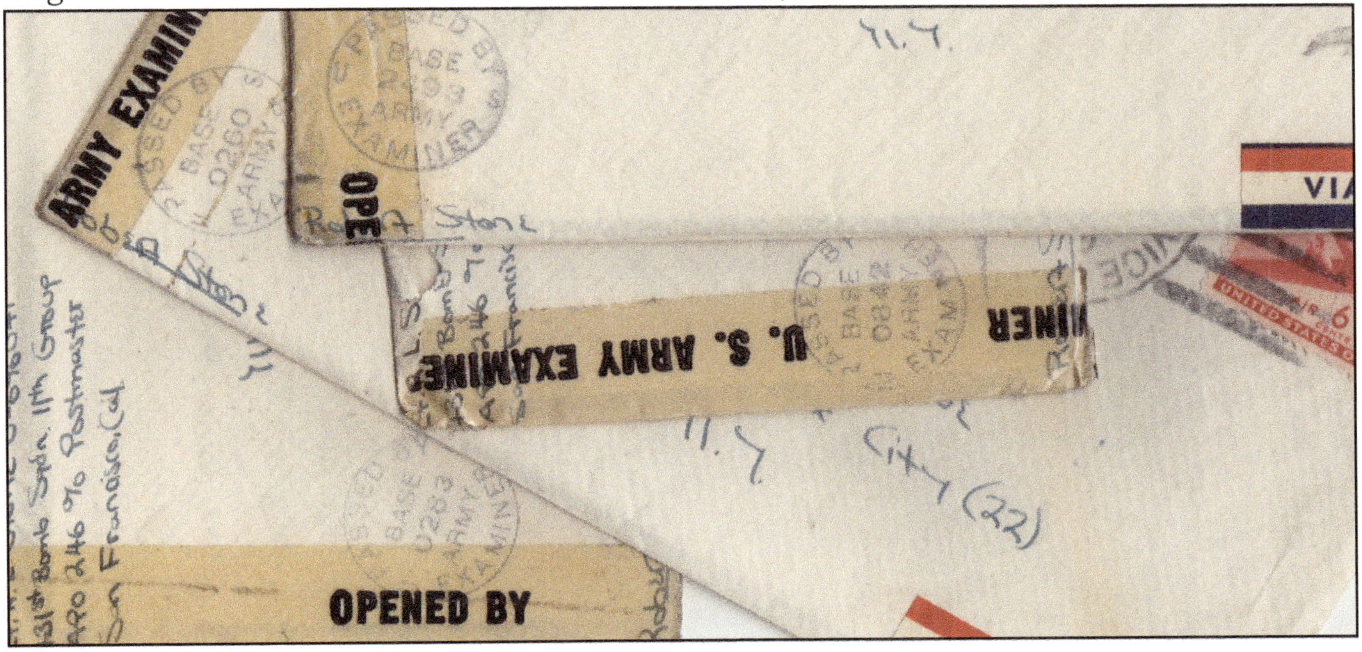

MARIANA ISLANDS

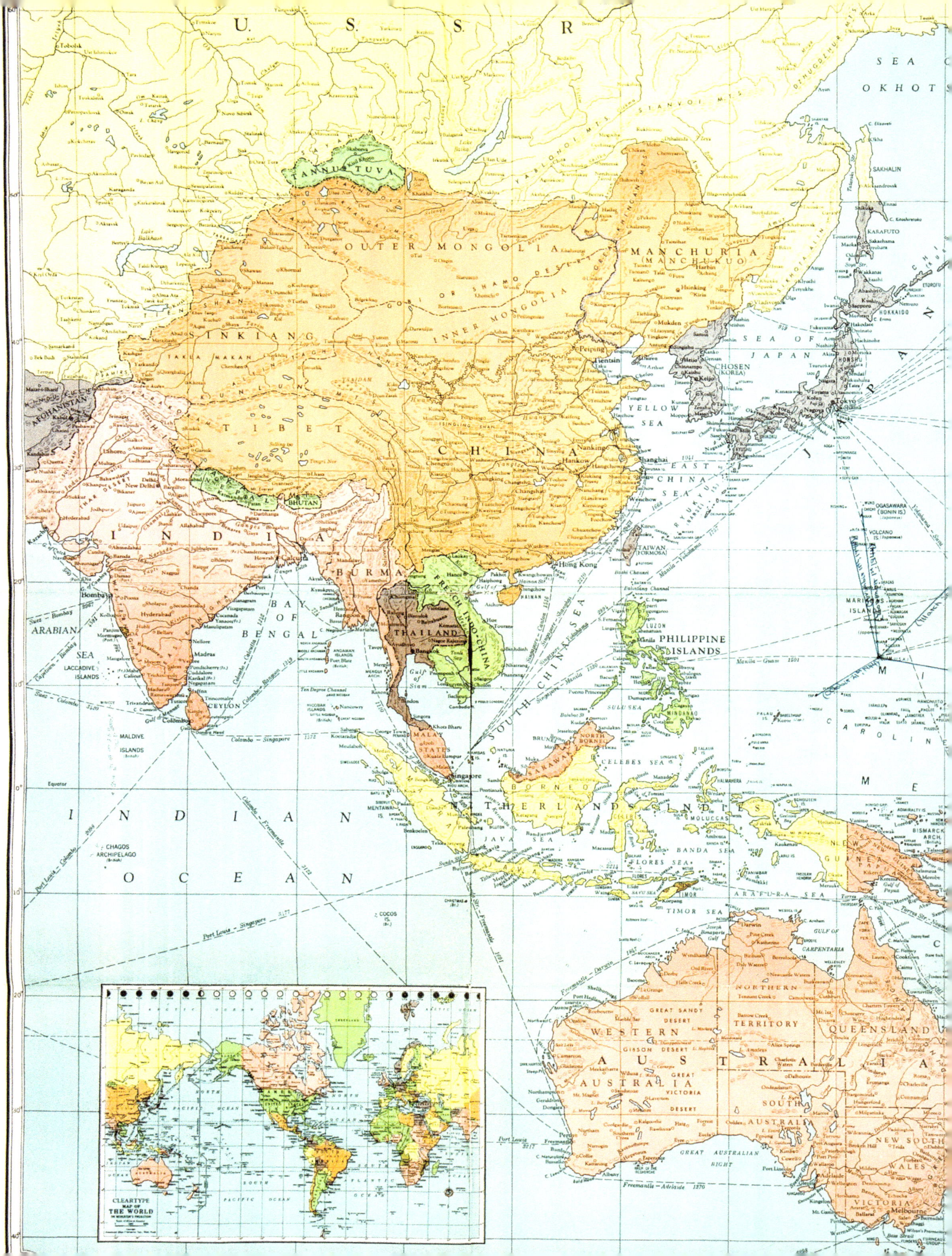

U. S. S. R
SEA OF OKHOTSK
TANNU TUVA
OUTER MONGOLIA
MANCHURIA
(MANCHUKUO)
INNER MONGOLIA
GOBI OR SHAMO DESERT
SINKIANG
TAKLA MAKAN
TIBET
CHINA
AFGHANISTAN
NEPAL
BHUTAN
INDIA
BURMA
THAILAND
FRENCH INDO-CHINA
CHOSEN
(KOREA)
SEA OF JAPAN
JAPAN
YELLOW SEA
EAST CHINA SEA
TAIWAN
(FORMOSA)
HOKKAIDO
HONSHU
SAKHALIN
KARAFUTO
Peiping
Tientsin
Nanking
Shanghai
Hankow
Chungking
Canton
Hong Kong
Mukden
Harbin
Hsinking
Tokyo
Bombay
Calcutta
Madras
Karachi
Delhi
Colombo
Bangkok
Singapore
Manila
Lhasa
Rangoon
Hanoi
ARABIAN SEA
BAY OF BENGAL
LACCADIVE ISLANDS
CEYLON
MALDIVE ISLANDS
CHAGOS ARCHIPELAGO
INDIAN OCEAN
ANDAMAN ISLANDS
NICOBAR ISLANDS
MALAY STATES
SOUTH CHINA SEA
PHILIPPINE ISLANDS
LUZON
MINDANAO
SULU SEA
CELEBES SEA
BORNEO
SARAWAK
NORTH BORNEO
NETHERLANDS INDIES
SUMATRA
JAVA
JAVA SEA
CELEBES
MOLUCCAS
BANDA SEA
FLORES SEA
TIMOR
TIMOR SEA
ARAFURA SEA
NEW GUINEA
PAPUA
BISMARCK ARCH.
MARIANAS ISLANDS
CAROLINE
OGASAWARA (BONIN IS.)
VOLCANO IS.
COCOS IS.
Equator
AUSTRALIA
WESTERN AUSTRALIA
NORTHERN TERRITORY
QUEENSLAND
SOUTH AUSTRALIA
NEW SOUTH WALES
VICTORIA
GREAT SANDY DESERT
GIBSON DESERT
GREAT VICTORIA DESERT
GREAT AUSTRALIAN BIGHT
GULF OF CARPENTARIA
Darwin
Perth
Adelaide
Melbourne
CLEARTYPE MAP OF THE WORLD

CLEARTYPE
GENERAL MAP OF
THE PACIFIC OCEAN
SOUTHEASTERN ASIA
AND AUSTRALIA
ON MERCATOR'S PROJECTION
STATUTE MILES
COPYRIGHT
AMERICAN MAP COMPANY, INC.
ORIGINATORS and SOLE MANUFACTURERS
MAP MAKERS
CLEARTYPE MAPS
PUBLISHERS
Trade Mark Reg.
NEW YORK
Map No. 9562
BERING SEA
GULF OF ALASKA
CANADA
UNITED STATES
ALEUTIAN ISLANDS (U.S.A.)
NORTH PACIFIC OCEAN
HAWAIIAN ISLANDS
POLYNESIA
MARSHALL ISLANDS
GILBERT ISLANDS
PHOENIX ISLANDS
ELLICE ISLANDS
FIJI ISLANDS
SAMOA IS.
TONGA IS.
COOK ISLANDS
SOCIETY ISLANDS
TUBUAI ISLANDS
MARQUESAS ISLANDS
TUAMOTU ARCHIPELAGO
NEW HEBRIDES
NEW CALEDONIA
NORTH ISLAND
SOUTH PACIFIC OCEAN
Tropic of Cancer
Tropic of Capricorn
Equator
INTERNATIONAL DATE LINE
San Francisco
Los Angeles
Seattle
Honolulu
(July 4th 1944)
(September 4th 1944)
(October 7th 1944)

COMBAT MISSIONS

1. October 21st the airfield at Yap	6 hrs. 20 min.
2. November 1st Navy escort in Bonins	13 hrs. 45 min.
3. November 9th shipping at Haha	12 hrs. 30 min.
4. November 11th airfields at Iwo	9 hrs. 35 min.
5. November 19th shipping at Chichi	10 hrs. 50 min.
6. November 21st installations at Haha	12 hrs. 15 min.
7. November 25th shipping at Chichi	11 hrs.
8. November 29th airfields at Iwo	9 hrs. 40 min.
9. December 3rd airfields at Iwo	11 hrs. 30 min.
10. December 8th airfields at Iwo	9 hrs. 40 min.
11. December 10th airfields at Iwo	9 hrs.
12. December 21st airfield #1 at Iwo	10 hrs. 10 min.
13. December 24th airfield #1 at Iwo	9 hrs. 45 min.
14. December 27th airfield #1 at Iwo	10 hrs.
15. December 29th airfield #1 at Iwo	10 hrs.
16. January 5th airfield #1 at Iwo	10 hrs.
17. January 8th airfield #1 at Iwo	10 hrs.
18. January 10th airfield #1 at Iwo	10 hrs. 20 min.
19. January 14th installations at Iwo	9 hrs. 30 min.
20. January 18th airfield #1 at Iwo	9 hrs. 25 min.

LIST OF 40 MISSIONS

COMBAT MISSIONS

21. January 21st airfield # at Iwo (10 hrs. 25 min)
22. January 24th installations at Iwo (10 hrs. 10 min.)
23. February 12th gun implacements at Iwo (10 hrs. 50 min.)
24. February 16th air support to task force (10 hrs. 10 min.)
25. February 18th air support to task force (10 hrs. 30 min)
26. February 27th Susaki Airfield at Chichi (12 hrs. 25 min)
27. March 1st Susaki Airfield at Chichi (11 hrs. 50 min.)
28. March 6th Susaki Airfield at Chichi (11 hrs. 25 min.)
29. March 10th Susaki Airfield at Chichi (10 hrs. 45 min.)
30. March 11th Susaki Airfield at Chichi (11 hrs. 05 min)
31. March 14th Susaki Airfield at Chichi (11 hrs. 50 min.)
32. March 18th Susaki Airfield at Chichi (11 hrs. 35 min.)
33. March 20th Susaki Airfield at Chichi (10 hrs. 50 min.)
34. March 22nd Susaki Airfield at Chichi (11 hrs. 25 min.)
35. March 27th Susaki Airfield at Chichi (10 hrs. 35 min.)
36. March 30th Installations + Airfield on Marcus (11 hrs. 35 min
37. April 5th Installations on Eten Is. Truk (8 hrs. 20 min
38. April 9th Installations + Airfield on Marcus (11 hrs. 35 min
39. April 13th Installations + Airfield on Marcus (11 hrs. 30 min)
40. April 19th Installations on Dublon Is. Truk (8 hrs. 10 min)

The Marianas
April 27th, 1945

Dear Dad & Bee—

Since my last letter I've been taking it very easy doing a little traveling around. I spent yesterday with Jack Naylor who asked to send his regards to you. I went out with him and watched his outfit fire their guns. As always 'twas fun to visit with Jack.

Still haven't gotten over the wonderful feeling of completing my missions. Somehow you're on top of the world and you haven't a worry. It's a terrific relief of tension to be finished up.

I still don't know when I'll be leaving the Marianas but ordinarily it takes a little over two weeks for your orders to come through. Actually time is of little consequence now—a few days one way or the other don't matter much. A couple of days ago I went up to Barry's old outfit, and found he'd been gone about a week. The boys seemed to think that he'd gone back by boat instead of flying back. No doubt, by now you've had some word from him.

The last couple of days I've spent out in the sun trying to get rid of my bar room gabr. It's gotten very warm out here

APRIL 27, 1945

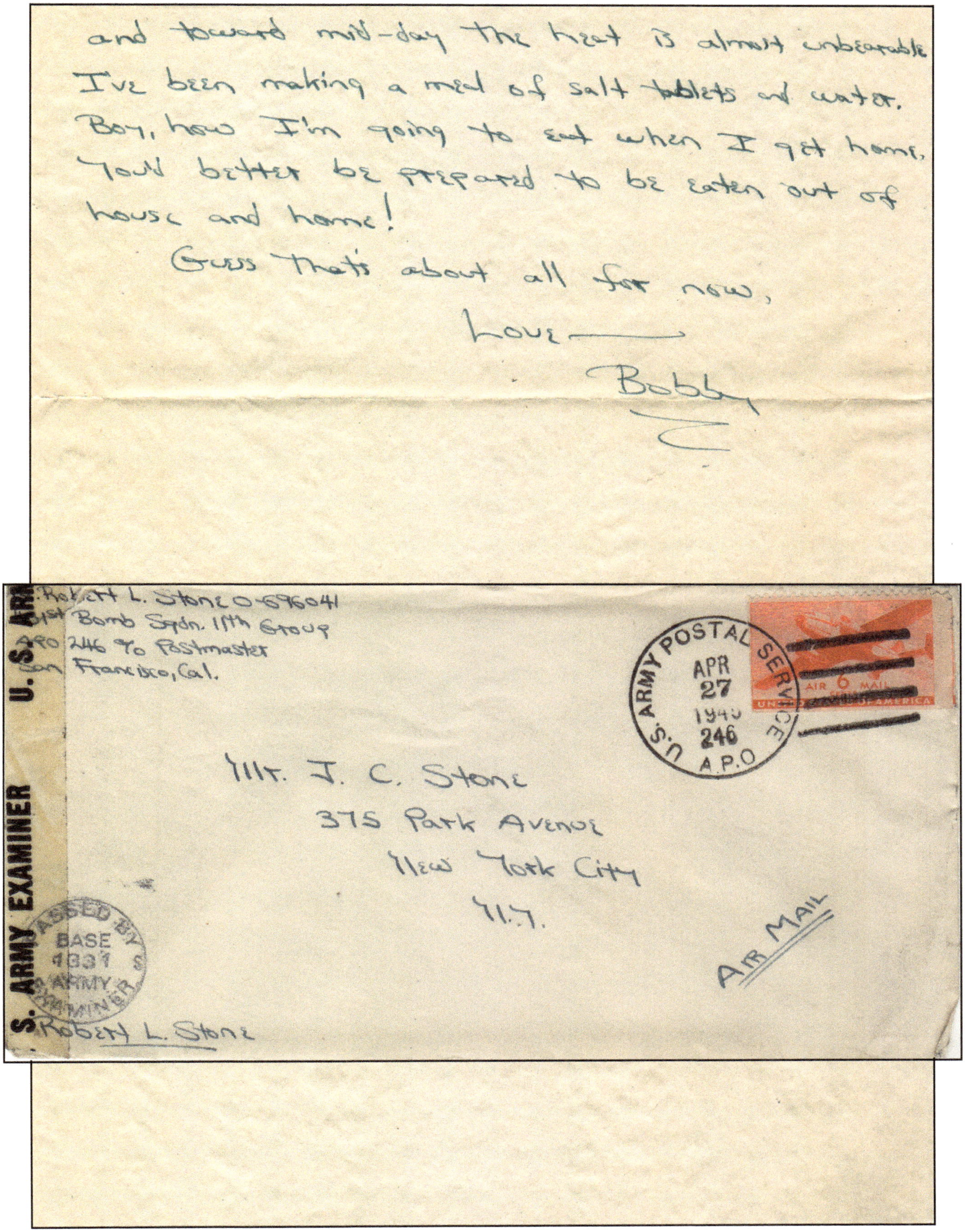

and toward mid-day the heat is almost unbearable
I've been making a meal of salt tablets and water.
Boy, how I'm going to eat when I get home.
You'd better be prepared to be eaten out of
house and home!

Guess that's about all for now,

Love —

Bobby

Robert L. Stone O-696041
Bomb Sqdn. 11th Group
246 % Postmaster
Francisco, Cal.

U.S. ARMY POSTAL SERVICE
APR 27 1945
246 A.P.O.

AIR 6 MAIL
UNITED STATES OF AMERICA

Mr. J. C. Stone
375 Park Avenue
New York City
N.Y.

AIR MAIL

U.S. ARMY EXAMINER

PASSED BY U.S. BASE 4331 ARMY EXAMINER

Robert L. Stone

The Marianas
April 30th, 1945

Dear Dad + Bee—

The last couple of days have found me the glad recipient of a number of packages. Many, many thanks for the five rolls of film which came through in fine shape. It came in the nick of time because I'm all out and have no way of acquiring any down here. The various canned delicacies really hit the spot. The chicken is particularly good for making tasty sandwiches. Our chow has been at a fairly low ebb, and so we usually supplement with a snack between times.

A million thanks for sending the "Bay Rum,"[58] Dad. You don't know how close I came to throwing it out because I thought it was a loaf of bread that had gotten moldy. All of us got a real kick (both ways) out of your ingenious job of concealment. It was swell and arrived unbroken—many thanks, Pop.

The last couple of days we received some bad news as to our immediate return. Oahu is so overcrowded that we'll have to remain down here for an indefinite period of time. The crew that finished right before

APRIL 30, 1945

page 2

us got by alright but we're stuck. There are five crews of us waiting to return and we just sit around. There are twenty-four new crews in the squadron making a total of ninety-six officers, none of which we know. We feel like strangers down here when actually the new crews are the strangers.

At the moment I'm as red as a lobster all over my body. We've been lounging around in the sun getting the so-called "forty mission tan." Had a rotten experience down at the beach two days ago when I had $170 stollen from my wallet. All the money was removed except a travelers check and two Philippine bills. Except for all my money being removed, the wallet was left intact. Needless to say I'm fairly well irritated about the whole thing but I haven't a chance in the world to recover it. It was at an officers beach house, but there were a couple of strange enlisted men wandering around that day and that's that!

I can't get too darn upset because we still all feel wonderful about finishing our missions. I guess I used up all my good luck on a couple of close calls

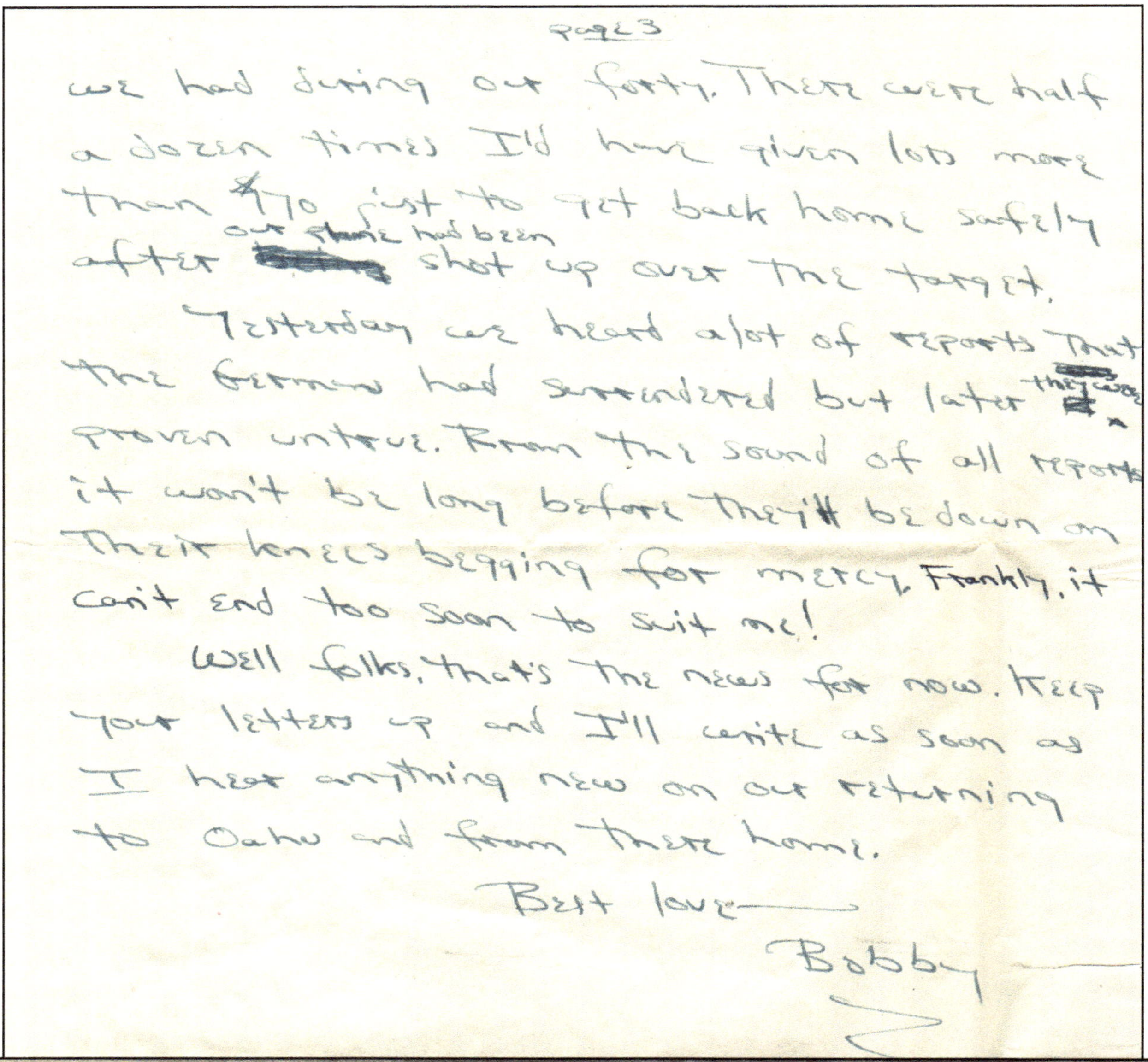

page 3

we had firing out forty. There were half a dozen times I'd have given lots more than $70 just to get back home safely after our plane had been shot up over the target.

Yesterday we heard alot of reports that the Germans had surrendered but later they were proven untrue. From the sound of all reports it won't be long before they'll be down on their knees begging for mercy. Frankly, it can't end too soon to suit me!

Well folks, that's the news for now. Keep your letters up and I'll write as soon as I hear anything new on our returning to Oahu and from there home.

Best love—

Bobby

APRIL 30-MAY 3, 1945

The Marianas
May 3rd, 1946

Dear Dad—

Received your letter this morning with the over generous check for a party. You know how much I appreciate it and can't adequately thank you for it Dad. I've already cashed it into travelers checks so that I'll have the money for a real blow-out when we hit Honolulu or possibly Frisco. That's a party we've been waiting to throw for just about a year now and it couldn't be sweller than to have you sponsoring it!

Still no definite word as to our leaving here, but I don't think it should be too much longer. We are all very anxious to get out of this environment as it gets awfully routine after all this time. All we've been doing for the last week is lounge around in the sun, write a few letters, and in general take it easy. After my unfortunate experience on the beach I'm a little resentful about going back so I rarely go swimming. The more I think of it the madder it makes me to think that anyone would be so rotten as to steal another man's money. My faith in human nature really took a tumble to say nothing of my financial status. C'est la guerre!

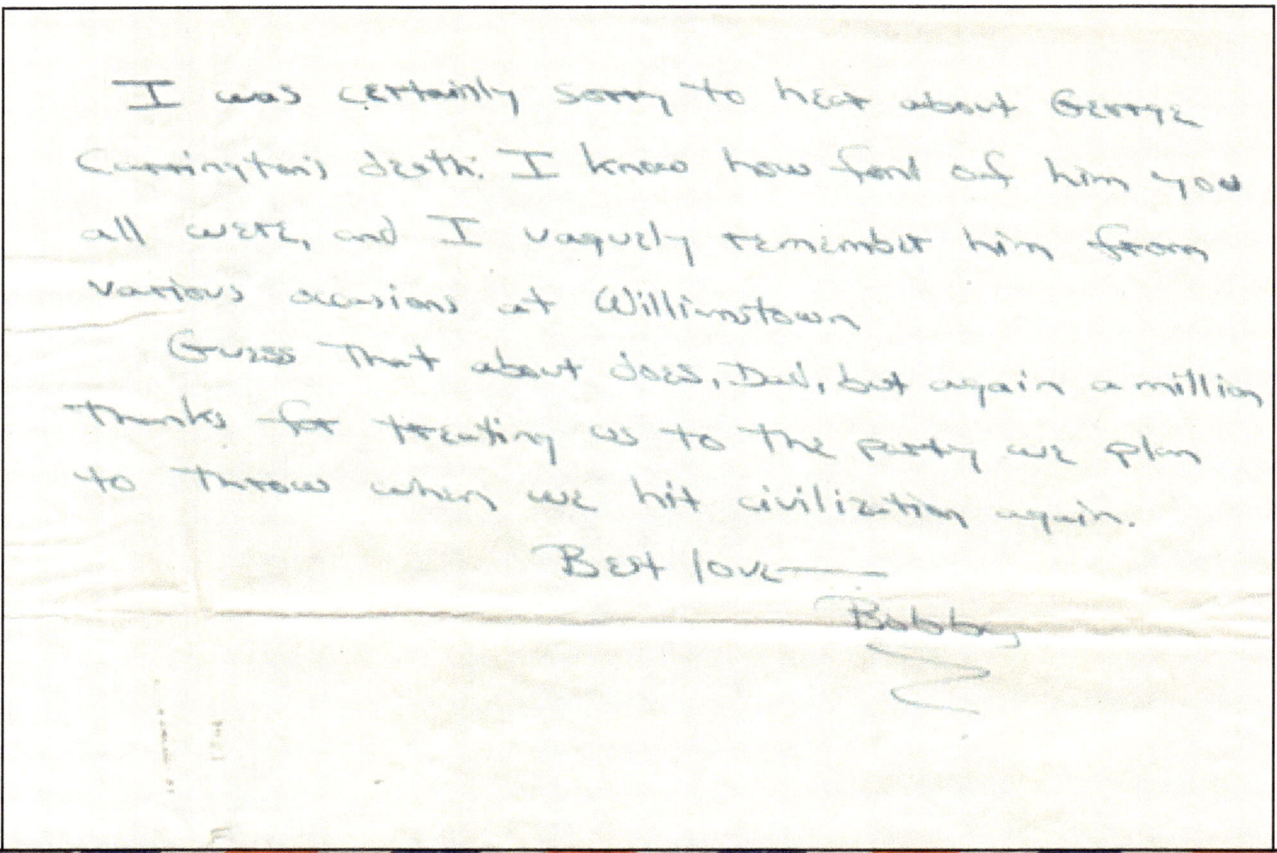

I was certainly sorry to hear about George Cunnington's death. I know how fond of him you all were, and I vaguely remember him from various occasions at Williamstown.

Guess that about does, Dad, but again a million thanks for treating us to the party we plan to throw when we hit civilization again.

Best love—

Bobby

MAY 3, 1945/SCRAPBOOK PHOTOGRAPHS

1.) The airfield on Yap Island. Our target on our first missio flown off of Guam.

2.) "Hellcat Honey" in the back-ground with #1 feathered.

1) The "Rapid Robin" on the way home from Iwo

2) The 431st in formation with Truk in the background. Down with the ball turrets, here come the fighters.

1.) Low-level shot of the north end of Haha Jima

2.) A glimpse of Iwo under the clouds.

1) The ship that was assigned to us when the 30th Group moved in and "Jenny" was sent back to Oahu.

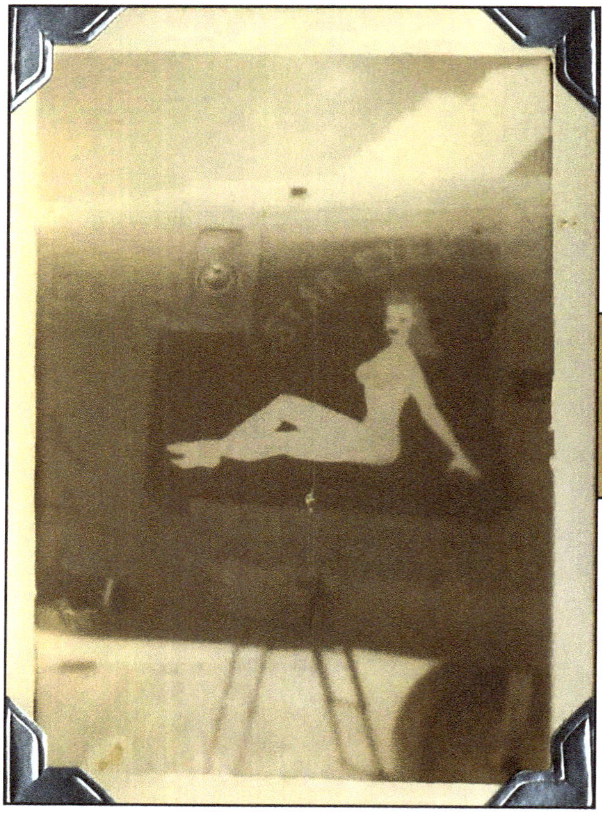

1) We flew Star Eyes on our first mission to Jap after bringing it down from Kwaj.

SCRAPBOOK PHOTOGRAPHS

"Birds Eye View," the "best ship" according to Bob was the one his crew was pictured with (p. 350).

1) The best ship on the line #864

2) Not for my grandchildren to look upon!

2.) Flew "Stripped For Action" on a couple of missions while Crampton was on rest leave.

1.) Flew "Hellcat Belle" twice and the second time we lost an engine over Iwo Jima and had to strip the ship. Made it back to Saipan after a grueling five hours of not knowing whether we'd make it or not.

SCRAPBOOK PHOTOGRAPHS

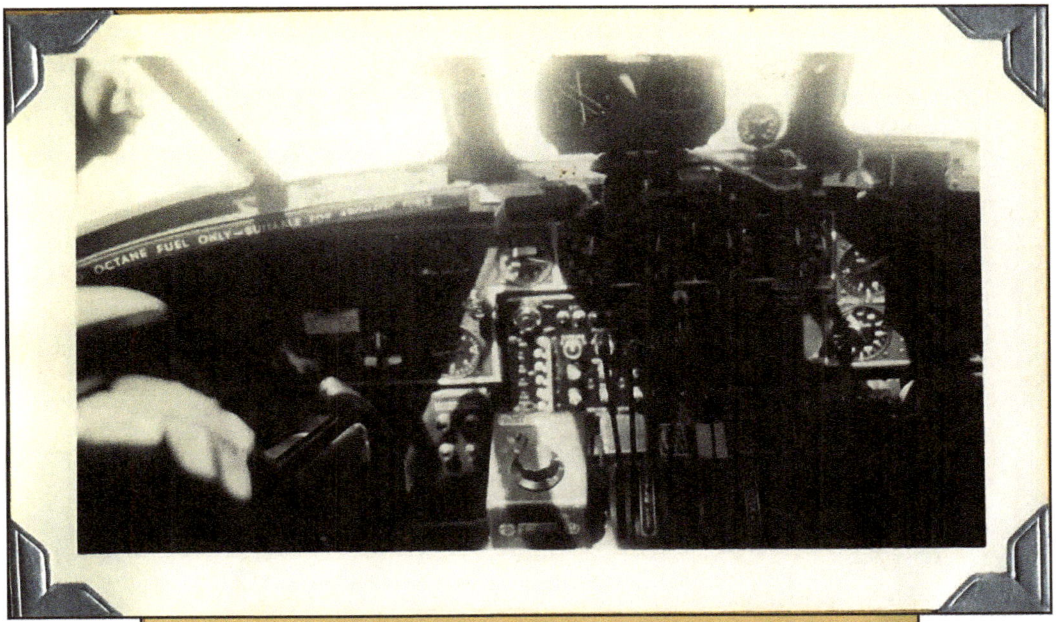

1) The instrument panel of the great lib

2) Drummond, keeping check on all the dials and instruments.

1) Close-up of the tail position.

2) Blurred shot of the waist gun position

At end of Bob's letters, see telegram from "Pop" Elkins to Bob, with 1945 holiday greetings.

GOING HOME

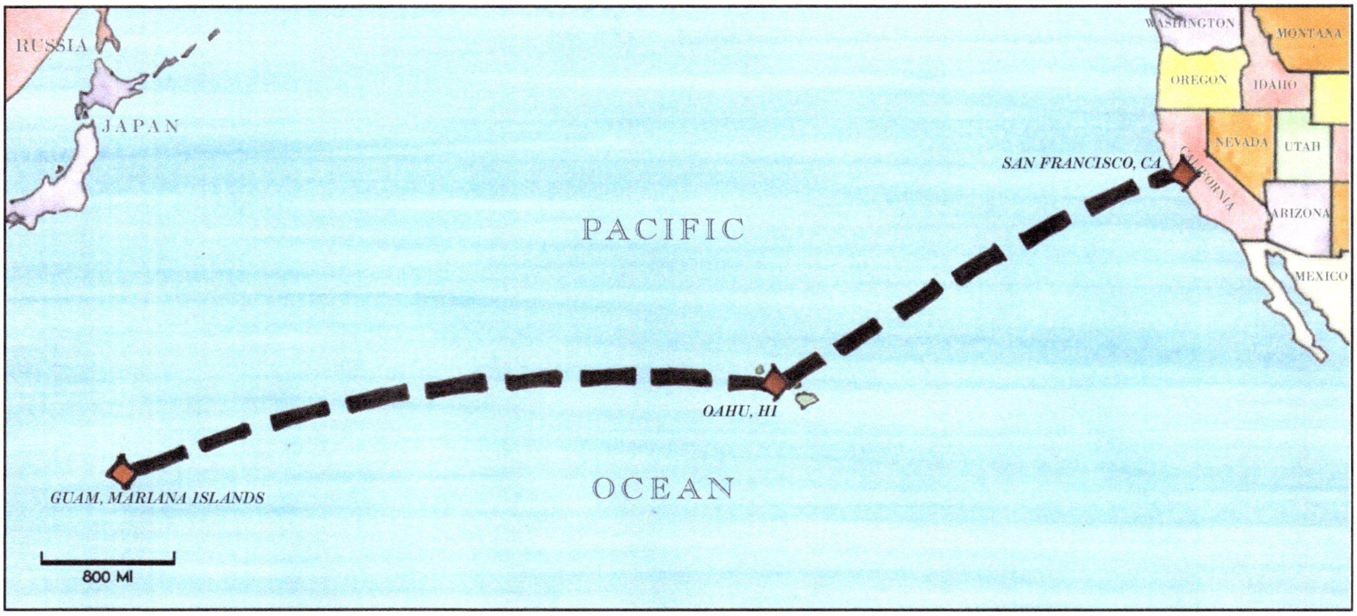

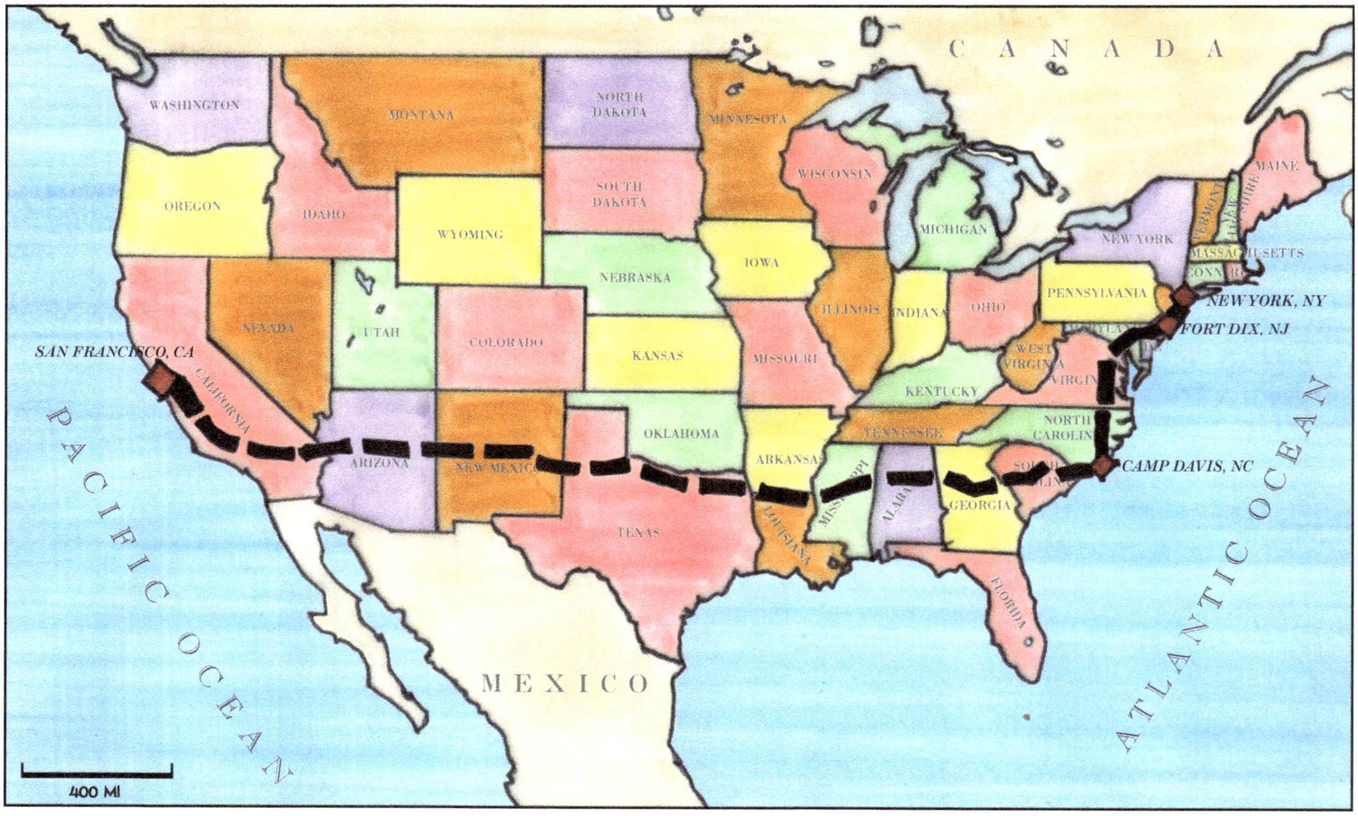

MAY 1945–DECEMBER 1945

Oahu, Hawaii
May 11th, 1945

Dear, Dad + Bee—

Just a line or two to tell you how swell it was to talk to you the other day. You can well imagine how wonderful it is to be out of the combat zone and back here where people live like human beings. It will still be a little while before we leave for the States so don't count the days. It seems that everyone goes home by boat now so that will take a little time too.

Had a big old brawl the other night on the money you send me, Dad. Believe me it was a mighty wet party and one we'd looked forward to ~~for~~ a long time. Again a million thanks ~~for~~ treating us, Dad. I only wish you could have been along.

At the moment we're living at the rest camp devouring lots of fresh food and gallons of milk. It's a real pleasure to eat good food once again.

Have been swimming several times and in general have been taking it very easy just enjoying the conveniences of civilization.

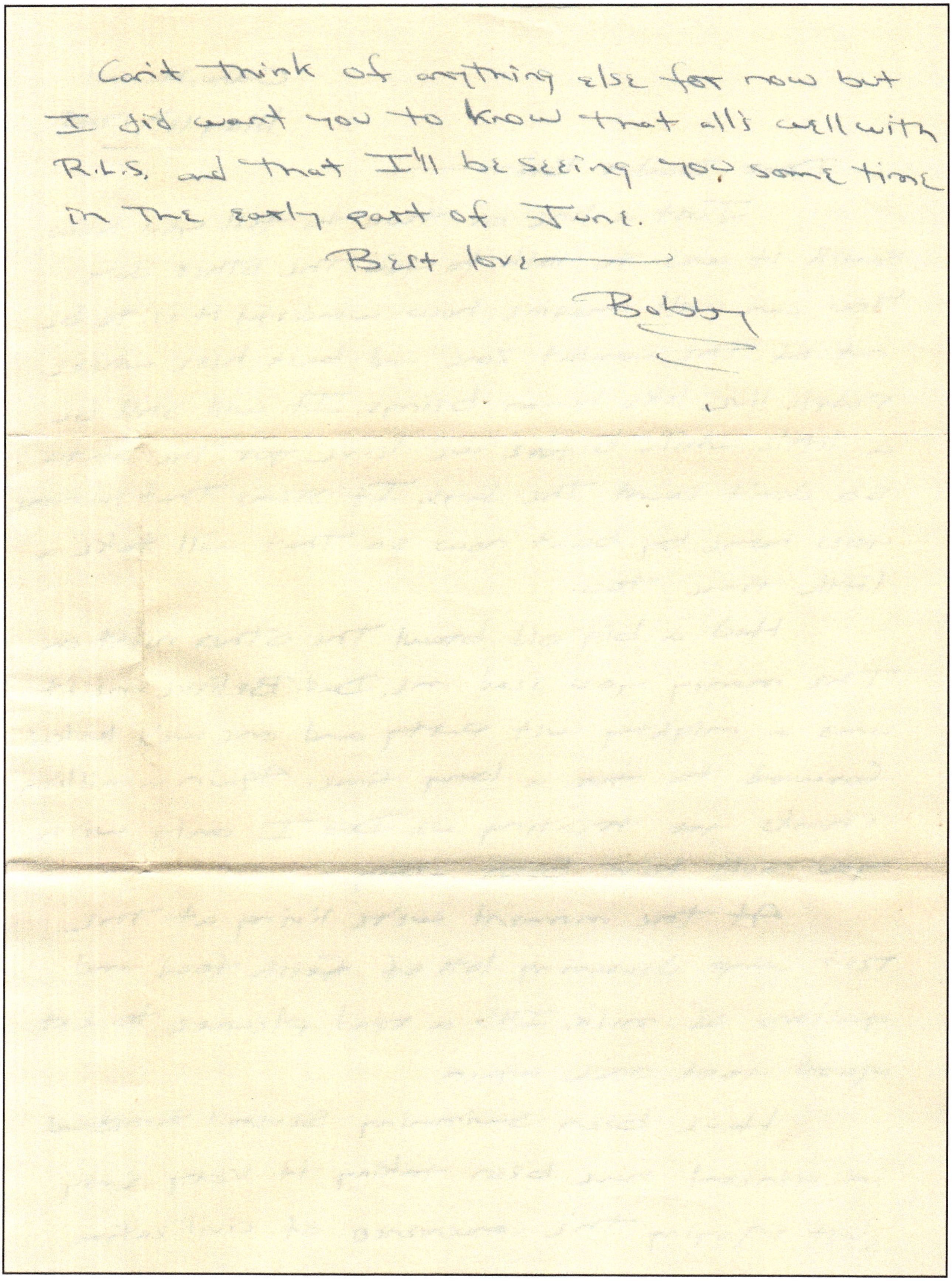
Can't think of anything else for now but I did want you to know that all's well with R.L.S. and that I'll be seeing you some time in the early part of June.

Best love—

Bobby

Oahu, Hawaii
May 15th, 1945

Dear Dad, Bee, & Bunny—

This morning one of my friends brought up a batch of mail from the Marianas and so a few lines are in order, even though I wrote you a few days ago. I was terribly surprised to learn that you'd heard of the completion of my 40th indirectly because I wrote you a long letter when I finished. I trust by now you've received it because I mailed about ten letters at the same time, and I can't understand you're not receiving it. Many thanks for all your letters of this morning. 'Twas swell of you to have written such a sweet letter, Bunny.

All goes well with this loafer, and I'm gaining weight each meal. We're living here at the rest camp eating colossal meals of nothing but fresh food and quarts of cold milk. No C-rations!!! The milk is a real treat after liquid refreshment of nothing but water or G.I. coffee for about a year now. To see us eat you'd think we were part of the starving Armenians.

Went in to see Mr. Kellett the other day and he asked after you, Dad. He's an awfully nice gent.

If all goes as I think it will, I ought to be on my way home in about ten days or so. Most of the boys have had to go by boat rather than air. Of course, we'd rather fly but for some reason they've cut out our air travel.

Well folks, that's about all for the moment but I'll write again if anything new comes up. Thanks for your various letters that I received this morning. If I don't write again from Oahu, you can expect a phone call from the West coast in about two weeks or so

Best love——

Bobby

Camp Davis
Saturday 14th, 1945

Dear Dad and Bee:

Really haven't much news to pass on as life is extremely dull down here. As I told you in my last letter I won't be able to get out of the service for the time being. Oh how the army sticks to its word! You've never seen a more disillusioned bunch of fellows as we have here.

Today I went to the classification part of my processing. They sent in a recommendation for me to be assigned to a place like Fort Dix and do some kind of administrative work. Frankly I doubt if this will be accepted as I have had no administrative experience, but I'll just have to wait and see. I'd give just about anything to be stationed at Dix. It will take about a week to find out if this assignment goes through. If it doesn't I believe I'll be sent out to Midland Texas (God forbid) to go through a refresher course. At the completion of the course which lasts six weeks you go into a pool and they try to find you some sort of a job. By that time they may have released us as essential and we can get out. You see, they have more of us than they need but for some reason they're not releasing us at the moment. Any job we get we'll just be marking time and so it won't amount to a damn. I won't ramble on any further because it's all so confused that it makes me mad to discuss it. To think that the army doesn't need us yet they insist on making us stay in the army and do nothing but bide our time.

I received a letter from you this morning, Dad, as well as one ## that I had written you. I forgot that airmail is eight cents in the states and so they returned my letter for two cents. No matter what happens I'll probably be here for another week at least, so please continue to write.

Just to prove that I wasn't exaggerating about this dump, they are no longer taking any returnees, and it will merely continue to be a German POW camp. Rain, mosquitos, and heat are the most outstanding thingsthat Camp Davis boasts and frankly I don't like any of them.

Last night a couple of us went into Wilmington for dinner and we were sadly disappointed. It's a typical small town overrun with soldiers and marines from Camp Lejeune.

Guess that's about all for now as I intend to talk to you tomorrow on Dad's birthday. Oh say, in my state of confusion since I've been down here I forgot to thank you for a perfectly swell leave at home. It was really great to get home and be with you again after all those months. You certainly did everything to make my stay just like old times what with theater and all. I don't need to say thanks a million because you know how much I appreciated everything you did for me. Enough said!

Best love,

Bobby

Camp Davis, N.C.
July 17th, 1945

Dear Dad and Bee:

There's really nothing new to write, but I thought you'd be interested to see the enclosed clipping from the morning's paper. Just trying to prove that my complaints about this dump are well founded. Frankly I'll never know how the Air Force ever got stuck with this white elephant when they have such swell places as Atlantic City, Miami, and Santa Monica.

There's nothing new about my assignment, but I ought to know something definite by the end of the week. I've got my fingers crossed that my job at a redistribution or separation center comes through. I'd certainly hate to be sent out to Texas, but I suppose that will be just my luck.

That's about all for now except that I hope you have a swell time at Alderbrook and that you catch lots of trout.

Best love,

Bobby

Davis Closing Order Leaves Future In Doubt

Announcement yesterday by the War Department that Camp Davis is to be discontinued as a convalescent and redistribution center for the Army Air Force personnel left in doubt the future of the mammoth installation in eastern North Carolina, where thousands of soldiers were trained for the war against Germany and Japan.

All construction work, totaling $1,600,000 in unfinished contracts, was ordered halted immediately. The work was ordered rushed to completion by Army engineers last week.

Camp Davis, in the general vicinity of Holly Ridge in lower Onslow county, was completed in 1941 at an original cost of about $17,000,000. It first was used as a training center for coast artillery, antiaircraft and balloon barrage units.

In the four years of its existence it has been expanded considerably. The Army Air Forces took it over a few months ago.

The future of the camp will be decided after it has been offered to other War Department agencies.

According to a statement by the AAF, through the Camp Davis public relations office, casuals now at the center, patients in the convalescent hospital and permanent personel will be moved to other AAF facilities as soon as possible.

Camp Davis, N.C.
July 20th, 1945

Dear Dad and Bee:

Still down here at Davis and as yet nothing is definite. At the moment I'm waiting on word about an assignment. So far I've been lucky as the devil. Except for me all the bombardiers coming through here have been sent out to the refresher course and pool at Midland Texas, much against their desire. After spending six weeks there they will get some sort of an assignment. For some reason, the fellow that interviewed me went to bat for me and is trying to get me a job that has to do with redistribution. He even made a phone call up to Louisville, which is the headquarters for all personnel redistribution, and he spoke to someone up there about me. I'm not completely sure of getting the job but at least it's a step in the right direction. The officer he spoke to told him to hold Lt. Stone until we heard from him, so right now I'm waiting with my fingers crossed. Why my interviewing officer even bothered to do all this for me I don't know as ordinarily they don't give a darn and just rush you right through to Midland and that's that. I must say it was one heck of a good break but it won't mean a thing if nothing comes through. All I can do now is wait and hope. Even in the army you run across a good man once in awhile and I was certainly lucky to hit one of the few.

Aside from the above there's nothing new. This place is definitely closing and they're not taking any more returnees. The other night I won a duplicate bridge turnament up at the officer's club. The prize was a free meal (for two people) in town at a darn nice place. I took a pilot friend of mine who came here with me.

That's about all for now, but I'll let you know as soon as I find out anything one way or the other as to my reassignment. I trust you're having a swell time and are catching lots of trout.

Best love,

Bobby

In August 1945, Bob was reassigned to Fort Dix, New Jersey. He worked as an Aide-de-Camp for Brigadier General Madison Pearson and Major General Leland S. Hobbs. Because he was so close to home, his letters were replaced by phone calls and visits.

8 THE FORT DIX POST

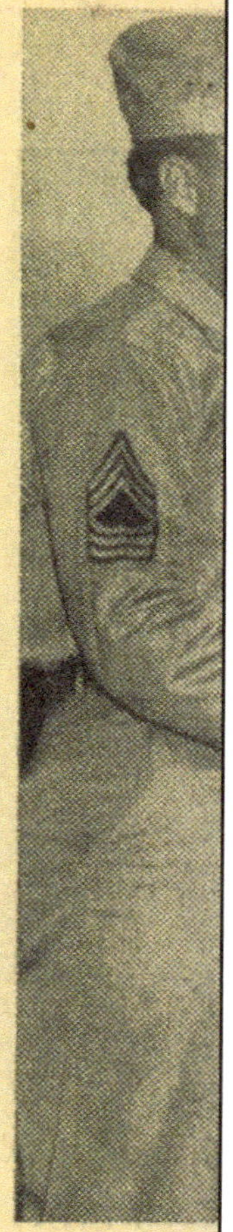

POST Photo by Sgt. Alfred D. Boehme

Pinning the Distinguished Flying Cross on his Aide, 1st Lt. Robert L. Stone, is Brig. Gen. Madison Pearson, Post Commander, during Retreat Parade ceremony last Wednesday. Others decorated were: (l. to r.) Pvt. Howard M. Course, Bronze Star; S/Sgt. Lester Orem, T/5 Joseph A. Wenzel, and Pfc John Lopke, Jr., Combat Infantryman Badges. Marine Lieutenant Stone, brother of the general's aide looks on as his brother receives the high award.

First M

Staff of the

The Fort Dix Post photograph of the "pinning" ceremony at Fort Dix, where Bob was awarded the Distinguished Flying Cross medal. Bob's brother, Jimmy Stone, is on the right.

SEPTEMBER 5, 1945

Photograph of pinning ceremony at Fort Dix, signed by Brigadier General Madison Pearson. Bob worked as an Aide-de-Camp for the General after the war ended. Bob's brother, Jimmy Stone, is second from left.

Bob's father, Jake Stone (3rd from the right) and his step-mother, Bee Stone (3rd from left) at the Retreat Parade Ceremony at Fort Dix, NJ where Bob was awarded his Distinguished Flying Cross award.

SEPTEMBER 5, 1945

The Retreat Parade Ceremony at Fort Dix on September 5, 1945. Bob is on the far right, facing the camera.

Brigadier General Madison Pearson (left), Major General Leland S. Hobbs (center), Bob is on the right. Bob served as Aide-de-Camp to both Generals at Fort Dix in 1945.

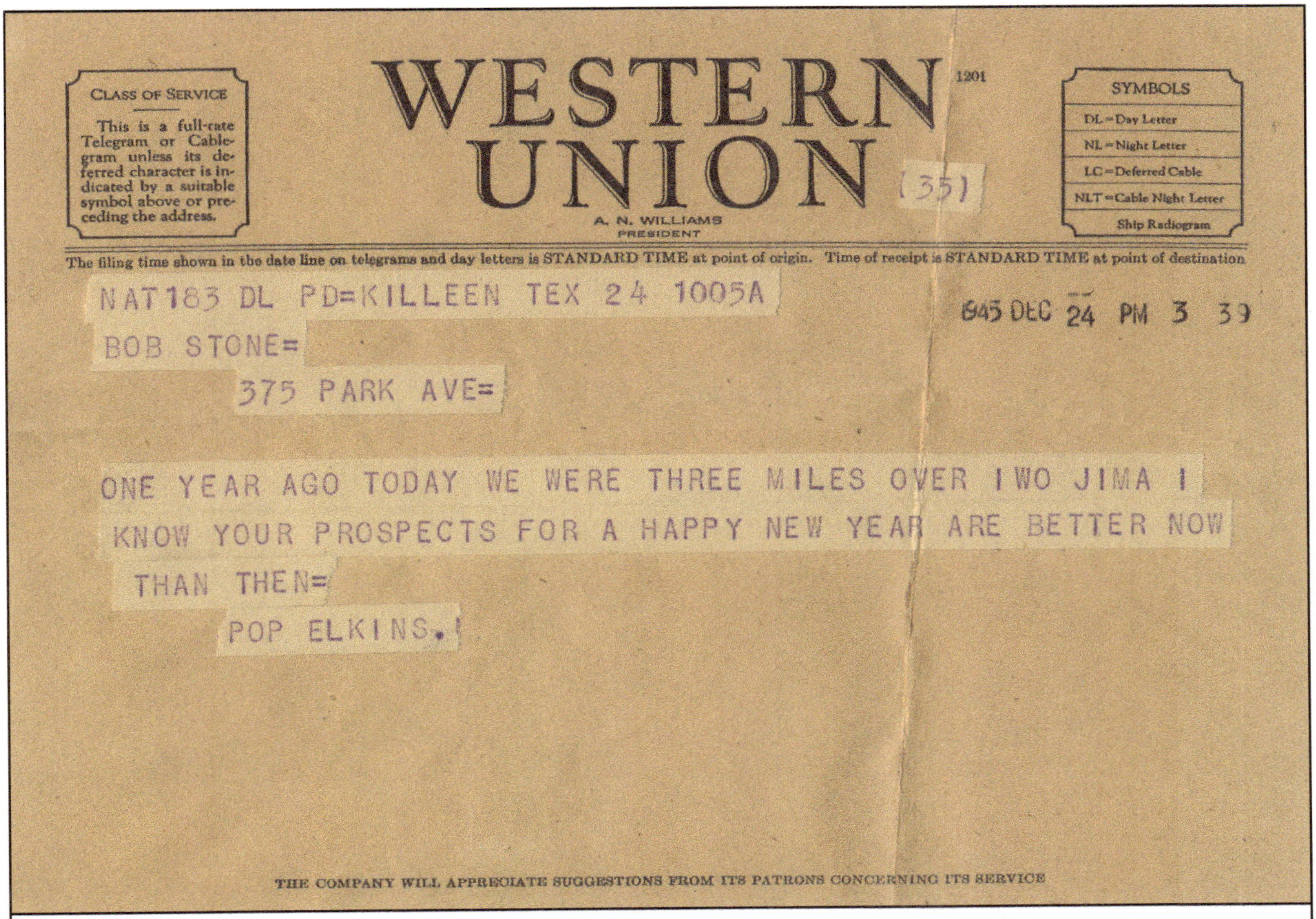

CLASS OF SERVICE

This is a full-rate Telegram or Cablegram unless its deferred character is indicated by a suitable symbol above or preceding the address.

WESTERN UNION

1201

(35)

A. N. WILLIAMS
PRESIDENT

SYMBOLS

DL=Day Letter
NL=Night Letter
LC=Deferred Cable
NLT=Cable Night Letter
Ship Radiogram

The filing time shown in the date line on telegrams and day letters is STANDARD TIME at point of origin. Time of receipt is STANDARD TIME at point of destination

NAT183 DL PD=KILLEEN TEX 24 1005A

1945 DEC 24 PM 3 39

BOB STONE=
375 PARK AVE=

ONE YEAR AGO TODAY WE WERE THREE MILES OVER IWO JIMA I KNOW YOUR PROSPECTS FOR A HAPPY NEW YEAR ARE BETTER NOW THAN THEN=

POP ELKINS.

THE COMPANY WILL APPRECIATE SUGGESTIONS FROM ITS PATRONS CONCERNING ITS SERVICE

Western Union telegram sent from "Pop" Elkins to Bob on Christmas Eve, December 24, 1945.

EPILOGUE

The cover of one of Bob's scrapbooks.

Bob's letters ended in July of 1944, when he was given his last assignment in the service as Aide-de-camp to Brigadier General Madison Pearson and then as assistant Post Adjutant to Major General Leland Hobbs at Fort Dix, New Jersey. Because he was so near to home his letters stopped; phone calls and visits were much more meaningful. Although his commanding officer recommended that he pursue a career in the army, he decided against that. He also knew he did not want to go back to Williams because he also felt that the academic work he had accomplished in the service was more than adequate. After working at Lehman Brothers before the war, he also knew that he didn't want to work on Wall Street. Most of all, he was anxious to get on with his life. He received a certificate from Williams that gave returning Veterans credit for the classes they had taken in the service and Bob was considered a member of the Class of '44.

At this point both of our lives were beginning to shape our futures. In Bob's case, as a twenty-three year old it was question of what to do next. For me as a nine-year old I had already embarked on a path that was to be as challenging to me as flying forty missions was for Bob. Of course my path did not include the inherent life or death danger, but it did need the same resolve, practice, determination, and ability in order to succeed.

I had discovered figure skating and was determined to be the best that I could be. There is a world of difference between being the best and being the best that one could become. When you are a nine-year old you are full of great enthusiasm and there are no limitations to what you think you can do and accomplish. With the support of my family, I became a competitive figure skater starting out in Juveniles and ending in Senior, National, and International Championships. To compete in Worlds or Olympics you have to pass the eighth level or the gold test of the U.S. Figure Skating Association. Free skating was easy and fun for me and I excelled at it: I could skate around the rink gathering speed and then take off on a jump and fly through the air—but unfortunately, it was a nightmare for me to do the school figures. As an eighteen-year-old, the school figures on the gold test were to me the equivalent of Bob's bombardier's wings and flying forty missions: it was a feat that was challenging, scary and ultimately satisfying, but one I would never want to go through again.

At that time in the skating world school figures counted for 60% of any competition or gold test, and took hours of practice even if you were good at them. My school schedule did not allow for many hours on the ice so I informed my parents when I was twelve that I wanted to attend the professional Children's School in New York City where all of my serious skating friends attended, and where their academics were arranged around their skating schedules. I was at a wonderful school that was academically rigorous, with an equally challenging athletic program, and a long school day. My parents were adamant that I remain there—so I had no choice.

While I was busy with school and skating Bob had been introduced by his Uncle Eddie to three young men who had outstanding service records and were forming a new management consulting firm called Cresap, McCormack & Paget in New York City. Bob was hired as a Staff Associate and was assigned to work on accounts ranging from Yale, Rutgers, and Vanderbilt to New York Hospital, United Airlines, Westinghouse, the IRS, The Hoover Commission, and the merging of the Army, Navy and Air Forces into the Defense Department. He always felt this was an invaluable opportunity and much more precious than an MBA as it was practical business experience. There was a lot of travel connected with the various consulting jobs and Bob hoped to stay in New York City, but did not want to marry and start a family until he had a job with less travel.

He met his wife, Mary Elizabeth Lee while working at Cresap McCormack & Paget. Mary's family owned the Lee Hat Company in Danbury, CT, and they married just before he joined the American Broadcasting Company (ABC) at the urging of a friend but to the dismay of his Dad. This was in 1952 in the very early days of television, and at a time when most executives were moved from the radio side of the corporation with no experience in television. So it provided an incredible experience for a young man with a good education, some business experience and ambition. He started as an account executive in the television sales network and was soon named Vice President and General Manager in charge of Channel 7, which was ABC's owned and operated T.V. station in New York City. Mary and Bob soon had a family of four children and in 1953 moved to an apartment building on East End Avenue in Manhattan.

At that same time I was living with my parents in the same East End Avenue apartment building where we had moved in 1943 after our year in New Jersey during the war. I was getting up early every morning to train at the old Madison Square Garden in mid-Manhattan before returning to school, which was just down the block on East End Avenue. In 1953, as Bob's family was about to move I graduated and spent the summer training in Lake Placid (several miles from Alderbrook), passed my eighth test in the fall, took the year off from school (unheard of in those days), and flew to St. Moritz in January with my mother to train with Howard Nicholson, my coach from Lake Placid summers.

In St. Moritz I was fortunate to be able to train with World and European Champions, and we soon formed a troupe that skated exhibitions around Europe before my new friends competed in the World Championships in Oslo, Norway. I was the first American skater to have permission to compete overseas in a free skating competition held in Villars, Switzerland. After Worlds, several of the U.S. women skaters returned home to college and I was invited to skate with the World Champions, U.S., Canadian and European Champions. We all toured in Europe together. It was a fabulous experience and one that I will always treasure—but my skating time in Europe convinced me that I should follow a different path.

My mother returned to the states in March and I continued to live with a family in Lausanne, Switzerland, before returning home in June—which is when I had to figure out what to do for the rest of my life. I was asked to write an article all about skating for a new magazine, Sports Illustrated, and so in the issue of January 3, 1955 my four-page article appeared titled "Black Ice and Flying Skates." From there I segued into forming one of the first womens' active sportswear companies with my mother. I designed skating clothes exclusively for Saks Fifth Avenue in our first year. Eventually, I designed for many sports including bowling, tennis, gardening and the designs were sold through many stores in the U.S. and Canada. My gardening overalls with foam kneepads and the first use of Velcro on non-military items were featured on the front page of Women's Wear Daily, and my bowling design was featured in a full-page ad on the back page. Eventually we sold the company and I worked as a designer for several years with a sportswear manufacturer, then got married and had two children… at which point I retired from the sportswear design world. However, when I bumped into my first department manager at Saks Fifth Avenue years later he told me: "Sheila—if you had stayed in business you would be a conglomerate now!"

Sheila at the Palace Hotel skating rink in St. Moritz

When you see how active sportswear has developed over the years he might have been right.

Around this time in 1959 Bob joined the National Broadcasting Company (NBC), then a division of RCA, as Vice President of Operations in television, and a year later was named Executive Vice President and General Manager of the television network. During this time, he handled the most important negotiations with the top stars at the network, and he persuaded and negotiated with Hollywood filmmakers to show their full-length movies on the small screen, which they were very reluctant to do. This was something brand new as up until that time most T.V. programming was handled through advertising agencies with clients paying for the half hour or hour long variety shows or situation comedies. He helped the network change from black and white programming to color, and was responsible for bringing Curt Gowdy[59] to NBC, where he became the top sportscaster for over thirty years.

During this time I was in an unhappy marriage with a happy result of two wonderful children—while Bob was in a happy marriage with the tragic result of his wife Mary developing breast cancer and dying in 1966. After fifteen years of marriage, Bob was left with four young children aged 9-12. I was divorced and living with my two children aged 5 and 7 in my parent's apartment, and so we were now both in the same building separated by several floors. We had mutual friends and our daughters were friends from the skating club, so our paths kept crossing and we soon discovered that they should be crossed forever!

In 1968, we married and had a combined family of six children aged 6 to 14 years old. At the time most of our friends remarked "how wonderful for the children" – we always smiled to ourselves hoping that that would be true because we knew it was so magical for us and we had over forty precious years together.

Our love for each other was amazing and was as if someone had cut a paper heart apart in a zigzag pattern and put the two halves back together into one—our two selves fit together perfectly. We adored each other and once we were married we were only apart for probably ten days during our forty-year marriage.

Vacationing in 1970's.

In 1971, Bob was asked to become President of the NBC radio division where his mission was to sell their six stations because they were losing money. As we pondered this opportunity we concluded that if he was successful he would be out of a job—but he was reassured by Robert Sarnoff, the head of RCA, that there would always be another challenge for him within the company. So he took the position and within the eleven months that he was there he sold the two weakest stations and made the four other stations profitable and they remained a part of the NBC family until the assets were sold in 1987 to Westwood One. Bob was made a director of NBC, and was on the board of the John Blair Company, a national media company.

In 1972 the Hertz Corporation, a rental car company which was a division of RCA, was going through a difficult business period. Once again he was called upon by the Chairman of RCA to resuscitate a business. When he became Chairman, Chief Executive Officer, and Chief Operating Officer, the company was making $21 million a year. Five years later when he left its annual pre-tax profit had increased to $200 million annually and contributed almost 25% of RCA's total annual profits. He hired 72 talented executives to fill 110 key management positions here and abroad and he hired the first African American to become a spokesperson for a large corporation. His name was O.J. Simpson—and at the peak of his football career Simpson became known as "The Superstar of Rent-a-Car," an advertising campaign that increased Hertz's profits by 50%.

Bob's reputation in the business world was as an efficient business manager who was particularly adept at removing ineffectual managers and hiring young, well-trained and eager replacements, and inspiring honest, hardworking management to succeed. He had learned from his Dad, his Uncle, and the bosses that he admired along the way that integrity, and hard work were needed to make a business successful. He had also witnessed on his forty missions the necessity of working together as a team and being able to trust one another. He was very demanding—but he was fair. For the first time in 1980, Fortune Magazine compiled a list of the "Ten Toughest Bosses" in American business and Bob, along with Jack Welch and Donald Rumsfeld were on this first list.

Bob at Columbia Pictures.

A quote accompanying the article describes his business acumen well. He always raised expectations and knew that the competent group he had recruited could always rise to the challenge. He once became annoyed when he heard that a young friend had quit his job because he didn't like the people with whom he was working. Bob's reply was "if I had only worked with people I liked I would have been unemployed and penniless."

In 1978, he was asked by Herbert Allen to join Columbia Pictures, which at the time was going through a difficult management period. He remained with them as Executive Vice President and Chief Operating Officer until 1983 at which time the company had been reorganized and earned enough respect in the business community to be purchased by the Coca Cola Company. During this time his responsibilities included the Columbia Pictures Television Division whose profits increased tenfold under his management. He remained a consultant to the company for three years and then retired to Williamstown, Massachusetts where Williams College is located, and where we had bought a home.

His association with Williams began at an early age because Jake, as a loyal alum, always brought his sons to football games and reunions. As the eldest son Bob was appalled to learn that the uniform for his Dad's reunion class was Scottish kilt so that many of his first visits to Williamstown were in a skirt! Because of his early association with Williams he personally knew seven of the College's presidents, and his two brothers, several nieces, nephews, and a granddaughter also graduated from the College.

Attending the 1983 Allen & Company conference in Sun Valley, Idaho.

He was always interested in young people whether they were seeking advice for the business world, or needing a fan on the sidelines to cheer them on the field. He took enormous pleasure in William's athletics always wearing his '92 hat, which signified a very special group of young women that he followed in all their sports for four years, and with a bit of encouragement from me, he realized the importance of supporting women's athletics before Title IX.

He created over five important scholarships at various schools and involved himself in many Williamstown community interests and projects including the Clark Art Institute, The Williamstown Theatre Festival, and the Williamstown Art Conservation Center, and most particularly the Williamstown Youth Center. In 2008, he helped to make the community aware of the desperate need for a new youth center and was a major force, through his actions and contributions, in its being built. The facility was completed in 2011 and now serves not only the young people of the town but the entire community.

In each of his jobs he made a difference, and he valued every true friendship in his life. He enjoyed watching all sports and we loved playing tennis and golf together, but his favorite sport of all was fly fishing, which he taught me along with all our children and many others over the years. We fished in the Adirondacks and Wyoming, Colorado and Idaho. His good friend Curt Gowdy said of him "I never met a fly fisherman I didn't like but I like Bob Stone the best." Even after I caught the biggest fish on one outing they continued to take me fishing with them.

In his marriage to Mary, Bob had four children: Robert Jr., Peter, Elizabeth, and Mary Patricia. When we married I had a daughter, Ali Adair, and a son, Richard Bartle. We have six grandchildren: Wendy and Kristen Stone, Lee and Zachary Trigonis, and Kate and Rob Aiello.

* * * * * * * *

After training in Madison, Wisconsin, Don was sent overseas to England for special land mine training before he was sent to Belgium, the Netherlands and Germany. He served with the British 2nd Armored Division in the Netherlands as a squad leader in the 1263rd Combat Engineers. He also served in the 8th Armored Division ("Hell on Wheels") at Remagen, Germany, and on the Elbe River with the 82nd Airborne. He fought at the Battle of the Bulge from December 16, 1944 to January 25, 1945 where along with other duties, he walked in front of tanks with a metal detector to locate buried mines. This battle incurred the highest number of U.S. casualties of any operation during the war, and took place just before the invasion of Iwo Jima in the Pacific.

When the war was over in Europe, Don remained overseas with the Army of Occupation in Germany through March of 1946. He was among the first soldiers to enter a German concentration camp and see the horrors first hand. Later one of his duties was to guard Nazi officers who were prisoners of war. He brought back to the States a German Dachshund puppy named Fleisch, sold to him by a young German boy for four cigarettes. He continued his education at Williams where the college held classes year round and he graduated—with Fleisch—in 1948, although they both remained members of his original class of '46.

After his graduation, and while they were both working in New York in 1949, he married Jean Lawson Stone, a wonderful, witty, intelligent, and beautiful blonde from Texas. Their loving marriage has continued for over sixty-six years.

After graduation he joined the firm of Asiel & Co. as a bond trader, and in 1950 became a member of the New York Stock Exchange (NYSE) as a trader and specialist. Also, at that time, he graduated from the New York University School of Business. Until 1968 he was a Partner at E. H. Stern & Company, then a Senior Partner at Lasker, Stone & Stern. In 1991 he became Chairman and Chief Executive Officer of Merrill Lynch Specialists, a group that, under his leadership, became the fifth largest of the Big Board's 42 specialist firms. From 1997-99 he was a Special Advisor to the Chairman at Merrill Lynch.

Don has worked on the exchange for over 50 years and he served as vice chairman for 11 years. During that period he served on over 14 committees most of which he headed, and he served on four SEC Advisory Committees. He was a Presidential Appointee to the National Advisory Drug Committee, and Adjunct Professor at NYU's School of Business, and also served as a Director, Chairman, Trustee and Board Member of numerous institutions ranging from the Hospital for Special Surgery, Save the Children Federation, the Bond Club of New York, the Federation of Jewish Philanthropies and many educational institutions, including Williams College.

He is an excellent fly fisherman and still enjoys Alderbrook, and is a highly respected fly fisherman in the Florida Keys around Islamorada. He also loves tennis, golf and swims every day.

Jean served as Police Commissioner and then as the Mayor of Scarsdale, New York from 1981 to 1983; during her tenure, there was a lawsuit about a religious display on public property in the village. The case received national publicity and was settled by the U.S. Supreme Court in 1985. She has done extensive community service in Westchester, New York most particularly for the Burke Rehabilitation Hospital, the Burke Medical Research Institute, and in the area of mental health. President Reagan appointed her to the Presidential Board of Advisors on Private

Initiatives in 1987. They have four children, Todd, Amy, Kate and William.

* * * * * * * *

Jimmy was accepted into the Marines in March of his senior year at Deerfield and as soon as he graduated his first training was at Parris Island; he continued the training program at Camp Lejeune and then he went on to Officer Candidate School in Quantico, Virginia. In the South Pacific he was a First Lieutenant in the First Marine Division, fighting on the beaches in the Battle of Iwo Jima. He narrated a video on view at the National WWII Museum speaking about his experiences as a very young officer leading soldiers in the attack on the island. Jimmy, after his discharge from the Marines returned to Williams College, where he graduated in 1948; he then worked in the oil department of Lehman Brothers in New York City until he left for Texas to study Advanced Geology at Texas A&M. While there he was recalled by the Marine Reserves during the Korean conflict and was discharged with the rank of Captain. He married Elizabeth Asbury and settled in Cincinnati, Ohio where in 1952 he founded and was Chairman of the Stone Energy Corporation, an independent oil producer operating in ten states. In the early 1970's he was involved in the urban renewal of the downtown business district of Cincinnati in a joint venture, through the Cincinnati Redevelopment Corporation, with John Galbraith. It entailed development of four major downtown city blocks, the 32-story DuBois Tower and the Fifth Third Bank Building.

In the 1980's he moved his company to Lafayette, Louisiana where it remains today, in the Riverstone office and park complex that he helped to develop. He was also a partner in building the Place St. Charles, a 55-story office building in downtown New Orleans.

Jimmy bought a home and moved to New Orleans in 1981 where he served as a director of the Hibernia National Bank of New Orleans, of Newpark Resources, and where he was a founder of The D-Day Museum (now known as The National World War II Museum). He remained loyal to the Marine Corps serving as a founding member and director of the Marine Corps Heritage Foundation in Quantico, Virginia, and as a board member of the Toys For Tots Foundation.

He also served on the Business Council of New Orleans and the River Region, and was a past trustee of the Tulane Medical Center, The New Orleans Museum of Art, the New Orleans Symphony, and the New Orleans Opera Association. Additionally, he served as a director of the NFL Rams. His company went public on the NYSE in 1993. For over sixty years he maintained a strong and lasting connection to Williams College as alumnus, active committee member, donor, father and grandfather of five graduates.

Through his first wife's family he developed a life-long interest in thoroughbred breeding and racing. His notable horses included Ardross, winner of the Gold Cup in England, and in partnership with Arthur B. Hancock III, his horse Menifee won the Blue Grass Stakes and was second in the Kentucky Derby and Preakness in 1999. He was married four times and died in 2007 leaving six children: Andrew, Thomas, Suzanne, Margaret, James, and Elizabeth.

* * * * * * * *

Jake was born in North Adams and went to nearby Williams College at age 16 on a scholarship. He graduated in 1914 and was a loyal alumnus who credited whatever success he had in his life to his education and the good friends he made at Williams. For these powerful reasons he wanted his sons to attend Williams. He also felt an obligation to give back to the college that had helped make his life so different from its humble beginnings; as a result he established several scholarship funds at the college so others could benefit as he had.

He joined Asiel & Co. after graduation and remained with them throughout his business career. Asiel was an established member of the New York Stock Exchange specializing in the equity, corporate bond, and preferred stock arenas. He took a leave of absence from the company during World War I and became a First Lieutenant in the First Infantry Division.

He helped to establish NYSE standards and procedures after the 1929 crash and served as a governor of the exchange from 1938 to 1940. He was also a director of Mount Sinai Hospital from 1940-1945. In the 1930's, with Robert Lehman of Lehman Brothers, he purchased several adjoining properties totaling 3,600 acres in the Adirondacks and created a fishing camp that they named Alderbrook.

At the start of World War II he wanted once again to serve his country in active duty but was turned down because of age and health reasons; however the Navy utilized his fervor and intelligence by making him a Lieutenant Commander in the Navy's Bureau of Supplies and Accounts where he served in New York City throughout the war years.

After the war he returned to Asiel & Co. where he specialized in the company's bond division and where he was a partner and he was a member of the NYSE. He was a fundraiser for Deerfield Academy, and Williams College, spent time on charities, and Wall Street committees and boards too numerous to mention.

He was a Trustee from 1958-64 and then served as a Trustee Emeritus of Williams College and he was one of the school's most dedicated alumnus. His three sons, five grandchildren, and three great grandchildren are all graduates of Williams.

He was a leading figure on the NYSE for over 50 years until his retirement in 1969. His second wife Beatrice Marks died in the 1950s and he subsequently married Eve Finsterwald. He lived in New York City, still on Park Avenue, and wintered in Palm Beach, Florida where he died at age 86. He is buried near his classmate, President James Phinney Baxter III, in the Williams College cemetery which is situated adjacent to the campus.

Jake and Isabel had three sons: Robert, Donald and James and when he married Beatrice, his two step-sons were Ken and Barry Marks.

* * * * * * * *

In 1945, Edward S. Greenbaum, Bob's Uncle Eddie, received the Distinguished Medal of Honor for his remarkable contributions during his time in the service when he served as Brigadier General and Assistant to Assistant Secretary of War Robert P. Patterson, who later became Secretary of War under Harry S. Truman.

Uncle Eddie was a mentor, and major influence in Bob's life. He graduated from Williams College where he met Jake Stone and he probably introduced Jake to his sister, Isabel, who became Jake's wife. After receiving his law degree from Columbia University in 1915 he founded a law practice with his older brother Lawrence, and Morris Ernst both fellow Williams graduates, and Herbert Wolff whom he met at Columbia.

Greenbaum Wolff & Ernst in New York City was, for over 60 years, a highly respected law firm that handled many high profile cases. Perhaps the most important case was the "U.S. vs. One Book Called Ulysses." The book by James Joyce had been deemed legally "obscene" and therefore could not be printed in America. The firm won the case for Random House and changed the literary scene in America forever by eliminating censorship.

In the 1960's one of his clients was Svetlana Allilueva, Stalin's daughter, who defected from the Soviet Union and became a naturalized citizen of the United States. He also was the lawyer for Harper & Row in its dispute with Jacqueline Kennedy over the publication of William Manchester's book "The Death of a President." The firm handled many literary clients over the years including Carl Sandburg, Tennessee Williams, and Edna Ferber, as well as politicians, and industrialists.

During his career he served on numerous committees most of which worked to improve the justice system through a variety of court reform efforts including court delay, jury trial, and the reorganization of the court system. Although he graduated from Williams and Columbia Law School his papers were donated to the Princeton University Library because his home was in Princeton, New Jersey and he had many ties to the University.

He was married to Dorothea (Aunt Dotsie), who was a renowned artist and sculptor whose work is on display in the Whitney Museum of Art, and the National Gallery in Washington, D.C. In 1915, as a teenager, she lost her father in the sinking of the Lusitania at the start of World War I. During World War II she was on an advisory committee on artists at the War Department and, in 1952, on the American delegation to the United Nations- sponsored International Conference on the Arts in Venice. In 1968, she was inducted into the National Institute of Arts and Letters. Eddie and Dorothea had two sons, David and Daniel.

* * * * * * * *

Ken received his B.A. degree from Amherst in absentia in 1942. In October of the following year, Ken and Bunny, who had met in dancing school in the 1930's, were married in Boston. He was assigned to the Destroyer Newcomb supporting the third and fifth fleet landings from the Marshall Islands to Iwo Jima. He was then transferred to the destroyer Heerman for fast carrier protection until V-J Day. He earned eight campaign ribbons for world-wide actions during his four years at sea, and then became an Executive Officer and Lieutenant Commander on a third destroyer.

When the war was over he graduated from Harvard Business School, and after returning to active duty with the US Naval Reserve, he entered the business world. He was first with Scott Paper, then with Lightolier, where he was a plant manager overseeing 600 employees. Ultimately he formed his own company, Advanced Packaging, Inc. that packaged food products for various companies.

Ken served as a scout leader, basketball coach, and in numerous and varied community associations. In his later years he was the President of the Northern Westchester Center for the Arts. This fine organization included a 63-member faculty that served 1,600 tuition paying students plus outreach clientele, and featured many community art exhibitions.

He was a tennis and sailing enthusiast all his life, and was captain of a tennis team for age 55-and-up players that was nationally ranked. Ken and Bunny had three children: Gregory, Lynn and Kathy.

* * * * * * * *

Barry graduated from Deerfield in June of 1943 and started classes that summer at Dartmouth. His class that consisted of 183 students was the smallest to enter the college since the 1800's. He enrolled in a Liberal Arts program, but the college offered elective courses in the V-12 Navy and Marines as well. At that time colleges and universities were asked to maintain a liberal arts curriculum for civilian students but to also devote college resources to the national war effort. He enlisted in the Marine program at Dartmouth and then trained at Parris Island, Camp Lejeune and at Officer Candidates School in Quantico, Virginia before he was sent to the Pacific where he fought at Iwo Jima.

After his discharge, Barry was an instructor from 1949 to 1964 at the University of Minnesota; later he taught Government and Great Issues at Dartmouth, was an Associate Professor at Brown University and a Fulbright Lecturer at University of Lille in France. In the 1960's he was professor and Chairman of the Department of Literature at the American University in Washington, D.C. He went on to teach at Rhode Island University in Kingston, Rhode Island until his retirement and early death at the age of 57. There is a Barry Marks auditorium in the Chaffee Social Science Center on the Kingston Campus of the University of Rhode Island.

He enjoyed sports, especially tennis, golf, and skiing. He was married to Gale Holman and together they had three children: Stephen, Pamela, and Dana. He remarried after a divorce from Gale.

* * * * * * * *

Mildred and Eddie Hilson were special friends of Jake's and became surrogate parents and then close friends of the Stone boys as they grew up. When Donny exclaimed in a toast at one of Mildred's parties that he planned to name his first born—male or female—"Mildred," the words evoked gales of laughter from the many guests attending the party.

Edwin I. Hilson, an investment banker with Wertheim & Co. died in 1952. At his death, his wife took his seat on the board of The Hospital for Special Surgery and five years later she was named Vice President, a title she held until her death in 1994 at the age of 96. She raised over $15 million for the hospital and, in addition, raised money for the American Cancer Society and the Museum of the City of New York; she was also an effective and well-known fundraiser for the Republican Party.

She loved to entertain and invited Presidents, Heads of State, Ambassadors, politicians, theatrical personalities and her many friends to the dazzling parties she held at their home at their Fifth Avenue apartment and later at the Waldorf Astoria Hotel in New York City.

President Eisenhower painted her portrait, and President Nixon played Happy Birthday on the piano at a gala party for her ninetieth birthday while 200 guests sang along at the St. Regis Hotel. She was an iconic figure in New York society and was always dressed in the latest haute couture designs. Of the Stone boys, Donny remained closest to Mildred until her death. Mildred and Eddie had two children: John and Mary.

* * * * * * *

After the war President Harry Truman sent a commendation to all servicemen saying: "To you who answered the call of your country and served in its Armed Forces to bring about the total defeat of the enemy, I extend the heartfelt thanks of a grateful Nation. As one of the Nation's finest, you undertook the most severe task one can be called upon to perform. Because you demonstrated the fortitude, resourcefulness, and calm judgment necessary to carry out that task, we now look to you for leadership and example in further exalting our country in peace." I believe that the extended Stone family more than fulfilled President Truman's directive "for leadership and example" in the years after the war.

When Bob died in 2009 we had a Celebration to honor his life which we held in Williamstown at Williams College. Many friends and family members spoke, in chronological order, about a part of his life they had known. His brother Don spoke of his childhood, and next to speak was 12-year-old Otis Baker.[60] Otis used Bob's war experiences as the subject of a school project and, because of his many questions, we were able to piece together and clarify many portions of Bob's letters. We are most grateful to Otis, who will be a freshman at Yale this fall. These are the words he spoke about Bob combined with details from his school project: "I first became friends with Mr. Stone when I was 8-years-old and I visited Williamstown with my parents. I've always loved coming up here and used to correct my brother when he told people we were going to visit The Rocks —"no, we're going to go visit The Stones." You can learn a lot about Mr. and Mrs. Stone just by the things they have in their house. There are skating pictures, old Coca Cola bottles, Williams College hats and of course, Mr. Stone's prized collection of ceramic cows. Upstairs at The Stone's house there are glass frames and cases filled with colorful ribbons and medals. I knew they were Mr. Stone's from World War II, but I wanted to know more.

So when my classmates were writing reports on food and dogs and cats, I decided to report on something really interesting: I would write about my very good friend Mr. Bob Stone and World War II.

I now know that lots of soldiers and veterans do not like to talk about their experiences in war. One of the soldiers in the book *The Greatest Generation* explained it best when he said, 'I figured, those who were willing to talk about combat had never really experienced it.' [61]

I didn't know any of this back in 2006 when I called Mr. Stone on the telephone. I didn't know that he had never talked about being a soldier and dropping bombs over Iwo Jima when he was just 20 years old to his friends, or his kids or even Mrs. Stone. But I called him up and told him my plan about writing a report on his experience in World War II, and my friend Mr. Stone said, 'that would be really neat.'

Bob with eleven-year-old Otis Baker (center) and his brothers, Satch (left) and Charlie (right).

When Mr. Stone was just 19 years old, he was studying in his room here at Williams College. He was listening to his radio when President Franklin D. Roosevelt announced that the Japanese had dropped bombs on our Naval ships at Pearl Harbor. Mr. Stone was so angered by the attack that he immediately enlisted. He didn't wait to be drafted into service, and he didn't stay in school like many might have today. Mr. Stone's father served in World War I and II, and Mr. Stone's uncle and two brothers served in World War II. Today, people would say, "Oh, of course he joined up, he came from a military family." But that's not true, Mr. Stone came from a family who believed in honor, duty and country.

After training, Mr. Stone graduated as a Second Lieutenant bombardier and was assigned to the Pacific where he and his crew flew missions bombing Chi Chi Jima, Yap, Truck, Marcus Island, and Iwo Jima, mostly on their plane "The Flying Jenny." Because he was superstitious, he always wore exactly the same clothing for his missions, and he carried a silver Saint Francis medal that a fellow flier had given him. St. Francis is the patron Saint of birds and the protector of men who fly, and Mr. Stone carried that coin in his pocket every day since 1942. He was proud to tell me that no one in the crew was ever hurt by bullets or shrapnel.

He did tell me about his scariest mission, which I will share with you. 'We had just bombed Iwo Jima and were leaving the target, which was 6 hours away from our base on Guam when several Japanese fighter planes called Zeros attacked us. Although we fought them off, we took a number of hits, as well as some hits from the thick flak we encountered when we flew over the island to drop our bombs. After a while flying back towards Guam, one of our four engines sputtered and stopped running. The pilot "feathered" this engine which means that he turned the propeller blades sideways so that they would cut through the air rather than being a total drag. A loaded B-24 cannot take off with only two working engines, but once in the air it can fly with only two engines.

With only three engines operating, the plane was flying much slower and was beginning to lose altitude, which made us consume more gasoline. All of a sudden there was total silence when all three engines stopped.

The silence was devastating and eerie.

We were all in a state of panic wondering what had happened and if the end was near—it seemed inevitable! After what seemed like a long time, but probably was only a couple of minutes, the engines caught hold and we were once again on our way to our base. We found out that in transferring fuel from the non-working engine to the working ones, an air lock developed which momentarily stopped the proper flow of gas and made the plane stall.

Because of our loss of altitude, we decided to lighten our load by throwing overboard anything we could such as: the ball turret (which was incredibly heavy), eight very heavy 50 millimeter guns, ten very heavy flak jackets (used for body protection) and a small gas engine used to start the plane's engines. Also, a great many boxes of unused 40-millimeter shells were deep sixed. There may have been more items that I don't recall any longer, but anything of any weight except the Norden Bomb Sight was jettisoned. The bombsight was top-secret equipment, very expensive, and very difficult to replace because it enabled the pilot to transfer the control of the plane to the bombardier who could then zero in on the targets more accurately. The reduction of all this weight helped us maintain altitude and at the same time use less gas. We continued along for about another hour or so hoping we would not lose altitude and not use up all our gas before we got to base. We also hoped that our three engines would continue to operate until we landed safely.

At this point, we decided to head to Saipan rather than our home base of Guam because Saipan was somewhat closer than flying back to Guam. With less than two hours left to reach Saipan, another engine conked out and had to be "feathered" leaving us with only two working engines—happily one on each wing. Now our big worry was whether we had sufficient gas to get to Saipan and whether we could maintain enough altitude to make a landing when we got there. Also, it was critical that the two remaining engines continued to operate properly. The next hour or so was really tense and scary as there was nothing else we could do except to hope that Saint Francis and Saint Christopher would do their job and protect us!

It was an enormous relief when we saw the lights of Saipan. We started our final approach and descent to the runway from a much lower altitude than normal. When the wheels hit the runway, we started to roll but only got half way down the runway when the other two engines stopped because we had completely run out of gas. This was an absolute miracle because if we had to fly another 100 feet to reach the runway we would have come down in the water and crashed! When the crew left the airplane, we all kissed the ground because we had been so fortunate in making it back safely to terra firma! The Flying Jenny was hauled away and never flew again because its engines and the body of the plane had been so badly damaged it was not worth repairing. Since this was our 32nd mission we were assigned another plane to complete our total of 40 missions.'

Mr. Stone and his crew were each awarded the Distinguished Flying Cross for this mission, the highest decoration awarded to Air Force flyers in combat. The Flying Cross is awarded to an officer or enlisted personnel of the U.S. Armed Forces who distinguishes himself in support of operations 'heroism or extraordinary achievement while participating in a flight.' The first person to be presented with this award was Charles Lindbergh after returning from his trans-Atlantic flight in 1927.

After his 40 bombing missions, Mr. Stone could have returned to a normal life back home in 1944. But until freedom was assured, there would be no such thing as normal life for Mr. Stone, so he stayed on as an aide to a General and a Major General until the end of the war.

Knowing Mr. Stone has taught me that history is not dates and numbers that you memorize. This past spring, I went with my family to Washington D.C. and visited the World War II Memorial and I saw the Enola Gay B-29 bomber that had dropped the atomic bomb "Little Boy" on Hiroshima to end the war. I always knew the plane was a big part of our country's history, but I felt attached to it because I had a friend who had flown in a plane like that, and his name was Mr. Stone."

****

There was a very rough spot in Bob's business career when he was forced to resign as CEO of Hertz because of corporate jealousy, and it took 16 months for him to find and be hired for an exciting new challenge with Herbert Allen and Columbia Pictures. To celebrate this wonderful job beginning in 1978, he bought me a beautiful Tiffany bracelet and wrote this two-

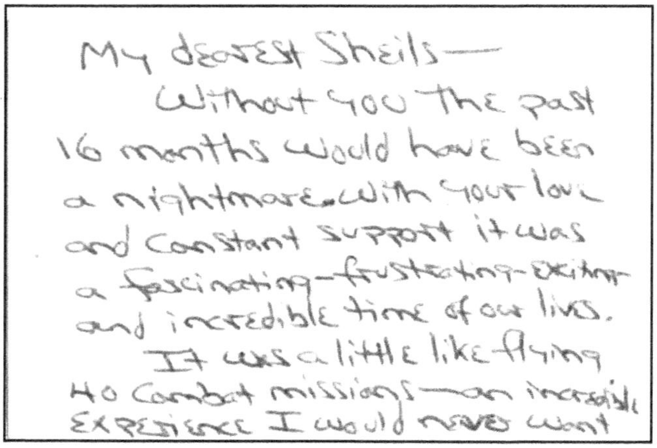

My dearest Sheils—
Without you the past
16 months would have been
a nightmare. With your love
and constant support it was
a fascinating—frustrating—exciting
and incredible time of our lives.
It was a little like flying
40 combat missions—an incredible
experience I would never want

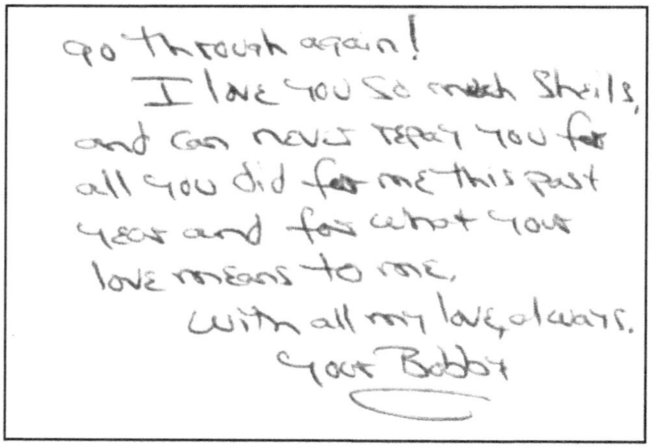

go through again!
I love you so much Sheils,
and can never repay you for
all you did for me this past
year and for what your
love means to me.
With all my love always.
Your Bobby

sided gift card to go with it, written in his distinctive handwriting.

When I think about all of this many years later, even though I was not in his life at the time, this loving note connected me to his 40 missions, and to a part of his life in which I did not exist. It made an amazing connection between our worlds then and now, and gave me an even more personal reason to write and assemble this book.

ENDNOTES

Introduction

1. p. 2, Brokaw, Tom. *The Greatest Generation*. New York: Random House Publishers, 1998. Print. (Marine Captain Joe Foss was the ultimate flying hero of WWII with 26 Japanese planes shot down defending American positions on Guadacanal. He was awarded the Medal of Honor personally by President Roosevelt and was featured on the cover of LIFE magazine. After the war he was elected to two terms as Governor of South Dakota, then the first Commissioner of the AFL, and later Head of the National Rifle Association. He wrote about how "the daily hell that was life on Guadacanal—the nerve shattering, life-or-death missions, combined with malaria and dysentery and poor food—was simply too much for most men." This was the life most of the troops in the Pacific lived but was not written about in letters home.)
2. p. 3, Ibid
3. p. 4, Ibid
4. p. 5, Ibid
5. p. 6, Ibid
6. p. 8, Ibid
7. p. 8, Ibid
8. p. 9, For photo of "E" Award Ceremony in Lansdale, PA in 1944, see Appendix.

Nashville

9. p. 15, We believe this letter should have been dated Thursday, February 10 or Friday, February 11.
10. p. 21, Lois and Phil Specter were friends of Bob's, from playing tennis at the Century Club in Purchase, New York.
11. p. 35, Don immediately started classes at Williams in a summer session after graduating from Deerfield in June 1942. When he entered the service in 1943, he was sent to Madison, Wisconsin.
12. p. 36, Bombardier. Dir. Richard Wallace. Perf. Pat O'Brien, Randolph Scott, Anne Shirley, Eddie Albert, Walter Reed and Robert Ryan. Warner Bros., 1943. Film.
13. p. 36, In 1943, the stanine tests (STAndard NINE) made selections for these positions with remarkable precision and they succeeded almost 100% of the time. Between July and October 1943, a new 18-week course went into effect at Childress and other training centers. Now candidates had to be proficient as dead-reckoning navigators, pilotage (map reading) and the use of the Norden and Sperry bombsights, which were extremely high tech and very costly.

14. p. 36, Information from: St. John, Phillip A.. *Bombardiers of WWII: A History.* Nashville: Turner Publishing Company, 1993. Print.

Ellington Field

15. p. 43, O'ma is Bee's mother—Bob's step-grandmother.
16. p. 52, SKOL was a very popular sun lotion in the 1940s. Sun bathing became a new craze in the 1930's and 40's as doctors praised its healing properties so that tanned skin became desirable and a sign of robust health and leisure, rather than outdoor labor. Tanning lotions like Skol were mostly alcohol and tannic acid that stained the skin and clothing giving only mild protection. Although Bob makes no mention of this—in the Pacific there was a sticky red veterinary petrolatum originally intended for animals to protect them from the harsh sun. After returning home airman and future pharmacist Benjamin Green formulated a moisturizing suntan cream based on this formula that in the 1950's became Coppertone. Eventually by the 1970's there were doctor warnings about sun exposure, and sunscreens with SPF labels replaced earlier lotions. Unfortuantely, this was too late for many of the veterans who developed skin cancers.[1]
17. p. 55, The "leading lady" Bob is referring to is Anne Shirley. The film *Bombardier* was filmed in the early 1940s at Kirtland Airforce base in Albuquerque, NM and Midland TX and released in 1943.
18. p. 57, "The boy's graduation" refers to Jimmy and Barry who graduated in the same class of 1943 from Deerfield. Jimmy immediately listed in the Marines. See endnote 22 for information on Barry.
19. p. 61, Pam Stern was one of Bob's first girlfriends.
20. p. 64, Both brothers were AWOL (Absent without Leave) so they could meet, but Donny was stopped by the MPs (Military Police) before he could leave his base.

Childress

21. p. 73, the "Bloomingdale" Bob refers to is Bloomingdale, New York, near Alderbrook (see endnote #20) in upstate New York.
22. p. 80, Alderbrook is a fishing camp in the Adirondacks near Saranac Lake, originally consisting of several farms put together by Jake Stone and Robert Lehman of Lehman Brothers. It was comprised of over 3,600 acres originally. Some land has been given to the Adirondack Park and the remainder is still in the family.
23. p. 82, The "complicated gadget" Bob is referring to is the Norden Bombsight.
24. p. 86, "Norden bombsight." Wikipedia: The Free Encyclopedia. Wikimedia Foundation, Inc. 28 April 2015. Web. 1 June 2015. <http://en.wikipedia.org/wiki/Norden_bombsight>
25. p. 109, O.D. stands for Olive Drab uniform color.
26. p. 112, Rationing books were issued to families in the United States for the purchasing hard-to-get items like shoes, sugar, butter, coffee, meat, tires and gasoline.

1 From "A Burning Desire," article for Chemical Heritage Foundation, Jane E. Boyd.

27. p. 131, B.O.Q. is Base Officer Headquarters.

March and Hammer Fields

28. p. 140, O.T.U. stands for Operational Training Unit.
29. p. 154, Ronnie and Doug were old friends of Bob's from New York City. Ronnie visited Bob at home when he was recuperating from his broken femur.
30. p. 164, I believe a lot of the typed letters were copied by Jake's secretary so they could be sent around to family members.
31. p. 164, Dr. William E. Gallie was a brilliant and innovative general surgeon with a particular expertise in orthopedics who preformed the first operation on Bob's leg in Canada after the car accident. He devised numerous new methods in surgery, including the transplantation of bone, the implantation of tendons, and skeletal traction in the treatment of fractures and dislocations of the spine.
32. p. 172, Mildred and Eddie Hilson were good friends of the family. The Hilsons knew that Jake was collecting Bob's letters and gave these letters to him to add to his collection. See biographies in the Epilogue.
33. p. 172, The Hilsons had two children: a son, John, who was in the service and a daughter, Mary.
34. p. 198, R.L.S. mistake in letter: Joe McGarvey should be Gerald William McGarvey, nicknamed "Mac" or "Bill."
35. p. 200, Information from: "The B-24 Liberator." The Bomber Warrior. n.d. Web. 18 August 2015. <http://thebomberwarrior.com/?page_id=53>

Oahu, HI

36. p. 223, For more information on V-mail communication, please see Appendix.
37. p. 234, According to historical records, Franklin Delano Roosevelt landed at Pearl Harbor on July 26, 1944 and left the Hawaiian islands on July 28, 1944.
38. p. 245, Before the notion of being politically correct was in vogue, *Time Magazine* of January 5, 1942 used the ethnic slur "Nips," which comes from the word Nippon, the Japanese name for Japan. "Japs" was another derogatory word, often used during the war years. Bob had a difficult time after his experiences thinking of the Japanese in politically correct terms.
39. p. 249, O.C.S. stands for Officer Candidate School.
40. p. 250, In the late 1930s, Jack Benny was the King of Radio with his own show, *The Jack Benny Program*, and he was one of the most popular and well-known entertainers who went on to star in T.V. and movies. During the war, he travelled extensively entertaining troops all over the world, and is credited with creating the forerunner of T.V. situation comedies. When Bob stayed in Room #5 at the Officers' Club in Honolulu, he was asked to leave early so Jack Benny could have the room.

Marshall Islands

41. p. 269, A.T.C. stands for Air Transport Command.
42. p. 271, Information on The Battle of Kwajalein: "War Bond." The History Channel. A&E Networks & The Walt Disney Company. n.d. Web. 18 August 2015. <http://www.history.com/topics/world-war-ii/battle-of-kwajalein> and About.com. IAC. n.d. Web/ 18 August 2015. <http://militaryhistory.about.com/od/worldwarii/p/kwajalein.htm>

Mariana Islands

43. p. 280, See Epilogue to see details on Ken's Navy experiences after Deerfield.
44. p. 286, See Epilogue to see details on Jimmy and Barry's Marine experiences after Deerfield.
45. p. 288, We are sure this letter is meant to be dated November 5, 1944 because the upcoming dinner with Barry is mentioned in the previous letter. The date that Bob wrote on the letter (October 5, 1944), he was in the Marshall Islands—or on his way to the Marshall Islands and was never able to meet Barry until they were both in the Mariana Islands.
46. p. 289, Wendell Willkie was the Republican nominee for President in 1940 and was defeated by F.D.R.
47. p. 295, This letter was written on the third anniversary of the Japanese attack on Pearl Harbor, which inspired Bob to volunteer.
48. p. 295, Robert Day Dean's was a caterer and confectionery on East 57th Street in New York City.
49. p. 301, Aunt Jane was Jake's sister married to Uncle Henry, who lived in Scarsdale.
50. p. 303, This letter to his Dad was written on Bob's 23rd birthday.
51. p. 307, "Recently we ran into some fairly tough opposition and had a couple of close calls—a wing and a prayer really hits it on the head, but as long as you make it back, that's all that matters." This is a typical description of frightening missions and probably the most descriptive that they were permitted to get, not wanting to scare their families or give away classified information. Raids during this period were mostly on Iwo Jima bombing the Japanese airfields and installations in preparation for the invasion of Iwo Jima.
52. p. 312, See Epilogue to see details on Don's Army experiences after Deerfield.
53. p. 312, A Stone tradition at Christmas time was Jake's reading of the editorial "Is There a Santa Claus?" which appeared originally in the New York Sun on September 21, 1897. A limited edition book of the article was published in 1947 and a copy was given to Bob signed by Edwin S. Friendly, the Vice President and General Manager of the Sun, who was their neighbor across the hall at 375 Park Avenue. The families were close and Mr. Friendly's son was a good friend of Bob's who in 1951 persuaded Bob to join him at ABC. Ed Friendly went on to produce *Laugh-In* and *Little House On The Prairie* among many notable projects for television. I still have the 70-year old book and we always read

it at Christmas time. I still keep up the tradition, although now I read it to myself. Also mentioned in letter on page 156.

54. p. 320, It is interesting that there is no letter home after the January 21, 1945 mission for which he was awarded the Distinguished Flying Cross at the pinning ceremony at Fort Dix on September 5, 1945.
55. p. 320, This letter of Bob's when he refers to his "next to last mission was a really rough one and all of us were pretty well scared" is quite understated, but he retold the story to Otis Baker many years later. (See Otis Baker's speech in the Epilogue.)
56. p. 333, The Battle of Iwo Jima took place between February 19, 1945—March 26, 1945. Bob's letter of February 20th and the newspaper article of March 2nd took place during this time period. This news article is probably referring to bombing raids over Iwo Jima in January, February, and the Susaki Airfield on Chi Chi Jima in February and March by the Liberator planes.
57. p. 346, Bill Struby, who was a friend of Bob's from Deerfield and Williams, was not Missing in Action and after the war roomed with Bob in New York City in their first apartment.
58. p. 358, The "Bay Rum" referred to is an aftershave and cologne made in St. Thomas and difficult to find during the war as shipping to and from the Caribbean Islands was only for essentials. However, when Bob mentions the "real kick" he and his buddies got from the rum, we wonder whether the cologne bottle was filled with the real stuff—courtesy of Jake's ingenuity.

Epilogue

59. p. 389, Over the course of Curt Gowdy's broadcasting career he was involved in the broadcast of 13 World Series, 16 Baseball all-Star Games, 9 Super Bowls, 14 Rose Bowls, 8 Olympic Games and 24 NCAA Final Fours. He also hosted the long running *The American Sportsman* TV show on ABC and provided historic commentary for PBS and HBO.
60. p. 397, Each speaker at the service was limited to two minutes so we have added a few details to Otis' speech that were in his original school project.
61. p. 397, Brokaw, Tom. *The Greatest Generation*. New York: Random House Publishers, 1998. Print.

Appendix

62. p. 413, Information on war bonds: "War Bond." Wikipedia: The Free Encyclopedia. Wikimedia Foundation, Inc. 21 June 2015. Web. 9 August 2015. <https://en.wikipedia.org/wiki/War_bond>
63. p. 416, Greenbaum, Edward Samuel. *A lawyer's job, in court, in the Army, in the office*. New York: Harcourt, Brace & World, 1967. Print.
64. p. 417, Public Papers of the Presidents: Harry S. Truman, 1945, p. 197

PHOTO CREDITS

All photographs
Robert L. Stone & crew members: all photographs except mentioned below

Covers
Mark McCarty: front and back cover photographs.

Front Matter
U.S. Army Air Forces, Barnard College, Deerfield Academy, U.S. Army Signal Corps: Images in "The Family," p.VIII

Nashville
Diane Taylor, Lane Plate, p. 31

Childress
United States Air Forces: AT-11 training plane, p. 85

March & Hammer Fields
Sheila M. Stone: St. Francis medals, p. 208

Oahu
U.S. Navy: General Douglas MacArthur, Franklin Delano Roosevelt, Admiral Chester William Nimitz, p. 235
Bettman/Corbis: Joe DiMaggio in AAF uniform, http://www.corbisimages.com/stock-photo/rights-managed/BE049799/joe-dimaggio-and-pee-wee-reese-at, p. 253
United States Army Air Forces: via http://www.flickr.com/photos/18532986@N07/4480632528/in/photostream, Bolivar Jr., p. 258
United States Air Forces: B-24 plane dropping bombs, p. 258

Mariana Islands
Mark McCarty: photograph of World Map, pp.352-353; navigation notes by Robert L. Stone

Going Home
United States Air Forces: Pinning ceremony, p. 381-383
United States Air Forces: Generals with Bob, p. 384

Epilogue
Unknown: Sheila Muldowny skating at St. Moritz, p. 388
Unknown: Sheila & Bob vacationing in the 1970's, p. 389
Unknown: Bob at Columbia Pictures, p. 390

Magic Photo: Sheila & Bob at Allen & Co. conference in Sun Valley, ID, p. 391
Sheila M. Stone: Bob with Otis, Satch & Charlie Baker, p. 398

<u>Appendix</u>
Unknown: Japanese attack on Pearl Harbor, Hawaii, p. 409
Unknown: The USS Arizona burning after the Japanese attack on Pearl Harbor, p. 409
U.S. Government: Franklin Delano Roosevelt delivers "Infamy" speech, p. 410
The National WWII Museum: stamp albums for war bonds, p. 413
Diane Taylor: World War II medals, p. 415
Jack W. Aeby: "Trinity" shot of the first nuclear test explosion, p. 416
U.S. Army: Atomic bombing of Nagasaki on August 9, 1945, p. 417
Unknown: President Harry S. Truman, p. 417

<u>End Matter</u>
Mark McCarty: Flag & hat, p. 419
Ali Adair: U.S. Marine Corp War Memorial, p. 420

Ali Adair: All section heading maps, diagrams & drawings

APPENDIX

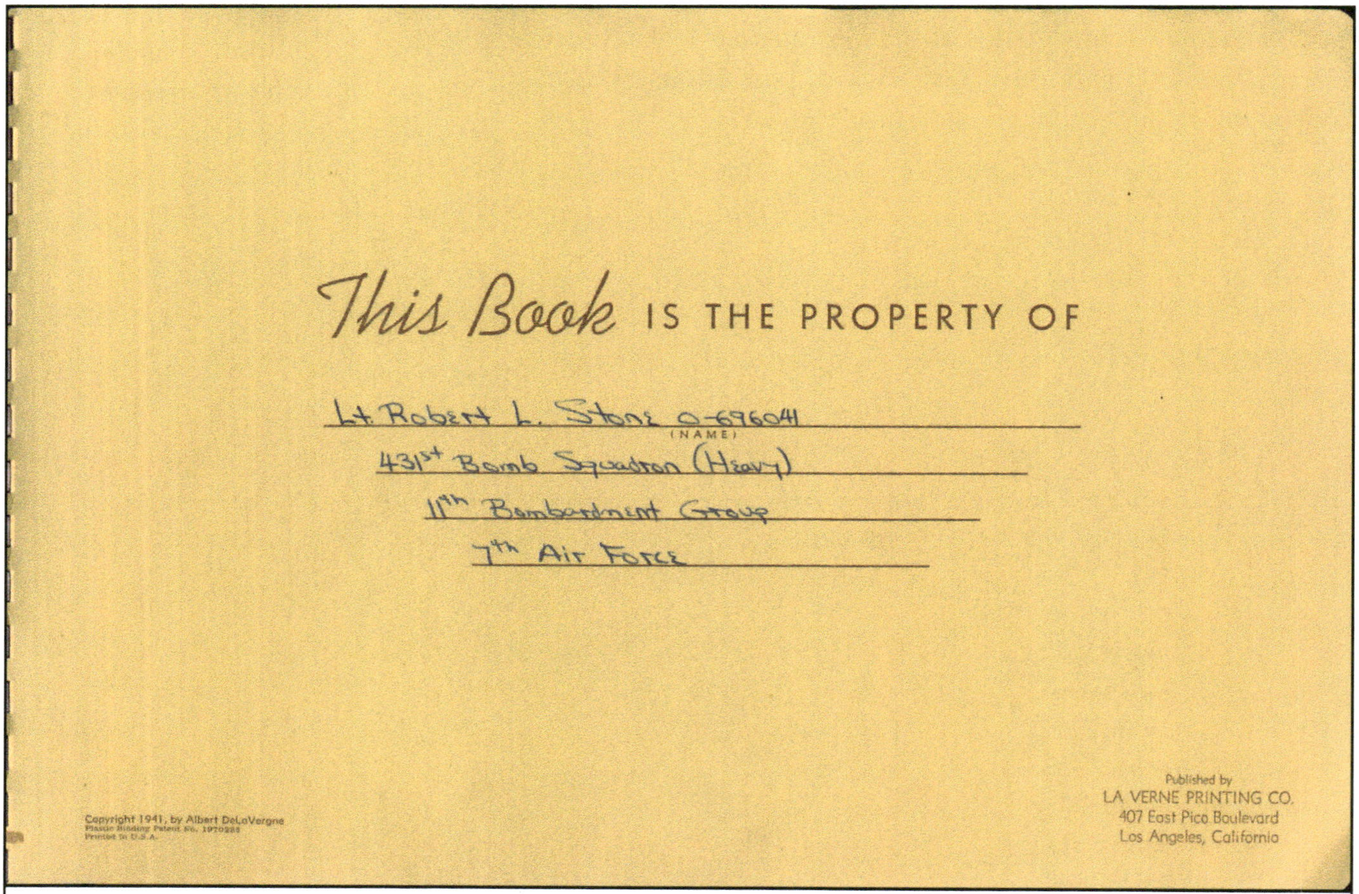

The inside cover of one of Bob's scrapbooks.

Destruction by Japanese bombs on our fleet at Pearl Harbor, on the island of Oahu, Hawaii on December 7, 1941. In the surpise attack, 2,493 soldiers lost their lives and 1,000 were wounded. This spurred many Americans to enlist—Bob was just one of many.

The USS Arizona burning from damage before sinking in Pearl Harbor. The USS Arizona Memorial is located above its sunken remains and is viewed by over 2 million visitors a year. It marks the resting place of 1,102 of the 1,177 sailors and marines killed on the ship that day.

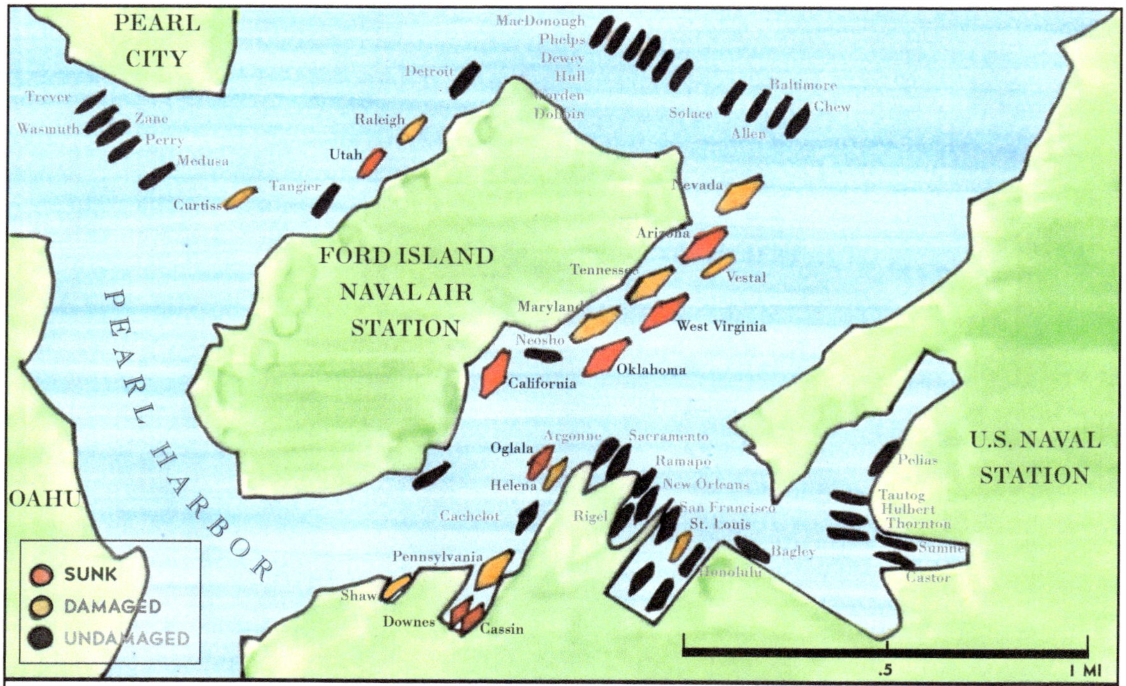

Map showing the devastation caused by the Japanese on Pearl Harbor.

December 8, 1941: Franklin Delano Roosevelt delivering a joint address to Congress that was broadcast on the radio telling us all that "Yesterday, December 7, 1941—a date which will live in infamy—The United States of America was suddenly and deliberately attacked by naval and air forces of the Empire of Japan." An hour later we declared war on Japan and its allies, Italy and Germany.

MILITARY RECORD AND REPORT OF SEPARATION

CERTIFICATE OF SERVICE

RG 7 17J 29

1. LAST NAME - FIRST NAME - MIDDLE INITIAL	2. ARMY SERIAL NUMBER	3. AUS. GRADE	4. ARM OR SERVICE	5. COMPONENT
STONE ROBERT L	0 696 041	1ST LT	A C	AUS

6. ORGANIZATION	7. DATE OF RELIEF FROM ACTIVE DUTY	8. PLACE OF SEPARATION
431ST BOMB SQUADRON 11TH BOMB GROUP 7TH AIR FORCE	26 AUG 46	SEPARATION CENTER FORT DIX NEW JERSEY

9. PERMANENT ADDRESS FOR MAILING PURPOSES	10. DATE OF BIRTH	11. PLACE OF BIRTH
375 PARK AVENUE NEW YORK CITY NEW YORK	19 DEC 21	NEW YORK CITY NEW YORK

12. ADDRESS FROM WHICH EMPLOYMENT WILL BE SOUGHT	13. COLOR EYES	14. COLOR HAIR	15. HEIGHT	16. WEIGHT	17. NO. OF DEPENDENTS
SEE 9	HAZEL	BROWN	5'8½"	145 LBS.	0

18. RACE: WHITE	NEGRO	OTHER (specify)	19. MARITAL STATUS: SINGLE	MARRIED	OTHER (specify)	20. U.S. CITIZEN: YES	NO	21. CIVILIAN OCCUPATION AND NO.
X			X			X		STUDENT X-02

MILITARY HISTORY

SELECTIVE SERVICE DATA	22. REGISTERED: YES	NO	23. LOCAL S. S. BOARD NUMBER	24. COUNTY AND STATE	25. HOME ADDRESS AT TIME OF ENTRY ON ACTIVE DUTY
	X			NEW YORK CITY NEW YORK	SEE 9

26. DATE OF ENTRY ON ACTIVE DUTY	27. MILITARY OCCUPATIONAL SPECIALTY AND NO.
23 OCTOBER 1943	BOMBARDIER 1035

28. BATTLES AND CAMPAIGNS

CENTRAL PACIFIC AIR OFFENSIVE JAPAN EASTERN MANDATES

29. DECORATIONS AND CITATIONS

DISTINGUISHED FLYING CROSS AIR MEDAL W/6 OAK LEAF CLUSTERS AMERICAN CAMPAIGN MEDAL ASIATIC PACIFIC CAMPAIGN MEDAL WORLD WAR II VICTORY MEDAL MERITORIOUS SERVICE UNIT PLAQUE

30. WOUNDS RECEIVED IN ACTION

NONE

31. SERVICE SCHOOLS ATTENDED	32. SERVICE OUTSIDE CONTINENTAL U. S. AND RETURN: DATE OF DEPARTURE	DESTINATION	DATE OF ARRIVAL
ADVANCED BOMBARDIER SCHOOL 7TH AAF GUNNERY SCHOOL	4 JUL 44	A P	10 JUL 44
33. REASON AND AUTHORITY FOR SEPARATION: RELIEF FROM ACTIVE DUTY RR1-1 46 ASF CIR 25 APR 46	22 MAY 45	U S A	29 MAY 45

34. CURRENT TOUR OF ACTIVE DUTY — CONTINENTAL SERVICE: YEARS	MONTHS	DAYS	FOREIGN SERVICE: YEARS	MONTHS	DAYS	35. EDUCATION (years): GRAMMAR SCHOOL	HIGH SCHOOL	COLLEGE
1	11	8	0	10	26	8	4	2

INSURANCE NOTICE

IMPORTANT IF PREMIUM IS NOT PAID WHEN DUE OR WITHIN THIRTY-ONE DAYS THEREAFTER, INSURANCE WILL LAPSE. MAKE CHECKS OR MONEY ORDERS PAYABLE TO THE TREASURER OF THE U. S. AND FORWARD TO COLLECTIONS SUBDIVISION, VETERANS ADMINISTRATION, WASHINGTON 25, D. C.

36. KIND OF INSURANCE: Nat. Serv.	U.S. Govt.	None	37. HOW PAID: Allotment	Direct to V.A.	38. Effective Date of Allotment Discontinuance	39. Date of Next Premium Due (one month after 38)	40. PREMIUM DUE EACH MONTH	41. INTENTION OF VETERAN TO: Continue	Continue only	Discontinue
X			X		31 AUG 46	30 SEP 46	$ 6.60	X	$	

42. RIGHT THUMB PRINT

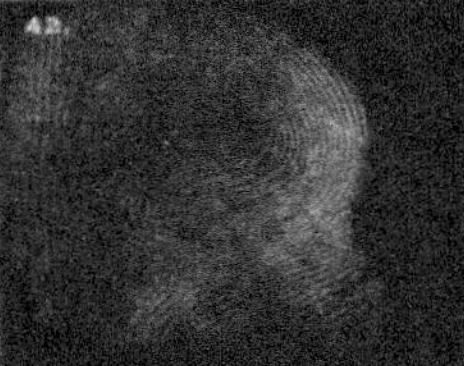

43. REMARKS (This space for completion of above items or entry of other items specified in W. D. Directives)

ASR SCORE (2 SEP 45) 96
BOMBARDIER NAVIGATOR
LAPEL BUTTON ISSUED
ON TERMINAL LEAVE FROM 18 JUL TO 26 AUG 46 INCLUSIVE

44. SIGNATURE OF OFFICER BEING SEPARATED	45. PERSONNEL OFFICER (Type name, grade and organization - signature)
Robert L. Stone	EDEL V SATTRE CAPT WAC ASST ADJ Edel V. Sattre

WD AGO FORM 53-98
1 November 1944

This form supersedes all previous editions of WD AGO Forms 53 and 280 for officers entitled to a Certificate of Service, which will not be used after receipt of this revision.

APPENDIX

U.S. AIR FORCES FORMS

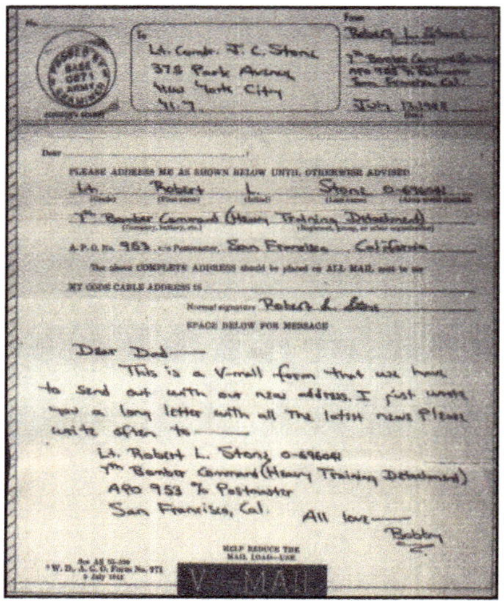

To
Lt. Comdr. J. C. Stone
375 Park Avenue
New York City
N.Y.

From
Robert L. Stone
7th Bomber Command
APO 953 % Postmaster
San Francisco, Cal.

July 13, 1943

Dear

PLEASE ADDRESS ME AS SHOWN BELOW UNTIL OTHERWISE ADVISED

Lt. Robert L. Stone 0-696041

7th Bomber Command (Heavy Training Detachment)

A.P.O. No. 953, c/o Postmaster, San Francisco, California

The above COMPLETE ADDRESS should be placed on ALL MAIL sent to me

MY CODE CABLE ADDRESS IS

Normal signature Robert L. Stone

SPACE BELOW FOR MESSAGE

Dear Dad—

This is a V-mail form that we have to send out with our new address. I just wrote you a long letter with all the latest news. Please write often to—

Lt. Robert L. Stone 0-696041
7th Bomber Command (Heavy Training Detachment)
APO 953 % Postmaster
San Francisco, Cal.

All love—
Bobby

HELP REDUCE THE MAIL LOAD—USE

W. D., A. G. O. Form No. 971
9 July 1942

V—MAIL

V-mail, short for Victory Mail, was the primary secure method for World War II soldiers stationed overseas to communicate. The original letter sheets (7" x 9-1/8") were sent through mail censors, copied to negative microfilm and printed back on paper to 60% of its original size (4-1/2" x 5-3/16") when it arrived at its destination. The system was based on the British Air-graph system, invented in the 1930s by the Eastman Kodak Company in conjunction with Imperial Airways and Pan-American Airways to reduce weight and bulk of air mail.

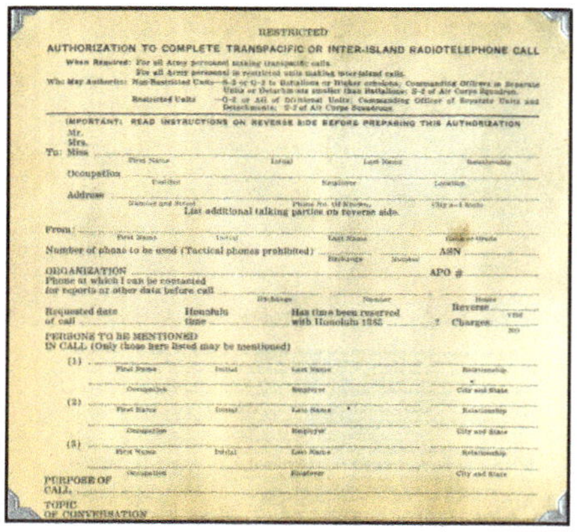

RESTRICTED

AUTHORIZATION TO COMPLETE TRANSPACIFIC OR INTER-ISLAND RADIOTELEPHONE CALL

IMPORTANT: READ INSTRUCTIONS ON REVERSE SIDE BEFORE PREPARING THIS AUTHORIZATION

To: Mr. / Mrs. / Miss
Occupation
Address

List additional talking parties on reverse side.

From:

Number of phone to be used (Tactical phones prohibited) ASN

ORGANIZATION APO #

Phone at which I can be contacted for reports or other data before call

Requested date of call / Honolulu time / Has time been reserved with Honolulu 1355? / Reverse Charges

PERSONS TO BE MENTIONED IN CALL (Only those here listed may be mentioned)

(1)
(2)
(3)

PURPOSE OF CALL

TOPIC OF CONVERSATION

Application for making a transpacific telephone call from Oahu, Hawaii to New York City.

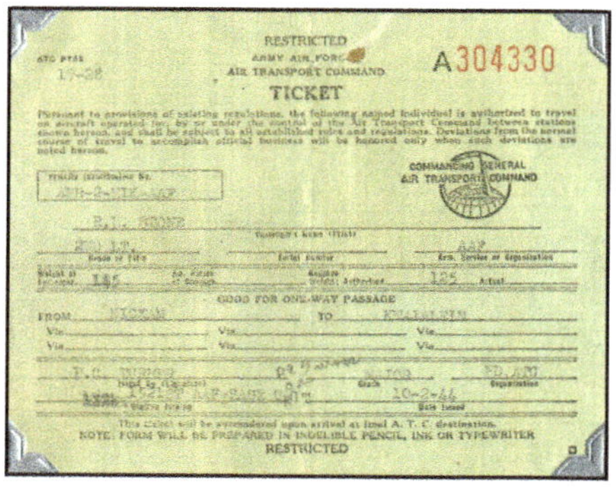

RESTRICTED

ARMY AIR FORCES
AIR TRANSPORT COMMAND

A304330

TICKET

COMMANDING GENERAL
AIR TRANSPORT COMMAND

GOOD FOR ONE-WAY PASSAGE

FROM HICKAM TO KWAJALEIN

This ticket will be surrendered upon arrival at final A. T. C. destination.

NOTE: FORM WILL BE PREPARED IN INDELIBLE PENCIL, INK OR TYPEWRITER

RESTRICTED

Army Air Forces Air Transport Ticket. This transport ticket took Bob from Hickam Air Force Base in Pearl Harbor, Hawaii to Kwajalein in the Marshall Islands via the Johnston Atoll. The Johnston Atoll is in the Pacific Ocean located about 860 miles southwest of Hawaii.

U.S. WAR BONDS

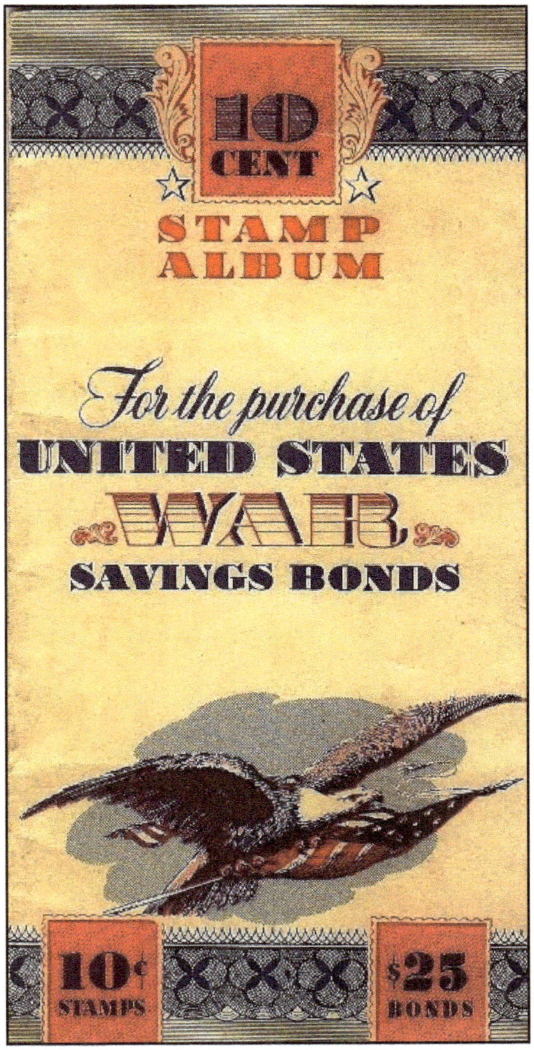

"The Minute Man of Concord" was for many years the symbol of the Savings Bond Program. He appeared on the cover of small paper books (roughly 3"x6") that you filled with stamps bought for varying amounts. These books made it possible for those who could not purchase an entire bond at once to accumulate enough stamps to purchase a bond. I had a several books over the years that I filled with 10 cent stamps until it was worth $18.75—then I took it to the Post Office and in exchange was given a bond that would be worth $25 in ten years. Now, $6.25 may not sound like a lot, but most Americans bought more than just $18.75 worth of War bonds.

The Government took that money to pay for tanks, planes, ships, uniforms, weapons, medicine, food, and everything else the military needed to fight and win. It was an investment in your country.

Everywhere they went, Americans were encouraged to help support the war effort by purchasing War Bonds. More than a quarter of a billion dollars' worth of advertising was donated to the campaign. Posters picturing Uncle Sam or a soldier on the battlefield implored people to do their part. Celebrities like Bob Hope, Jack Benny, Frank Sinatra, Bette Davis, and Marlene Dietrich travelled the country putting on live shows or radio programs promoting War Bond sales.

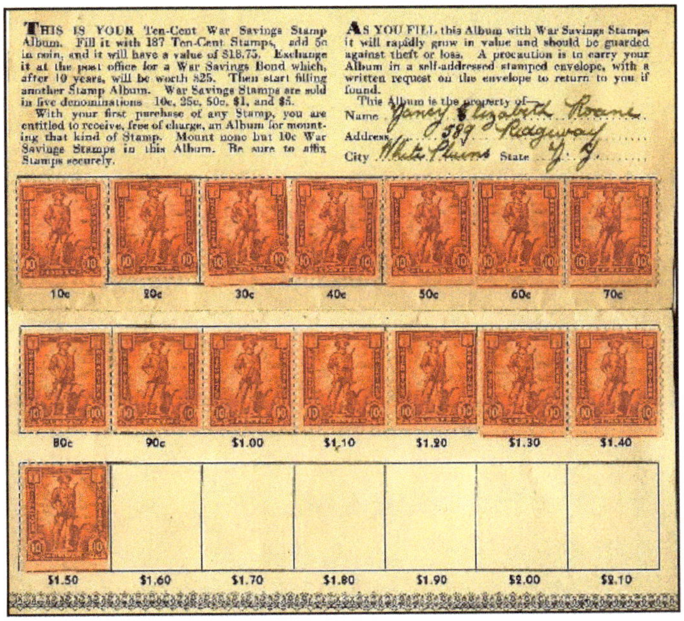

Popular contemporary art was used to help promote the bonds, such as Norman Rockwell's painting the Four Freedoms that toured in a War Bond effort that raised $132 million. Warner Brothers produced a theatrical cartoon "Any Bonds Today?" shown in movie theaters. Even Superman, Batman, Bugs Bunny and other cartoon characters got into the spirit, reminding young people that "we are all in this together." Over the course of the war 85 million Americans purchased bonds totaling approximately $185 billion.

I collected stamps using my allowance, Bob used his service pay to purchase bonds in larger denominations, and his Dad bought bonds for gifts. 62

The "E" Award Ceremony. My father, Sylvester "Syl" W. Muldowny, is on the far left.

CENTER: Two silver bars for 2nd Lieutenant; Distinguished Flying Cross Medal awarded for initial act of valor; UPPER LEFT: Air Medal, note two oak leaf clusters, one silver, one bronze. The silver cluster represents five additional awards for valor and the bronze cluster represents one, equaling a total of six awards; UPPER RIGHT: U.S. Army Air Forces Good Conduct Medal; PATCH, LEFT: Seventh Army Air Force; PATCH, RIGHT: U.S. Army Air Forces; BOTTOM ROW, ABOVE (left to right): Distinguished Flying Cross Ribbon, Air Medal Ribbon (with silver and bronze Oak leaf clusters), U.S. Army Air Forces Good Conduct Medal; BOTTOM ROW, BELOW (left to right): World War II Victory Medal, World War II Asiatic Pacific Medal (with three bronze stars for participation in Pacific campaigns), American Campaign Medal (for duty at Fort Dix).

First atomic explosion on July 16, 1945 at 5:29:45 A.M. at Alamogordo Air Base in New Mexico.

THE MANHATTAN PROJECT

The first atomic bomb was successfully tested at Alamogordo, New Mexico as the final test of the "Manhattan District" project. No one knew what the results of this test would be.

I remember Bob telling me that Uncle Eddie was involved in the plans called "Manhattan District" (later known as the "Manhattan Project") for funding and developing the atomic bomb for $1.7 billion, and explaining the rationale for using it in August of 1945. President Roosevelt had died in April and Harry Truman had replaced him in office. Instead of trying to paraphrase what I remember Bob telling me I will quote from Uncle Eddie's book:

Our new president, who had been told about "Manhattan District" by Secretary Stimson just after he had assumed office, was now in command. He had to make the decision.

We still had the gigantic task of defeating Japan. In order to do it we would have to land in Japan and then fight our way to final victory against a military strength, which, although weakened, was then estimated at five million men. Our war plan told us that it would cost us one million casualties to do this, and we would have to commit troops who had already been through years of devastating fighting in Europe. Our war-weary economy on the home front would have to be told that it must still go forward. And we were prepared to do just that. The operation was to be launched on November 1st. To support it, our people would have to endure the agonies of having millions of husbands, fathers, and sons shipped to the Far East for this hazardous undertaking.

All of this, Secretary Stimson believed, could be avoided by using the bomb. He had given months of soul-searching study to the problem, and he finally recommended that we use the bomb."[63]

And so it happened: Germany had surrendered on V-E Day May 8th; the bombs were dropped on Hiroshima and Nagasaki; the Japanese formally surrendered on V-J Day which was August 15th; finally, the war was over and most of our troops came home to their families and loved ones. But, most importantly, they arrived back home to a free country unscathed by the destruction of bombs where they could try to build a better world for everyone.

This photo shows the mushroom cloud created by the atom bomb called "Fat Man" over Nagasaki on August 9, 1945 that ended the war in the Pacific with the Japanese surrender on August 9, 1945. On August 6th the first atomic bomb called "Little Boy" was dropped from the B-29 the Enola Gay on Hiroshima as a warning—but the Japanese did not surrender until the second bomb was dropped. The Enola Gay left from Tinian in the Mariana Islands near Saipan where Bob's plane was forced to land on his "scariest mission."

HARRY S. TRUMAN

> *"The Japanese began the war from the air at Pearl Harbor. They have been repaid many fold"* [64]

In Bob's words: "I did not meet anyone in the war who had been a friend before I joined the Air Force. However, the entire crew became friends because we all relied on one another to fly successful missions—our lives depended on it! One member of the crew and I became good friends and have stayed in touch at least through lengthy Christmas cards each year—this man came from Texas and was a great pilot. When the war ended, Bill McGarvey stayed in the Air Force to fly jet fighters and retired as a Major General." Note written in May 2009 by Bill McGarvey, co-pilot of the "Flying Jenny" on Bob's missions.

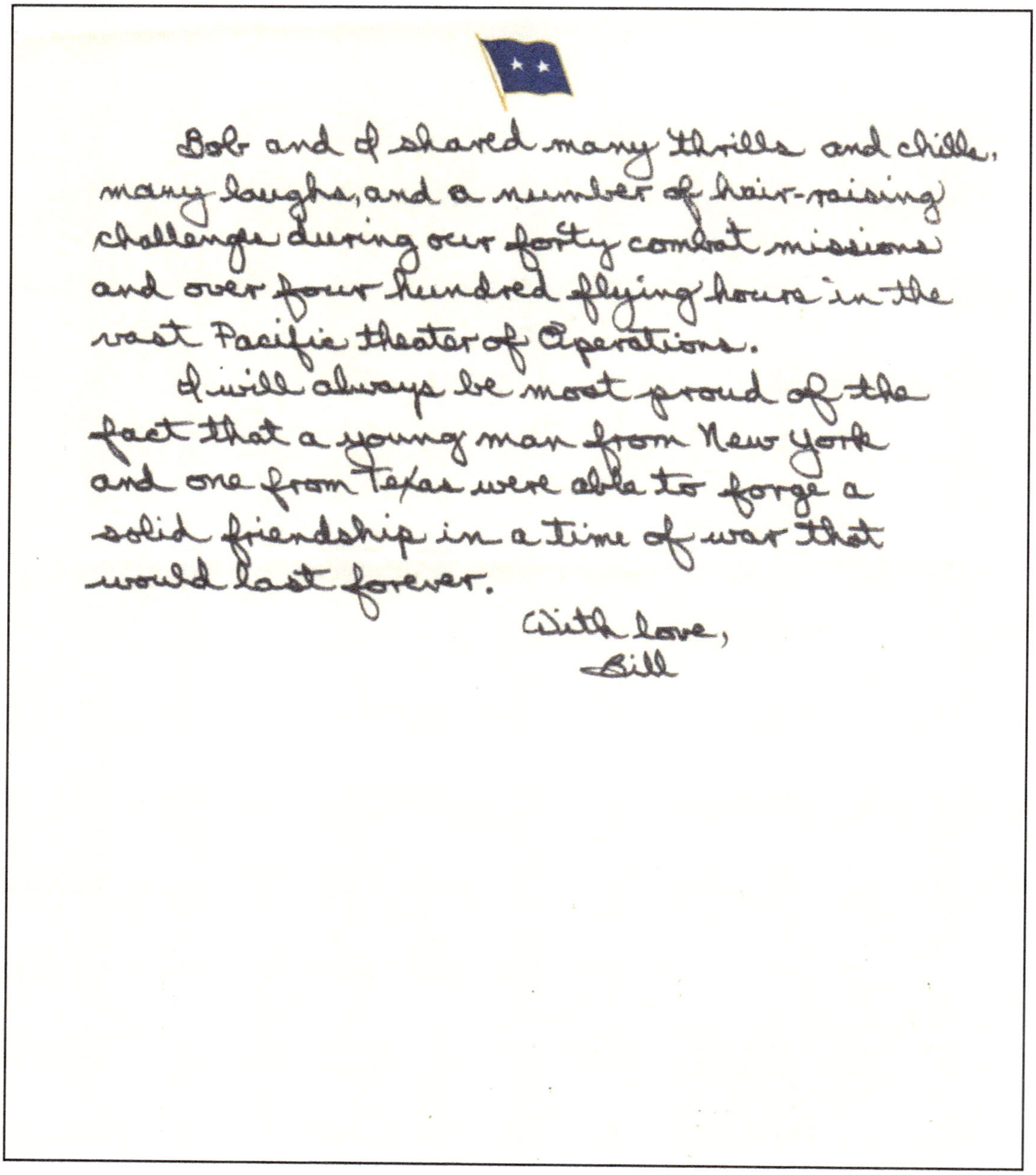

Bob and I shared many thrills and chills, many laughs, and a number of hair-raising challenges during our forty combat missions and over four hundred flying hours in the vast Pacific theater of Operations.

I will always be most proud of the fact that a young man from New York and one from Texas were able to forge a solid friendship in a time of war that would last forever.

With love,
Bill

19 W 92
WILLIAMS

The United States Marine Corps War Memorial, also known as the Iwo Jima Memorial, at the entrance to Arlington National Cemetery in Arlington, Virginia. The statue is based on an iconic image of the second flag-raising on Mount Suribachi on the island of Iwo Jima on February 23, 1945. Note "1945 Iwo Jima" on the left of the base.

In lieu of buying our book we hope you will consider a gift to the Wounded Warriors Project that helps the men and women who have served in a war and were not as fortunate as those in our family. If you are writing a check, please be sure to put "Event ID#P47729" in the memo.

Contributions may be made to:
Wounded Warrior Project
P. O. Box 758517
Topeka, Kansas 66675-8517
Attn: Community Events, EVENT ID#P47729

Or go online to our Wounded Warrior Project page:
https://fundraise.woundedwarriorproject.org/rtt/Fundraising/individual/25512316

ABOUT THE AUTHORS

SHEILA MULDOWNY STONE

Sheila Muldowny Stone, while at The Brearley School in New York City, won several figure skating championships. After graduating, she became a USFSA Gold Medalist and trained in Europe where she won the Swiss International Championship and skated exhibitions with the U.S. World Team. In the 1950's she wrote for Sports Illustrated in its first year of publication and started Sheila Muldowny Designs, one of the first active sportswear companies. Her label was one of only three labels allowed in Saks Fifth Avenue merchandise at the time. She designed practice outfits for the 1956 Olympic figure skating team in Cortina d'Ampezzo, Italy, so that the judges and spectators could easily identify the American skaters before the competition began. When she and Bob were married in 1968 they had a combined family of six children ages 6 to 14. During this time in NYC she was a mother and corporate wife and was active in the Parents League of New York, becoming president for three years. In 1981 the couple bought a home in Williamstown, Massachusetts, and since then she has supported Williams College womens' athletics (most particularly field hockey and lacrosse), the Williamstown Youth Center, the Williamstown Art Conservation Center, the new Williamstown Theatre Festival Guild, the Clark Art Institute, the Williamstown Rural Lands Foundation, and she is a partner in Archirazzi. For the past several years she has been working on this book with her daughter and treasuring these memories of her beloved husband.

ALI ADAIR

Ali Adair graduated from Middlebury and holds a Master's Degree in Architecture from the New School of Architecture and Design; she is LEED AP BD+C accredited. She has worked as a reporter, assignment editor and producer in newspaper, radio and television in Vermont and California, and also worked in the entertainment business, primarily in International Film Distribution at Warner Bros. She optioned the book High Stick by Ted Green of the Boston Bruins, who made a miraculous recovery from a near-fatal head injury, and she wrote a screenplay on the story. This led to producing a documentary in the late 90's about concussions in the sport of ice hockey before it became a hot topic. She interviewed over twenty members of the 1969-1970 Stanley Cup team members including Bobby Orr and Phil Esposito, and after 9/11 she wrote a memorial piece about Ace Bailey that was published in the LA Times. She started a design business, Archirazzi, which capitalizes on her combination of professional skills as a photographer and graphic designer to produce unique artwork; her calendar design, developed for the company, has been granted a U.S. patent. Her photographs have been featured in many publications here and abroad. For the past few years she has been working on the graphic and organizational process for this book. She is in the process of acquiring her architecture license and she lives in Washington, D.C. with her cherished border collie, Bailey, named after Ace.